P9-CCC-104

Emotional Intelligence in

COUPLES THERAPY

A NORTON PROFESSIONAL BOOK

Emotional Intelligence

IN

Couples Therapy

Advances from Neurobiology and
the Science of Intimate Relationships

Brent J. Atkinson

W. W. NORTON & COMPANY
New York • London

Copyright © 2005 by Brent Atkinson

All rights reserved
Printed in the United States of America
First Edition

For information about permission to reproduce
selections from this book, write to
Permissions, W. W. Norton & Company, Inc.,
500 Fifth Avenue, New York, NY 10110

Production Manager: Leeann Graham
Manufacturing by Haddon Craftsmen

Library of Congress Cataloging-in-Publication Data

Atkinson, Brent.
    Emotional intelligence in couples therapy : advances from neurobiology and
the science of intimate relationships / Brent Atkinson.
        p.   ; cm.
Includes bibliographical references and index.
ISBN 0-393-70386-X
1. Marital psychotherapy. 2. Neuropsychology. 3. Neurobiology. 4. Emotions.
I. Title.

RC488.5.A88 2005
616.89′1562—dc22   2005047281

W. W. Norton & Company, Inc., 500 Fifth Avenue, New York, N.Y. 10110
www.wwnorton.com

W. W. Norton & Company Ltd., Castle House, 75/76 Wells St., London W1T 3QT
1 3 5 7 9 0 8 6 4 2

to Lisa

Contents

Acknowledgments

I OWE A TREMENDOUS debt of gratitude to my wife, Lisa, for her support and inspiration through all phases of the development and articulation of the ideas set forth in this book. Lisa has companionship abilities that I can only approximate, and I have become a more emotionally intelligent being through my relationship with her. Thank you, Lisa, for the hundreds of drafts you enthusiastically read, for the countless hours of processing our own relationship and for the special way you understand me.

Very special thanks to my children, Heather, Brian, Jessica, and Grace, for all the years of love and support. Thank you Heather, for your instinctive compassion for those who are in need. Your tender heart has been a source of inspiration for me for over twenty years. Thank you Brian, for being openly proud of me, and for somehow understanding from an early age that you don't have to prove yourself to anybody. How did you do that? Thank you Jessica, for the daily hugs, and for trusting me enough to be honest with me. Your ability to talk about your feelings already exceeds mine. Thank you Gracie, for the little dance you do when I come home at night, and for how earnestly you keep saying the same thing to me over and over until I finally understand!

The clinical methods described in this book have been subjected to years of field-testing by a group of extremely talented therapists — my colleagues at the Couples Research Institute; Lisa Atkinson, Paul Weiss, Julie Szekely, Jeff Lata, Kari Wittmann Lata, and Paula Kutz. These individuals contributed immeasurably to the ongoing development of the PET-C approach, and practice it better than any clinicians I know. Their fingerprints are all over this book.

Special thanks to my friend and colleague Teresa McDowell for her support and pivotal contributions in the early phases of the development of PET-C. A gifted researcher, Teresa watched countless hours of my clinical work and helped me understand what I was doing!

Thank you Deborah Malmud, for seeing the importance of this book before it was written, and for your editorial guidance through the entire process. Thank you Michael McGandy and the rest of the Norton staff for your meticulous work on the manuscript as well. I'm also grateful to Margot Smith and Stephanie Nelson for their assistance in the final phases of manuscript production, and to each of my graduate assistants who helped me with papers which paved the way for this book.

Thank you Marian Sandmaier and Rich Simon, for helping me bring to life the material in Chapters 2 and 3.

Thank you Tony Heath, for standing with me through every triumph and tribulation I've had in the past twenty years, and for embodying the nonjudgmental attitude discussed throughout this book.

Thank you Harv Joanning, for seeing potential in me when I was 25 years old, and thank you Brad Keeney for the hours of dreaming and scheming about how to do something truly worthwhile.

Emotional Intelligence in

COUPLES THERAPY

INTRODUCTION
New Answers to Old Questions

THIS BOOK INTRODUCES a new way of understanding and navigating relationships, and provides a guide for therapists to help distressed couples improve their lives together. The new approach results from advances in two independent fields of scientific inquiry: neuroscience and the science of intimate relationships. New studies in relationship science have identified with a high degree of precision what people who succeed in their relationships do differently than those who fail, taking much of the guesswork out of the question of what makes a relationship work. Meanwhile, ground-breaking discoveries in the field of affective neuroscience provide new answers to the age-old question of why people persist in outmoded ways of thinking or acting, even when they know it would be in their own best interest to change.

ADVANCES IN THE SCIENCE OF
INTIMATE RELATIONSHIPS

Researchers in the mid-1980s set out to find what it is that people who succeed in their marriages do differently from those who fail. In the first year of these studies, such entities as attitudes, communication styles, expression of anger and tenderness were measured. Participants were installed in a lab apartment with videocameras in every room except the bathroom that recorded their daily lives. The couples were asked to discuss specific topics while their heart rates were monitored and their physical movements were measured. Blood samples were taken at various points in the conversations. After the study finished, the participating couples were tracked for several years to see how they were doing—which couples were divorced, which were unhappily married, and which had thriving marriages. Not only did the researchers succeed in pinpointing the interpersonal habits that distinguish people who succeed from people who fail in their marriages, but they found that some interpersonal habits are so crucial that the absence of them virtually guarantees marital failure. By measuring the relative presence or absence of specific interpersonal habits, researchers found that they could predict the likelihood of a marriage's success or failure with 91% accuracy (Gottman & Silver, 1999)! People who have these crucial habits almost always end up in happy marriages, whereas people who don't almost always end up divorced or unhappily married.

These studies are revolutionizing our understanding of intimate relationships. Before them, marriage therapists had to proceed on the basis of what they thought couples needed, or what generally accepted theories in the field told them to do. Now, for the first time, we have scientific evidence about what it is that couples who succeed and those who fail actually do differently. This information has been filtering into public awareness through books such as John Gottman's *Why Marriages Succeed or Fail* (1994a), *The Seven Principles for Making Marriage Work* (Gottman & Silver, 1999), and *The Relationship Cure* (Gottman & De Claire, 2001). These studies present compelling evidence that there are personal prerequisites for succeeding in intimate relationships. Those who want to succeed in love must have specific interpersonal abilities, and we now know exactly what these abilities are. If people have these abilities, the chances are very good that they will be treated with respect and admiration from their intimate partners. If they don't have them, the evidence suggests that the future of their relationships will be quite dim.

Some of the most important interpersonal habits involve things that people must be able to do *without the help of their partners*. In fact, they must be able to do these things precisely when their partners are making it most difficult to do them. Researchers have discovered that the way people respond when they feel misunderstood or mistreated by their partners dramatically influences the odds that their partners will treat them better or worse in the future. All people in lasting intimate relationships feel misunderstood or mistreated at one time or another. At these times, some people respond in ways that make it likely that their partners will treat them better in the future, and some people respond in ways that dramatically increase the odds that they will be even more misunderstood or mistreated. The way people respond to the worst in their partners plays a central role in determining whether or not they will experience something better from them in the future. These studies suggest that people can dramatically influence the way their partners treat them. This is because a person's level of motivation has so much to do with how a partner interacts with him or her. People are almost guaranteed love relationships in which they feel respected and valued if they have certain interpersonal abilities. The good news is that when people find themselves in relationships in which they feel consistently misunderstood or mistreated, they don't have to wait around, hoping that their partners will start treating them better. They can largely take the matter into their own hands. They cannot control their partners, but they can dramatically influence the odds that their partners will treat them better in the future. How? *By making sure that they are responding well to the things their partners do or say that are upsetting them right now.*

In Chapter 3, we'll take a detailed look at what "responding well" means. Some of these habits that predict relationship success are obvious. It doesn't take a rocket scientist to figure out that people who tend to start out discussions with harsh criticisms won't be any more likey to succeed than those who are unwilling to accept influence from their partners when making decisions. Some of the important predictors have more to do with what a person is *thinking* than what she or he says or does. Two different husbands may each apologize and adjust their plans when their wives criticize them harshly for forgetting an important appointment. One husband will end up divorced, and the other will remain happily married. Why? While husband 1 apologizes and adjusts his plans, inside he's thinking "She shouldn't get so upset over such a little thing; If it's not one thing, it's another!; She's never satisfied!; I would never act like that if she forgot something!; She's just like her mother!" In contrast, husband 2 is thinking, "Why is she so upset?; There must be more going on here than meets the eye; My forgetting about this must mean something to her that I don't really understand; I've got to find out the emotional logic behind her reactions." Although the outward actions of the two husbands look the same (apologizing and accepting influence), clearly these husbands have vastly different attitudes. Attitudes are as potent as behaviors when predicting relationship success or failure.

In all of my years working with couples, I have rarely encountered a couple in which one partner was meeting the prerequisites when the other partner wasn't. Granted, the shortcomings of one partner are often more public or provocative than the shortcomings of the other (i.e., one partner flies into rages and throws things while the other tries to placate and calm down the raging partner), but when all of the prerequisites are considered, we find that partners in distressed relationships are generally a match for each other. But partners entering therapy rarely see things this way. Inwardly, if not outwardly, people generally think that the shortcomings of their partners are more serious than their own. Usually, this is because there are certain "dysfunctional" things that their partners do that they know they don't do themselves. What they don't realize is that there are many different interpersonal habits that are predictive of relationship success or failure. They tend to focus on the particular dysfunctional habits of their partners, not realizing that some of their own habits are just as powerfully corrosive to the relationship. Fortunately, people who are able to see and modify their own dysfunctional habits will most often find that their partners follow. This is due to the powerful combination of abilities that people destined for relationship success have. They require that they be treated with respect, but they make it easy for their partners to treat them with respect at the same time.

The bottom line is this: If people want their partners to treat them better, they need to think and act like people who usually get treated well by their partners. Researchers have studied people who naturally elicit respect and cooperation from their partners, and have identified exactly how they do it. There are specific skills and attitudes involved in knowing how to bring out the best in others, and there is evidence that people who know how to do this are more successful not only in their intimate relationships, but in most areas of their lives. Of course, we all have the ability to do this sometimes, but the people who succeed in getting respect and admiration from their partners can do it even when they feel really misunderstood or mistreated. These are the moments that separate the men from the boys, and the women from the girls, psychologically speaking. If people can't stay on track in these times, they are probably not going to be among those who end up with partners who understand, respect, and care about them. However, if they develop the ability to respond well during these times, they will find that their partner will begin treating them in a whole different way.

At our couples clinic, each week we encounter people who tell us stories about how poorly they have been treated by their partners. After spewing the details of their mate's most recent episode of incredibly selfish or disrespectful behavior, they usually look at us as if to say, "Now how am I supposed to respond to that?" Half of these people are already convinced that there is no good answer to this question. In fact, they resent even having to ask the question, believing that they shouldn't have to deal with this situation in the first place. But the evidence suggests that if they continue dismissing the question, they will kiss their relationships goodbye. Marital success has more to do with responding well when one's partner seems selfish or inconsiderate than it has to do with avoiding actually being selfish or inconsiderate in the first place. It is not that selfish or disrespectful behavior doesn't matter, it does: Repetitive, selfish behavior is destructive in relationships. The problem is that people are not very reliable judges of what truly selfish behavior is, the reason being that there are hundreds of yardsticks for measuring selfishness, and people tend to use their own, not their partners' yardsticks. Let's take a hypothetical example: A wife accepts an invitation to go out with her friends on Friday night without consulting her husband. The husband considers this to be really inconsiderate, and feels justified in criticizing her harshly for it. But the fact is, this wife wouldn't be upset at the husband if he made similar arrangements with his friends without consulting her. In fact, the wife has a quite different ideal for how a relationship should be. In her view, partners should each be free to make other arrangements unless plans between the two of them have been specifically made. She wouldn't dream of being so selfish as to try to restrict his freedom by asking him to consult her every time he wanted to plan something with his friends. Obviously, he doesn't see it that way, and he lets her have a piece of his mind! Well, if she wasn't behaving selfishly before he harshly criticized her, now she is! She slams the door in his face. Feeling perfectly entitled to his contempt, the next time he sees her he is sneering at her for her childish tantrum. Needless to say, her response to his contempt isn't exactly what he was hoping for.

And so the story goes. It began with the husband's *perception* that his wife was being inconsiderate. If he had been able to respond differently, she may have been willing to try to work out a more mutually satisfying plan. But he felt perfectly justified in his reaction. After all, hadn't she done the selfish thing first? But she doesn't see it that way. She believes that he is the one who was selfish, trying to control her by limiting her freedom to schedule time with her friends. Of course, his priority of collaboration isn't any more selfish than her priority of mutual freedom. As the discussion unfolded, she didn't respond any better to the perception that he was being selfish than he did to the perception that she was being inconsiderate, and so the whole thing blew up. But it all would have been avoided if both of them had been able to stand up for themselves without putting the other person down. We will take a close look at how people who succeed in their relationships do this in Chapter 10.

The track record for professional marriage counseling is not particularly impressive (Gottman, 1999). A massive *Consumer Reports* survey in 1995 (Seligman, 1995) revealed that, among consumers of various kinds of psychotherapy, consumers of marital therapy were the least satisfied. I believe that marital therapies have been relatively unsuccessful at least in part because therapists often inadvertently reinforce the notion that intimate partners can succeed in their relationships without meeting the prerequisites. Therapists support this notion each time they attempt to help partners get more of what they want from each other even though they are going about trying to get it in ways that are clearly predictive of marital failure. For example, to help her get her point across, a therapist might reframe a wife's harsh criticism as a desperate cry for connection. Or, a therapist might help a wife view her husband's stony silence as his decision to confine himself to a life of loneliness rather than attack his wife. Often, therapists make progress with couples by going back and forth, softening one partner a little bit, then softening the other, then back to the first partner, and so on. As each partner experiences the other as a bit more willing to give, they become more willing themselves, and things gradually get better. If a therapist is sufficiently skilled in this softening process, couples can make remarkable progress in a relatively short period of time. However, each partner may leave therapy thinking that the progress happened because their partner finally became more reasonable. It is possible for marriage therapy to "succeed" without either partner developing any more ability to respond well when feeling misunderstood or mistreated. Beneath the tenuous progress, they might still have the same attitude that they entered therapy with: "I'll change my reactions to my partner if my partner changes his reactions to me." People who have this quid pro quo attitude generally don't get treated very well for very long (Gottman & Silver, 1999; Murstein, Correto, & MacDonald, 1977), and this may be why there is such a huge relapse problem among couples who improve during marital therapy. While therapists are busily helping partners capitalize on small increases in the reasonableness of their mates, they are reinforcing assumptions that will eventually undo the progress. Those who believe that things improved because the therapist got their partners to change often leave couples therapy with an uneasy feeling about their progress. They feel relieved that their partners finally got a clue, but also feel just as unable to influence the state of their relationship as they did before therapy. Each of them is haunted by the unspoken question: "What's to keep my partner from starting to treat me poorly again?"

On the other hand, partners who use therapy to increase their abilities to respond to each other in ways that are predictive of success leave therapy with an entirely different feeling. Such partners have confidence that the relationship changed in large part because they became better at meeting the prerequisites for a happy relationship. They have seen the powerful, positive impact that the hard-earned changes in their attitudes and actions have had on their mates. They have come to realize that, to a large extent, the future of their relationship is in their own hands.

The approach to couples therapy described in this book begins with the assumption that, if people want to succeed in their intimate relationships over the long haul, they must meet the prerequisites for relationship success. They must accept the assumption that the single most powerful thing they can do to get more respect and caring from their partners is to more fully develop the ability to think and act like people who stand a chance of getting respect and caring. They must become more concerned about how they respond to the upsetting things that their partners say or do than they are about the upsetting things their partners are saying or doing.

The new information about the prerequisites for relationship success should be of great interest to all therapists, regardless of theoretical orientation. Narrative therapists will be pleased to learn that new studies confirm that the beliefs and stories that people have about their relationships exert a powerful influence on their success or failure. Cognitive–behavioral therapists will not be surprised to learn that people destined for relationship success think and act differently from those destined to fail. Emotionally focused therapists will find support for their assumption that successful partners own and express attachment-related bids for connection more often than unsuccessful partners, and Bowenian therapists will find support for the idea that relationship success is related to the ability to stand up for one's own viewpoint without putting the other person down. But the studies on factors that predict relationship success will also help therapists of various orientations refine the focus of their interventions. For example, there are *particular types* of relationship narratives, attributions, and differentiating moves that almost always destroy relationships and other types that ensure relationship success. These studies have identified the specific moves that people in successful relationships make when they need to stand up for themselves, and they have identified how successful partners make and respond to bids for connection.

ADVANCES IN AFFECTIVE
NEUROSCIENCE

Developing the habits that support relationship success is probably the single most important task a person can accomplish in his or her lifetime. Evidence suggests that those who succeed in their marriages will live an average of four years longer than those who don't (Gottman & Silver, 1999). They will have an average of 35% less illness, have healthier immune systems, will be substantially less likely to become violent, homicidal, or suicidal, and less likely to experience an emotional or mental disorder. They will even have a lower risk of being involved in automobile accidents. The children of those who succeed in their marriages will have fewer health problems, better academic performance, more social competence, less depression, fewer problems with social contact, more ability to regulate their emotions, lower heart rate physiological reactivity when experiencing negative emotions, and lower quantities of stress-related hormones circulating in their bodies (Gottman, 1994b). Many people assume that the cost of improving their marriage will be too great for them in personal terms. They assume that, in order to keep their partners happy, they will have to "give in" most of the time. But the evidence simply doesn't support this notion. People who meet the prerequisites get more cooperation from their partners, not less. Given the huge benefits and minimal costs, why do so many people go through life failing to develop the habits that would virtually guarantee their success in one of life's most important endeavors?

New answers to this question have recently emerged from the study of the human brain. There is a mounting body of evidence suggesting that people keep doing things that they know they shouldn't do, and they fail to do things they know they should do because their brains are programmed to make decisions for them. New studies reveal how the brain becomes conditioned to respond automatically to certain cues by activating neural response programs that propel people into specific patterns of thinking and action. The human brain is equipped with seven such neural response programs, each set up to produce powerful internal states that dictate how people respond in any given situation. For the most part, people don't volunteer for these internal states, they simply find themselves under their influence. When any one of them is activated, a person may lose the freedom to choose her thoughts and actions freely. It is as if, at that moment, someone else is in charge. She cannot act differently because she's in the grips of a neural state that is preprogrammed for a specific purpose. In order to respond differently, she must first experience a shift in brain states.

In Chapters 1 and 2, we will take a close look at the ground-breaking neuroscience studies that have identified the brain's neural response circuits. There is a good deal of evidence suggesting that the brain gets wired for specific kinds of neural activations very early in life, and that once the activation patterns are set, they can persist throughout a person's life. These automatically activated neural operating systems can be the greatest advantage a person has in navigating the demands of everyday life, but they can also be the source of a person's distress. When things go well, people automatically experience the motivation to love, to care, to seek comfort, and to defend themselves precisely when they need to. But sometimes the required neural operating system doesn't kick in when needed. For example, people don't miss loved ones when apart from them, they don't feel empathy when others are upset, or they just don't enjoy opening up to others. When the appropriate internal states don't show up on cue, the best they can do is fake it. A husband might not exactly be lying when he says, "I miss you, honey," but the "missing" may be more theoretical than heartfelt, and at some level his wife will know this. He is saying the right words, but they are hollow. Other times, neural states that produce defensiveness or withdrawal kick in precisely when people need to be open-minded or engaged with their partners.

When intimate relationships become distressed, there are nearly always problems with the conditioned activation or suppression of each partner's neural operating systems. Research on internal response circuits suggests that problems come in three varieties: (1) When a person gets caught in the "pull" of an internal response circuit, and is unable to do what is needed (e.g., when the "anger program" kicks in, and a person just can't listen to his partner when it would ultimately be to his or her benefit to do so); (2) when a person avoids doing or saying requisite things because to do so would likely trigger an uncomfortable internal response circuit in him or her (e.g., when a person is unable to admit when he's wrong, because doing so triggers an anxious or vulnerable state in him); (3) when a requisite response state simply doesn't show up (e.g., when a person needs to respond to his partner with tenderness or caring, but he finds himself preoccupied with other things).

The discovery of the brain's neural operating systems is of huge importance for those of us who are trying to make sense of why partners often persist in self-defeating interactions, even when they know that it would be in their best interest to change. People fail to think and act in ways that promote relationship success because they repeatedly find themselves in the wrong frame of mind when certain types of thinking or action are needed. They cannot sustain requisite attitudes or actions because the juice that fuels these attitudes and actions isn't there. The wrong brain state shows up, and they find themselves with attitudes and urges that take them in the wrong direction. To get better at meeting the habits that enable relationship success, our clients must first develop more ability to influence their own internal states. Many times, the problem isn't knowledge (they often know very well what they need to do), or ability (they've done it many times before), the problem is *motivation*. Precisely at the moments when they need to think or act differently, they don't feel like it. They're not in the mood, because something that has happened has activated a brain state that simply doesn't support the kind of thinking and action needed to promote relationship success. They can try to override the internal state and act in ways that aren't supported by it, but this is a bit like trying to accelerate from zero to 60 miles per hour while driving in fourth gear. A person might be doing all the right things (letting the clutch out slowly while giving it some gas), but he won't be able to get where he wants to go unless he shifts into first gear before accelerating. All of the effort in the world won't keep the car from stalling out unless this person shifts first. Most of the time, relationship problems stem from gear-shifting problems, or more precisely, state-shifting problems. Anyone who wants more cooperation, respect, or caring from his or her partner must get better at the ability to shift internal states when the requisite states don't automatically show up.

The discovery of the brain's neural operating programs helps explain why psychotherapies sometimes fail to promote lasting change. New narratives, attributions, and behaviors learned in therapy will only persist to the extent that they become woven into the fabric of neural response programs that automatically swing into gear during the course of daily living. Further, because the brain operates in state-specific ways, new ways of thinking or acting while in one brain state will not necessarily persist when another neural state becomes active. Regardless of the type of change a therapist is trying to promote, it will only last when the change becomes integrated into the brain's conditioned response patterns.

In his book *The Emotional Brain* (1996), neuroscientist Joseph LeDoux suggested that successful psychotherapy literally rewires the brain for more flexibility by forging new neural networks that were not previously associated. Psychotherapy can create new levels of neural integration in the brain by promoting the growth of new neurons, the expansion of existing neurons, and changes in the connections between existing neurons (Cozolino, 2002). Problems arise when various parts of the brain aren't communicating well with each other. Daniel Siegel noted:

> Mental functioning emanates from anatomically distinct and fairly autonomous circuits, each of which can be dis-associated from the function of others. . . . Various mental processes may thus be functionally isolated from one another with the blockage of integrative circuits. (1999, pp. 319–320)

Siegel provided an example of how psychotherapy promoted new levels of neural integration within the brain of an attorney whose career was threatened by her angry outbursts with clients:

> Within these states in the therapeutic session, her experience of being "out of control" was joined by the reflective and supportive dialogue with her therapist. She was able to listen in her agitation but remained hyperaroused. However, she now had two objects for her attention—her internal state and the external dialogue. As time went on, she was able to begin to reflect on the nature of her own mental processes. She could picture her circuits with an excessive flooding of activity; she could notice her tense muscles contributing to the feedback to her mind that she was furious. . . . Therapy allowed her to experience emotionally flooded states, and within that state of mind, she could use relation and imagery to "lower the energy of her circuits" and the tension in her body. Her metacognitive cortical capacities were strengthened and made more accessible during her rages in ways that were not possible before. Such capacities allowed her to use previously inhibited pathways during this state of mind to alter the way she processed information. What had been a blockage in information processing and an inhibition in the flow of energy now became more adaptive states of mind. Her capacity for emotional regulation, and thus for self-regulation, became more flexible and more effective. (1999, 261–262)

The kind of neural integration experienced by Siegel's client is similar to that experienced by distressed partners who participate in the clinical approach described in this book.

As I have worked with couples over the years, I have often been struck by how predictable and rigid their reactions to each other are as they struggle to influence each other. To any outside observer their reactions are clearly counterproductive. When they are calm, clients often readily acknowledge that these reactions need to change, but when they get upset, it is as if the part of their brain that knows this gets shut off. They get caught up in internal states that dictate their reactions to each other. In couples therapy, we help clients develop the ability to use their brains more fully during stressful situations. We do this by helping them use previously neglected parts of their brains precisely at the moments when their old, emotionally driven neural response programs are "up and running." As we help them do this over and over again, new neural connections are formed, enabling their brains to respond in a different way. They become more able to use their whole brains as they navigate difficult circumstances in their relationships.

THE BOOK

This book is divided into two parts. Part I provides a detailed exploration of the exciting discoveries we have touched on here. In Chapters 1 and 2, groundbreaking studies in the field of affective neuroscience are explored that provide new clues about why people persist in self-defeating ways of thinking or acting, even when they want to change. Studies described in Chapter 1 challenge the long-held assumption that cognition is the primary organizer of human experience. A host of studies suggest that our brains are set up to favor the influence of emotion. Chapter 1 invites the reader into the world of Susan and James, a couple whose relationship was hijacked by the activation of overly self-protective neural states that dictated their interactions. We will review what brain scientists have learned about how the brain's self-protective states operate, and take a look at how this information can be used to short-circuit the activation of these states.

In Chapter 2, we move on to explore the lives of Loretta and Jack. Unlike James and Susan, Jack and Loretta weren't fighters. Rather, they suffered from a lack of emotional connectedness in their marriage, and had drifted apart. In Chapter 2, we will review findings that suggest partners fail to connect because they have limited access to the brain's intimacy-producing states. Researchers have discovered that our brains are equipped with four special-purpose internal response systems which, when activated, naturally draw people closer, and produce strong emotional bonds. The text will demonstrate via Loretta and Jack how I used this information to jump-start dormant intimacy-producing neural states in the couple. This helped Loretta and Jack to experience genuine desire for emotional and sexual connectedness.

Chapters 1 and 2 explore the question of *how* people change, but in Chapter 3, we move on to explore *what* people in distressed relationships need to change, describing studies that suggest there are prerequisite abilities that people must have in order to succeed in their relationships. For example, we will explore how effective partners stand up for themselves without putting their mates down, and we will review the specific moves made by people who both require that they be treated with respect and at the same time make it very easy for their partners to treat them with respect.

The second part of this book is devoted to a detailed description of the methods and assumptions of Pragmatic/Experiential Therapy for Couples (PET-C), an approach that helps partners rewire their brains for more flexibility, enabling them to meet the prerequisites for relationship success. In Chapter 4, we will review the phases of PET-C, the assumptions that inform the approach, and the basic tasks that skilled PET-C therapists accomplish. We will look at how PET-C is used to facilitate greater awareness of the brain states that often prevent partners from implementing the habits that predict relationship success, and how PET-C helps partners develop the ability to shift into brain states that make needed thinking and action possible. We will explore the integrative nature of PET-C, compare it with other prominent approaches to couples therapy, and consider how PET-C incorporates aspects of other clinical models into its unique theoretical base.

In Chapter 5, we will look at how the PET-C therapist uses assessment sessions to develop a clear picture of the patterns of automatic internal state activation-suppression that characterize each partner's interaction in the relationship. We will look at methods that can be used by therapists to uncover the pathologizing explanations that clients often use to make sense of upsetting aspects of their partners' thinking or actions, and show how therapists can identify various forms of contempt that partners often secretly harbor. We will also detail methods for assessing the extent to which each partner is currently engaging in the 10 habits that predict relationship success, the specific issues over which partners are gridlocked, the bigger issues at stake behind each partner's position on gridlocked issues, and significant past hurtful experiences that each partner has experienced in the current or past relationships.

When couples begin therapy, partners are usually caught in mutually reinforcing patterns of interaction, fueled by the automatic activation of self-protective internal states in each partner. A state in one partner automatically activates a predictable state in the other, which triggers or perpetuates a predictable state in the first partner, and so on. In Chapter 6, we will review three levels of intervention that can be used to help partners shift internal states during therapy sessions, freeing them to interact in ways that are predictive of relationship success.

Most people who are in distressed relationships believe that, for their relationships to improve, somebody must convince their partners that they need to change. In Chapters 7 and 8, we will review how the PET-C therapist uses state-shifting interventions to help partners become receptive to the idea that the best way to change their partners is to change themselves. Once partners become committed to changing their own habits of reacting in upsetting situations, a

second phase of therapy begins in which each partner receives personalized tutoring in the skills of emotional intelligence, using his or her own relationship
as a workshop for practicing these skills. In Chapters 9 and 10, we will review
how the PET-C therapist helps clients become expert in responding effectively
to their partners in any upsetting situation that occurs. Clients generally enter
Phase II faintly aware of the extent to which their interactions with their partners are governed by the automatic patterning of internal state activations inside
of them. Here clients learn to recognize cues that signify the activation of specific internal states, and they become more adept at recognizing the "triggers"
for these mood states.

Awareness of the internal states that govern one's reactions in upsetting situations is crucial, but often not sufficient to promote lasting change, because at the
moments when clients need to use this awareness, they are often caught in neural
states that carry their thoughts in a different direction. Once activated, a neural response program has a momentum of its own. In order to engage in different thinking and action when it is needed, the client must develop the ability to think and
act differently *in the moments when the state is active*. In Chapter 11, we will review how PET-C therapists help clients accomplish this through repetitive practice designed to recondition automatic internal reactions. Through these practices, clients rewire interfering internal states for more flexibility, making it possible
for them to think and act in ways that are predictive of relationship success.

When the second phase of PET-C is successful, partners begin experiencing
increased respect and cooperativeness. Critical as these changes may be, they
will not be enough to ensure a couple's lasting happiness. Long-term studies on
relationships suggest that the absence of fighting on its own is not sufficient to
predict good relationship outcomes. Couples who succeed don't just stop fighting, they form powerful positive emotional bonds. They become best friends, experiencing warmth, fondness, and admiration for each other on a daily basis.
Each of our brains is equipped with four executive operating systems which,
when active, naturally produce feelings and motivations that draw intimate partners emotionally closer to each other. In Chapter 12, we will review how the
therapist can help partners increase access to these intimacy states.

Interest in the PET-C model has grown considerably in the years since it was
first introduced (Atkinson, 1998, 1999, 2001), and several training formats are
now available for those who are interested in developing expertise in it. From
our training experiences, we have identified a number of factors that contribute
to the success of individuals becoming skilled PET-C practitioners. Chapter 13
highlights some of the insights we have gleaned on this topic, and some of the
training methods we have used.

CONCLUSION

New studies on factors that predict relationship success point to the critical role
that emotion plays in the course of intimate relationships (Gottman, 1999). Un-

til recently, we understood relatively little about emotional processes in the brain, but since the mid-1970s neuroscientists have made dramatic progress in uncovering the mysterious mechanisms of emotion. Let me say clearly at the outset that almost nothing about the brain processes involved in emotion can be stated with absolute authority. Affective neuroscience is still an infant field, which means that many conclusions are still in the realm of correlation and possibility. And high-tech tools notwithstanding, the task of mapping the emotional brain is a staggeringly complex undertaking. Each human brain houses up to 100 billion neurons, each of which is capable of making thousands of connections with other neurons. Attempting to understand this intricate, electrochemical mesh *of* emotion, a concept that itself encompasses an enormously complex set of phenomena, is a truly daunting task.

Nonetheless, as the "black box" beneath our craniums is slowly and painstakingly being pried open, its contents deserve our close inspection. For while more time and research will be needed before new discoveries become widely accepted, new perspectives on the emotional brain hold the promise of more potent and effective ways of doing therapy. This new knowledge has transformed my clinical work with couples, inspiring an approach that empowers emotion and thought to work in common cause, rather than at cross-purposes, to help people manage their most volatile feelings. Whatever a therapist's current orientation, be it cognitive, behavioral, affective, or some blend thereof, I believe that the newly charted links between our neural circuitry and our most primitive passions merit open-minded and thoughtful consideration.

PART I
Scientific Basis

CHAPTER 1

Affective Neuroscience and the Emotional Revolution

O N A HUMID EVENING last September, Susan, 27, and James, 36, burst into our office looking like two high schoolers in the grip of a classroom giggle fit. Usually serious and reserved, James explained between chuckles that he had been telling Susan a funny anecdote about his boss. Still chortling, Susan tried to compose herself, then eyed her husband and they both began laughing again. I glanced at my wife and cotherapist, Lisa, for a microsecond and gave her a raised-eyebrow version of a high five: This had all the earmarks of an easy session. After a bit more banter, we steered the conversation to the main order of business—the state of their six-year marriage. Susan began to recount an incident that had occurred a few days before, when James had volunteered Susan to drive his daughter to a birthday party so that his ex-wife wouldn't be inconvenienced. "I felt used," Susan said bluntly. So far, so good, I thought—she is simply stating her feelings. Then looking directly at her husband, she continued: "But what upset me even more was your reaction when you saw that I was unhappy. You started defending her!"

With these words, Susan's voice began to shake and she ducked her head, staring at the flowered pattern of the tissue in her fist. When she looked up her eyes were narrowed and her face flushed a deep, mottled crimson. "You are so full of crap!" she spit out. "You're too weak to stand up to her, then you look at me as if I'm the one with the problem. God, what a sucker I am to stay with you!"

James rolled his eyes and sighed elaborately, then turned toward us. "You see what I have to deal with here?" he asked beseechingly. It was as though he had lit a match to his wife's innards. "Oh, that's good, James!" sneered Susan. "Blame me again! This is classic. You're such a fucking wimp!"

James didn't respond. In fact, I wasn't even sure he had heard her. His whole body seemed to contract as he turned toward the office picture window and stared unseeing through it, his mouth a taut line. Though he sat very still, I could hear the ragged sounds of his breathing. The relaxed, affable man who had entered our office 10 minutes earlier had simply vanished.

Looking back, I realize it was pure wishful thinking to equate this couple's initial good cheer with an easy session. In fact, over the years I have often been struck by how swiftly and dramatically the moods of intimate partners can change in the midst of an interaction, as though some internal switch gets flipped that compels each partner to react in a particular, almost predetermined way. In a previous session, James had jokingly called Susan "Sybil," noting that whenever she became deeply upset, she entered "the zone," a place from which she could only react with white-hot wrath. At times, that rage turned physical: during one particularly savage fight, she had knocked James unconscious by pushing him into a wall. Yet, in my observation, Susan was not the only partner prone to meteoric mood shifts. James's predictable response to Susan's rage—a lightning-fast retreat into his own zone of tuned-out, protective distance—was every bit as sudden and intense as his wife's.

In the past, the goal of our therapy with a couple like Susan and James would have been to teach them habits of thinking and behaving that are highly predictive of relationship success, and hope that they would actually use these abilities when therapy was over. For example, we would have coached Susan to launch her complaint without criticizing James, to become determined to understand the logic behind James actions, acknowledge the understandable aspects of his feelings, and stand up for her own feelings without putting James down. Similarly we would have helped James assume that there was something at least partly legitimate about Susan's complaint, assure her that he cared about her feelings, and be willing to work toward a mutually satisfying solution. These methods, and most others used in couples therapy today, assume that our rational brains are in charge of our emotions, that what distinguished Homo sapiens from so-called "lower" animals is our capacity to reason before we react.

But what if the human brain isn't actually wired that way? What if our neural circuitry programs us instead to rage and cower and collapse in grief in a second, before we ever get a chance to fashion an "I" statement or otherwise think things through? With the help of ever more refined imaging techniques that generate vivid portraits of the brain in action, a new generation of neurobiologists is in the process of documenting that our cerebral topography actually favors emotionality, not reason. Thinking still counts, but not nearly as much as we have always assumed.

THE EMOTIONAL BRAIN

Since the early 20th century, it has been assumed that cognition is the most powerful organizer of human experience (LeDoux, 2000). According to this view, the way we *think* about things determines how we *feel* and *act*. The "cognitive priority" view emerged in sharp contrast to the Freudian view that preceded it. According to Freud, our emotions and actions are the result of unconscious drives and feelings of which we may not be aware, and often have little direct control over. The cognitive paradigm emerged as a comforting counter to the animalistic view of humans implied by the Freudian perspective. The cognitive view sees humans as being unlike other mammals, in being consciously in charge of their experience.

The cognitive revolution was inspired by early discoveries about the brain. Neuroscientists learned that, although certain parts of the human brain are almost identical to the brains of primates such as bonobos or chimpanzees, a part of the human brain is not shared by animals—the neocortex (MacLean, 1990). The limbic brain appears to be the source of basic emotions and urges, and is sometimes referred to as the "emotional brain." In contrast, the neocortex gives humans the ability to think in abstract terms. Given that the neocortex is three times larger than the emotional brain, it has been assumed that thinking must be more powerful than emotion in influencing human experience. The neocortex enables humans to use language, symbolic thought, and abstract thinking. It was assumed that because the neocortex is what makes humans unique amongst mammals, it must also be the part of the brain most responsible for organizing human experience. Decades ago, Joseph LeDoux, who was prominent in research into the origins of emotions applied to the National Institutes of Health (NIH) for a grant to study brain processes involved in fear, his application was rejected outright (Johnson, 2004; Rosenthal, 2002). The burning question of the day was how do we think, not how do we feel.

The climate in the neuroscience community has changed dramatically in the past two decades. LeDoux finally got his grants, and others followed. Spurred by the discoveries of Nobel laureates Arvid Carlsson, Paul Greengard, and Eric Kandel, the field of neuroscience has entered what many scientists believe to be a revolution in thinking about the fundamental processes that organize human experience (Rosenthal, 2002). Let's take a look at some of the discoveries that have prompted such an amazing shift in perspective.

NEURAL ARCHITECTURE FAVORS EMOTIONAL INFLUENCE

Many major researchers in affective neuroscience agree that in terms of neural architecture, the direction of influence is clearly in favor of emotion being the primary organizer. If cognition were the primary organizer of human experience, one would expect to see many more neural projections from the thinking brain to the emotional brain than vice versa, but this is decidedly not the case. Neuroscientist Joseph LeDoux summarized: "The wiring of the brain at this point in our evolutionary history is such that connections from the emotional systems to the cognitive systems are stronger than connections from the cognitive systems to the emotional systems" (1996, p. 19). In fact, neural projections from the brain's emotional centers are wired to nearly every other part of the brain, and influence each stage of cognitive processing, whereas many phases of cognitive processing do not project to the emotional centers (LeDoux, 1996). This means that, structurally speaking, emotion can influence what we pay attention to, and how we interpret what we see. "Because emotions are fundamentally linked to appraisal-arousal mechanisms in both the right and left hemispheres, they influence all aspects of cognition, from perception to rational decision making" (Siegel, 1999, pp. 185–186). "Emotion is not just some 'primitive' remnant of an earlier reptilian evolutionary past. Emotion directs the flow of activation (energy) and establishes the meaning of representation (information processing) for the individual. It is not a single, isolated group of processes; it has a direct impact on the entire mind" (Siegel, 1999, p. 263).

No doubt, the brain privileges emotion because the neocortex, the phylogenetically most recent part of the brain developed out of the older limbic brain structures (hypothalamus, hippocampus, and amygdala). It is generally agreed that the circuits of the limbic brain developed over 500 million years ago, while the human neocortex began evolving just 5 million years ago, and the current version of the human neocortex has existed for approximately 60,000 years (Ornstein, 1991). LeDoux pointed out: "Consciousness and its sidekick, natural language, are the new kids on the evolutionary block—unconscious processing is the rule rather than the exception throughout evolution" (1996, p. 71). The limbic brain has neural connections to every part of the neocortex. Natural selection "does not produce novelties from scratch. It works on what already exists" (Jacob, 1977, p. 1164). Evolution works by modifications that expand the effectiveness of existing structures rather than by replacing them. "Evolution . . . creates unique behavioral solutions to the problem of survival in different species, but it may do so by following a kind of 'if it ain't broke, don't fix it' rule for the underlying brain systems" (Le Doux, 1977, p. 125). In the course of evolution, the limbic brain wasn't replaced by the neocortex. Rather, the existing abilities of the emotional brain expanded to adapt more effectively to the world. The neural fingerprints of the limbic brain are all over the neocortex. The limbic brain retained its ability to "use" or influence this new structure of the brain in the service of its goals.

RATIONAL DECISION MAKING IS
DEPENDENT UPON EMOTION

Conventional wisdom suggests that, when we have important decisions to make, it's best to avoid being swayed by our emotions, and instead approach things in a logical, rational way. Studies conducted by Antonio Damasio and his colleagues at the University of Iowa have revealed that those who are most able to keep their emotions out of the decision-making process make *terrible* decisions (Damasio, 1994).

A Vermont railroad worker, Phineas Gage, had a tamping iron blown through his head in the summer of 1848. The iron went up through his cheek and exited the top of his head, landing more than 100 feet away. Gage was thrown to the ground, stunned, but fully awake. Fellow workers watched wide-eyed as Gage was transported by ox cart, jabbering to others along the way and to the local physician, John Harlow, who reported that Gage told him about the accident with a perfectly rational demeanor while he examined Gage's skull. Harlow reported that he was able to insert one finger in the hole in the top of Gage's head and the other finger in his cheek, bringing the fingers together in the middle of Gage's head! But all the while, Gage appeared unaffected.

Time passed, and it became clear that Gage was indeed affected, but yet the impact of the damage was not as expected. His intellectual and motor faculties appeared fully functional, it was his social interactions that began to change. Before the accident Gage was praised by his supervisors as their most valued employee, able to make apt decisions, and manage his workers with sensitivity and efficiency. After the accident, "Gage was no longer Gage" (Damasio, 1994, p. 8). The rest of his life was characterized by impulsiveness, irresponsibility, outbursts of rage, and a foul mouth. He couldn't hold a job, and finally landed with Barnum's circus, earning a wage as an eccentric attraction. Gage's last years were spent drinking and brawling.

Although the importance of Gage's particular kind of brain damage was not understood right away, his skull has been an object of intense study by affective neuroscientists (Bower, 1994a; Damasio, Grabowski, Frank, Galaburda, & Damasio, 1994; Shreeve, 1995). Damasio and his colleagues at the University of Iowa Medical Center identified a group of brain-damaged patients who exhibited behavior that was strikingly similar to that of Gage. Like Gage, following brain damage, these patients evidenced no impairments in intellectual or motor abilities, but they experienced a sharp decline in their ability to make good decisions, failing to prioritize events well, and acting irresponsibly. For example, one of Damasio's patients, Elliot, had been a good husband and father, had a good business-type job, and was described by others as a role model for younger colleagues. But after a surgery that removed part of his brain, Elliot had trouble getting started in the morning, and he couldn't keep to a schedule. He failed especially at jobs that required prioritizing; spending too much time with whatever captivated his attention at the moment. Eventually, Elliot was fired, and he lost other jobs as well. His business ventures failed miserably and he ended up filing for bankruptcy. His wife couldn't understand why such a competent person could act so irresponsibly, and his subsequent marriage failed.

Damasio and colleagues assessed Elliot's perceptual ability, short-term memory, long-term memory, new learning, language, ability to do math, attention span, and working memory, all of which were normal. Standardized psychological and neuropsychological tests were also normal. Damasio eventually realized that he had been overly concerned with the cognitive and motor abilities of Elliot and the other patients, and had not paid much attention to their emotions. At first glance, there was nothing unusual about Elliot's emotions. He was emotionally reserved, but had a dry and witty sense of humor. Further analysis revealed, however, that

Elliot described his life tragedies with a kind of detachment. In fact, Damasio found himself suffering more when listening to Elliot's stories than Elliot himself. Elliot recognized this, and told Damasio that his feelings had changed from before his surgery. He knew that situations that had once evoked strong emotion no longer caused any reactions, positive or negative. Damasio tested this, using skin conductance experiments. People normally exhibit regular, predictable skin conductance reactions to both unexpected, alarming conditions, such as loud noises, and to viewing emotionally disturbing pictures, such as scenes of human suffering or devastation. Elliot didn't show any reactions to disturbing pictures at all. His skin conductance recordings for each of the emotionally charged slides were uniformly flat. He could recall the pictures in perfect detail and sequence, and could describe how sad or awful the situations in the pictures were, but he felt nothing.

The skin conductance tests were repeated with 11 other patients who, like Elliot, had sustained damage to the ventromedial sector of the prefrontal lobes, and who demonstrated the Gage syndrome in their decision making. Their reactions to the slides were identical to those of Elliot.

Damasio had finally found the impairment in brain functioning he was looking for. These patients didn't experience emotion like the rest of us. But what do logical decision making and emotional processing have to do with each other? Damasio's Somatic-Marker hypothesis says that when a decision is made, various possibilities flash through the mind. As each possibility is considered, the body responds, generating a gut feeling. For example, when a bad outcome is connected to a possible course of action, the individual gets a bad feeling. Sometimes this feeling enters awareness, and sometimes it does not, but at some level, it automatically forces attention on the negative outcome to which a given action may lead, and functions as an automated alarm signal warning of danger ahead. This signal may lead the person to immediately reject a particular course of action and choose an alternative. There is still room for a rational cost–benefit analysis, but only after automated somatic markers drastically reduce the choices. Negative markers serve as alarms; positive markers serve as beacons of incentive. Somatic markers do not deliberate for the individual, they assist deliberation by highlighting some options. Logical consideration of all options in various situations would take forever. Somatic markers provide immediate direction and motivation (Damasio, 1994, 1998, 2001).

The absence of somatic markers may leave an individual adrift with no motivation to move one way or the other, as was the case with Elliot and the 11 other subjects in Damasio's study. They were unable to anticipate consequences as the average person would do. Without the feelings that, for most of us, come automatically as we ponder different possibilities, Elliot and his cohorts began acting more or less on the basis of what they wanted at the moment. Damasio (2002) summarized: "Without emotion, we're left at the mercy of fact and logic, and that's just not good enough."

Support for the somatic marker hypothesis comes not only from Damasio's neurological laboratories, but also from research on patients suffering from antisocial personality disorder (also known as psychopaths), who are known for making decisions that harm others. They steal, they kill, they rape, and they lie. Studies suggest that they are often intelligent, too. Several studies suggest that, like Damasio's patients, these patients have an impaired experience of emotion (Kaihla, 1996). For example, in one study, psychopaths exhibited a significantly lower physiological response to emotionally charged words than normal individuals did (Patrick, Cuthbert, & Lang, 1994). Other studies show that psychopaths who know they are about to receive an electric shock show less physiological signs of fear that nonpsychopaths (Hare, 1965, 1978, 1982; Hare & Craigen, 1974; Hare, Frazelle, & Cox, 1978; Ogloff & Wong, 1990). Damasio has suggested that psychopaths may have a dysfunction within the same overall system which was impaired in Gage, and in Elliot and the 11 other patients in his study. The difference is that, whereas in the case of Gage and Damasio's patients the dysfunction occurred in adulthood, it is possible that some psychopaths could have a dysfunction in emotional processing that dates back to the early years of life, stemming from prenatal brain development or early brain development governed by parent-infant attachment experiences (Anderson, Bechara, H. Damasio, Tranel, & A. Damasio, 1999).

Damasio explained that somatic markers have two avenues of influence, one through consciousness, and another outside consciousness. Neurologically, it is possible for the physiological mechanisms accompanying emotion to be activated without our being aware of it. Apparently, emotions can come on strong, or they can simmer beneath the threshold of awareness. Many studies show that people often aren't aware of experiencing emotion when physiological signs of emotion are present, for example, as measured by galvanic skin conductance (Goleman, 1995; Kagan, 1994; LeDoux, 1996; Weinberger, 1990). We all know that strong emotion biases thinking. However, Damasio understands the brain as being set up so that subtle, undetected emotional responses can bias cognitive processes just as surely, without the thinker's awareness of the influence, creating the possibility that a person may think she or he is being perfectly rational when that is not the case. LeDoux noted, "Emotional responses are, for the most part, generated unconsciously. Freud was right on the mark when he described consciousness as the tip of the mental iceberg" (1996, p. 17). As Robert Ornstein put it:

> Emotions set our agenda, and they do so largely without our being aware of them. Far from being disorganizing, they are the focal point of the mental system's activity: They govern our choices, they determine our goals, and they guide our lives. We are, for the most part, in most of life their servants, and we are not usually conscious of them." (1991, p. 96)

When I first read about Damasio's studies in 1994, I knew that the implications were profound, but even Damasio himself couldn't have imagined the widespread impact that his work would have. His discoveries have been cited by virtually every neuroscientist in the field of affective neuroscience, and have been featured in a recent PBS documentary, *The Secret Life of the Brain* (Damasio, 2002).

Since Damasio's initial studies, additional research has begun to tease apart the specific prefrontal structures that are most responsible for the experience of emotion (Hornak et al., 2003). The findings of Damasio and others have challenged the notion that responsible people rely more on thinking when making decisions and irresponsible people go more with their feelings. The evidence suggests we all go with our feelings (Mayer, Nabiloff, & Munakata, 2000; Tranel, Bechara, & Damasio, 2000). In those extraordinary cases in which feelings truly are kept out, the results are disastrous. Before these studies, a "rational person" was considered to be a person who has the ability to set aside emotion and make a decision based on logic. Damasio's work has suggested a new definition of what it means to be rational: *Rationality depends on the ability to experience (and be influenced by) emotion both in reaction to present situations, as well as when remembering past situations and visualizing future situations.*

THE BRAIN MECHANISMS THAT GENERATE EMOTION

Damasio's studies provide compelling evidence that rationality is dependent upon emotion, but where do emotions come from in the first place? Affective neuroscientists have long suspected that there is a brain structure that triggers emotional reactions quickly and independently of the thinking brain. It is basic knowledge among experimental psychologists that animals can learn emotional reactions through conditioning or association. For example, if you pair any sound or sight repeatedly with an aversive condition such as a shock, a rat will learn to be afraid of the sight or sound, regardless of whether the shock continues or not. Humans learn this way too, in laboratory settings as well as real life. For example, a Vietnam veteran who experienced traumatic situations in combat may experience a surge of anxiety years later when a helicopter flies overhead. Or a person who was in an auto accident in which the horn got stuck in the on position may later have a fear reaction when hearing the blare of car horns (LeDoux, 1994).

The amygdala, a small, almond-sized structure located at the top of the brainstem near the bottom of the limbic lobe, is responsible for emotional learning. Evidence comes from both animal and human studies (Adolphs, Tranel, Damasio, & Damasio, 1994, 1995; Aggleton, 1992; Barinaga, 1992; Bechara et al., 1995; Blanchard & Blanchard, 1972; Bower, 1994b; Cahill, Prins, Weber & McGaugh, 1994; Cahill, Babinsky, Markowitsch, & McGaugh, 1995; Cahill et al., 1996; Clark, 1995; Davis, 1986, 1992a, 1992b; Davis, Hitchcock, & Rosen, 1987; Decker, Curzon, & Brioni, 1995; Fendt & Fanselow, 1999; Kapp, Whalen, Supple, & Pascoe, 1992; LeDoux, 1986, 1992a, 1992b, 1992c, 1993a, 1993b, 1994, 1995, 2002; Rasia-Filo, Londero, & Achaval, 2000; Rolls, 1990). If the amygdala is destroyed, all learned emotional responses vanish. Without the amygdala, mammals cannot generalize emotional experiences. A rat who was previously conditioned to expect an electric shock when hearing a specific tone will "forget" this learning if the amygdala is damaged. A rat with a lesioned amygdala will even nibble at the ear of a cat (Blanchard & Blanchard, 1972).

Emotional Memory

The amygdala also plays a crucial role in generating emotional memory in humans. Until recently, it was thought that the hippocampus was the most important brain structure involved in memory. New studies suggest that there are different types of memory, and that different brain structures play prominent roles in these different types of memory (LeDoux, 1994). The hippocampus is indeed responsible for declarative memory (memory about facts and details), but the amygdala is most responsible for emotional memory (LeDoux, 1996). Bechara, Damasio, and colleagues studied three patients with different types of brain damage: one had bilateral damage to the amygdala but not the hippocampus, one had bilateral damage to the hippocampus but not the amygdala, and a third had bilateral damage to both the amygdala and hippocampus. In a series of controlled trials they compared the performance of these three individuals with control subjects who had no known brain damage (Bechara et al., 1995). Each of the subjects was exposed to common fear conditioning trials in which colored slides were shown in random order. A blue slide was always paired with a loud blast from an air horn. Emotional reactions were recorded via galvanic skin conductance tests. The patient with amygdala damage and an intact hippocampus could remember intellectually which slide was paired with the horn, but this patient's *body* did not remember. The patient registered no physiological signs of fear conditioning. For the individual with hippocampus damage, but intact amygdala, galvanic skin tests revealed a continuing emotional reaction to the blue slide, but this individual could not remember which slide was paired with the horn during the trials. The person with bilateral damage to both the amygdala and hippocampus did not develop fear conditioning, and could not remember which slide was paired with the horn.

These studies and others (Adolphs et al., 1994; Bower, 1994b; Cahill et al., 1995; Iidaka et al., 2003; LaBar, LeDoux, Spencer, & Phelps, 1995; Tranel & Hyman, 1990) provide evidence that the amygdala is responsible for emotional associations, while the hippocampus is responsible for memory of facts, context, and details. As LeDoux put it, "The hippocampus is crucial in recognizing a face as that of your cousin. But it is the amygdala that adds that you don't really like her" (cited in Goleman, 1995, p. 20). The amygdala detects features of current circumstances and decides if they are close enough to former, emotionally significant experiences to warrant an emotional response in the present situation. All of this happens instantaneously, no cognitive processing is required. The amygdala draws on a history of emotional conditioning, and relies on gross generalization in making decisions about whether or not to trigger an emotional response. Its method is "quick and dirty," and its generalizations are "sloppy" (Goleman, 1995). The emotional state triggered by the amygdala may be exactly the same, regardless of whether it is a spouse who is angry with you or your father, who abused you in years gone by.

These findings could be very important when paired with evidence that the amygdala matures faster in newborn infants than does the hippocampus (Jacobs & Nadel, 1985; LeDoux, 1994, 1996; Rudy, 1993; Rudy & Morledge, 1994; Schore, 1994). This means that during early childhood, when relationships with caregivers have such profoundly life-shaping impact, the amygdala is busy making emotion-charged associations about events that the embryonic hippocampus is insufficiently developed to record. Neurologically speaking, it is likely that the emotional dispositions that accompany individuals through life are conditioned early, when the amygdala is making associations and the hippocampus isn't yet sufficiently developed to make sense of things. Adults, then, can be plagued by chronic, debilitating emotional outbursts linked to past events that they neither remember nor have any way of recovering, because one cannot recover a memory that has never been recorded. Perhaps this is one reason why many clients seem so unwilling to relinquish their convictions that their explosive reactions to current spousal behavior—a wife's propensity to flirt at parties, a husband who forgets to call when he's going to be late—is entirely appropriate. There may be no early memory of attachment distress to trace such reactions to.

But this amputation of emotion from its historical origins may take place at any point in our lives. During severe stress, hippocampal functioning can be inhibited, as massive levels of stress hormones are released along with catecholamines such as epinephrine and norepinephrine, resulting in the possible blocking of a memory from being encoded (Siegel, 1999). Studies by Bruce McEwen, a researcher on the biology of stress at New York's Rockefeller University, indicate that even in a mature hippocampus, severe stress can cause a shriveling of dendrites, the stringy, branching ends of neurons that are largely responsible for the initial phases of long-term memory formation (McEwen, 1992; McEwen & Sapolsky, 1995; Magarinos, McEwen, Fluegge, & Fuchs, 1996). Excessive and chronic exposure to stress hormones may lead to the death of neurons in the hippocampus (Siegel, 1999), severing people from conscious memories of stressful experiences that often shape their later emotional reactions. Studies have shown that in trauma survivors, such as victims of chronic childhood abuse and Vietnam veterans with posttraumatic stress disorder, the hippocampus is measurably shrunken (Bremner & Narayan, 1998).

In stark contrast, stress enhances the functioning of the amygdala (LeDoux, 1996). As blood levels of stress hormones shoot up, the amygdala seems to kick into overdrive, thereby facilitating extremely potent learned fear. So if a person endures a severely stressful situation, he or she may forget the distressing incident itself, yet become emotionally hyperactive to future events that are unconsciously even slightly reminiscent of the original, triggering situation. Hence, a client may have forgotten that she was raped repeatedly by her uncle, yet become panicky and tearful whenever her husband approaches her for sex. Or a man may verbally attack his wife whenever he perceives that she is being "distant" from him, having altogether forgotten that as a small child, his depressed mother regularly retreated to her locked bedroom, leaving him utterly alone for hours at a time.

The Neural Back Alley

People who cannot remember the origins of emotionally charged experiences are not the only ones who can be influenced by the amygdala. A person who remembers emotionally significant experiences can be impacted by them just as surely. This is because, in terms of neural architecture, the amygdala receives incoming information, and can trigger emotional reactions before the information ever reaches the "thinking brain" (LeDoux, 1994). For years, it was assumed that information about the world travels via the eye, ear, and other sensory organs through the thalamus to the sensory processing areas of the neocortex where the signals are processed and sorted for meaning and object recognition. From the neocortex, it was assumed that signals are then sent to various limbic structures, including the amygdala, which trigger the appropriate emotional responses throughout the body. While confirming that sensory signals indeed travel this path, LeDoux discovered a "neural back alley," where incoming signals are also routed through the thalamas, then bypass the neocortex by crossing a *single* synapse straight to the amygdala (Barinaga, 1992; Goleman, 1995). This means that the amygdala gets a look at all incoming information before it is processed by the neocortex. LeDoux discovered this neural arrangement by destroying the entire audio cortexes of rats, then subjecting them repeatedly to a tone paired with an electric shock (Johnson, 2004). He found that the rats learned to fear the tone, even though the tone never registered in their audio cortexes. The rats learned an emotional reaction without any higher cortical involvement. Next, LeDoux injected a tracer substance into the thalamus, allowing him to see where the neurons in the thalamus send their fibers. He found that the thalamus projects to four subcortical regions. He made individual lesions which interrupted the information from the thalamus to each of these regions. Three of the lesions had absolutely no effect. But disconnection of the fourth area, the amygdala, from the thalamus prevented conditioning from taking place. LeDoux had located a pathway from the thalamus to the amygdala that bypasses the cortex altogether (LeDoux, 1996). The neural back alley enabled LeDoux's rats to generate emotional reactions without any higher cortical involvement. LeDoux explained: "Anatomically the emotional system can act independently of the neocortex . . . Some emotional reactions and emotional memories can be formed without any conscious, cognitive participation at all" (cited in Goleman, 1995, p. 18).

Unconscious Emotional Influence

Many controlled laboratory studies have confirmed that, indeed, adults experience emotional reactions triggered by stimuli that they are not aware of

(Bornstein, 1992; Kagan, 1994; Kihlstrom, 1987; Kunst-Wilson, 1980; LeDoux, 1996; Mathews & MacLeod, 1986; Ohman, 1999; Ohman & Soares, 1993; Zajonc, 1980, 1984). For example, in one study, patterns of letters were flashed on a screen using exposure durations that were too short to allow verbal identification. Some of the patterns were paired with an electric shock, transforming the meaningless letters into emotionally significant stimuli which elicited skin conductance responses. When the letter patterns that had been previously paired with a shock were presented too quickly to be consciously perceived, the subjects still had emotional reactions (LeDoux, 1996). Subsequent neuroimaging studies suggest that the right side of the amygdala may be responsible for processing stimuli that are not consciously perceived (Morris, 1999). Studies such as these suggest that the amygdala perceives and appraises significance much more rapidly than the conscious mind, again explaining why we may experience emotional reactions in the apparent absence of triggering stimuli in real life. A split-second shift in a lover's expression may vanish too quickly to be consciously recognized, but may nevertheless trigger an emotional reaction that thoroughly influences the tone of future interactions.

We tend to assume our reactions in any given situation are based on a more or less rational assessment of the merits of the particular situation. But our reactions are just as likely to be influenced by the instantaneous, automatically activated, emotionally based reactions that bias our thinking processes in certain directions. Because the shorter, subterranean pathway from the thalamus to the amygdala transmits information twice as fast as the more circuitous route involving the neocortex, by the time the neocortex gets into the act, the amygdala-triggered reactions may invade the neocortex itself, recruiting its centers for logic and judgment to support the emotional decisions the amygdala has already made. Some neuroscience experts believe that this is more often the case than not.

Most of us can think of many examples in which it seems that people have motives that are much more emotionally driven than they are willing to admit. For example, we often suspect that the ostensibly well-reasoned positions of politicians arise more from their basic emotional commitments (e.g., will this viewpoint get me reelected?) than a rational consideration of the facts. But this doesn't stop politicians from believing that their positions are fact-driven. Robert Ornstein summarized the relationship between emotional motivations and reason in the brain:

> Mental processes, I have come to believe, are not organized around thought or reason but around emotional ideals: how we feel we want something to be. . . . The relationship between emotional drives and reason is like the relationship between an entrepreneur and her lawyers. The entrepreneur knows what she wants to do and employs the lawyers to tell her how. Engineers and architects may be called upon to carry out the plan, provide the proper procedures, and supply other "rational" parts of the design, but the direction springs not from the lawyers or the architects but from the entrepreneur. (1991, p. 95)

Our brains are not set up to inform us accurately as to why we may feel the way we do. Emotionally based motivations often occur without conscious awareness. Beliefs and values may arise just as surely from a person's former emotionally significant experiences as they do from a reasoned assessment of the facts. But because the brain mechanisms that generate emotion are not subject to conscious awareness, we tend to conclude that our reactions are fact-driven. LeDoux noted:

> The fact that emotions, attitudes, goals, and the like are activated automatically (without any conscious effort) means that their presence in the mind and their influence on thoughts and behavior are not questioned. They are trusted the way we would trust any other kind of perception. In other words, the perception in oneself of an attitude (disguised as fact) about a racial group can seem to be as valid as the perception of [the] color of their skin. (p. 63)

The vast influence of emotional drives over the rest of the brain explains why distressed partners can have such radically different interpretations of the "facts" during arguments. Each wants to believe that his or her viewpoint is based on what has actually happened, but the partners are often unaware that their emotional commitments bias their conscious perceptions. For example, it may seem perfectly clear to one partner that arguing is unproductive, while it is obvious to the other that arguments are necessary in successful relationships. Why do partners have such radically different takes on "the truth" about relationships? It is likely that the first partner has a history of emotionally uncomfortable experiences during arguments, while the second has experiences of the relief of anxiety through arguments. Often, partners don't realize that their perceptions and interpretations are influenced by their histories of emotional conditioning, and instead continue to insist that the other's viewpoint is objectively "wrong." The approach to helping couples described in Part II of this book involves helping partners become more aware of the emotional needs and longings that drive their perceptions and the rigid positions they take during disagreements. Indeed, awareness of one's emotional world is a hallmark of what researchers have defined as "emotional intelligence" (Salovey & Mayer, 1990). Emotional intelligence involves more than intellectual know-how, and is a more powerful predictor of life success than a person's IQ (Goleman, 1995; Rosenthal, 2002). Emotional intelligence involves knowing and managing one's emotions, motivating oneself, recognizing emotions in others, and using these abilities skillfully in relationships (Goleman, 1995).

NEURAL HIJACKING

Let's return to Susan and James, the couple introduced at the beginning of this chapter. Emotional influences aren't always subtle, or undetectable, in fact, sometimes distressed couples are taken over by emotional storms that they are very much aware of. Susan knew that her explosive attacks were often unreasonable, and James realized that his emotional shutdowns were unproductive. But in the midst of upsetting situations, each seemed unable to prevent the emotional takeovers that tyrannized their relationship. What was happening in their brains?

Goleman (1995) has explained that the amygdala sometimes acts like an emotional sentinal, constantly alert and scanning every experience for signs of trouble: Is this bad? Could it hurt me? If the information registers as dangerous enough, the amygdala broadcasts a distress signal to the entire brain, which in turn, triggers a cascade of physiological responses, from a speeded-up heart rate to rising blood pressure to mobilized muscles to the release of the fight–flight hormones, adrenaline and noradrenaline. Indeed, the amygdala's extensive web of neural connections allows it to capture and drive much of the rest of the brain—including its centers for thought (Goleman, 1995). Within milliseconds, we may explode with rage or freeze in fear, well before our conscious mind can even grasp what is happening, much less persuade us to take a few deep breaths and maintain our cool. This cranial takeover can occur because neuroanatomically speaking, our thinking brain is simply outmatched by the competition. At the same time that emotion-laden signals are zooming down our neurological express route—what LeDoux (1996) called the "low road"—the same data is being transported via the customary, well-trodden "high road" from thalamus to neocortex to amygdala. But because the shorter, subterranean pathway transmits signals twice as fast as the more circuitous route involving the neocortex, the thinking brain simply can't intervene in time. By the time the neocortex gets into the act, the damage has been done—and family and work relationships are in shreds. To make matters worse, by this time amygdala-triggered emotional information has invaded the neocortex itself, overwhelming its centers for logic and judgment. As a result, the person's emotion-flooded thoughts about the situation are apt to feel entirely accurate and justifiable at the moment.

This telling new glimpse of the topography of the brain helped to explain the moments with Susan and James when we could see that they were honestly struggling to think and behave differently, but simply couldn't make the shift. On one occasion, we watched James trying to listen empathetically to Susan, but when she let him know that she was sick and tired of his shirking the housework, bam! Before we could reframe her statement, James' amygdala was sounding its sirens and suddenly he was yelling that she's the slob, not him, in fact, she's let herself go big time and is goddamned fat! And as he's shouting all this, his face is turning the color of boiled lobster, his heart is practically leaping out of his chest, and he is sweating heavily. Depending on your theoretical orientation, you might say this man had just contacted his "wounded child," or that he had been sabotaged by his "problem story," or that he was reenacting a hurtful, family-of-origin script. But at the level of brain wiring, his neocortex just got hijacked by his amygdala. When the amygdala tries to judge whether a current situation is hazardous, it compares that situation with its motley collection of past emotionally charged events. If any key elements are even crudely similar—the sound of a voice, the expression on a face—it instantaneously unleashes its warning sirens and sometimes an accompanying emotional explosion.

The gradually emerging portrait of the emotional brain gives us an illuminating window on why many clients find it so difficult to contain their reactivity in committed love relationships. If the amygdala's original purpose was to act as our emergency alert system, leaping into action in response to life-or-death threats, it is apt to activate with particular vigor in intimate partnerships, which are so entangled in primal need. When our partner says or does something that telegraphs "This person doesn't love me! This person is leaving me!" our amygdala scrambles blindly, frantically to the rescue.

The central role of this hair-trigger brain mechanism in creating marital misery is persuasively suggested by psychologist John Gottman's research at the University of Washington (1999; see Chapter 3). By hooking up couples to a battery of physiological sensors while they discussed sensitive subjects, Gottman documented that during highly toxic arguments, partners' bodies became flooded by brain-mediated bodily changes, including a quickened heart rate, stepped-up sweat production, tensed-up muscles, and the release of stress hormones. The split-second nature of these changes—an angry spouse's heart rate can accelerate 10 to 30 beats per minute in the space of a single heartbeat—strongly indicates a cranial coup d'état originating in the amygdala.

And like most coups, this one can wreak ugly consequences. For Gottman further found that these classic bodily signs of an emotional hijacking were highly correlated with specific kinds of conflict behaviors—criticism, contempt, defensiveness, and stonewalling—that, in turn, strongly predicted later divorce (see Chapter 3). In his observation, the trajectory of divorce often originates with frequent, nasty arguments that eventually cause both partners to develop a kind of bioemotional hypersensitivity to each other.

As we have seen, when the amygdala deems a situation to be an emotional emergency, it lights up the entire brain and body with bioemotional fireworks before the neocortex ever gets into the act. It is in precisely these kinds of volatile, felt-crisis situations, which intimate partnerships, in particular, seem so readily to create, that cognitive therapies are at a serious disadvantage. But many clinicians, including myself, have spent untold sessions trying to get fuming couples to engage in some kind of well-established communication technique, such as "active listening," only to watch the whole thing fly apart when one partner says something seemingly reasonable—"I feel that the kids don't get enough of your attention"—which feels, to the other, like a poison arrow to the heart. And in those moments, when the office is vibrating with fury and the clinician feels more like a rookie referee at a mud-wrestling match than an authoritative, multidegreed professional, the bulging bag of reframings, restoryings, and other sweet reason techniques is worse than useless.

So where does the bad-news tale of limbic mayhem leave therapists? If an element of our humanity as unalterable as brain architecture favors emotion over rationality, why even bother to try to help clients master their most volatile and disabling reactions? The answer to this question is suggested by the discoveries of affective neuroscientists such as University of Wisconsin psychologist Richard

Davidson (Davidson, 2001a, 2001b, 2003; Davidson, Putnam, & Larson, 2000). Davidson, along with a host of others, found that the left prefrontal cortex, which is located just behind the forehead, plays a critical role in moderating emotional reactivity and shifting operating modes (Davidson, 2001a, 2001b; Fox, 1994; Goleman, 1995; Hariri, Bookheimer, & Mazziotta, 2000; Morgan, Romanski, & LeDoux, 1993; Nobre, Coull, & Frith, 1999; Raine et al., 1998; Robbins, 2000; Siegel, 1999). The prefrontal lobe lies at the crossroads between the cognitive and limbic brains, and appears to be the part of the brain that is able to reduce the longevity and intensity of neural hijackings and thereby to limit the fallout. This part of the brain contributes heavily to a person's ability to be aware of his or her internal states. The prefrontal cortex acts as an emotional "clutch" that disengages the sympathetic nervous system and engages parasympathetic "brakes" (Siegel, 1999). As a client increases awareness of his or her internal states, the prefrontal lobes become more active, and able to modulate emotional intensity.

A primary goal of the therapeutic approach described in Part II of this book is to help activate each client's prefrontal lobes, enabling the client to shift from the defensive, isolating brain circuits that generate rage and fear to the connecting, healing circuits that mediate nurture and sorrow. Giving immediate and thorough attention to clients' defensive neural systems, we coach clients to sympathetically and respectfully interact with those brain states until they feel safe enough to switch to more vulnerable states.

In our experience, this internal sense of safety is the linchpin of change for couples. For only when an individual feels no longer threatened by his or her partner (i.e., threatened by the annihilating prospect of abandonment) will the amygdala shut off its internal alarm system, freeing the individual to authentically shift to an intimacy-promoting neural state. So, unlike therapeutic models that zero in immediately on changing thinking or behavior, we don't ask clients to change how they think about, or behave with their partners until they feel safe enough to interact in a more vulnerable way.

This is not to suggest that cognitive and behavioral strategies are unimportant to effective therapy. In our clinical work, the cognitive structure of the brain, particularly the prefrontal cortex, is a central player. The key difference between our approach and explicitly cognitive–behavioral models is that rather than using cognition to harness the limbic brain, we put it to work helping the amygdala to gradually relax its defenses. To do anything less, we believe, is to paddle against our neural currents.

PUTTING NEURAL KNOWLEDGE
INTO ACTION

As Lisa and I sat with James and Susan in our consulting room, we well knew that "helping the amygdala to relax" was the last thing they had in mind. What was clear, however, was that each partner was far too stuck in his or her respective emotional circuit, Susan in rage, James in fear, to make any immediate shift to a more intimacy-promoting state. Before that could happen, each partner would need to get on much better terms with the feelings that had so violently seized him or her. We responded, therefore, as we customarily do when couples encounter extremely "hot" emotional states, by calling a temporary time-out on conjoint work to conduct some one-on-one emotional exploration.

Leaving Lisa and Susan to work together in our office, I asked James to join me in a consulting room down the hall. There, I suggested that if he was willing to explore his inner experience a bit, he might be able to learn to respond to Susan in a way that would help her to treat him well in return. He agreed to try, warning me, however, that self-awareness wasn't his "thing." Like many men I work with, James had done a good job of numbing his body to the telltale, physiological signs of an emotional hijacking—the knotted muscles, the racing heart, the queasy stomach—and consequently, during his fights with Susan, he often had trouble knowing what he felt at all. His lifelong stance, he admitted, was to keep a "stiff upper lip" in the face of trouble—he saw no other options.

"None?" I inquired. "Who taught you that?" After a few moments of silence, he began to talk of his junior high football coach, whom he remembered as single-mindedly intent on forcing him and his teammates to perform endless calisthenics until their bodies screamed for relief. The coach would then stride up to the player with the most tortured expression, get right in his face and shout: "What do you feel?" On cue, the player would yell back: "Nothing, sir!" to the loud cheers of his teammates. On one broiling afternoon on the football field, James heard those rousing cheers for himself, and he recalled now how curiously proud he felt of his stoic denial of his own body. Shaking his head, he admitted: "I guess I learned the lesson well."

I assured him that it would be possible, necessary, in fact, to relearn to recognize his feelings. In an important way, I explained, the body was the voice of the emotions, eloquently communicating critical information about our current emotional state. Tightened muscles and a sick sensation in the gut, for example, typically accompany fear, while rage is characterized by an upsurge in aggressive energy and increased body temperature. Learning to readily identify an "emergency" brain state via its characteristic physiological signals is the first, crucial step of our approach, because brain studies suggest that the moment one becomes aware of one's internal state, the prefrontal lobes are activated, which in turn, can begin to moderate the response. I suggested to James that the next time he and Susan began arguing, he should try to notice any changes happening in his body.

At the next session, Susan and James stalked into our office, their signature brain states already activated. Susan was furious at James for forgetting to buy her flowers for their anniversary; James, already withdrawn, slumped sullenly into his corner of the sofa. As soon as Lisa and I got the gist of their current conflict, James and I took off again for a private tête-à-tête.

Before I had even closed the door behind us, James reported that he was feeling an uncomfortable tightness both in his stomach and his lower jaw, sensations he had noticed several times over the past week whenever Susan had become angry with him. At my suggestion, he checked his current pulse rate and was stunned to find it had soared to 85 beats per minute, in contrast to his usual, resting rate of 68 bpm. In fact, the dramatic jump in heart rate closely mirrors that of experimental animals in the "freeze" state after their fear systems have been electrically stimulated. James, whose clenched-jaw, stonewalling response to Susan's fury had a distinctly frozen quality, was clearly in the midst of a full-fledged, brain-mediated fear response.

I encouraged him to notice how his state of mind seemed to kick in all at once, as if a part of him just stepped forward and took over. He replied that he had already noticed this happening a few days earlier, when Susan was nagging at him about the state of their finances. "I actually tried to respond to her, you know, say something sympathetic about the bad day I knew she'd had," he reported. "But somewhere inside, I'd just gone cold." I suggested that he might think of that frozen, steely part of himself as a little guy within him whose job it was to defend him against Susan's attacks.

In our experience, personalizing emotional states is a powerful way of helping people to accept their survival-driven emotions, which prepares them to interact respectfully with them. For this personalizing strategy, we are indebted to Dick Schwartz's Internal Family systems model (1995), which conceptualizes conflicting behaviors as inner family members, each with its own distinctive personality and function. In our work, we personalize particular bodily responses, such as a constricted throat or a nauseated stomach, that correspond to a client's emotional state. While I was encouraging James to view his knotted stomach as a difficult but fanatically loyal friend, Lisa, two doors down the hall, was similarly helping Susan to understand her rage response—particularly a characteristic throbbing sensation behind her temples—as a desperate, love-hungry little kid inside her who was frantically trying to get her husband's attention. The next step would be to help each of them consult with these inner defenders about the possibility of letting down their respective guards.

At this point, proponents of systems therapy may well be raising their collective eyebrows, thinking: This is couples work? My response is that while we do a lot of individual work with intimate partners, we are very definitely doing couples therapy. In our experience, the hair-trigger defense system of the emotional brain is such that for many couples, learning to regulate brain states is all but impossible in each other's presence; nobody can calm down long enough to do the kind of quiet, deeply focused work that is necessary to allow an emotional system to shift. Particularly early in therapy, each partner is far more likely to chronically trigger the other's already hyperaroused limbic system than help to soothe it, a pattern that may lead many couples to prematurely quit therapy, convinced that theirs is a "hopeless case."

Consequently, our customary modus operandi is to do a lot of individual work during the first several sessions, until each partner develops enough skill in shifting brain states to rejoin his or her partner in the consulting room. At that point, couples begin to practice making these shifts in "real time," in the midst of au-thentic interactions. In this way, work on the internal system of brain states pow-erfully supports work on the external system of a relationship in action.

Over the next several sessions, Lisa and I stepped up our roles as personal coaches, helping Susan and James learn to shift their self-protective brain states to those mediating nurture and sorrow. We knew that when the sorrow neural system is electrically stimulated in animals, they emit distress vocalizations sig-naling a kind of mammalian separation anxiety, which in turn, triggers a "mov-ing toward" response from nearby animals. This is, of course, the same primal dance we endlessly try to choreograph in our therapy offices: if he would only drop his Lone Ranger mask, we would bet the ranch that she would reach out to him. The catch, of course, is that nobody wants to go first. Using methods we will examine fully in Chapters 7 and 8, I helped James see that it was completely in his own best interest to increase awareness of his emotional world.

Once James saw the wisdom in the process of inner exploration, I spent sev-eral sessions coaching him through conversations with his stonewalling "de-fender," in an effort to help it to feel safe enough to let down its guard. Progress was gradual and halting. Then, toward the end of one particularly slow-moving session, I brought up how James's typical response to Susan, sullen stonewalling, had not managed to blunt her fury so far. He nodded, admitting that, in fact, his icy withdrawal seemed to aggravate his wife even more. I suggested that James notice how his inner sentry reacted when I asked: "What have you got to lose by trying something new, like reaching out to Susan?" This was a delicate moment: I was asking James to engage his prefrontal cortex to entertain a new thought, without asking him to willfully redirect his current thinking. His hand on his stomach, James closed his eyes and focused his attention within. Perhaps 15 sec-onds passed before he opened his eyes and looked at me. "It's okay," he softly said.

"You're sure it's okay with him?" I asked, pointing in the direction of his stom-ach. "Yeah, he's okay," nodded James. He looked relaxed and younger, some-how less defended. His inner watchdog, he told me, had acknowledged that shutting down had only gotten him a redoubled dose of Susan's rage, the terrify-ing experience of an all-out attack that had activated his defense system in the first place. If there were a better way to stave off these assaults, his defender told him, it would do its best to stand aside. "I'm ready," James said quietly.

Susan was on her way to being ready, too. While James and I had been doing our work, Lisa and Susan had been making steady progress in helping Susan's inner defender feel safe enough to expose the intense yearning for love that hid behind her fury. As each partner's neural defense system gradually relaxed its hold, we began spending less time on one-on-one coaching and more time in conjoint sessions, helping them to practice real-world interactions without flip-ping into their respective fury and fear states.

Then one evening, Susan and James walked into our office in utter silence. They had had a violent argument two days before and had barely spoken to each other since. The issue at hand was James's relationship with his younger brother,

Sam, and his sister-in-law, Claire, who lived only a few streets away from them. Susan had long felt resentful toward Sam, whom she felt took advantage of James's helpful nature, but even more hostile toward Claire, a stunningly beautiful local fashion model. James denied feeling attracted to Claire, but Susan had not believed him since the night she had seen James flipping through the pages of her modeling portfolio, which included some nude pictures.

Susan was furious now because, on the first day of a recent, heavy snowstorm, James had called to say he was stopping on his way home from work to help Sam and Claire dig out their driveway before coming home to help Susan shovel out so she could attend an evening yoga class. An hour later, when Susan walked the half-mile to her in-laws' house to drag her husband home, she was incensed to find James and Claire working in the driveway and laughing companionably together, with Sam nowhere in sight. That evening Susan never made it to her yoga class; instead, she raged hard and long at James, accusing him of caring more about his brother's long-legged, exotic-looking wife than about her.

As our session began, Susan warned that this was a horribly painful issue for her. As she began to recount the incident, within seconds she was breathing so hard and fast that I thought she might start hyperventilating. "James," she managed between jagged breaths, "do you have any clue what you're like when you get within sniffing distance of Claire?"

I quickly looked at James, who had turned his gaze downward and was sitting stock-still. I feared he was shifting into a full-scale shutdown. But after a long moment he looked up again at his wife. "Susan," he began softly, "I don't give a damn about Claire." When Susan hooted bitterly at this, James shook his head in frustration. But he didn't fold. "When Sam called me to help out, I just didn't think," he went on. "I should have."

When Susan turned away in disgust, James looked suddenly desperate. "Look, Susan," he said pleadingly, "when you get mad at me like this, it's awful." She looked back at him, clearly surprised. "It makes me feel sick inside," he admitted to her. "I feel kind of lost." As Susan continued gazing at him, he touched her arm. "But whatever I did, I'm sorry I hurt you."

At this, Susan's face began to crumple. "You did hurt me, James," she cried out. Tears spilling down her cheeks, she jumped up and fled the room. For a moment, James looked stunned and disoriented: A tearful Susan was not what he had expected. Then he, too, abruptly rushed out into the hallway, where his wife was weeping. "God, Susan, I really didn't know what a big deal this was to you," we could hear him say. "Will you help me understand?" As she continued to sob, we stepped out into the hall in time to witness James enveloping his wife in a bear hug and whispering into her hair: "It's you I want."

It was a moment of great tenderness, one of those exchanges of naked need and open-hearted nurture that remind a couples therapist why he or she has chosen this work. Yet ultimately, the melting moment of bonding that we had just witnessed was not what made us feel optimistic about James and Susan's futures. For we knew that such jolting shots of connectedness, however real and deep, would inevitably fade; stinging disappointments and misunderstandings would arise again. What encouraged us most was that in the midst of this highly charged interaction, James had demonstrated the ability to shift from a reaction of fearful withdrawal to a warmly empathetic state that, in turn, allowed Susan to shift from her own state of fury to one of sorrowful hurt. We knew that if they were to construct an intimate bond that could truly sustain them—and not remain on a neural roller coaster of endless highs and lows—they would need to continue the difficult and delicate work they had begun. Little by little, they were teaching their brains to trust.

Susan and James's therapy spanned six months. In the initial phases of therapy, Lisa and I relied heavily on methods we have developed for helping clients shift from self-protective to vulnerable states (Chapter 6). A critical transition in therapy occurred when James and Susan each became convinced that the best way to change their partner was to change themselves. We devote as much time as is necessary to help partners come to this conclusion. Successful therapy hinges upon each partner's motivation to influence their own automatically activated mood states. Methods we use to crystallize each client's motivation are discussed at length in Chapters 7 and 8. Like most of our clients, it was of great value for Susan and James to develop a clear picture of the kind of attitudes and behaviors that are highly predictive of relationship success (see Chapter 3).

TOWARD A PSYCHOTHERAPY RESPECTFUL OF THE EMOTIONAL BRAIN

There is little doubt that in psychotherapy today, the neocortex is where the action is. While a few emotion-centered approaches are still holding their own, they hardly represent the field's dominant direction. Instead, pressured by increasingly meager third-party reimbursements, clinicians have been scurrying to get trained in therapy models that promise the speediest possible results. And by and large, the briefest models tend to be those that zero in on retooling beliefs and behavior, based on the premise that changing thoughts and actions will, domino-style, cause feelings to change. Early forms of marriage and family therapy assumed that, by changing rigid behavioral sequences of interactions, symptoms could be alleviated and family members would feel better. More recently, particularly with the influx of social constructionist thought, there is an assumption that if clients change their outdated stories or beliefs about themselves, their problems, and their lives, a change in their actions and feelings will follow. In short, these models take for granted that the neocortex is firmly in charge of the limbic system.

We all know that, indeed, sometimes thoughts can influence feelings. If you are confronting a situation that is emotionally salient but not perceived by you as a life-or-death matter—let's say, you've noticed a worrisome drop-off in client hours—that information would register in your neocortex, and you'd mull the situation over, come up with thoughts that make you feel better, or generate an action plan that might change things for the better. If you were to apply a solution-focused approach to this matter, your neocortex might help you make a mental list of ways you have successfully beefed up your practice in the past and secure a commitment to try those strategies. Using a narrative model, you might challenge your culturally fueled assumption that making more and more money is necessary. Within a traditional cognitive model, you might try to battle any rumination about imminent professional disaster with a tough-minded counterargument. Given the right conditions, each of these interventions would likely spur your rational brain to signal the amygdala to respond with, perhaps, mild anxiety leavened with a strong, motivating shot of hope. In short, when the neocortex can provide input to the brain's emotions centers, they are just as powerful as the situational cues that automatically trigger emotional reactions.

Of course, the trouble is that often, cognitive interventions work only when we're relatively calm in the first place. As we have seen, when we deem a situation an emotional emergency, the amygdala lights up the entire brain and body with bioemotional fireworks before the neocortex ever gets into the act. It is in precisely these kinds of volatile, felt-crisis situations—which intimate partnerships, in particular, seem so readily to create—that thinking-brain therapies are at a serious disadvantage. At such times, I have tried my best to help people change their thinking and interactions with little success. In these situations, I had little doubt that if they could change certain behaviors, beliefs, or thought patterns, they would feel better. Often, they thought so, too. Under stress, they just couldn't do it.

Influenced by the model of the mind emerging from the studies such as those reviewed in this chapter, I began formulating therapeutic methods that were more respectful of the centrality and power of emotions in organizing human behavior. These methods assume that a shift in emotional state is often necessary before new thinking or actions are possible. Here are some of the principles for working with emotion that guide the couples treatment methods described in Part II of this book.

Help Clients Cultivate Greater Awareness of How Emotions Influence Their Reactions to Each Other

The reactions of intimate partners arise from gut feelings about how they want things to be, and their ideas about how they can get there. Gut feelings can arise without any conscious thought, based on genetic emotional dispositions, early attachment experiences, and ongoing significant emotional experiences through life, which "program" their brains to produce feelings in future situations. Our brains are not set up to inform us of the extent that our reactions are based on our emotional conditioning histories. Consequently, clients tend to think that their reactions to each other are based solely on present circumstances that they are consciously aware of. As clients become more aware of the emotional bias inherent in their interpretations of each other, they become more able to drop their critical judgments of each other, and more able to express the needs and longings that lie beneath their reactions. As we'll see in the second part of this book, awareness and expression of needs and emotional longings is essential if partners are to form secure emotional bonds.

Treat Emotional States as If They Had Minds of Their Own

Brain researchers tell us that it's possible for emotional states to become activated for reasons we may not at first be aware of. As we'll discuss in Chapter 2, it's possible that emotional command circuits may be carrying out pre-programmed agendas without our full awareness. My clinical experience bears out these conjectures. When clients approach emotional states with a "not-knowing" attitude, willing to listen to what may be going on inside of them, they often come away with a greater sense of understanding and satisfaction, and they are more able to calm the emotional states, or help them shift. Conversely, when clients assume that it is perfectly clear what they are feeling and why, new understanding or change in emotional states may be more difficult to achieve. It is helpful to approach an emotional state with the curiosity and respectfulness with which you might approach another person whom you wanted to know more about.

Give Attention to Emotional States Before Pursuing Other Therapeutic Goals

Earlier in my work, I spent many frustrating hours trying to help family members listen to each other more attentively, speak to each other more kindly, fight more fairly, negotiate with each other more realistically, and give each other more benefit of the doubt, all the while knowing that they often weren't in the right frame of mind for the tasks I had in mind. I now know that I must address the emotional state of each client first. If a client is in an emotional state during a therapy session that seems incompatible for the task or thinking needed at the time, I will help the family member explore the emotional state first, until the needed shift occurs. Then we focus on thinking and acting differently.

Focus on the Stance Clients Take Toward Their Emotional States

People vary considerably with regard to how they react to various emotional states (both their own emotional states and the states of others). Some people are uncomfortable because they get too close to their emotions—they wallow in emotional states, or are dominated by them, and can't get breathing room. Others tune emotions out so thoroughly that they are barely aware of how emotional states organize their lives. It is my observation that those who are most able to get cooperation from their emotions as well as intimacy with others learn to approach their emotional states in a way that promotes good contact with the states, but some separateness as well. Learning how to accept emotional states as they are is the first step toward helping the states shift or become easier to be with.

There is something similar about learning how to relate to one's own difficult emotions and learning how to relate to difficult people. Both kinds of learning involve attentiveness to one's own reactions in relation to another, regardless of whether the "other" is inside one's skin or outside.

Work with Emotional States When They Are Active

Early family therapists such as Minuchin, Satir, and Whitaker learned that old patterns are most amenable to change when they are "up and running." These therapists found that they could be most helpful if they were able to assist families in a "hands on" way, by facilitating enactments in which redundant interactional patterns were activated and challenged in the context of ongoing therapy sessions. Similarly, I have found that an individual's stance toward an emotional state is most amenable to change when the person is actually experiencing the emotional state, not just talking about times when the state was active. For the therapist, this means developing greater attentiveness to emotional states that naturally occur in therapy, as well as greater skill in helping clients activate certain states.

Seek Cooperation From, Not Control Over Emotional States

Since Freud, psychotherapists have been trying to help clients harness their emotions through ego strength and willpower. Studies such as the ones reviewed in this paper suggest that the ego is ill equipped for this task. The emotional brain has the neurological position of greatest influence. Those who believe that they are controlling their emotions are probably unaware of how emotions organize their values, beliefs, choices, and actions. However, recognition that we can't control our emotions doesn't mean that we are without potential influence. There is an important difference between attempting to control one's emotions and seeking cooperation from them. If approached in a respectful, accepting way, troubling emotional states generally shift into calmer versions of the same state or yield to other states that are needed. Such shifts are usually achieved by gentle and compassionate exploration of inner states rather than the force of conscious willpower.

CHAPTER 2

Wired for Love

I WAS COMPLETING MY FIRST semester of a doctoral family therapy practicum when Bruce and Ginger were assigned to me for marriage counseling. Within five minutes, I knew that I was going to like working with them. Like me, they were both poor graduate students. Brandon, their 2-year old son, was almost the same age as my daughter Heather. In fact, Brandon and Heather were classmates at the university child development lab. But what really drew me in was the way they lit up when I asked them to tell me about Brandon. Twenty-five years later, I still remember one occasion when Bruce and I met alone. Before we began the session, he told me how he'd snuck into Brandon's bedroom the night before and just sat, watching the little guy sleeping in the moonlight. What I remember most vividly was the tender quality in Bruce's voice. I could relate to this, because as a father, many times I had felt similar emotions toward my own child.

As a therapist, I had little experience to help me with Ginger and Bruce, but enough sense to know that the way that they talked about their son was a good sign. There was love and tenderness inside each of them. I always started sessions asking about Brandon, because it I thought it might "prime the pump," and by some magic, the tenderness would transfer to each other. But each time they began talking about their relationship, some internal switch got flipped, and they seemed like different people. The tenderness or playfulness that had characterized their previous talk vanished, eye contact broke off, and a dead seriousness entered the room. I remember saying to them, "What I need is a remote control device that I could use to switch each of you back to the channel you were in when you were talking about Brandon."

Little did I know that, at that very moment, in a different part of the country, a team of brain researchers had already developed just such a remote control device. Incredibly, these researchers had found that they could turn on and off whole parts of patients' personalities with the flip of a switch. By implanting electrodes deep within specific regions of patients' brains, then applying electrical pulses, researchers were stunned to see the moods, desires, and concerns of patients change dramatically. Stimulated individuals were temporarily transformed from calm experimental subjects into intensely angry, fearful, lustful, driven, lonely, playful or compassionate individuals. Activation of any one of these circuits transformed subjects' thinking, beliefs, perceptions, interpretations and motivations within a few seconds. In a series of studies by Robert Heath of Tulane University School of Medicine, individuals' moods, perceptions, and behavior shifted dramatically in response to the stimulation of particular limbic structures (Heath, 1963, 1972, 1992; Heath & Mickle, 1960; Moyer, 1986). In one study, upon stimulation, a subject flew into a rage and felt suddenly offended, and threatened to "kill the physician who was closest to him at the time" (Heath, 1992, p. 341). In another study, published in the *New England Journal of Medicine*, a woman was moved to tears and experienced profound depression in response to stimulation (Bejjani et al., 1999). In an earlier study, a 34-year-old woman who had an electrode implanted in the septal region of her brain found herself in a "sexual motive state," culminating in multiple orgasms within a few minutes, without external stimulation of any sort (Heath, 1972).

These case reports and others dating back to the 1950s (Amano, Tanikawa et al., 1982; Gloor, 1972; Gloor, Oliver, Quesney, Andermann, & Horowitz, 1982; Halgren, Walter, Chrelow, & Crandall, 1978; Heath, 1963, 1972, 1986, 1992; Heath & Mickle, 1960; Higgins, Mahl, Delgado, & Hamlin, 1956; Hitchcock & Cairns, 1973; Mark & Ervin, 1970; Mark et al., 1969; Ervin & Sweet, 1972; 1975; Meyer, McElhaney, Martin, & McGraw, 1973; Monroe & Heath, 1954; Nashold, Wilson, & Slaughter, 1969; Obrador & Martin-Rodriguez, 1979; Panksepp, 1985; Richardson, 1972; Sano, 1975; Sem-Jacobson, 1968; Sheer, 1961) provided initial clues that the brain is equipped with a number of special-purpose circuits which, when activated, create powerful mood states that dramatically influence perceptions, interpretations, and motivations. These mood states become active only when the older parts of the brain are stimulated, those parts shared by all mammals (Heath, 1986; Panksepp, 1982, 1985, 1986, 1991, 1992a, 1992b). Indeed, these mood states can be activated in animals as well as in humans, and most of what we know about the mechanisms involved in the brain's mood states comes through animal research (Panksepp, 1989).

Neuroscientist Jaak Panksepp and his colleagues at Bowling Green State University mapped the neural circuitry of seven "special-purpose" mood states in the brain (Panksepp, 1998). Panksepp calls these specialized neural networks "executive operating systems." The word *executive* means that, when active, these mood states exert a control function, creating a *state of mind* that makes it easier for people to accomplish specific tasks important for survival. According to Siegel, a "state of mind" involves "a pattern of activation of recruited systems within the brain responsible for (1) perceptual bias, (2) emotional tone and regulation, (3) memory processes, (4) mental models, and (5) behavioral response patterns" (Siegel, 1999, p. 211). When a particular state is active, it "recruits" perceptions, feelings, memories, attitudes, and actions that will make it more likely that the individual will accomplish the goals that the state is set up to attain. With the activation of any particular state, some types of thinking and actions come naturally, and it is nearly impossible to engage in others unless a switch in circuits takes place.

Each of the brain's seven executive operating systems likely evolved during different periods of our evolutionary history and were retained because they provided distinct evolutionary advantages (Table 2.1). LeDoux explained: "Different classes of emotional behavior represent different kinds of functions that take care of different kinds of problems for the animal and have different brain systems devoted to them" (1996, p. 127). Activation of any one of these special-purpose emotional states will automatically produce motivation to accomplish critical tasks necessary for survival, such as escaping from danger, aggression, curiosity, learning, eagerness, directed purposefulness, caretaking, affiliation, creativity, skill-development, and reproduction. Two of the brain's seven executive operating systems are activated by the amygdala, and produce powerful attack and withdrawal states, like those experienced by Susan and James in Chapter 1. But humans are not only equipped for self-protection, but wired for connection with other human beings as well. Our brains are equipped with four executive operating systems that draw us together, propelling us into strong emotional bonds. When these neural systems are operating freely, we experience feelings of tenderness, the longing for emotional contact, the desire for spontaneous and joyful interaction with others, and the ecstasy of sexual union. However, just as the brain's self-protective circuits can misfire, so can these intimacy-producing circuits. When relationships are distressed, the circuits that move partners toward intimate bonds become dormant, leaving partners without the emotional connection that once sustained them. Without these powerful circuits active in their brains, attempts to connect are destined to fail. Caring acts become just that—caring *acts*.

Panksepp's early paper on the brain's executive operating systems produced 29 commentaries and rebuttals from prominent emotions researchers in a 1982 issue of the journal *Behavioral and Brain Sciences* (Panksepp, 1982). Many of these researchers had previously rejected the idea of categorically discrete emotions. In recent years, however, Panksepp's work has gained wide recognition amongst neuroscientists.

Most of the time, we assume that we are consciously directing our experience, but brain studies suggest that, during the course of everyday life, we may be unaware of subtle shifts in the mental states that guide our perceptions and actions. Ornstein maintained that our lives are largely run by the agendas of pre-programmed neural programs:

> The working mind "in place" executes its job as if it had always been there, then disappears, to be replaced with another "recruit," one with different memories, priorities and plans. And "we," our conscious self, hardly ever notice what has occurred. We know what is on our mind . . . but we have no capacity to know what is in our mind—which mind "program" is acting for us at any given time. (1991, p. 210)

TABLE 2.1
Executive Operating Systems: A Summary

A summary of the groundbreaking research leading to the discovery of the brain's neural operating systems can be found in neuroscientist Jack Panksepp's book *Affective Neuroscience* (1998). Two of the brain's seven executive operating systems are activated by the amygdala, and produce self-protective thinking and action. Panksepp calls these systems, RAGE and FEAR. He uses capital letters to remind readers that he is not simply talking about the emotions of rage or fear—executive operating systems involve more than emotion. When any particular EOS is active, perceptions, interpretations, priorities, and motivations become recruited in the service of accomplishing whatever goals the system is programmed to accomplish.

Creatures who are able to affiliate and work together are more likely to survive than those who simply fight or flee from danger. Fortunately, nature endowed each of us with four specialized neural circuits that, when activated, produce a natural desire to draw closer to others. A final EOS provides the motivation to explore, learn, and act upon the world around us. Here's a summary of all seven of the brain's executive operating systems.

> **RAGE:** Activation of this executive operating system produces feelings ranging from frustration to intense anger, thoughts that overflow with blame and scorn, memories of past transgressions, and the urge to strike at the offending agent. *Evolutionary Advantage*: Self-protection.
>
> **FEAR:** Activation of this operating system produces feelings ranging from anxiety to intense fright, thoughts on a continuum from worried to catastrophic, and motivation to escape existing circumstances. *Evolutionary Advantage*: Motivation to escape danger
>
> **SEEKING:** When this system is active, people experience curiosity, interest, anticipation, craving, expectancy, engagement, excitement, eagerness, directed purpose. It leads people to energetically explore their worlds, seeking for resources. It produces an invigorated feeling of anticipation we experience when we actively seek accomplishments and rewards. *Evolutionary Advantage*: Motivation to learn, effective agency in the world.
>
> **LUST:** When activated, this system produces feelings of sexual arousal, thoughts oriented toward sexual fulfillment, and urges to engage in sexual activity. *Evolutionary Advantage*: Motivation to reproduce.
>
> **CARE:** This system produces spontaneous feelings of warmth, tenderness, and concern for others, (i.e., the welfare), and urges to act in nurturing ways toward others. *Evolutionary Advantage*: Protection of one's own.

(continues)

TABLE 2.1
Executive Operating Systems: A Summary (Continued)

PANIC: Normally activated by separation from important persons or circumstances, feelings associated with this neural command system include variations of loneliness, sadness, and disappointment. When the PANIC system is activated, it produces thoughts centering around the obtainment of social contact and urges to move toward possible sources of comfort. *Evolutionary Advantage*: Motivation for affiliation, solicitation of support.

PLAY: Activation of this brain circuit triggers the urge to vigorously and spontaneously interact with others. The accompanying emotion can be characterized by joy or delight, and thoughts are generally positive in nature. *Evolutionary Advantage*: Releases neuropeptides that promote social bonding, motivates creativity, experimentation; intrinsic healing properties of physical agents released in play.

While all of us are born with the basic neural structure for each of the seven executive command systems, the way they become wired up in each of us is tailored by our unique histories of emotional conditioning. The types of circumstances that activate command circuits, the threshold for activation of any circuit, and intensity of activation varies across individuals. Many studies suggest that early attachment experiences play an important role in establishing automatic patterns of EOS activation and suppression into motion that often stay in place across a lifetime (Panksepp, 2001).

As noted in Chapter 1, emotional states can be activated by cues that we are unaware of at an unconscious level and they can dramatically influence our perceptions and attitudes without our realizing it. Subjects in the brain stimulation studies "believed" the validity of their mood induced perceptions and interpretations, even though they knew that the feelings were activated through electrical stimulation. In daily life, we tend to trust our feelings and interpretations too, even though the feelings we experience may have more to do with our history of emotional conditioning than a well-reasoned interpretation of present events.

So radical is this shift in perspective, that the *American Psychologist* devoted most of a 1999 issue to a review of studies that challenged the conventional notion that our thoughts and actions are the result of conscious, willful intent (Park, 1999). In her editorial introduction, *"Acts of Will?"* Denise Park wrote:

> The theory and data presented in these articles represent recent fundamental breakthroughs in the understanding of motivations, free will, and behavioral control. . . . The premise of all four articles is this: There are mental activations of which we are unaware and environmental cues to which we are not consciously attending that

have a profound effect on our behavior and that help explain the complex puzzle of human motivation and actions that are seemingly inexplicable, even to the individual performing the actions. (Park, 1999, p. 461; see also, Bargh & Chartrand, 1999; Gollwitzer, 1999; Kirsch & Lynn, 1999; Tallis, 1999; Wegner & Wheatley, 1999)

Of course, the idea that we may be less rationally in charge of ourselves than our experience leads us to believe isn't exactly new. In a *Newsweek* interview, Jaak Panksepp and Antonio Damasio agreed that neuroscience research had confirmed an idea put forth by Sigmund Freud nearly a century ago: "there are unconscious drives shaping our behavior without the mediation of our conscious minds" (Guterl, 2002, p. 50; see also Panksepp, 1999).

The presence of these seven prepackaged executive operating systems in the brain explains why our thoughts and moods can seem so contradictory at times. When a circuit is activated, a person may experience dramatically different thinking and motivation than she or he was experiencing only moments before. Denise Park summed it up nicely, "Often enough in my life I have done things I had not decided to do. Something—whatever it may be—goes into action; "it" goes to see the woman I don't want to see anymore, keeps on smoking although I have decided to quit, and then quits smoking just when I've accepted the fact that I'm a smoker and always will be" (Park, 1999, p. 461). Brain studies suggest that the internal conflicts and contradictions we experience are rooted in our multipurpose neural states. We have not one mind, but many minds. Robert Ornstein pointed out:

> A set of minds swings in and out: One system, then another, then a third takes hold of consciousness. Once recruited for a purpose, the mind in place performs as if it had been there forever, then steps aside, to be replaced with another "actor," one with different memories, priorities and plans. . . . This is one reason why we don't act the way "we" want ourselves to. Since minds shift, "we" are not the same person from moment to moment, not the same "self" at all. The idea most people have that they are consistent in the diverse situations of their lives is an illusion, one caused by the structure of the brain. (1991, p. 11)

Most of the time, the fact that many of our thoughts and decisions are influenced by automatic processes that operate outside of our awareness is to our benefit, because these neural operating systems are conditioned to "kick in" at the right time. We automatically experience tenderness when others are in pain, we experience anger when someone is trying to take advantage of us, and we become anxious when we sense danger. But it doesn't always work this nicely. Sometimes, just when we need it most, the needed internal state is nowhere to be found. When relationships are distressed, there are nearly always problems with the automatic activation and suppression of the internal states within the brains of clients. People keep doing things in relationships that they know they shouldn't do, and fail to do the things they know they should do because their brains are programmed to make decisions for them. Their neural circuits are *conditioned* to respond automatically to certain cues by activating internal response programs that propel them into specific patterns of thinking and action.

For the most part, people don't volunteer for these internal states, they simply find themselves under their influence. When any one of them is activated, individuals may lose the freedom to choose their thoughts and actions freely. It is as if, at that moment, someone else is in charge. They cannot act differently because they are in the grip of neural states that are preprogrammed for a purpose different from the one needed at the moment. In order to respond differently, people have to first experience shifts in brain states.

Back in 1982, I knew that something very fundamental was missing in Ginger and Bruce's interactions with each other. I remember the steely quality to an apology that Bruce offered to Ginger during one session. The words were apologetic, but there was no remorse. Bruce's apology wasn't coming from the right place inside. Inside both Bruce and Ginger's brains, the internal states that naturally produce intimacy were dormant, and without access to these states, they didn't stand a chance. Although I tried my best to jump-start Bruce and Ginger's feelings for each other, I didn't have the knowledge or tools for the task. Ginger and Bruce separated, and eventually divorced.

Years later, when I had forgotten all about Ginger and Bruce, Jack and Loretta walked into my office with the same kind of stony silence that had doomed Bruce and Ginger 20 years earlier, but this time I was equipped with an understanding of what was happening in each of their brains, and had a plan for what to do about it.

Loretta looked very different from the way I had remembered her. "I don't think I love him anymore" she said softly. Loretta hadn't said anything softly during the course of our couples therapy, which had ended a year earlier. Loretta, 31, was a feisty and successful, red-headed realtor whose presence ordinarily commanded attention. She had the slender frame and fine facial features of a model. Her husband, Jack, 33, was a manager for a software development company. Jack looked like a more muscled version of Pierce Brosnan from the 007 movies, but his personality was anything but James Bond. Jack was more of a creature of habit than an adventurer. He used routine to his advantage, however, and worked out in the gym five days per week. Jack was initially attracted to Loretta's forceful and energetic style. However, after marrying her, Jack was horrified to learn that Loretta was the sort of person who would become angry at the drop of a hat, and would "fly off the handle" at the smallest irritation. At first, Jack prided himself in his ability to give in, and "not need to have his way," but in the second year of marriage he began pointing out to Loretta that her tantrums were really emotionally immature. By the third year, Loretta and Jack found themselves stuck in a pattern in which Loretta would become upset at Jack about something (according to Jack, it didn't matter what—she "needed" something to be upset about) and Jack would become indignant and criticize her barbaric approach, often launching into lectures about how arguing should be done, calmly, rationally, without being swayed by feelings. Feeling his contempt, Loretta would react defensively. The arguments escalated until the couple sought therapy.

When I first met them, they were at war, and Jack was threatening divorce. Jack and Loretta's reactions to each other were lightning fast and 100% predictable. Loretta knew that when she attacked Jack, he would almost certainly belittle her for it. And Jack knew that his tendency to take the moral high ground threatened Loretta to the point where she could do little but intensify her attack. But when offended, neither Jack nor Loretta was able to resist the urge to play out their part in this escalating spiral. It was as if a different part of their personalities took over and the real Jack and Loretta were just along for the ride.

During four months of couples therapy, Jack and Loretta's therapy resembled that of James and Susan, described in Chapter 1. Each came to understand the nature of the neural takeovers that were dictating their interactions with each other. Each of them became more able to recognize when they were caught in an internal brain storm, and learned how to short-circuit the unfolding of the storm. Once Jack and Loretta learned how to escape the pull of these powerful overly self-protective internal states that had previously held them captive, they made rapid progress in finding ways to understand each other's points of view during arguments. But they didn't stop there. They also began opening up to each other about their disappointments, dreams, and hopes, something they hadn't done since the early years of their relationship. When Loretta and Jack ended therapy, their marriage appeared to be back on track. They stopped therapy by missing two appointments, then simply left me a message letting me know that they were doing fine, and thanking me sincerely for "saving their marriage." Jack and Loretta were confident that the changes they had made would last. I wasn't as optimistic, and I had tried to tell them so, but they thought I was just being overly cautious. Now, over a year later, Loretta and Jack were sitting in my office again. This time they weren't at each other's throats, but frankly, they seemed worse off than before. When I first met them, they were full of fight. Now the anger had turned into resignation, and they really seemed serious when they said they were thinking about divorce.

What happened? Loretta told the story. When they left therapy, they had a new lease on life. For the first time, they felt like they had some control over the devastating fights that had nearly destroyed them. Loretta had broken her habit of attacking Jack when she felt mistreated or misunderstood. Jack had learned to refrain from taking the moral high ground when they disagreed. These changes had continued. Even now as they sat in front of me talking about the possibility of divorce, each of them seemed grateful that they no longer had to tolerate this kind of punishment from the other. The fighting had really stopped, but the newfound tenderness they had experienced for each other began waning within months of leaving therapy. The trouble began when Jack got a promotion at work. His new job was stressful, and he became discouraged and preoccupied. This was alarming to Loretta, but she refrained from attacking him, and instead she tried to be supportive. Jack didn't seem to want support, and instead he became more withdrawn. Loretta felt lonely, and she tried to talk to Jack. Feeling their relationship slipping, he apologized and promised to take more time off to do fun things together. For a while, they made every Friday night "date night." But they often ended up just watching a movie and then going to bed. They were going through the motions, but it seemed as if the "juice" was gone in their relationship. Jack still brought Loretta flowers, and made it a point to compliment her at least once each day. But the compliments didn't seem to "take." Eventually they stopped even going to movies together. Gradually, Loretta turned her focus from Jack and became more involved with her own friends. Jack felt abandoned by her, but he also felt relieved. Loretta seemed content. Months later, he was devastated when he found that she had developed a special relationship with a male coworker. While he was preoccupied with one of the most difficult challenges of his professional life, Loretta was becoming enchanted with a man who was much less professionally successful than Jack. Loretta explained that this man was the opposite of Jack in many ways. He was easygoing, playful, and fun. She insisted that they weren't romantically involved, but Loretta explained that this relationship made her realize that she needed things that she just didn't think Jack could give her. She was considering a divorce.

Jack and Loretta went further in their first round of therapy than many couples. After allowing me to help them short-circuit the executive operating systems that were compelling them to hurt each other, they each developed the ability to do this on their own. They literally reconditioned the neural circuitry that had been propelling their conflicts. A year later, they had retained this important ability. However, while it kept them from returning to the dangerous escalations that characterized their previous relationship, this ability did little to help them maintain their emotional bond. When they began therapy, the internal operating systems necessary for intimacy were shut down in each of them. Before they dropped out of therapy, I jump-started these circuits, and once they became active, Jack and Loretta made a profound connection with each other. However, they left therapy before developing the ability to maintain access to these critical internal circuits. When life got stressful, they lost their emotional bond. They tried to do caring things for each other, but without the ability to activate the internal states that power intimacy, they were just going through the motions.

If we are going to help couples increase their abilities to connect with the powerful internal motivational states that naturally generate emotional bonding, we must help them set up reconditioning practices. But first we must first understand the nature of the states that we are trying to activate.

CARE

From the beginning of their lives, humans and other mammals are protected by the activation of a neural operating system in their mothers' brains that Panksepp called CARE (Panksepp, 1998). Before the birth of their first child, women commonly worry about their future adequacy as mothers, but such doubts typically vanish, as if by magic, soon after the birth of the baby. This is because all mothers have a neural operating system that is preprogrammed to produce caring motivations and behaviors. They don't have to learn how to nurture their young. It happens naturally. The CARE system is responsible for the subtle feelings that humans call acceptance, nurturance, and love, feelings of social solidarity and warmth. The initial clue that there was a preprogrammed intrinsic brain system for nurturance was the fact that transfusion of blood from a female rat that had just given birth could instigate maternal behaviors in a virgin female rat (Panksepp, 1998). The CARE system is activated by neurochemicals such as oxytocin and prolactin, which rise precipitously just before a mother gives birth. Scientists have discovered that the CARE circuit can be activated just as surely by introducing oxytocin and prolactin directly into certain areas of the brain (Keverne & Kendrick, 1992; Pedersen, Ascher, Monroe, & Prange, 1982; Rosenblatt, 1992; Uvnas-Moberg, 1998). Virgin female rats treated with these chemicals fly into a flurry of caring behaviors, probably to the confusion of young pups nearby who are the unsuspecting recipients of the virgin's newfound maternal urges. Other studies show that instinctive maternal behaviors can also be blocked by giving new mothers drugs that prevent oxytocin from being absorbed (Van Leengoed, Kerker & Swanson, 1987). Although the most dramatic activation of this brain system can be seen in new mothers, all humans, both men and women, have the CARE neural operating system, waiting to be activated. Considerable evidence suggests that, across all mammalian species, females have more vigorous CARE circuits in their brains than males (Berman, 1980; Panksepp, 1998). This was certainly the case with Jack and Loretta. Whereas Loretta could be moved to tears listening to a sad story, Jack often ridiculed weakness in others. Jack believed that mature people should be self-sufficient, and he hated when Loretta seemed to look to him as if it were his responsibility to comfort her when she was upset. She was often furious with him even before she sought his support, anticipating that he would fail to give it, or worse yet, act as if she was wrong for wanting it in the first place. One of my primary goals early in therapy was to connect Jack with his CARE circuit. To accomplish this, however, I knew that I first had to help both Loretta and Jack make better connection with another intimacy-promoting executive operating system that each of them had limited access to, the neural response system PANIC.

PANIC

When the PANIC circuit is activated, humans experience feelings ranging from mild loneliness to intense separation distress. The effect is always to promote an urge for emotional contact with others. This neural circuit is particularly active in the younger members of all species, who must depend upon the protection of others for survival. However, there is an abundance of evidence that in healthy adults, the PANIC circuit remains active throughout life, providing the motivation for human contact. Nature's plan doesn't involve emotional self-sufficiency. Scores of longitudinal studies suggest that individuals who cut themselves off from the need for emotional comforting from others don't function as well as individuals who continue to experience a need for emotional comforting throughout their lives (Siegel, 1999). When soothing emotional contact is consistently available, individuals develop a sense of security that allows them to avoid wasting energy being overly vigilant to danger (Cozolino, 2002). Neuroscientists believe that the PANIC system is central to the forming of secure emotional bonds that buffer individuals against stresses throughout their lives (Panksepp, 2001). When the PANIC system is aroused, humans and animals seek reunion with others who help create the feeling of a "secure neurochemical base" within the brain (Nelson & Panksepp, 1998). As Panksepp put it, "social bonding involves the ability of organisms to experience separation distress when isolated from social support systems and to experience neurochemically mediated comfort when social contacts are reestablished" (1998, p. 274).

The PANIC system is calmed through the release of specific neurochemicals, the chief of which are the internal opioids such as endorphins and enkephalins (Panksepp, 1998). These neurochemicals are released though intimate social contact, especially direct physical contact (Keverne, Martensz, & Tuite, 1989; Montagu, 1978). When the PANIC circuits in animals are electrically stimulated, they emit "distress vocalizations" (DVs) which are identical to those emitted naturally by young animals who are separated from their mothers (Panksepp, 1980). One of the easiest ways to reduce DVs in experimental animals is to put mirrors on the wall of the test chamber. The animals calm down when they believe they are not alone. The same effect can be observed when music is pumped into the test chamber. Music simulates the comfort of audiovocal contact with other animals (Panksepp, Bean, Bishop, Vilberg, & Sahley, 1980). This may be one of the reasons why people love to listen to music—it keeps them company (apparently, chickens have their favorites in "mood music," too, as evidenced by a notably positive reaction to the 1980s Pink Floyd recording, *The Final Cut*; Johnson, 2004).

The PANIC circuit can also be dramatically calmed through the administration of external opiates such as morphine or heroin (Carden & Hofer, 1990; Kalin, Shelton, & Barksdale, 1988; Panksepp, Herman, Conner, Bishop, & Scott, 1978). In fact, brain researchers hypothesize that one reason why certain people become addicted to external opiates such as morphine or heroin is because they are able to artificially induce feelings of comfort similar to those normally achieved by the socially induced release of endogenous opioids. This also explains why opiate addicts tend to socially isolate themselves except for when they need to find another fix, and opiate addiction is most common in environments where social isolation and alienation are endemic (Panksepp, 1998).

There are many experiments that have shown that the DVs have a powerful effect in activating the CARE circuits of other animals, even if the DVs are recorded. Not all crying comes from the PANIC system—both humans and animals respond to pain, hunger, and irritation by crying, but these cries can be distingushed from separation-induced DVs on both neuroanatomical and neurochemical bases. Adult animals instinctively know the difference (Panksepp, 1998).

This is probably why Loretta's tears of anger and frustration had little effect in activating Jack's CARE circuit. However, Loretta also came into contact with sorrowful tears more easily than Jack, which isn't surprising. Considerable evidence suggests that the PANIC circuit is more vigorous in most female mammals, especially as the years go by (Panksepp & Miller, 1996).

People vary considerably with regard to the degree to which they experience PANIC, and in their relative abilities to self-sooth and benefit from comfort offered by others. In recent years, compelling evidence has emerged suggesting that early experiences with caregivers can have a dramatic effect on such abilities (Cozolino, 2002; Fonagy & Target, 1997; Schore, 1994, 1996, 2001a, 2001b, 2001c; Siegel, 1999, 2001). All infants and young children readily experience and express distress when they are separated from desired people or objects. Investigations into early processes related to emotional attachment reveal that children whose parents fail to respond consistently in comforting ways learn to detach from their need for human contact, and that this detachment can persist throughout their lives. Jack fit this profile. On the other hand, children who experience inconsistent, unpredictable parental comforting may experience a chronic activation of the PANIC system, and develop into adults who are continually looking for the kind of comfort that they never got enough of as children. In many ways, this was Loretta's experience. Early in her life, Loretta's mother was occasionally very nurturing to her, and Loretta knew how good emotional comfort could feel. But her mother had many problems of her own, and often she was not there when Loretta needed her most. On these occasions, as many children do, Loretta learned to escape the pain of uncomforted PANIC by activating her RAGE. By the time Loretta met Jack, she had learned this lesson well. When Jack failed to respond to her PANIC, she automatically shifted to RAGE.

When caregivers respond to the emotions of developing children in ways that help soothe negative states and amplify positive ones, children develop the ability to fully experience both positive and negative emotions, and their brains also learn how to soothe stressful states. These children develop secure attachments. Studies suggest that the brains of securely attached children develop differently from the brains of insecurely attached children, specifically in the orbital prefrontal cortex, the area of the brain most responsible for emotional regulation (Schore, 1994, 1996, 2001a, 2001b). Schore summarized this point:

> During the first and second years of life, the infant's affective experiences, especially those embedded in the relationship with the primary caregiver, elicit patterns of psychobiological alterations that influence the activity of subcortically produced trophic bioamines, peptides, and steroids that regulate the critical period growth and organization of the developing neocortex. Interactive attachment experiences of psychobiological attunement, stressful misattunement, and stress-regulating repair and reattunement that maximize positive and minimize negative affect are imprinted into the orbitofrontal cortex. . . . During the critical period of maturation of this system, prolonged episodes of intense and unregulated interac-

tive stress . . . result in structurally defective systems that, under stress, inefficiently regulate subcortical mechanisms that mediate the physiological processes that underlie emotion. (1996, p. 59)

It is likely that neither Jack's nor Loretta's brains had the benefit of optimal critical-period interactions with their parents. Fortunately, the brain is open to changes throughout life, particularly in the orbital prefrontal area (Siegel, 1999). Loretta's brain would need to learn how to soothe her PANIC circuit, and Jack's brain would need to allow feelings of emotional need emanating from the PANIC to emerge.

ACCESSING CARE AND PANIC IN THERAPY

In my therapy with Jack and Loretta, I succeeded in accessing CARE in Jack by helping Loretta stay with her PANIC rather than switching to RAGE. Jack immediately sensed when Loretta's distress vocalizations were coming purely from her sorrow and loss (PANIC circuit) rather than from her frustration with him (RAGE circuit), and with my help, he was able to respond empathically. However, I knew that Jack wouldn't be able to maintain this on his own. He had no point of reference from which he could even fathom the kind of comfort that Loretta was seeking because he had never experienced it himself. During our early sessions, I helped Jack have a taste of this experience by facilitating his contact with just a bit of the disappointment and sadness he felt about losing Loretta's trust. Loretta's empathic response was immediate, reminding me of the studies in which mother rats instantly responded to distress vocalizations in their young. Jack was confused and somewhat embarrassed by Loretta's response to his display of weakness. However, I was able to facilitate more of this process in each of three subsequent sessions just before they decided to end therapy.

This part of my work with Jack and Loretta involved an ironic twist that is typical of my work with couples. Loretta was dying for more emotional understanding and support from Jack, and Jack wasn't really wanting emotional comforting from Loretta. Yet my main strategy was to connect Jack with his emotional need (which he didn't really want) and ask Loretta to delay getting support even longer (which she had been wanting all their married life). Experience working with the internal CARE and PANIC states of individual partners has taught me that a person cannot respond very well with CARE unless they have experienced the comfort of someone else in response to their own emotional need. Loretta's CARE was available from the beginning, and she often attempted to give it, but not in response to Jack's PANIC, because Jack's PANIC was rarely available, not even to himself, let alone Loretta. Long ago Jack had learned to disconnect from his own loneliness and had given up on his hope that he could be comforted by someone else when he was distressed. In the last few sessions of our first round of therapy, when I accessed Jack's PANIC and Loretta responded with CARE, both he and Loretta knew that something profound had happened. They had made a deeper connection than ever before. Jack had his first experiences in allowing himself to need emotional support from Loretta, and to allow himself to be comforted by her. If he stayed on track, this would shortly enable him to understand how to comfort her as well. Because they left therapy, they never got that far. Jack got as far as allowing me to access his PANIC, but he stopped far short of reconditioning his habit of shutting down his need for emotional comfort. As he and Loretta returned for therapy, I knew that this would be one of my primary goals.

Jack and Loretta were slumped on my couch, their bodies angled away from each other and their voices utterly drained of energy or affection. "Jack, what's going on?" I asked after Loretta had wrapped up her summary of their troubles. "You seem sort of sad." He straightened up immediately. "No," he demurred, "I think Loretta's probably right. We're just too different to make a go of it." As I allowed these words to hang in the air for a moment, I noticed that his eyes looked glassy, a sign that his separation-distress circuit was firing. "Jack," I asked softly, "How are you feeling right now?" His eyes filled and he remained silent for perhaps 20 seconds. Then, his voice wavering, he said: "I don't know what I'm going to do without her."

At this, Loretta spontaneously reached over and touched his hand. "I don't want to hurt you, Jack," she said gently. I imagine that her oxytocin had begun to flow, but she couldn't yet sustain it. "I'm not sure I can go on like this," she continued, her voice rising in irritation. "When you hang out with your damn computer every night of the week."

I stopped her short. "He needs you now, Loretta," I encouraged her. Following my lead, Jack added: "I know I didn't let you in Loretta, and I'm sorry." Loretta snapped: "Yeah, that and three bucks will get you a cup of coffee at Starbucks." Jack looked hopeless. "You're right, Loretta," I said. "Nothing will change until Jack learns how to let you in. And I can show him, if he wants." Jack bit his lip, then nodded. I pulled out my appointment book and scheduled a meeting with him.

I opted for a one-on-one session because I didn't want to forever facilitate emotional closeness between this couple, reinforcing an endless dependency on me. Instead, I wanted to teach Jack to contact his need for Loretta entirely on his own (I would teach Loretta a similar process). Later, I would bring them back together to help them put their new skills into practice. In my experience, a stint of individual work is indispensable to the kind of brain reconditioning couples need to avoid relapse.

In our individual sessions, I helped Jack use his conscious mind to tune into his emotions. Researchers in affective neuroscience all agree that our rational, thinking minds play a relatively weak role in the overall setup for how decisions are made. As Ornstein put it, "Consciousness comes in late; it is potentially powerful but is usually a weak force in most of our minds, easily overridden by circumstances, by eloquent people, by lower forces of the mind, by automatic routines" (1991, p. 226). Not only is consciousness a relatively limited resource in the overall mental scheme, neuroscientists like Ornstein believe that we often

squander what little we have, missing the most important and potentially powerful use for the conscious mind. We do this by directing conscious attention outward, rather than inward. We use our conscious minds to attempt to solve problems that our external worlds present us with. It is not that this is a bad idea. We
have solved many problems that potentially threaten human extinction by using
our conscious minds to develop vaccinations against disease, shield ourselves
from the elements, and find ways to secure the resources we need to live comfortable lives. However, as compelling as these accomplishments may be, we
have made precious little progress in increasing personal happiness and interpersonal harmony, as evidenced by the soaring divorce rate, and the societal conflicts that threaten our lives. In fact, the jury is still out on the question of
whether the added level of consciousness that humans possess will turn out to
be adaptive, or fatal to our species. Some of our most astounding accomplishments have also created the conditions that threaten our planet as we go about
our daily lives. For example, our rational capabilities have resulted in the cre-
ation of powerful engines that enable us to travel around the world in hours, but
the polluting byproducts of combustion engines now threaten life on earth. We
figured out how to preserve food by refrigerating air, but the CFCs used in the
process have created huge holes in the earth's protective ozone. We have learned
to control pests with a variety of chemicals that now make much of the earth's
water unfit for consumption.

I am not suggesting that we discontinue the use of our conscious minds to try
to solve external problems. I am simply suggesting that in our zeal to direct conscious attention outward, we may be missing the most important use of consciousness, which is to know the internal states that drive our actions, and to use
conscious attention to help them shift when needed. To do this, we will have to
give up the illusion that we are consciously in charge of ourselves, and start paying attention to the internal states that really run the show. Once we are aware
of our emotional world, there is potential for exerting some conscious influence.
We can help our internal states to shift, and coax dormant states into activity.
This is exactly what I had in mind for Jack and Loretta.

Alone with Jack, I began with a bit of teaching, describing in simple terms
how his brain was already set up for intimacy. I let him know that he could learn
skills that would allow him to more readily get in touch with connection-pro-
moting feelings such as sadness and disappointment. At this, Jack grinned and
shook his head. "I can't believe I'm sitting here about to learn how to feel depressed. This is a good thing?" We shared a good laugh, and then I clarified. "A
little bit of sadness is a good thing," I said. "It's not something to be afraid of."
The first step would simply be getting into the habit of noticing everyday disappointments and allowing himself to fully feel them.

In doing this work with clients, many therapists may wonder whether it is really necessary to explicitly refer to the role of the brain. Can't we just help people learn to shift their moods without muddying the conversational waters with
neurospeak? Probably, we can, but I have found that rather than turning off

clients, most are intrigued and even relieved by the impact of brain processes on thoughts, emotions, and behavior. It has a way of softening blame as clients begin to understand that the brain, in its natural, unruly state, does things that its "owner" may not really want or approve of. This doesn't mean we allow clients to pass the emotional buck ("Whoops, my rage circuit made me do it!"), but it does encourage a bit more compassion toward oneself and one's partner. It also offers a potent message of hope. Clients learn that no matter how emotionally shut down, self-protective, or stuck in anger they or their partner may now be, they still have the potential to restore intimacy.

I tell my clients, however, that they will have to work hard to make it happen. I told Jack, for example, that I would be giving him regular homework assignments, such as paying close attention to his feelings as they came up, especially the more vulnerable ones—and writing down how his body felt as he experienced them. I explained that if he could learn to tune in to his body's telltales signs of loneliness, a tightened throat, a sick feeling in his gut, he could then do something to relieve it. I encouraged Jack to think of his daily awareness work as a spiritual practice, a regular inventory of self that would slowly help him discover what he most valued and needed.

Jack's work was complicated by the fact that his brain had already figured out a way to compensate for the limited comfort he experienced from direct, nurturing contact with others. People like Jack, who have limited access to the kind of satisfaction and comfort that comes from direct, nurturing contact with others, often experience an overabundance of satisfaction emanating from another executive operating system that brain scientists call SEEKING.

SEEKING

The SEEKING circuit motivates human beings to energetically explore their worlds and produces a state of mind in which people are focused, attentive, and fully engaged. When the SEEKING circuit is active, people engage in the pursuit of meaningful resources (Panksepp, 1998). They experience feelings of interest, curiosity, and an invigorated feeling of anticipation that can replace uncomfortable feelings such as anxiety, restlessness, or disappointment. When SEEKING, people often forget about their worries because they are too busy solving their problems. But SEEKING was probably retained through the course of evolution for additional reasons. Individuals with vigorous SEEKING circuits are more likely to be successful in manipulating the world, and hence, more likely to survive. The experience of the SEEKING state is rewarding in itself. The feeling that comes when focusing one's energies and attention in the pursuit of something meaningful is enjoyable, even if the goals pursued are never attained. Researchers have hypothesized that extraverted individuals may have particularly active SEEKING circuits (Depue & Collins, 1999). Mihalyi Csikszentmihalyi (1990) called the state of mind produced by the SEEKING circuit, "Flow." When a person is in the Flow state of mind, they temporarily lose self-consciousness, and enter fully into a goal-directed process that recruits all parts of the brain in the service of goal attainment. Csikszentmihalyi suggested that, while the pursuit of a meaningful goal is part of the Flow experience, *attainment* of the goal is not necessary to produce Flow. Time spent in the SEEKING state is satisfying, regardless of the concrete external rewards that SEEKING enables. It's the thrill of the chase.

When a person's access to social comfort is partially shut off, they will rely more heavily on goal pursuit and attainment for satisfaction. This was the case with Jack, who had experienced a very limited amount of the kind of satisfaction that comes from receiving emotional nurturing from others. Predictably, Jack spent an inordinate amount of time SEEKING. To Loretta, it seemed as though Jack was always on some mission that excluded her. She claimed that Jack's idea of fun was doing yard work together. Jack disagreed, claiming that he was perfectly capable of relaxing, but preferred to "work first and play later." But "later" never seemed to arrive. There was always something that needed to be done. In short, Jack was a man who spent large amounts of time in the grips of an overly active SEEKING circuit to the relative exclusion of his intimacy-producing circuits. His overly active SEEKING was both the result and cause of his partially shut-down intimacy circuits: His reliance on SEEKING developed because the other avenue of satisfaction (direct nurturing contact) was closed off to him. But now his reliance on SEEKING to soothe himself was the main obstacle to gaining greater access to intimacy. At the first pang of anxiety, restlessness, or disappointment, Jack would fly into a flurry of goal-directed activity. This process happened so fast and automatically for Jack, that he wasn't even aware of it.

CALMING AN OVERLY ACTIVE SEEKING CIRCUIT THROUGH ACTIVATION OF EMOTIONAL NEED

For several weeks, I coached Jack to pay attention to difficult or stressful feelings that came up during his everyday life, and to notice how strongly the urge to get busy and fix things came over him whenever he felt stressed. He learned to sit quietly with these feelings, and treat these parts of his experience (the feeling of frustration and the urge to solve the problem) like guests who had come to visit him for a few moments. Because Jack wasn't accustomed to paying attention to his internal experience, he had very little ability to distinguish one feeling from another. In the beginning, he could describe the feeling only as "good" or "bad." Knowing that Jack had a hobby of sampling fine wines, I explained that developing skill in distinguishing feelings is much like becoming an expert in any specialized area such as becoming a wine connoisseur. When Jack was 15 years old, all wines tasted the same. As the years passed, Jack began to distinguish the wines he liked from the one's he didn't, but he couldn't say exactly why. The more he tried the wines, learning their names and paying close attention to the subtle differences, the more he began to distinguish the differences between them. It had never occurred to Jack that it might be worthwhile for him to become a connoisseur of his internal experience. Once he decided it was a good idea, he made rapid progress. He found that when he paid close attention, he was able to distinguish different types of "good" and "bad" feelings. For example, at first, Jack described all negative feelings as "frustration" or "stress." I gave him a list of feelings and asked him to see if, when he was feeling frustrated, he could find other words that described his feeling more precisely. Was there a hint of disappointment along with the frustration? Or how about embarrassment? Did he feel any worry, or anxiety? As Jack paid closer attention, he found that, not only could he better distinguish what he was feeling, he found that he actually felt more of these feelings. The more he paid attention, the more his emotions came to life.

An important part of my work with Jack involved moments when Jack allowed himself to pay attention to feelings he was having while in my presence. Our therapy sessions became a safe place for Jack to connect with, and more fully experience, his feelings, without fear of being judged. The process of allowing vulnerable feelings to emerge was a new experience for Jack, and it was stressful, but tolerable. Cozolino (2002) suggested that this combination is optimal for successful change in psychotherapy to occur. Under the right conditions, moderate levels of stress can stimulate new neural growth and integration. As Jack connected with uncomfortable feelings, my calming presence allowed him to tolerate these feelings, and to self-soothe without detaching from them. In a sense, I was becoming an important attachment figure for Jack. My presence was having the same effect on his emotional development as the presence of a well-attuned caregiver has on the development of a young child. Within the secure confines of our relationship, Jack was learning the skills of emotional intelligence.

After Jack had faithfully practiced these new awareness skills for several weeks, I encouraged him to begin acting on them. With Loretta's permission, Jack began to call her whenever he felt lonely, sad, or disappointed. Then, during a joint session, Jack recounted an incident at work in which he had inadvertently offended a client and lost an important account. In the middle of the story, he fell silent for a moment, and then told Loretta that he felt a kind of queasy, hollow sensation in his stomach. "I'm sorry, honey," responded Loretta quietly. "I can imagine how that feels." Loretta instinctively scooted toward Jack on the couch and put her arm around him. Instantly, his whole body tightened in an instinctive attempt to short-circuit his vulnerability, I guessed. I asked him to pay attention to the tension in his body, then to simply notice the softness of Loretta's hand on his neck. Closing his eyes, Jack visibly relaxed, resting his hand on Loretta's knee. After about 30 seconds, I asked him to check again how he was feeling. "Warm and calm," he reported, surprise edging his voice. Chuckling softly, he added: "I must be high on those opioids you were talking about!"

It was a pivotal moment. Before, Jack hadn't even noticed that he usually resisted the comfort Loretta offered. Afterward, he began to consciously allow himself to be soothed by Loretta's gentle support, and a few sessions later, he reported that he often missed his wife during his long workdays and looked forward to being with her in the evenings. Before long, Jack began to spontaneously ask Loretta about her own emotional ups and downs.

This didn't come easily. At first, when Loretta loudly voiced her frustration about some problem she was experiencing, he lapsed into his old style of lecturing her that she simply shouldn't get so upset. But gradually, Jack discovered that if he simply gave his wife his unreserved, sympathetic attention, she usually became calmer and clearer after a few minutes. To his surprise, he found himself beginning to enjoy giving her support. I no longer needed to help Jack jump-start the process of comforting his wife; he was activating his CARE circuit on his own. Jack's experience jibes with brain research suggesting that each time neurons fire in a new pattern, those neural pathways get strengthened as though new emotional grooves are being dug in the brain (Hebb, 1949). No question, Jack was getting into the groove of connection.

Of course, intimacy takes two. I also worked with Loretta individually, assigning homework in which she stopped to reflect on each interaction with Jack that triggered her own default mode anger. I asked her to try to identify what important need, belief, fear, or dream was at risk when Jack didn't give her the attention she craved.

At first, Loretta firmly resisted thinking in these terms. Her husband could be an insensitive jerk, end of discussion! But as she repeatedly stopped and listened to herself whenever she felt Jack withdrawing, and paid close attention to her body's signals at these moments, she began to identify deeply rooted fears of invisibility and aloneness. The more she practiced, the more she was able to pause in the face of conflict, identify her fear, then speak to Jack from her yearning rather than from her anger. From a neural perspective, she was learning how to keep her PANIC system up and running, which was exactly the signal her husband needed to stimulate his CARE circuit. Finally, Loretta and Jack were beginning to do the intimacy tango and better yet, they were now learning the dance steps on their own.

Over the course of three months, Loretta and Jack reestablished the emotional intimacy they had only tasted in the first round of therapy. This time, however, they had developed the ability to consciously put themselves into internal operating modes from which intimacy naturally flowed. As a result, I had much more confidence that the intimacy would last. However, I wasn't through with them yet. While each of them had learned how to consciously influence the previously conditioned activation patterns of their PANIC and CARE systems, I had noticed that two other neural systems critical to emotional bonding were partly shut down, PLAY and LUST.

PLAY

When I first read about the brain's seven executive operating systems I was surprised to find that one of them is devoted exclusively to instigating play. It is easy to see why each of the other EOS survived the challenges of evolutionary time. RAGE promotes self-protection, FEAR facilitates withdrawal from danger, SEEKING motivates exploration and mastery of the external world, CARE and PANIC create secure attachment, and LUST promotes the passing of genes from generation to generation. But play? How does play enhance chances of survival? Like CARE and PANIC, the PLAY circuit appears to play an important role in facilitating social bonding (Johnson, 2004; Panksepp, 1998). When the PLAY circuit is active, internal opioids are released throughout the brain, and when released through nurturing contact serve the function of calming an active PANIC circuit. (Panksepp & Bishop, 1981; Vanderschuren, Niesink, & Van-Ree, 1995; Vanderschuren Stein Wiegant & VanRee, 1997). Internal opioids are now believed to be one of the prime neurochemical movers in the construction and maintenance of social bonds (Panksepp, 1998). Experimental studies reveal that mammals consistently prefer to spend time with others in whose presence they have experienced high brain opioid activity (Agmo & Berenfeld, 1990; Panksepp Neson, & Bekkedal, 1997).

When the PLAY circuit is electrically stimulated, individuals experience urges toward vigorous and spontaneous social interaction, often accompanied by a sense of joy. Panksepp uses words like *carefree* and *rambunctious* to describe the state of mind resulting from an activation of the PLAY circuit in rats (1998). In contrast to the SEEKING state of mind, which is focused, planned, and goal directed, PLAY involves a make-it-up-as-you-go kind of interaction where individuals place priority on getting unplanned responses from each other. There is evidence, across mammalian species, that females are somewhat more playful than males (Panksepp, 1998). When I first described each of the brain's intimacy circuits to Loretta, she remarked that PLAY was probably her strongest circuit. She was certain that her friends would use the word *fun* to describe her. Loretta maintained that a sense of humor was required to survive growing up with three older brothers who incessantly teased and played practical jokes on her. In the early days of their relationship, Jack seemed to love her penchant for wrestling, tickling, and chiding. No doubt, this kind of affectionate contact released internal opioids in each of their brains and facilitated a feeling of closeness. When the neural hijackings began, however, playfulness ended. Like many partners who get into ruts, Loretta still wanted closeness to Jack, but seemed to forget that there were several avenues to pursue connection, play being one of them. When she felt lonely or down, she would approach Jack and try to tell him about the things that were stressing her. This seemed like a sensible approach, but as we have discussed, Jack often had a difficult time responding in a way that was satisfying to Loretta, often dismissing her feelings by telling her she shouldn't let things bother her so much. Of course, this cued Loretta's rage circuit.

I remember the look on Loretta's face the day I posed a simple question to her: "When you're feeling disconnected or lonely, why do you always try to get sympathy from Jack?" She looked at me as though I had lobsters crawling out of

my ears. "You've been telling us for months that we need more emotional support from each other! Now you're saying I shouldn't expect that?" Anticipating
her response, I smiled and teased her, repeating her words in a play-mocking
tone back to her. She smiled immediately, recognizing that I was trying to get a
rise out of her, and quipped, "Okay smart ass, where the hell are you going with
this?" I replied, "What I mean, Loretta, is that you always use the same approach
to connect with Jack, when there are several avenues available to you." I went
on to explain that she seems to forget all about her strong suit—playfulness.
When she was feeling lonely or upset, would it be possible for her to make an
internal shift and connect with her playfulness as a means of making contact
with Jack? Loretta looked confused, and sat silent, frowning for a few moments.
Gradually, her expression changed, and she then told me about a time she remembered when she did exactly that. It was one of those days when everything
that could go wrong was indeed going wrong. She rushed to her car after work
thinking that she couldn't wait to vent to Jack when she got home. But on the
way home, she got so sick of herself that she realized what she really needed was
to just forget about the whole damned day and do something to take her mind
off of it. When she got home the first thing she did was pinch Jack in the ass.
Jack responded by tackling her, and they romped gleefully with each other for
15 minutes until they were laughing so hard that Loretta had to stop because
she thought she was going to pee her pants! Loretta admitted that this was probably better than any kind of serious, supportive conversation they might have
had. As it turned out, she did confide in Jack later in the evening, and at that
moment, he was able to be sympathetic. What happened? Loretta had connected with Jack in a different way.

This memory inspired Loretta to try this approach several times in the weeks
that followed. It worked so well that I was tempted to end therapy, but for the
fact that I knew there was still one avenue for connection that was not operating
at full potential in their relationship. This avenue involved the brain system that
promotes sexual connection. During their months of therapy, Jack had made
several comments about Loretta's lack of sexual interest.

LUST

In the past I had couples cases in which sex was sometimes mentioned only in
passing. If the couple didn't report sex as a pressing problem, we didn't explore
it. As evidence has mounted regarding the important role of sex in solidifying
emotional bonding, however, I have taken it upon myself to probe further into
sexual relationships. Research suggests that there are tremendous advantages to
couples who maintain a robust sexual life.

Probably the most important finding about the neural operating system that
brain scientists call LUST, is that activation of this system in both men and
women elevates oxytocin levels throughout the brain. In animal studies, it has
been shown that free access to sexual gratification can lead to an enormous

threefold elevation of oxytocin in some parts of the male brain (Panksepp, 1998). Oxytocin is centrally involved in activating the CARE circuit. Thus, sex primes the brain for activation of nurturing motivation. Animal studies confirm this. Increased sexual activity diminishes the tendency of male rats to kill the young in a territory that they have successfully invaded (Hausfater & Hrdy, 1984; Mennella & Moltz, 1988). In fact, the administration of oxytocin to experimental animals reduces all forms of aggression (Panksepp, 1998). It has been documented that societies that are permissive of premarital sex are generally low in adult physical violence (Prescott, 1971). Panksepp has written, "Considering the importance of oxytocin in sexual behavior and the mediation of mother–infant bonds, we must suspect that sexual interactions among consenting adults may neurophysiologically facilitate the consolidation of social attachments, thereby promoting the more nurturant forms of human love" (1998, p. 259).

It should be noted that, while activation of LUST can lead to activation of CARE, activation of CARE also makes the activation of LUST more likely, especially in women. It is commonly thought that men can have sex without intimacy and that women are less likely to operate this way. Indeed, there are neurochemical reasons for this. Oxytocin plays a greater role in facilitating female sexual interest than male sexual interest. For men, sexual eagerness is mediated by the neuropeptide arginine-vassopressin, which is also known to have a role in the activation of aggression (Sachser, Lick, & Stanzel, 1994; Schurman, 1980). Perhaps this is why men are often experienced as more conquest-oriented in their sexuality. For men, oxytocin levels peak during ejaculation (Carter, 1992), which may be why women often enjoy the company of men most during the "afterglow" period following sex. Due to the release of oxytocin, men are most naturally motivated to act in nurturing ways after sex.

When I approached the topic of sex with Loretta and Jack, Loretta confessed that part of the difficulty she was having with sexual interest was that she saw Jack as a sexual aberrant. Across the course of their relationship, Jack had pushed Loretta to do things like dress provocatively in public so that he could watch how other men looked at her, or make love in public places where they might get caught. He constantly wanted her to act out sexual fantasy situations. For example, in one of his favorite fantasies he wanted her to dress and act like a doctor who got "carried away" while she was giving him an exam. In her view, there was no end to Jack's sexual imagination. He had ordered countless sex toys, tried to get her to watch porn movies with him, and even attempted to persuade her to try a threesome at one point. She made it clear that this turned her off, but he persisted in pushing his desires on her again and again. At first, she worried that he would be unfaithful to her if she didn't acquiesce, but over the years he had shown no signs that he would actually be unfaithful. At one point Loretta stopped having sex altogether with Jack until he promised that he would just try to enjoy normal sex. He stayed on good behavior if Loretta made him wait about two months between sexual encounters. But when they began to have sex more frequently, he always returned to his push for experimentation.

In a conjoint meeting, I spent time asking each of them to try to pay attention to exactly what it was inside that kept them from being comfortable with their partner's sexual desires. What was it that kept Jack from enjoying sex without provocative adventure? And what was it that Loretta objected to most about trying Jack's experimental sexual attitude? Jack loved my question, and went to great lengths to explain to me that it wasn't the particular sexual activities that were important to him. It was the sense of adventure, the daring aspect. He wanted his closest buddy to go with him into forbidden territory. For him, the sharing of these fantasies and adventures was a very intimate thing, something you would only do with a person you trusted wholeheartedly. Jack clarified that he would never actually want to act out his sexual fantasies in real life. He admitted that if he thought that Loretta would actually want to be with the other men he fantasized about her being with, he would be shaken. Loretta had never heard Jack talk this way about the situation before, and hearing him created a new frame of reference for her.

Loretta also gave serious consideration to my question, and was able to clarify that she wasn't as bothered by the actual activities that he wanted as she was about his intense push for them to happen. He simply wouldn't take "no" for an answer. It wasn't that he wanted these activities, it was that he had to have them, and something didn't seem right about that to her. Why the urgency? It felt like Jack was saying that sex with her was so boring that only a fantasy could salvage it. As she spoke, I was struck by how much progress she had made in staying with her sadness rather than her old mode of anger and resentment. Her voice wavering, Loretta explained, "I just wanted you to want to be with me." Jack sat thoughtfully for a few moments. Then he responded softly, "I feel embarrassed and humiliated to not have heard you this clearly until now, Loretta." There wasn't a trace of defensiveness in his voice. He went on to try to explain one more time that he pushed because he couldn't imagine anything quite as exciting and intimate as going on these daring adventures together. The intensity wasn't because he had to have it. What he felt intense about was trying to convince her that it could be so much fun to do these things together. For him it would mean that their relationship had entered a new level of trust, one that he had always dreamed of having. Loretta sat silently with her sadness. Jack took the hint, and dropped his attempts to explain himself. After a minute of silence, Jack looked over as if studying the sadness in Loretta's face, then simply said, "I feel awful that I've made you feel this way. I don't ever want to do that again." The tenderness in his voice brought tears to Loretta's eyes. The session ended and they left without speaking.

Jack and Loretta had heard each other differently in that session. In the car on the way home, Jack assured Loretta that even if she never wanted to go on any of his crazy sexual adventures with him, sex with her was twice as good as it could ever have been with anyone else, and he assured her that he would find a way to be okay with the disappointment of her not wanting to play sexual games with him. When they returned for their next session, I knew something was different by the way they walked down the hall to my office. This was the most relaxed I'd ever seen them. Loretta explained that in the previous session she sensed for the first time that Jack had felt bad about how he made her feel. I knew she was right. Jack's heartfelt words at the end of the session had "CARE circuit" written all over them. They were the real deal. Loretta explained that he had also seemed vulnerable when he was explaining why the sexual games and activities were important to him, and for the first time she believed that for him, they really might be a vehicle to intimacy, an experience that only the two of them would share. She said that she sensed his pain at being misunderstood, and felt badly about that. Somehow this shifted her perspective, and she decided to surprise Jack one night by explaining to him that his wife had hired her to be his masseuse. As the massage progressed, she took sexual liberties with him, grinning and apologizing along the way. Beaming, Jack added that she stayed perfectly in character for a full 45 minutes! Loretta confessed that Jack's excitement about the experience actually turned her on.

I wasn't surprised. In many ways, Jack and Loretta's sexual awakening was typical of what many couples experience in therapy. Once the constraints are removed which keep the LUST circuit from being activated, sexual intimacy often flows naturally. Of course, It's not always this easy. Loretta and Jack's constraints were fairly limited, but strong enough to have brought their sex life to a standstill. Once Loretta was able to understand Jack differently, she was able to avoid the thoughts that shut down her LUST circuit (e.g., He finds me boring, he's treating me like an object, etc). Once Loretta got new understanding of Jack (he wants to share a daring experience with his best friend, for him, it would be a way of feeling closer to me) she was able to hold onto it. Loretta was unusual in this way. More often, I find that partners have to practice trying out new ways of thinking over and over again before they arise spontaneously when they are needed most.

Jack and Loretta ended therapy shortly after this session. Later that year, I got a Christmas card in Jack's handwriting, letting me know that Santa Claus had visited their house and given Loretta some "special favors" as well as Christmas presents! During our one year follow-up assessment, Jack's score on the Locke Wallace Marital Adjustment test was holding at 110 and Loretta's was 124. In our follow-up interview, Loretta noted that Jack had actually stopped pushing the sexual experimentation theme as much, and that their sex life had never been better. We routinely ask each partner at follow-up, "If your partner started acting the way she or he used to act when things were going badly, what would you do?" Both Jack and Loretta explained that they were confident that if they could stick with their sadness rather than feeding the resentful and angry feelings that might arise when their partner was misunderstanding them, they were confident that their partner would eventually respond.

CONCLUSION

Jack and Loretta's therapy illustrates a fundamental principle that guides our work with couples. It is necessary to help couples to learn not only to modulate their RAGE and FEAR systems, but also to build up their emotional bank accounts via strengthening access to "intimacy circuits," those controlling nurture, separation distress (which spurs us to seek connection), play, and sexual interest. While other mammals may have no need for such tinkering, we human beings, with our more complicated craniums, are uniquely gifted at getting our emotional wires crossed. Our early childhood experiences, intercut with the everyday storms and stresses of marriage, may spur us to feel furious with our spouse when no actual threat exists, or distant when our partner badly needs nurture, or sexually frozen on the very night the kids are at their grandparents, the champagne is chilled, and Barry White is pouring sweetly out of the stereo, doing his best to get us in the mood.

A couple might go through the motions of connection as Jack and Loretta did when they set up regular "date nights," but if they don't know how to activate their intimacy circuits, their hearts simply won't be in it. I believe that this is why so many couples wind up like Jack and Loretta, relapsing quickly and convinced that the "juice" has irretrievably leaked out of their marriage. While couples are in therapy, good clinicians help them effectively calm their anger and fear circuits as well as stimulate the more vulnerable, connection-generating states. The therapist acts as a kind of neural chiropractor, making regular, finely tuned adjustments to each partner's out-of-sync brain. But once couples leave therapy and face the slings and arrows of intimate partnership on their own, they all too readily revert back to their deeply conditioned, default brain states. The next time their partner is critical or distant or sharp-tongued, they're apt to flip back into their neural safety zone of anger or fear—in a split second. Moreover, once they've plunged into one of these intimacy-zapping states, they may find it difficult to shift out again at will. If they aren't truly in the mood, that is, in the right brain state, for intimacy, all the flower deliveries and date nights, and diaphanous nightgowns in the world aren't likely to bring a couple back into connection.

This points to a key benefit of behavioral brain science for clinicians: it helps us identify the real target of our work—brain-mediated mood states. Cognitive or behavioral interventions work only when they influence "Big Seven"-type shifts. Even the best-rehearsed self-statements or the most insightful restorying may fail to trigger confident, intimacy-seeking, or collaborative internal states. Without the needed mood states to sustain them, new stories will fade, and new behaviors will eventually peter out. Brain science encourages us to not settle for changed thinking or actions without evaluating whether these changes activate internal states that naturally pull us toward intimacy.

Helping clients shift mood states is essential, but it's not enough. We need to give our clients the tools to shift from one brain state to another entirely on their own. If the new affective neuroscience shows therapists anything, it is the critical importance of our role as teachers of emotional literacy. Notwithstanding the clinical scenarios that many of us were schooled on, featuring therapy masters who transformed a couple or family with a single, brilliant directive, the new behavioral brain science suggests the profound improbability that such "aha" moments will have any staying power. Our neural habits are far too deeply ingrained for that. Instead, we need to help our clients develop practices for reconditioning their automatically activated neural habits. This is no quick or casual undertaking, to be wrapped up in a couple of role-play exercises. Exerting an impact on lifelong neuroemotional conditioning requires serious training, much as athletic or musical ability is honed through constant skill building and practice. When clients first experience the dramatic effects that often follow internal state shifts, it's tempting for them to conclude that they have "arrived." Usually, however, the work has just begun. Lasting change requires new emotional habits that are formed by making the same internal shifts over and over.

CHAPTER 3

The Prerequisites for Relationship Success

THE STORIES OF James and Susan, and Jack and Loretta in Chapters 1 and 2 were presented to illustrate the most important assumption behind the treatment model described in the chapters that will follow: Distressed partners will often be unable to succeed in their relationships unless the automatic activation and suppression patterns of their neural states are reconditioned. The majority of partners who seek couples therapy will need to rewire their brains for more flexibility if they want to make lasting changes. The methods we use to help couples with this rewiring process will be detailed in future chapters. For the moment, let's take a different angle. If a person was able to get enough cooperation from his/her emotions to be able to interact with his/her intimate partner in ways that would lead to a happy, stable relationship, what would it look like? How do people who have good "neural flexibility" use it in their relationships?

In Chapter 1, I introduced you to the exciting new developments in the field of marriage research, in which researchers have identified attitudes and actions that strongly predict the success or demise of a relationship over time. Let's take a closer look at these studies. At this point, there have been seven longitudinal studies examining the variables that predict marital outcomes (Carrere, 2000; Gottman, 1994a, 2002; Gottman & Levenson, 1992, 1999, 2000; Gottman, Katz & Hooven, 1996; Gottman, Coan, Carrere, & Swanson, 1998; Jacobson & Gottman, 1998; Levenson & Gottman, 1983, 1985; Levenson, Carstensen, & Gottman, 1994). The general method used in these studies was to measure any variables that researchers thought might possibly be related to how couples' relationships fare over time, then follow the partners over many years, tracking how their marriages progress in terms of happiness and stability. These studies included newlyweds, couples in the first seven years of marriage, violent marriages, and long-term couples in their 40s and 60s (Gottman, 2002). Some of the studies were conducted in an apartment laboratory at the University of Washington. Couples lived at this lab for 24-hour periods, with cameras recording everything that happened between them. The studies employed a multimethod approach, measuring three domains: Interactive behavior (coding partners' behavior and emotion as they interacted in various contexts), perception (studying individual perceptions of self and other through questionnaires, video recall procedures, attributional methods, and interviews), and physiology (measuring autonomic, endocrine and immune system responses). Researchers found that variables in each of these domains predict marital outcomes.

Researchers recorded many different types of conversations: They observed couples talking about how their day went after they had been apart for at least eight hours; they observed them talking about, and trying to resolve, areas of continuing disagreement between them; and they observed them talking about enjoyable topics as well. During some conversations, they also recorded the physiological responses of each partner as they talked to each other. Specifically, they gathered data on respiration, electrocardiogram, blood velocity to the ear and the finger of the nondominant hand, and skin conductance and gross motor movement via a "jiggle-ometer" attached to the base of their chairs. Researchers used Holter monitors from SpaceLabs (used to conduct physiological measurements of NASA astronauts) and their beat-to-beat computer program for analyzing the couple's electrocardiograms. The researchers also measured urinary stress hormones, and took blood samples for standard immunological assessment.

In one procedure, researchers had partners review videotapes of previous conversations and asked them to recall what they were thinking and feeling at different points during the conversation. Researchers also asked them to guess what their partners were thinking and feeling. The researchers sometimes replayed interviews of specific moments (selected on some salient dimension, such as their rating, their behavior, or their physiology). The interview of specific moments asked people how they perceived the moment—how they were feeling, how they thought their partner was feeling, and what their goals were during that moment. They also filled out questionnaires about these moments. From these procedures, researchers learned that there were two basic categories of negative reactions: an "innocent victim" type of perception, associated with whining and defensiveness; and a "righteous indignation" perception, associated with contempt.

Researchers also developed interviews to gather each partner's perceptions of the history of their marriage, their parents' marriages, their philosophies of marriage, and their levels of comfort with the basic emotions. Researchers developed an interview for the purpose of gathering data on the rituals, roles, life dreams, goals, symbols, and myths that guided each partner's search for meaning.

Videotapes of conversations were analyzed using objective coding systems with trained observers who looked for such elements as specific verbal and nonverbal communications—facial expressions, voice tone, gestures, body positions and movements, and the distance between the partners.

When researchers had measured everything they considered relevant, they sent the couples back to live their lives, and followed them carefully for many years. (Gottman, 1999, pp. 26–27)

Gottman has summarized what he sees as the most salient of the predictive variables in his books, *The Seven Principles for Making Marriage Work* (Gottman & Silver, 1999), *Why Marriages Succeed or Fail* (Gottman, 1994), and *The Relationship Cure* (Gottman & DeClaire, 2001). From the myriad of variables that predict the fate of relationships, and drawing from Gottman's own ways of summarizing the most important of these, we have identified five prerequisites that are both central to predicting relationship success, and practical in the sense that they are easily understood and learned. These prerequisites are a measuring stick that we use in our clinical work to assess the ongoing progress of each partner. They anchor the pragmatic focus of Pragmatic/Experiential Therapy for Couples (PET-C).

Over time we have settled on 10 specific skills that help individuals accomplish the prerequisites (see Table 3.1). In his therapy with couples, John Gottman takes a "smorgasboard" approach with couples (Gottman, 1999). That is, he offers them a variety of options that might work in helping them meet the prerequisites. We have taken a different approach, focusing instead on a limited number of specific habits that we feel confident will work. Our clients seemed to be overwhelmed when presented with too many choices, and learned better by focusing on a few specific abilities. In this chapter, the five prerequisites for relationship success that provide direction for PET-C will be summarized, and 10 habits that enable clients to meet these prerequisites will be discussed.

PREREQUISITE 1: SOFT STARTUP

One of the most important things we know about people who are destined to succeed in their relationships is that they deliver complaints differently from those who are destined to fail. Researchers have found that 96% of the time the outcome of an argument can be successfully predicted after watching only the first three minutes of an interaction between partners (Gottman, 1999; Gottman & Silver, 1999). People who want the cooperation and respect of their partners are able to express their dissatisfactions well, they know how to bring their complaints up gently. They don't beat around the bush, and they don't sugarcoat what they have to say, but they do avoid criticizing or talking down to their partners. Researchers call this ability, a *soft startup* (Gottman, 1999, 2002). A soft startup is a simple statement about something the person doesn't like, or something he or she would like to see changed, with an explanation as to why this is so. A soft startup might involve a statement like, "I'm really upset that you forgot we were going to play cards with Rick and Cindy Saturday night. I was embar-

TABLE 3.1
The Prerequisites for Relationship Success and Ten Habits
that Enable Partners to Meet Them

MANAGING CONFLICTS

Prerequisite 1: Soft Startup
Predictive Habit 1: Avoiding a Judgmental Attitude
Predictive Habit 2: Standing Up for Yourself Without Putting Your
  Partner Down

Prerequisite 2: Accepting Influence
Predictive Habit 3: Finding the Understandable Part
Predictive Habit 4: Giving Equal Regard

Prerequisite 3: Effective Repair
Predictive Habit 5: Offering Assurances

Prerequisite 4: Respecting Your Partner's Dreams; Holding on to Your Own
Predictive Habit 6: Understanding and Explaining What is at Stake

CONNECTING DURING NONCONFLICT TIMES

Prerequisite 5: Five Positives for Every Negative
Predictive Habit 7: Curiosity about Your Partner's World
Predictive Habit 8: Keeping Sight of the Positive
Predictive Habit 9: Pursuing Shared Meaning
Predictive Habit 10: Making and Responding to Bids for Connection

---

rassed when it was clear to Cindy that you didn't know." In contrast, a harsh startup involves criticism or contempt. Criticism involves the tendency to go beyond a simple statement of feelings to a global statement or implication about your partner: "How can you be so insensitive?" "You never forget about things that are important to you, but you can't remember things that are important to me! You live in your own little world!" Contempt goes even further, and anger turns to disgust, resulting in statements like these "I should have known that you'd screw things up again"; "Why do I even bother with you?"; "You're just like your mother!" A person with contempt puts him- or herself on a higher plane than the partner.

There are situation-specific forms of contempt and global forms of contempt. The situation-specific kind of contempt involves thinking that one's values, preferences, or viewpoints are better or more correct than those of one's partner, in any given situation. Global contempt involves the generalized tendency to think of one as better (more mature, more responsible, less selfish, less to blame) than one's partner. There are universally recognized facial expressions of contempt, which often involve a raising of the eyebrow combined with the raising of the upper lip, as in a sneer (Gottman, 1999). Contempt is powerfully corrosive to relationships. In fact, of all of the factors that have been found to predict divorce, contempt is the most powerful predictor. Happy marriages are virtually contempt-free (Gottman, 1999). In one study, researchers observing videotapes of couples arguing turned off the sound and just coded facial expressions of contempt. They found that nonverbal expressions of contempt on the part of husbands predicted the extent of infectious illness in their wives during the following four years. Interestingly, they did not find the reverse to be statistically true; that is, nonverbal expression of wives' contempt did not predict illness in husbands, unless a loneliness variable was included. Only lonely husbands whose wives were contemptuous had more infectious illness in the following years (Gottman, 1994a).

People who meet the soft startup prerequisite avoid both criticism and contempt. In our work with couples, we have found two foundational abilities that, when present, enable partners to easily meet the soft startup prerequisite. The first has to do with attitude, and the second requires a specific kind of behavior.

Predictive Habit 1: Avoiding a Judgmental Attitude

Beneath both criticism and contempt lies a general tendency to assume that, if you are upset, somebody must have done something wrong. Marriage researchers have discovered that most of the time this assumption is unwarranted, and that when partners are upset with each other, neither partner has done anything that is intrinsically wrong (Gottman, 1999). Sixty-nine percent of marital upsets arise from conflicting values, priorities, beliefs, or personal tendencies for which there is no generally accepted standard (Gottman, 2002). Marriages start to slide when partners assume there is a "correct" standard to which they are entitled to hold their partners accountable. For example, consider the following questions.

- How much arguing is acceptable in marriage?
- How much money should be spent on what type of things?
- How much of life should be planned out versus "make-it-up-as-we-go?"
- Should we work first, then play, or play along the way?
- To what extent is it all right to socialize with members of the opposite sex?
- To what extent is it appropriate for a married person to wear sexy or revealing clothing in public?
- Who should do what chores around the house, how often?
- How neat and organized should a couple's life be?
- How much time should be put into career versus family?
- How important is it for the couple to talk about feelings?
- How much, and what type of discipline should be used with the kids?

- How much time should married people spend together versus time with friends?
- How much time should be spent with extended families?
- How much should partners keep each other informed as to where they have been, and with whom?
- What kind of sexual activities are acceptable (or expected)?
- How much financial risk should be taken?

Gottman's studies (2002) suggest that there are a wide variety of legitimate opinions that partners can take on such questions. There are happily married and unhappily married risk-takers, and both happily and unhappily married conservatives. Some couples who place high value on personal freedom are happily married and some are not. Some happily married couples argue a lot and some couples who argue a lot end up divorced. Happily married partners differ on scores of important values and priorities, but they have one thing in common: They avoid assuming that their partner's values, priorities, or opinions are wrong, and instead assume that there are many potentially legitimate ways to live life. People destined to succeed understand that if you assume the worst of your partner, you'll get the worst from your partner. Instead, they give their partners the benefit of the doubt; they assume that there is a legitimate reason for their partner's words or actions, even if they don't know what it is yet. Beneath even seemingly provocative behavior on the part of their partners, they assume that there are legitimate dreams or priorities that their partners are trying to obtain. In contrast, when people who are destined to fail in their relationships are faced with words or actions from their partners that are upsetting to them, they assume that their partners are acting this way because they have misguided reasoning, priorities, motivations, or intentions, or that their partners have faulty personality characteristics (e.g., "my partner is just lazy, controlling, irresponsible, insensitive, etc."; Gottman, 1999; Holtzworth-Monroe & Jacobson, 1985; Notarius et al., 1989).

Many of us grow up feeling that we don't have the right to be upset with someone unless that person did something wrong. So, when we find ourselves upset, we tend to automatically assume that the other person did something wrong—otherwise, we wouldn't feel entitled to be upset (Wile, 2002)! Successful people find a way out of this dilemma, realizing that it is normal for people to get upset with each other when their expectations are at cross-purposes. Nobody has to be wrong.

Predictive Habit 2: Standing Up for Yourself Without Putting Your Partner Down

Dropping the idea that one's partner is wrong doesn't mean that one has to give in. People who are destined to succeed believe that their own opinions and expectations are just as important as those of their partners. Rather than criticizing or trying to prove their partners wrong, people who are destined to succeed in their relationships simply ask their partners to "move over and make room for me." They ask their partners to meet them half way. Successful partners both require that their feelings be respected, and make it easy for their partners to be respectful at the same time. They make it easy for their partners to be respectful by refraining from assuming that their partners are wrong. They require that their feelings be respected by avoiding criticism of their partners and instead ask their partners to work toward solutions that take both of their preferences into account (Gottman, 2002).

When couples are distressed, it is most always the case that neither partner has the ability to stand up for him- or herself without putting the other person down. Instead, partners criticize and never state exactly what they want, try to present their own point of view as the only reasonable option, or give in to their partners while secretly thinking bad things about them. People who swear that their partners are control freaks are often amazed to learn that their partners are actually willing to compromise when they are asked to "move over and make room for me" rather than be judged or criticized. Of course, this doesn't always happen. Sometimes, even in situations where one partner avoids judging the other, and instead simply asks the other to "move over," the other won't move over! This is the real test. It is often at this point that the first partner loses focus and slides back into judging the other, or giving in. The result is a predictable negative slide. People who are destined for success refrain from making a big deal of it when their partners don't seem willing to meet them half way. They simply hold their ground and continue to insist that their opinions or priorities be given equal consideration.

To return to to the story of Susan and James from Chapter 1, there wasn't anything soft about the way Susan typically delivered her complaints to James. As therapy progressed, I thought that most of her complaints were valid, but she undermined her potential influence by her criticism of James. Although James often capitulated to Susan to avoid her wrath, her approach drove the thing that she wanted most from James further away, namely, for him to see her complaints as legitimate. Rather than telling James that his actions upset her and asking him to work toward a solution that would take her feelings into account, she usually set out to convince James that he was wrong to do or say what he did. She became furious with James for volunteering her to drive his daughter to a birthday party instead of asking his ex-wife to do it. Susan immediately assumed the worst of James:

- "He stands up to me all the time, but he won't dare upset the little princess over there!"
- "I'm not going to play their sick little game."

With thoughts like this in her head, it was impossible for Susan to accomplish a soft startup. In order for a soft startup to become a possibility, she'd have to find a way to suspend her critical assumptions about him, which is what people who are destined to succeed in their relationships do. If Susan was going to find a way to meet the soft startup prerequisite, she'd need to find a way to propose different possibilities to herself, such as:

- "Maybe I don't have all the facts yet."
- "Maybe there's a reason why he did this that I don't yet understand."
- "Maybe James didn't do anything *wrong*. It's just way different from what I wanted. Maybe not everybody would be as upset as me in this situation. In fact, James probably wouldn't be as upset if the roles were reversed."
- "I have the right to be upset even if James didn't do anything wrong."
- "I have a right to ask James to take my feelings seriously even if he doesn't agree with me. My feelings should count just as much as his."

There are probably two reasons why Susan had gone so long without putting any serious effort into trying to get these kinds of thoughts into her head. First, she had no idea that it would strengthen her influence. In fact, she assumed that if she let go of the idea that James was wrong, she'd lose her leverage with him. Gottman's studies (2002) on marriage suggest that this is an erroneous assumption of major proportions. When Susan's therapist described the overwhelming evidence suggesting that partners are more likely to be influenced when they feel less criticized, Susan became interested. But her interest did little to help her actually think or act differently because just when she needed to think and act differently, it was the last thing she *felt* like doing. A state became activated in her that was completely incompatible with giving James the benefit of the doubt. To make progress in meeting the soft startup prerequisite, Susan first had to become convinced that it was actually in her own best interest to do so, and then she had to learn how to short-circuit the internal state that kept her from thinking and acting differently. Educating her about the soft startup prerequisite was necessary in order for her to even consider finding a way to move in that direction, but the real work involved helping her learn to shift from the internal state that kept her from approaching James in a different and more effective way. Susan's access to her anger was an asset to her in helping her have the courage to stand up for her own feelings, but she consistently overshot her goal by putting James down, and it backfired for her.

PREREQUISITE 2: ACCEPTING INFLUENCE

People who want to succeed in their relationships must not only be able to deliver complaints softly (and firmly, if necessary), they must also be able to respond well to their partners' complaints. When their partners stop criticizing and ask them to work toward solutions that respect each of their positions, they must be willing to work toward mutually satisfying solutions. The willingness to accept influence is a powerful predictor of marital outcomes. There is evidence that, although wives tend to begin complaints more harshly than husbands, husbands are generally less willing than wives to accept influence (Gottman, 2002). Research shows that the willingness of husbands to accept influence *alone* predicted marital success 80% of the time (Gottman, 1999). On the other hand, researchers were surprised to find that the willingness of wives to accept influence did not distinguish those destined to succeed versus those destined to fail because wives in both categories tended to accept influence quite well (Gottman, 1999). Some husbands did accept influence and some didn't, but those who didn't accept influence ended up divorced or unhappily married.

People who reject influence tend to do it in two ways. The first is defensiveness. People who respond defensively fail to acknowledge anything reasonable about their partners' requests and instead counter nearly every point their partners make. The second common way of rejecting influence is stonewalling. People who stonewall simply refuse to engage in conversation when their partners complain. They sit in silence, or they just walk away. Studies suggest that husbands stonewall much more than wives (Gottman, 1994b; Gottman & Silver, 1999), and that the reason for this may be related to biological differences between men and woman. There is evidence suggesting that negative emotional intensity is more punishing to men than women (Gottman, 2002; Gottman & Silver, 1999). Husbands' bodies kick into diffuse physiological arousal (DPA) at lower levels of negative emotional interchange than their wives' bodies. DPA is generally an uncomfortable physiological experience. When it occurs, the brain's fight or flight response is activated: The heart rate increases by at least 10 beats per minute and individuals experiencing DPA become hypervigilant to signs of danger. A person experiencing DPA interprets situations as more threatening than a person not experiencing DPA. At higher levels of DPA, an individual is less able to respond to complaints by accepting influence. Studies suggest that husbands who eventually divorce have heart rates higher by up to 17 beats per minute than husbands whose relationships succeed (Gottman, 1999). Not only do husbands experience DPA during lower levels of negative emotional interaction than wives, it takes husbands longer to calm down once DPA occurs.

While husbands' threshold for kicking into DPA tends to be lower than that of wives, both husbands and wives experience DPA during arguments, and finding ways to physiologically soothe oneself or one's partner is often necessary in order for either soft startups or accepting influence to occur. Specific methods clients can use to soothe the fight–flight internal states will be discussed at length in Part II of this book. For now, we will assume that an individual has this ability to self-soothe. After soothing him- or herself, how would such an individual go about accepting influence? In PET-C, we teach two powerful methods for accepting influence: "Finding the Understandable Part," and "Giving Equal Regard."

Predictive Habit 3: Finding the Understandable Part

When disagreements arise, most of us tend to think of our own position as reasonable and our partner's position as unreasonable. However, at some point in the argument, those who succeed manage to find something understandable about what their partner is saying or wanting, even if they can't agree overall (Gottman & Silver, 1999). In order to receive understanding, first one must give understanding. Many partners are hesitant to acknowledge anything understandable about their partner's point of view, thinking that if they give an inch, their partners will take a mile. People destined to succeed in their relationships don't worry about this, because they know that they can always stand up for their own point of view later. They know that just because they acknowledge something legitimate about their partner's point of view doesn't mean that their own point of view isn't legitimate, too. They are able to first acknowledge the understandable part of their partner's opinions and then stand up for their own opinions, if needed. In our experience, partners who have difficulty acknowledging the understandable part of their partners' feelings often also have difficulty standing up for their own feelings effectively. In couples therapy, partners must often learn to do both of these things at the same time. An individual will only be able to acknowledge the understandable aspects of a partner's feelings if he or she is confident that he or she can stand up for his/her own.

Predictive Habit 4: Giving Equal Regard

Finding the understandable part is a relatively simple and moderate form of accepting influence, giving equal regard is the most powerful form. The best relationships operate like democracies: one person, one vote. When people go to cast their votes in a democratic society, nobody stands at the polling place deciding if their reasoning is good enough to allow their votes to count. Their opinions count equally, regardless of what anyone thinks of their reasoning. The same is true in successful marriages. Successful partners give equal regard, regardless of whether they agree with each other or not. They may argue tooth and nail for their own points of view, but in the end, they are willing to work toward finding mutually satisfying solutions. Either explicitly or implicitly, people destined for relationship success deliver the following message to their partners: "You don't really have to explain yourself. If that's how you feel, then I'm going to make room for your feelings, too. You're my partner, and your feelings should count as much as mine, even if I don't agree with them." In contrast, people who are destined to fail in their relationships are often only willing to give equal regard if they feel that their partners' points of view are compelling enough to merit concessions. Of course, the problem is that most of us rarely find our partners' points of view as compelling as our own.

In successful marriages, the willingness to give equal regard does not necessarily come at the front end of an argument. In fact, sometimes when researchers looked at the arguing style of partners destined to succeed, they could not distinguish them from partners destined to fail. The differences only became clear later, after each partner had exhausted his or her efforts to convince the other. Both successful and unsuccessful partners often argue vigorously for their own points of view, and often show little regard for their partners' viewpoints during the argument. However, in the end, successful partners are willing to give equal regard. When people are confident that, when the dust settles, their partners are going to be willing to give them equal regard, they can each argue persuasively along the way with less risk that the other person will take offense.

In our work with couples at our clinic, we have found that partners have difficulty "finding the understandable part" or "giving equal regard" unless they are also able to "avoiding judgmental thinking" and "stand up for themselves without putting their partners down." It was clear to me that James was every bit as critical and judgmental of Susan as she was of him. The difference was that he rarely expressed his judgments of Susan directly. Inside, however, he often dismissed her complaints out of hand. Early in their marriage, James had come to the conclusion that Susan was not the sort of person who could be reasoned with, and he began assuming that most of her complaints were overly emotional, knee-jerk reactions that couldn't be taken seriously. Outwardly, James would often end up accepting influence, but inwardly he thought of her as a selfish child. This resulted in James saying things like, "Okay, fine! I'm sorry! Is that what you want me to say?" or "Whatever, Susan. You're going to do what ever you want anyway." This, of course, infuriated Susan.

James progressed in therapy by developing the ability to do the opposite of what he had been doing. That is, rather than assuming that her complaints were without merit, but giving in to her demands anyway, he began searching for and acknowledging the understandable part of her feelings, offering to meet her half way, and, perhaps most importantly, refusing to cave in and allow his feelings to be dismissed by her.

When I first began talking to James about the shift in thinking and ways of interacting with Susan that would be needed if he was going to be more successful in influencing her, he immediately recognized the vastness of the task in front of him. It went against all of his instincts. Of course, his "instincts" were set by the automatic shifting of internal states that happened inside of him whenever Susan became upset. James experienced a powerful activation of the FEAR circuit each time Susan acted in a threatening way, and this fear shut down the natural anger that most people feel and express when they are being attacked. Instead of meeting anger with anger, James battened down the hatches and retreated to a place inside where he felt buffered from Susan's emotional blows. I knew that it would do little good to point out to James how he could stand up for himself while accepting influence as long as he was in the grip of his FEAR circuit. Susan needed to feel strength and investment from James that equaled her own. He would need a great deal of practice in shifting from FEAR to RAGE, then to CARE. Paradoxically, as James became more able to meet Susan's anger with his own, and more confident that he would not allow himself to be dominated, he became more tolerant of her anger, and more able to recognize the logic behind many of Susan's feelings that he had previously dismissed. This is often the case when partners begin to do a better job of standing up for themselves. When people allow themselves to be violated by angry attacks, they are besieged by feelings of contempt for their partners. Only when they no longer fear annihilation can they afford to really listen to their partners and acknowledge the understandable aspects of their partner's feelings. James is a good example of a partner who simply could not accept influence until he learned to shift internal states.

PREREQUISITE 3: EFFECTIVE REPAIR

As we noted previously, at particular points in arguments they witnessed, marriage researchers often had difficulty distinguishing partners destined to succeed from those destined to fail. This finding needs further explanation. If there is one thing that's clear from research on marriages, it is that arguments don't have to be pretty in order to be productive. In fact, they can be downright ugly, so long as partners stay relatively free of contempt (Gottman, 1999, 2002). Partners destined to succeed are often defensive, bull-headed, and unresponsive to their partners. The difference is that, after a failed argument, partners who succeed in their relationships are effective at repairing the damage, whereas partners destined to fail rarely repair. This finding is of vast importance, because it means that partners who want to succeed don't necessarily need to do better in the first round of arguments. It is more important to be good at repairing than to avoid getting off track in the first place.

How do successful partners go about repairing arguments that have failed? Researchers set out to find the answer to this question by keeping track of everything partners did that seemed to have the effect of steering conversations into the repair direction. Their findings were frustrating, because it seemed that the same words or gestures that moved some partners toward repair failed to move others. For example, sometimes an apology works and sometimes it doesn't. In the end, they found that the effectiveness of any repair attempt could not be predicted by the quality of the repair move itself (Gottman, 1999). There is only one thing that was found to reliably predict the success of a repair attempt: The degree of positivity present when the partners weren't fighting. The repair attempts of those who communicated higher levels of love and admiration to their partners when they were not fighting were more successful than the attempts of those who communicated less love and admiration. Studies suggest that there is something like an emotional bank account in relationships that dramatically influences the likelihood that repair attempts will be successful. A robust emotional bank account creates positive sentiment override PSO (Weiss, 1980). Conversely, a depleted emotional bank account creates negative sentiment override (NSO). When negative sentiment override prevails, people in relationships fail to recognize the repair attempts of their partners (Gottman, 2002). Or, if they do recognize them, they are too stressed by the lack of positivity in their relationship to be influenced by them. On the other hand, positive sentiment override creates goodwill, and makes it more likely that partners will notice and accept repair gestures from each other (Gottman, 1999).

The relationships of couples entering therapy are often characterized by negative sentiment override. Not only are they unable to resolve conflicts, but they are also unable to interact positively when they are not arguing. Ideally, the best way to proceed in such relationships is to increase positive interaction during nonconflict times. Of course, this is easier said than done. When fresh hurts and misunderstandings linger or when resentment festers from unresolved hurts from the past, the last thing partners feel like doing is expressing caring toward their partners between fights.

Our approach in situations like these is two-pronged: First, we help partners find small ways to express as much positivity toward their partners as they can tolerate, hoping that any increase in their emotional bank account will translate into a more positive sentiment override, which in turn will enable partners to accept repair moves from each other. Predictive habits 7 to 10, discussed below, provide specific ways for partners to increase positivity. Second, we have found a specific repair move that is often effective, even when a relationship is characterized by negative sentiment override: offering assurances.

Predictive Habit 5: Offering Assurances

Whenever an argument seems to be stuck or unproductive, one of the most effective things a person can do is to stop and ask him- or herself, "Does my partner think I'm saying that she is *wrong*?" or "Does my partner think I'm saying 'It's my way or the highway'?" When arguments are unproductive, the answer to these questions is almost always "yes." We have found that the most powerful thing a partner can do at this point is to simply offer an assurance, by saying something like, "Look, I was pretty worked up back then, and I'm sure you felt criticized by me, but I don't really think there's anything wrong with what you did. It's just different from what I wanted." Another example of an assurance might be, "I know we have a difference of opinion about how to prioritize things here, and I don't want you to get the idea that I'm saying that things have to be entirely my way. I'm willing to work with you on this." Of course, partners can't offer assurances if they are thinking judgmental thoughts about their partners. If a partner is saying one thing but thinking another, the person's partner won't believe him or her. The offering of an assurance is completely dependent upon a partner's ability to shift from a judgmental to nonjudgmental attitude. However, those who are able to shift to a nonjudgmental attitude and then offer assurances will be successful in repairing the argument a high percentage of the time.

The finding that repair is just as effective as the ability to avoid nonproductive arguing is good news, given the way our brains are wired. Few of us have the ability to escape the pull of the RAGE or FEAR circuits when we feel freshly offended or threatened. Even as they were ending therapy feeling much better about their relationship, Susan and James continued to have arguments in which Susan slipped back into attack mode, and James stonewalled. The difference was that, over time, each partner had developed the ability to shift from the attack/defend states, then try the conversation again.

PREREQUISITE 4:
RESPECTING YOUR PARTNER'S DREAMS;
HOLDING ONTO YOUR OWN

Sometimes, the reasons why partners become upset with each other run deeper than the present circumstances. When partners persist in doing or saying things that upset each other over and over again, there is often something more at stake than meets the eye. Many times, each partner often feels that if they did what their partner wants, they would lose something very important to them. It is not so much present circumstance that is upsetting as it is what the present situation symbolizes (Gottman, 1999).

Each partner enters the relationship with implicit dreams or expectations about how they want things to be. When a person's partner is wanting something that threatens a basic need or expectation that this person has, then refusal to cooperate may result. But sometimes it is not even what the partner wants that bothers this person, it is the fear of where things might be headed if the partner's wishes prevail. Successful partners are able to look beneath the present circumstances and identify the hopes, dreams, fears, and expectations that are at stake for them and their partners.

Predictive Habit 6: Understanding and Explaining
What Is at Stake

Partners who are destined to succeed in their relationships learn to assume that, whenever they have the same arguments over and over again, there is something important and legitimate at stake for each of them that is going unrecognized (Gottman, 1999). In our work with couples, we help partners develop the habit of looking for the important dreams and fears that lie beneath the stalemates over specific issues.

When Jack and Loretta entered therapy the first time (see Chapter 2), they got along well during the week, but ended up fighting almost every weekend. Jack expected that Saturdays would be spent with the two of them doing household chores. He couldn't understand why Loretta always seemed to object to working on the basic tasks that were necessary to maintain the lifestyle they had chosen. He often criticized Loretta for being lazy, and unable to delay gratification. The partners usually ended up in a stalled argument about whether these tasks really need to be done or not. To Jack, Loretta's arguments seem absurd and irrational. He concluded that she just wanted him to do all the work. On the other hand, Loretta believed that Jack was a control freak who thought that he should set the agenda for the entire weekend.

Neither partner was able to realize that the other's behavior was rooted in a legitimate, but different, dream about how relationships should be. Jack was a "work first, play later" kind of person. Everything he had accomplished in his life emerged from this philosophy. He entered the marriage with a dream that two people were better than one, because they could accomplish the work faster, and this would then allow more time to enjoy leisure later. Loretta was an "enjoy life as you go" type person. She believed that there would always be more work to do, and unless time was deliberately set aside for relaxation and fun, it would never happen. She grew up with parents who were each highly successful, but had little affection for each other. When Jack insisted on spending weekends doing chores, Loretta felt her dream of a fun-filled life together slip away. On the other hand, Jack had a hard time relaxing until the work was done. On those occasions where he gave in to Loretta and tried to spend Saturdays with her, he was agitated. Loretta took this as evidence that he didn't really enjoy spending time with her. Neither of them was able to understand that, beneath the other's behavior was a legitimate, but different, dream of how relationships should be. When their dreams came into direct conflict, they argued about the wrong things. Loretta argued that the lawn didn't really need to be mowed, even though Jack would look out the window and point to evidence to the contrary. The couple was gridlocked until each came to understand what was at stake for the other beneath the seemingly "lazy" or "controlling" behavior. With my help, Jack was able to explain to Loretta the anxious feeling he got when important tasks were postponed. Jack grew up in a single-parent home in which his mom was unable to accomplish all of the tasks needed to effectively run their household. Growing up, Jack felt embarrassed when he compared his family to most of the neighbors, and he learned that he could feel better if he stepped in and helped his mom organize the family. Now, in his own family, Jack carried an underlying fear that chaos would emerge, and he felt compelled to stay on top of household tasks.

Once Jack was more in touch with why he felt so strongly about postponing work that needed to be done, he stopped criticizing Loretta and talking as if it were obvious that tasks needed to be done before relaxing. He developed the ability to remind her that it just made him really anxious when important tasks were postponed. In short, he stopped requiring that she buy into his dream of how things should be and started asking her to help him feel less anxious. In turn, Loretta was able to explain to Jack that she felt anxious and insecure when, after a whole week of going their separate ways, Jack didn't seem to want to connect with her on the weekends. She was able to acknowledge that there really wasn't anything wrong with Jack's agenda. Rather, she was just worried that they would work and work and never really connect. Once each partner recognized the legitimate dream that was at stake for the other, they stopped arguing about whether or not Jack's agendas were really necessary or not, and they got better at offering mutual assurances that they would try to honor each other's dreams and fears. For example, each time Jack suggested Saturday tasks, he assured Loretta that if they weren't done by noon, he would try to let them go until the next day. In turn, when Loretta proposed a leisurely morning together, she assured Jack that she would be willing to devote the entire afternoon to "getting things done."

PREREQUISITE 5: FIVE POSITIVES FOR EVERY NEGATIVE

If there is one thing that is clear from the decades of research identifying predictors of marital success, it is that the key to lasting relationship success has more to do with what happens when partners' aren't fighting than it does with what happens when they are fighting (Gottman, 1999). Research suggests that the absence of destructive fighting is no guarantee that relationships will succeed. In fact, studies suggest that only 40% of couples who divorce cite intense fighting as a major cause, whereas 60% report a gradual drifting apart as the main culprit (Gottman, 2002). People who stay happily married over the long haul have became great friends, and regularly express fondness and admiration for each other. A consistent finding across studies is that partners destined to succeed engage in at least five positive interactions for every negative interaction that happens (Gottman, 2002). Successful relationships are not free of negative interactions, they simply have more positive ones, and the abundance of positive ones has the effect of overriding the negatives. A close look at partners who succeed reveals that these positive interactions take several forms. Predictive habits 7 to 10 reflect some of the major ways that people who succeed in their relationships connect with their partners.

Predictive Habit 7: Curiosity about Each Other's Worlds

Researchers have known for some time that 67% of couples experience a drop in marital satisfaction after the birth of the first child, but 33% do not (Gotterman, 1999). What separates these two groups? One of the strongest predictors is the extent to which partners keep in touch with each other's worlds as they go through this transition (Gottman, 1999). The worlds of new mothers change dramatically when a baby arrives. Husbands who enter into the new world of their wives end up in happier, more stable marriages. On the other hand, new mothers who avoid becoming so absorbed with the new baby that they lose interest in their husbands' worlds end up in happier marriages as well.

Curiosity about one's partner's world isn't necessary only during the transition to parenthood. People who succeed in their relationships maintain curiosity about their partners throughout the course of their relationship. Studies suggest that partners who are destined to succeed are better able to answer questions like:

- What is my partner looking forward to the most in the next week?
- What has my partner done that she is most proud of lately?
- What has been most disappointing to my partner lately?
- What is at the top of my partner's wish list for home improvement?
- What compliment has my partner received from a person other than myself in the past few days?
- If my partner could follow her heart right now and do one thing she otherwise wouldn't, what would it be?
- Who does my partner consider a major rival or enemy?
- What is most frustrating about my partner's job lately?
- When is a time when something happened that made my partner doubt herself?
- What is the most challenging part of my partner's daily routine?
- If my partner could make her parents understand one thing before they died, what would it be?

People who succeed in their relationships make it their business to know these kinds of things about their partners. Researchers say that people who succeed devote more "cognitive room" to their partners than those who fail (Gottman, 1999). As they go through their separate days, they spend more time thinking about what their partner might be doing, and they remember to ask about what a partner's day has been like when the couple is reunited.

Predictive Habit 8: Noticing and Acknowledging the Positive

People destined to succeed in their relationships are more aware of the positive things that happen in their relationships, and they acknowledge them more often (Gottman, 1999, Gottman & Silver, 1999). For example, they acknowledge and express appreciation for the small things that their partners do each day, which are often taken for granted. Taking care of the children might be just part of the agreed upon division of duties in a marriage, but when a wife has had a particularly challenging day with the kids, a husband destined to succeed will let her know that he appreciates the effort she put into the day. Similarly, even though a husband has agreed that he will accept responsibility for reading to the children each night before bed, wives destined to succeed let them know that they appreciate their husbands for being willing to do this.

When marriages become distressed, studies show that partners underestimate the positive things that happen between them by about 50% compared to objective observers who rate the positive things that happen (Robinson & Price, 1980). Many positive things happen each day that escape the attention of those who are destined to fail in their relationships. On the other hand, people who succeed take advantage of opportunities to express appreciation. For example, a husband who is destined to succeed will notice his wife laughing on the phone, and later remember to tell her that he thinks she is a good buddy to her friends.

People destined to succeed are also more likely to remember positive memories that have happened in the recent or distant past, and bring them up to enjoy again. People headed for relationship failure do not do this nearly as much. In fact, one poor prognostic indicator is when partners actually re-write history, omitting the good memories (Gottman, 1999). Even though at one time they had good memories of specific occasions, when the relationship reaches a certain point of distress, they no longer want to acknowledge anything positive. They change the memory in their minds over time, or they pick out a particular nonpositive detail in an otherwise positive memory and dwell on it, canceling out the good that happened.

In Part II, we'll look at exercises intended to help partners become more curious about each other's worlds, and increase attention to the positive aspects of their relationship, however, increasing positivity in a relationship isn't as simple as learning to say or do the right things.

Relationships don't work because partners say the right things to each other, or act nice toward each other. They work when each partner senses that the other feels tenderness, fondness, longing for contact, sexual attraction, or enjoys the other's presence. Relationship success depends upon the extent to which each partner experiences the internal activation of CARE, PANIC, LUST, and PLAY in their relationship (see Chapter 2). Unless these brain circuits are firing, exercises designed to nudge partners to be more curious about each other, or more complimentary toward each other will fail to have their intended effect. We do not simply ask partners to be nicer or more interested in each other, we attempt to connect them with internal states from which tenderness or interest naturally emerge.

Having said this, let me now add that we consider exercises that suggest ways that partners can be more curious, positive, and attentive to each other to be an invaluable part of our work. Knowledge of the specific kinds of positive things that people do in successful relationships often serves as a wake up call for partners. It often helps them realize that their relationships don't have enough positive connection to predict success over the long haul. This realization can help partners become motivated to do the work of learning to activate their intimacy-producing internal states. Once they have increased their access to these internal states, knowledge of the predictive habits helps them guide their newfound motivation in directions that will most likely make a difference.

Predictive Habit 9: Pursuing Shared Meaning

Having a successful intimate relationship involves more than just "getting along." Roommates can get along just fine, but intimate partners who are emotionally connected have a sense that they are on a journey together (Gottman, 1999). They have a shared sense of purpose, a common mission. There is a sense of loyalty and agreement to uphold their mutually agreed upon goals and values. People destined to succeed talk freely about their hopes and dreams, and encourage their partners to do the same. In small, everyday ways, they communicate to their partners, "I want to be on your team, because I think you're pretty darned cool, and I think that together, we can have a better life than I could by myself."

People who are destined to succeed look for ways to work with their partners to build a unique culture, complete with its own rituals. They do not sacrifice their own individual identities for the sake of the group, but rather try to find a way to mesh what is important to them with what is important to their partners. If their own dreams come into conflict with those of their partners, they work hard to find solutions that incorporate both partner's dreams. They realize that if they squash their partners' dreams in pursuit of their own, they will lose perhaps the most important dimension of their relationship: a sense of mutual loyalty and adventure.

Because different things are meaningful to different people, the development of shared meaning can be a difficult process. Only those who meet each of the prerequisites discussed thus far will succeed. It took all of the abilities that Jack and Loretta (Chapter 2) had developed through months of therapy to succeed in creating a jointly meaningful sex life together. But after years of struggle, misunderstandings, critical judgments, and hurt feelings, Jack and Loretta did find a way to merge their vastly different hopes and dreams. Partners like Jack and Loretta, who succeed in creating shared meaning in many areas of their lives, travel through life with the feeling that they have a trustworthy and loyal companion constantly by their side. They have the knowledge that they are never without a safety net.

Predictive Habit 10: Making and Responding to Bids
for Connection

Throughout daily life, in both small and large ways, people who are destined to succeed in their relationships both make and respond to bids for connection (Gottman, 1999; Gottman & DeClaire, 2001). When their partners make observations or share information with them, they engage, showing their interest in what their partners are saying. Bids for connection are embedded in seemingly insignificant communication. For example, a wife remarks to her husband that she's going shopping for some summer clothes. This is a small bid for the husband's attention. The husband, busy reading the paper, can respond in one of two ways. He can either engage, for example, by putting down the paper momentarily and asking her what kind of clothes she's looking for, or not engage, keeping his nose in the newspaper. In the beginning of relationships, partners make dozens of bids and responses each day. Sooner or later, however, one or the other partner may begin to experience the other as unresponsive to their "bids." If this person becomes critical of his or her partner, the partner may become even more unresponsive over time. People destined to succeed use all of the abilities described in this chapter to repair failed bids, and their relationships remain emotionally connected. People destined to fail may simply stop making bids, and their relationships head down the cascade toward isolation and alienation.

People who are really good at making and responding to bids initiate small connecting moves many times throughout each day. A skilled "connector" might think of something he can do to make his partner's load a little lighter, take time to initiate a plan for the two of them to do something fun together. She might spend time thinking or learning about something important to the partner, notice something in his day that she knows he would be interested in—then remember to tell him about it later. He might remember to ask her about something specific he knows will be happening in her day, ask her to do something with him (a bike ride, walk, etc.), take responsibility for making (ordering) food for his partner, or leave a voice-mail message or an e-mail to let his partner know he is thinking about her. Connection making is an art, and those who are destined to succeed in their relationships have mastered it.

There are specific moments when it is especially important to make and respond to bids for connection. These are moments when one or the other partner is feeling upset or vulnerable because of stressful or challenging circumstances in their lives. In these circumstances, skilled partners are good at asking for and giving support. They understand that many times, what stressed people need is not help in solving their problems so much as understanding, sympathy, or support. Attempts to cheer one's partner up often backfire, because the person who is feeling bad interprets the "cheering" attempts of his or her partner to be evidence that the "cheering" partner is uncomfortable with the "feeling bad" person's feelings and wants the "feeling bad" person to "get over it." Well-intended comments like,

- Don't let it get you down!
- I'm sure everything is going to work out.
- You just can't let things get to you like that.
- Things aren't as bad as they seem.
- It could be a lot worse.
- Let's look at the bright side.

are often heard as

- I can't handle your being so upset!
- I don't really want to know how you are feeling.

- You should be able to handle things without getting so upset.
- You're too sensitive.
- You're overreacting.
- You shouldn't feel that way!
- Enough said, now let's move on!

It is not that advice or "focusing on the positive" comments are never helpful, it is a matter of timing. People who are skilled in responding to bids help their partners feel understood first, then help their partners explore different avenues for dealing with the problem situation, but only if their partners request help. Often, advice giving or problem solving isn't even necessary, because when people feel understood and supported, they often feel better, and know what to do on their own. Feeling understood is often the most critical factor in feeling better.

How do successful people help their partners feel understood and supported? Several categories of responses are particularly helpful:

Asking for More Details

- What about the situation was the most upsetting to you?
- What was that like for you? What were you thinking? How did you feel?
- What did you do?
- What did you feel like doing?
- Why do you think that happened?

Giving Sympathy

- I'm sorry you had a hard day.
- I think you've had a harder day than me. How about if you just try to relax for a while and I'll take care of the kids.
- I don't like it when people treat you that way.

Communicating Loyalty

- I'm on your side.
- We're in this together.
- I'll help you if you want me to.

Giving Affection

- Why don't you come over here and let me rub your shoulders for a few minutes?
- Here, you put your feet up while I get you something to drink.
- Let me hold you for a minute.

The motivation to make bids for connection arise naturally from the brain's PANIC circuit, and the ability to respond with tenderness or empathy to a bid for connection emerges from the CARE state. Unless these brain circuits are active, saying or doing supportive things will have minimal effect. A person cannot listen sympathetically unless they feel sympathetic. As is true for each of the other predictive habits, partners will only be able to do them if they are able to activate compatible internal states.

CONCLUSION

The five prerequisites for relationship success and the 10 habits that support them described in this chapter them provide concrete direction for couples seeking to improve their relationships. They provide the pragmatic focus of Pragmatic/Experiential Therapy for Couples. Although each relationship is unique, we believe that the studies on predictors of marital outcomes provide compelling evidence that there are some abilities that all of us who want to succeed in our intimate relationships must have. The way that each of us applies these abilities will be unique to our own personalities. However, we believe that each person doesn't have to "reinvent the wheel" when seeking for ways to improve his or her relationship. Existing evidence strongly suggests that some ways of navigating relationships work better than others. While relationships are infinitely complex, the habits necessary to succeed in them are not. They are precise, well-defined, and learnable. Our therapeutic goals always involve an increase in the specific habits that predict relationship success, and a decrease in habits that predict relationship failure.

The problem for many of us is that, for a variety of reasons, our brains are wired up in ways that prevent us from meeting the prerequisites for relationship success. Through less-than-optimal early attachment experiences, emotional conditioning across the course of our lives, or due to the current reciprocal interactive patterns partners get themselves into, some of the brain circuits required to fuel these prerequisites have become dormant, and other brain circuits fire when they need to be quiet. The problem is complicated by the fact that the misfiring inside our brains often escapes our notice. We keep trying to think and act differently in relationships, not realizing that the brain circuitry needed to generate new patterns of thinking and action is malfunctioning. In part two of this book, we'll take a look at an approach for helping partners recondition their brains for more flexibility, enabling them to more fully meet the prerequisites for relationship success described in this chapter.

PART II
Pragmatic/Experiential Therapy for Couples

CHAPTER 4

An Overview of Pragmatic/Experiential Therapy for Couples

I N PET-C, WE HELP partners become aware of how their thoughts and actions are governed by internal neural states that they are often unaware of. We help each partner learn how to (1) shift out of internal states which block attitudes and actions predictive of relationship success, and (2) increase contact with internal states that support attitudes and actions needed for relationship success.

THE SIX BASIC ASSUMPTIONS OF PET-C

1. *Focus on increasing attitudes and behaviors predictive of success, and decreasing behaviors predictive of failure.* Specifically, a goal of PET-C is to increase each of the 10 habits that enable partners to meet the prerequisites for relationship success, (see Chapter 3).

2. *Even when they know what to do to succeed, intimate partners are often unable to do these things. Many times, the problem isn't knowledge, it's motivation.* PET-C assumes that there are always two questions facing individuals who want their relationships to improve: (a) What needs to happen? and (b) Why isn't it happening? PET-C looks to the studies identifying predictors of marital stability and satisfaction (Chapter 3) for answers to the first question, and to the neuroscience studies (Chapters 1 and 2) for answers to the second question.

3. *Distressed intimate partners are frequently unable to do what is needed because they are caught in automatic, conditioned internal states that perpetuate unhelpful thinking and action, and block needed thinking and actions.* When intimate relationships become distressed, there are nearly always problems with the conditioned activation or suppression of each partner's neural operating systems (see Chapters 1 and 2).

Research on internal response circuits suggests that problems come in three varieties: (a) When clients get caught in the pull of an internal response circuit, and are unable to do what is needed (e.g., when the "anger program" kicks in, and the clients just can't listen to their partners when it would ultimately be of benefit to do so); (b) when clients avoid doing or saying needed things because to do so would likely trigger an uncomfortable internal response circuit in them (e.g., when clients are unable to admit that they are wrong, because doing so triggers an anxious or vulnerable self-state); and (c) When a needed response state simply doesn't show up (e.g., when clients need to respond to partners with tenderness or caring, but find themselves devoid of genuine feeling).

4. *The internal states of intimate partners are often mutually reinforcing. A state in one partner automatically activates a predictable state in the other, which triggers or perpetuates a predictable state in the first partner.* The couple's relationship functions as a system: a movement in any part of the system triggers a predictable response from the other part. When partners are distressed, the systemic nature of their relationship perpetuates a cycle that is difficult for either partner to break out of.

5. *If one partner can shift his or her conditioned internal state, the other partner will also be better able to shift.* The systemic interrelatedness of intimate partners is a blessing as well as a curse. A change in one part of the system will trigger changes in other parts of the system.

6. *To get more understanding or cooperation from a partner, the most effective thing a distressed partner can do is to more fully develop the ability to influence his or her own internal states during key intimate situations.* This assumption arises from studies that have identified predictors of marital satisfaction and stability. There is a very high probability that an individual who meets the prerequisites for relationship success will end up with a partner who has respect, affection, and admiration for him or her, and the ability to meet the prerequisites is directly related to individuals' ability to influence his or her own internal states during key situations. Individuals who meet the prerequisites are able to activate and regulate their self-protective states (RAGE, FEAR) when needed, and also connect with internal states that naturally lead to intimacy (CARE, PANIC, PLAY, LUST; see Chapters 1 and 2).

THE DUAL FOCUS OF PET-C

In PET-C, a dual focus is maintained throughout therapy. First, partners become intimately familiar with the attitudes and actions that are needed in order for them to succeed in their relationships. This is the pragmatic aspect of our therapy. We find that often, partners really do not know how to respond effectively when their partners do things that are upsetting to them. Our goal early in therapy is to remedy this gap in knowledge. Through a variety of specific exercises and procedures, each partner learns the ability to, at least in theory, know how best to respond in difficult situations that arise with the other person. This knowledge is crucial, but it is not enough. Knowing the attitudes and actions that are needed, and acquiring them are two entirely different matters. The experiential part of our work involves helping partners to become more aware of the brain states that prevent them from engaging in needed thinking and action, and helping them develop the ability to shift into brain states that make needed thoughts and actions possible.

THREE PHASES OF PET-C

Therapy occurs in three overlapping phases. The ordering of the phases is not set in stone, and couples progress through them at different rates.

Phase I: The Therapist Helps Partners Shift from Defensive to Receptive States, Then Helps Them to Make Needed Changes in Their Thoughts and Actions

In Phase I of PET-C, therapists create internal shifts in the service of two goals. First, the therapist helps each partner shift from defensive or aggressive internal states in order to make it possible for both to interact differently and break out of specific gridlocks that hinder their relationship. Through this process (illustrated in the case examples in Chapter 6), couples often experience dramatic positive momentum in therapy. However, the positive momentum is almost entirely dependent on the therapist's active role in making the internal shifts take place in each partner. Unless partners develop the motivation and ability to shift internal states on their own, they will relapse when the therapist isn't there to help them. In the later part of Phase I, the therapist uses his or her ability to create internal shifts to help clients become motivated to develop the ability to make internal shifts, and become better able to meet the prerequisites for relationship success, on their own.

Phase II: Partners Do the Work Previously Done By the Therapist

In Phase II, each partner enters a personalized training program in the skills of emotional intelligence, using the relationship as a workshop for learning these skills. The therapist helps each partner to (a) develop the ability to recognize situations that typically trigger states that bring about nonproductive thinking or actions; (b) develop a plan for shifting out of such states; and (c) develop and implement a strategy for repeatedly practicing this plan.

Phase III: Building the Emotional Bond at
Nonconflict Times

In the third phase, the focus shifts from deintensifying internal states that block respectful interaction during disagreements to the activation of internal states that produce playfulness, spontaneity, sexual interest, the desire for emotional closeness, and genuine interest in one's partner. Some couples are ready for Phase III at the outset of therapy. However, most clients are not ready for the level of vulnerability required in Phase III until they are convinced that their partners have laid down their weapons, and it is safe to bring more vulnerable feelings into their relationships.

CRITICAL TASKS IN PET-C

Help Partners Shift from Defensive to
Receptive Internal States

Most partners enter couples therapy feeling misunderstood, criticized by their partners, and worried that the therapist is going to blame them for the relationship problems. Because of this, they are often at least somewhat defensive, and sensitive to any cues that might indicate therapist disapproval. The success of PET-C hinges on the ability of the therapist to help each partner shift from defensive to receptive internal states. The methods we use to accomplish such shifts (detailed in Chapter 6) center around the therapist's ability to connect with internal states that convey empathy, tenderness, and respect for the client. Each partner experiences understanding and caring from the therapist, even while the therapist is speaking directly to each of them about the ways in which they fall short of meeting the prerequisites for relationship success. Although clients may react defensively at first, gradually they become more receptive because the therapist avoids becoming argumentative, combative, or controlling. Clients receive critical feedback, but they don't *feel* criticized, lectured, or talked down to. Most clients can handle direct talk about their shortcomings if they feel that the therapist genuinely likes them, recognizes their strengths, and operates from internal states that exude patience and loving concern. When clients feel the therapist is in their corner, they trust him or her, even though they might find the words the therapist offers difficult to hear.

It is often not easy for the therapist to maintain a nurturing internal state, especially when clients become angry or indignant. Chapter 13 details the training PET-C therapists receive which helps them increase their own abilities to respond well to challenging clients. The task of helping partners shift from defensive to receptive states occurs throughout therapy, but is especially important in Phase I.

Help the Partners Develop the Belief that They Can
Powerfully Influence the Way Each Treats the Other

Most clients entering couples therapy tend to focus on how they think their partners should be changing rather than on what they need to change about their own patterns of thinking and acting. Partners will not focus on themselves unless they become convinced that changing themselves is the surest way to change their partners. The PET-C therapist helps each partner see that, indeed, this is the case. Clients are encouraged to consider that they haven't been able to get what they want from their partners because they haven't developed the required abilities. If they want more cooperation or respect, they must think and act like people who know how to elicit cooperation and respect. The therapist helps clients believe that they can powerfully influence the way they are treated by developing the abilities that virtually guarantee relationship success. Referring to the research described in Chapter 3, and drawing upon his or her knowledge of each partner's relationship habits, the therapist helps partners to understand exactly how they routinely sabotage their own efforts to get respect or cooperation from their partners. The therapist communicates confidence that she or he knows exactly how each client can get more cooperation or understanding, and backs up this claim with vivid descriptions of the kind of attitudes and actions that are needed. Clients will be able to receive this information only to the extent that the therapist is able to maintain a noncombative, nurturing internal state, avoid arguing with clients, and instead encourage clients to accept only what truly makes sense to them. Methods useful in helping clients believe in their own interpersonal impact potential will be described in Chapters 7 and 8.

Know Which Predictive Behaviors and Attitudes
are Needed at Key Moments

Part of the success of PET-C lies in the therapist's ability to describe and illustrate for partners exactly the attitudes and actions that will increase the odds that they will get more respect and cooperation from their partners. Skilled PET-C therapists are intimately familiar with the prerequisites for relationship success and the 10 PET-C habits that support them (see Chapter 3). In our training programs, we show trainees dozens of videotapes of couples arguing, stopping the tapes at random points, and asking two trainees to step into the roles of the partners they have been watching. We ask one trainee to continue the style of nonproductive arguing of one partner, while the other partner attempts to finish the argument in a way that would be predictive of success. We do this over and over again until trainees feel confident that, at any point in an argument, they know precisely which predictive habits are needed, and are able to model these habits down to the smallest detail. In our experience, clients are tremendously heartened when they realize that their therapist has spent hundreds of hours learning how successful people navigate their relationships, and can show them precisely what is needed at any moment. In Chapters 9 and 10, we'll look at how the PET-C therapist gives each client personalized tutoring in the habits of relationship success.

Help Each Partner Develop the Ability to Shift Internal States

In the first phase of PET-C, the therapist influences internal state shifts in each partner. Once partners have shifted to the needed internal states, the therapist then helps them interact in ways that meet the prerequisites that predict relationship success. By the end of Phase I, partners are ready and motivated to begin a training program designed to increase their abilities to shift internal states as needed. How can a person who has a life-long pattern of reacting ineffectively in the face of a complaint, unlearn this pattern? Effective PET-C therapists are skilled in the methods of internal shifting and reconditioning internal activations. These methods are described in detail in Chapter 11.

Know Which Session Format is Needed at Any Moment

While the overall goals of PET-C are consistent for every couple entering therapy, the immediate goals pursued in specific sessions and phases of therapy vary. Some session formats facilitate some goals better than others. Sometimes individual sessions are best, other times conjoint sessions are necessary. Many times, conjoint sessions need to be broken up by "repair breaks" during which the therapist meets with each partner separately, providing help to enable a shift in internal states. Effective PET-C therapists are skilled in knowing which session format is needed at particular points in therapy.

Help Partners Connect with Internal States that Naturally Produce Intimacy

Early in therapy, the PET-C therapist is busy helping partners develop the ability to short-circuit internal states that fuel nonproductive escalations between partners. However, successful partners go beyond merely treating each other more respectfully. They become more skilled in activating internal states that naturally produce intimacy. To establish a robust emotional bond, each partner learns how to connect with internal states that promote spontaneous, play interaction, sexual desire, tenderness, and emotional need (see Chapter 2 for descriptions of Panksepp's concepts PLAY, LUST, CARE, and PANIC). Increasing access to the intimacy states requires different internal moves than decreasing the fight (RAGE) and flight (FEAR) states. Skilled PET-C therapists help partners both short-circuit RAGE and FEAR-based interactions, and connect with states that naturally move partners closer to each other (see Chapter 12).

*As the Therapist, Know How to Shift Your Own Internal
States as Needed When Working with Clients*

During therapy sessions, specific cues and interactions will sometimes automatically trigger the therapist's own internal states in ways that are not always productive. Effective PET-C therapists develop a fine-tuned ability to move consciously toward internal states from which they naturally communicate tenderness and empathy. At times, they also allow themselves to be honest about the level of frustration and anger they feel toward clients. However, they are also able to shift out of these states rapidly when the situation calls for it. PET-C therapists undergo extensive training in the art of internal awareness and influence (see Chapter 13).

THE PRAGMATIC/EXPERIENTIAL METHOD

Throughout the second and third phases of PET-C, our approach to helping couples is guided by the following operating procedure: Start off in pragmatic terms, and then move on to the experiential as needed. Drawing from research identifying the habits necessary for relationship success, we take a pragmatic focus by directly modeling, illustrating, or describing how partners can get more cooperation and respect from each other. We give specific, concrete suggestions about how each partner can best respond to the other during conflict situations. Of course, partners will be able to follow these suggestions only to the extent that they are able to get into internal states that support these predictive habits. When partners are not able to do this, we shift to giving direct attention to short-circuiting internal states that prevent needed thinking and actions, or activating internal states necessary for needed thinking and actions. This is the experiential aspect of PET-C.

With most clients, there are some situations that require only that they become clearer on how to react effectively. In these situations, once they know what to do and believe it will helpful, they are able to do it. However, the same clients may become overwhelmed in other situations, and unable to react effectively, even though it may be perfectly clear that their reactions are self-defeating. At this point, the experiential aspect of PET-C comes into play, and the therapist begins working with the client on gaining greater awareness of, and ability to influence internal states. We have found it helpful to consider that clients have a range of situations within which they can operate with emotional flexibility if they really try. If a situation falls within the person's "range of emotional difficulty," clients can calm down, become less defensive, or shift to a more empathic state, just by concentrating or relaxing. Most partners entering therapy are not operating at the top of their range of emotional flexibility. As they learn more about how effective reactions look and sound, clients will naturally move toward the top of their ranges, using some of the emotional flexibility they have been neglecting.

Most clients have a limit to their range of emotional flexibility, however. If a situation is stressful enough, it may be beyond their ability to handle it effectively with the emotional regulation skills they currently possess. Many times, clients seem truly at the mercy of the automatic patterning of internal states. In such situations, clients cannot shift, even if their lives depend upon it, and we must help them gain greater awareness of and ability to influence their internal states. Most partners entering therapy can shift in some situations and not others. Therefore, at some point in therapy, both the pragmatic and experiential aspects of PET-C are needed.

In the pragmatic/experiential method, we begin by assuming that partners can make needed internal shifts as they become clearer about the changes in thinking, attitude, and behavior that are needed. We don't want to begin training in the art of internal shifting if they already have the ability to do it. We direct attention to internal states only when needed, but always if needed.

AN INTEGRATIVE APPROACH

PET-C can best be described as an integrative treatment model. We find many of the dichotomies that characterize contrasting theoretical approaches unnecessary, favoring certain aspects of experience and excluding others. Many traditional dichotomies are bridged in PET-C.

Strength vs. Pathology Focus

Clinical approaches are often distinguished by the extent to which they focus on building strengths versus remedying dysfunction. Proponents of strength-based approaches argue that focusing on eliminating negative habits can create a therapeutic atmosphere in which clients come to see themselves as fundamentally flawed rather than whole. Rather than focusing on what's wrong, these approaches favor building on what's going right. Critics of strength-based approaches counter, arguing that an exclusive focus on strengths can amount to a denial of reality—a kind of "putting one's head in the sand." Sometimes, people benefit from being confronted with the fact that they are behaving in self-defeating ways. An exclusive strength focus can amount to inadvertently colluding with clients in their perceptions that there is nothing problematic about their dysfunctional habits.

We find the either–or aspect of the strength–pathology dichotomy to be unnecessary. Acknowledgment of one's shortcomings is often the first step toward constructive change. Given a supportive and nonjudgmental therapeutic atmosphere, we have found that clients can both tolerate an acknowledgment of their dysfunctional habits and experience a renewed sense of empowerment. However, ignoring the strengths clients bring can result in a lack of full empowerment. PET-C capitalizes on the power of acknowledging weaknesses as well as the benefits of enhancing the strengths that clients bring to therapy.

Objectivism vs. Relativism

Closely related to the strength versus pathology dichotomy is the objectivism versus relativism dichotomy. Objectivists believe that there are real dynamics that exist within clients and in their relationships, and that the job of the therapist is to identify them and help clients change them. Objectivists believe that real-world dynamics can be objectively observed and measured. Relativists, on the other hand, believe that there are no independently existing dynamics in clients or their relationships. For relativists, there are no "healthy" or "dysfunctional" patterns; rather, we create "health" and "dysfunction" by the ways we choose to interpret situations. Relativists object to the notion that the therapist's assessments (i.e., "you are conflict-avoidant") are an objective and accurate portrayal of real dynamics, and tend to favor therapeutic approaches that encourage clients to discover what is true for them.

I have discussed my views on the objectivist/relativist debate extensively elsewhere (Atkinson, 1992a, 1992b; Atkinson & Heath, 1987, 1989, 1990a, 1990b, Atkinson, Heath, & Chenail, 1991). Here I will simply say that in PET-C, we bridge the objectivist–relativist dichotomy by holding onto the possibility that real relationship dynamics exist (i.e., some ways of understanding and navigating relationships really *are* healthier than others), while still acknowledging that there is no way for us to know this for sure. Given our assumption about the lack of certain knowledge, we agree with relativists that each person must decide for him -or herself what to believe. In PET-C, we present a strong case for our understanding of how relationships work. However, we encourage clients to make up their own minds about what to believe. As the reader will see in the following chapters, if clients disagree about our assessment of their relationship habits, we encourage them to go with what they honestly believe rather than take our word for it.

Therapist as Expert vs. Client as Expert

Another dichotomy that is bridged in PET-C involves the extent to which the therapist eschews or embraces the role of expert. The position taken by therapists on this dichotomy often closely parallels their objectivist–relativist assumptions, with the objectivist therapist gravitating toward an expert role and the relativist therapist eschewing the role of expert in favor of the notion that the client should be the sole authority on his or her own experience. In PET-C, we embrace both positions (Atkinson, 1993). We assume the role of expert in our assessments and specific recommendations to clients about how they can improve their relationships. However, although we view ourselves as having expertise in a particular way of understanding and navigating relationships, we are not expert in the sense of knowing whether or not partners should accept our assessments or recommendations. At any particular point in therapy, as PET-C therapists present information about the prerequisites for relationship success, they may look very much as though they are assuming the expert role. We are not the least bit reluctant in our attempts to persuade partners to consider the merits of the viewpoints we believe to be valid. However, we place a high priority on encouraging clients to follow their own intuitions about what they need, and we encourage clients to seek other perspectives if the one we are offering doesn't seem right for them.

Challenging vs. Supportive

Skilled PET-C therapists are equally comfortable challenging the assumptions that clients bring into therapy, and providing safety and support for the feelings of each partner. In PET-C, our goal is for partners to experience some of the most profound understanding and empathy that they have ever experienced in their lives, while at the same time experiencing the most powerful challenge. This is only possible when the therapist is able to deliver challenges from a noncritical internal state. If the therapist is combative or critical, partners will most likely not change. In our experience, a combination of unwavering support and relentless challenge is not only desirable, it is absolutely necessary if the couples therapy is to be effective. If the support isn't there, partners will often be caught in defensiveness. If the challenge isn't there, partners will often continue with assumptions and habits that doom their relationships to failure. PET-C therapists take a straightforward, pull-no-punches approach with clients, but do so from a noncritical internal state. To do this, therapists must be highly skilled at influencing their own internal states throughout therapy.

Growth Oriented vs. Problem Solving

PET-C is ultimately geared toward helping partners grow personally by developing greater awareness of their emotional worlds and greater abilities to attend to their internal states in a way that enables them to change conditioned internal response patterns that inhibit them from getting what they want from life. However, these same abilities also help them solve the specific problems they enter therapy complaining about. In this sense, PET-C is both a growth-oriented and problem-solving therapy. We begin therapy by pledging our support in helping each partner solve the immediate problems facing them (e.g., "My partner is treating me poorly"). Then, we help partners come to understand that the best way to solve their problems is to grow personally. For example, partners may enter therapy with the goal of getting their mates to be less critical and blaming. We help such partners understand that the best way to achieve this goal is to develop the ability to respond to their mates' criticisms in a way that will lead to less criticism from their mates. Thanks to the research discussed in Chapter 3, we know how people do this: They change their partners by changing themselves. Although it is admirable to be motivated to become a better person for the sake of one's own personal growth, it is not necessary. People usually grow personally in order to get more of what they want out of life. Fortunately, the motivation to grow as a person and the motivation to get more of what one wants from one's partner are not incompatible goals.

Cognitive vs. Behavioral vs. Experiential

Therapies are often categorized by the extent to which cognitions, behaviors, or emotions are a focus of intervention. However, the studies reviewed in Part I of this book suggest that thoughts, feelings, and actions are all organized by neural states (executive operating systems) that operate behind the scenes, prompting certain thoughts, feelings, and actions and inhibiting others. When cognitive therapies work, we believe it is because cognitive interventions have successfully helped clients shift neural states. Sometimes, these neural states shift when clients remind themselves that they need to shift, or when clients develop new ways to interpret their partners' behavior. This comprises intervention at the cognitive level. Other times, internal states shift when clients simply begin acting differently (e.g., a client apologizes, even when he doesn't feel like it, but then afterwards feels an internal change). This happens when behavioral therapies are effective. Other times, states shift when we simply experience them more directly, something that happens in experiential therapy. However, we have all encountered situations in which one or more of these intervention types fails to influence internal state shifts. For example, a client can remind himself that his fear is irrational (cognitive intervention) but the fearful state remains. This client might also plunge ahead with needed action in spite of the fearful state that produces an urge to withdraw, but the fearful state might persist anyway. The client might even experience his fear more vividly, but sometimes this only intensifies the fear. In PET-C, we use a unique combination of cognitive–behavioral–experiential interventions, but we do not regard changed thoughts, feelings, or actions as successful unless they produce the kind of shifts in neural state activation–suppression patterns that we believe are necessary for lasting change to occur. In other words, we constantly check the effect of any cognitive, behavioral, or experiential intervention on the patterning of internal states.

Planned vs. Spontaneous

PET-C is a highly structured therapy, yet the success of any given session depends upon factors that cannot be predicted ahead of time. The pragmatic aspects of the therapy are comfortable for therapists who prefer structure, and the experiential aspects of the therapy are most appealing for therapists who are at home with ambiguity and spontaneity. The most successful PET-C therapists develop the ability to work comfortably with both structure and improvisation.

In each session, the therapist begins with a plan, but relies heavily on his or her intuition to know when to halt the plan and attend to client reservations. The therapist bases interventions on a sense of what's happening with the client's internal state. For example, in Phase I of PET-C, the therapist follows a careful plan aimed at helping each partner shift internal states, then moves each client toward thoughts and actions that are predictive of relationship success. However, in order to help clients shift internal states, skilled therapists follow their intuitions to sniff out any resistance clients have to the ideas the therapist proposes. Therapists then follow the client's lead down unpredictable paths as they seek to soothe defensive states. If they attempt to forge ahead with the plan of trying to get clients to think and act in ways that are predictive of success, they will fail. Skilled therapists suspend their plans and follow the client. At some point, however, PET-C therapists return to the original plan. Skilled PET-C therapists are both highly organized and also comfortable with allowing therapy to become temporarily disorganized.

Biological vs. Psychological vs. Social

PET-C embraces the premise that our thoughts, feelings, and actions are largely determined by the way our nervous systems are set up. The neural operating systems that are a target of PET-C intervention are biological systems. At the biological level, dopamine can enhance the vigor of the SEEKING circuit, whereas benzodiazepines can inhibit an overly active FEAR circuit (Panksepp, 1998). There is evidence that some individuals are genetically wired with varying thresholds for the activation of certain neural operating systems. However, the activation of neural states is also highly dependent upon psychological factors, such as the way a person learns to think or react when internal states are automatically activated. Biological systems are amenable to biological, psychological, and social interventions. For example, studies suggest that the physical maturation of the human brain is highly influenced by a child's interactions with his or her primary caregiver (Schore, 2001a, 2001b). The brains of young children who have highly attuned caregivers develop differently from those whose caregivers are intrusive or unresponsive. Specifically, securely attached children who have highly attuned caregivers evidence more complex development in the prefrontal area of the brain—the area responsible for emotional regulation (Seigel, 1999). Social interaction continues to shape brain development throughout life. In PET-C, partners learn how to rewire their nervous systems, and they also learn how to interact with their partners' nervous systems in ways that make intimate responses more likely, and they learn how to avoid activating states in their partners that result in antagonistic reactions.

In PET-C, we intervene at psychological and social levels to promote the restructuring of internal state activations in each partner.

Historical vs. Present Focus

Therapies can be classified according to the extent to which they focus on help-ing clients explore their past, and the extent to which they maintain a focus on changing their present circumstances. In PET-C, our goal is to help clients change internal state activation–suppression patterns in their current day-to-day experience. For many clients, this does not require extensive exploration of their past. However, in virtually all cases, some past exploration is instrumental in helping clients gain greater awareness of and ability to influence their internal states. In general, we promote reprocessing of past emotional experiences only when more direct, present-oriented efforts fail.

COMPARISON WITH OTHER CLINICAL APPROACHES

PET-C has been influenced by or has parallels with, a variety of other perspec-tives. Most obvious is the influence of John Gottman's research, which provides the focus of the "pragmatic" aspect of PET-C, which shares some commonali-ties with the way that Gottman organizes his marital therapy (Gottman, 1999). For example, Phase II of PET-C parallel's Gottman's marital therapy in its em-phasis on the teaching of specific skills. Also shared is the idea that new skills must be practiced in therapy when automatic emotional reactions are active. However, PET-C diverges from Gottman's marital therapy in the level of atten-tion it gives to the skills involved in shifting to internal states that support the predictive attitudes and behaviors.

Our focus on the internal states that govern the interactions of intimate part-ners arises from the brain studies described in Chapters 1 and 2. As we became more convinced of the importance of helping clients increase their abilities to shift internal states, we looked for existing therapeutic methods for working di-rectly with emotion, and we began developing our own. Among existing meth-ods, we found Eugene Gendlin's Focusing method (Gendlin, 1981, 1996), and methods from Dick Schwartz's Internal Family Systems model (IFS; Schwartz, 1995) most useful. PET-C's Level III methods described in Chapter 6 are par-ticularly influenced by Schwartz's and Gendlin's methods. Gendlin does not consider Focusing to be a therapy model, but rather a powerful method for bringing people into helpful contact with their internal experience. It is incor-porated for precisely this purpose in PET-C. Schwartz's IFS model is a coherent clinical approach with its own assumptions, only some of which are shared by PET-C. However, many IFS methods can be seamlessly integrated into the PET-C agenda. Focusing, IFS, and PET-C share in common the goal of culti-vating a respectful inner relationship between conscious "self" and the more au-tomatically activated internal states. We believe that Gendlin's "felt sense" and Schwartz's "internal parts" refer to the brain's executive operating systems, which are a target for change in PET-C.

PET-C has also been influenced by the principles of problem formulation and problem resolution developed in the 1970s by the associates of the Mental Research Institute (MRT; Fisch, Weakland, & Segal, 1982; Watzlawick, Weakland, & Fisch, 1974). The MRI group based their clinical model on the notion that "the attempted solution maintains the problem." This notion is fundamentally compatible with the PET-C formulation: The way that people respond when they feel misunderstood or mistreated often sabotoges their goals of getting more cooperation and respect from their partners. The architects of the brief MRI approach suggested ways to help clients reverse their attempted solutions, but felt it was unnecessary (or perhaps not possible) to develop detailed descriptions of universally applicable components of attempted solutions that actually work. Of course, the MRI associates were operating in the pre-Gottman era, and had limited empirical data to draw upon at the time. PET-C takes advantage of empirical evidence regarding the attempted solutions that almost always work.

Astute readers will find a Bowenian influence in the PET-C formulations. Like PET-C, Bowen believed that the way in which individuals function in relationships is heavily influenced primarily by automatic patterns of emotional reactivity (Bowen, 1978). Bowen's insights are remarkable, in that they predate much of the brain research described in Chapters 1 and 2. One of the habits for relationship success, "standing up for yourself without putting your partner down," is quite consistent with Bowen's notions about how a well-differentiated person interacts in relationships. Our applications of this principle have been considerably enriched by the Bowen-influenced writings of Harriet Goldhor Lerner (1985, 1989), who gives lucid examples of the importance of an individual "having a bottom line" in relationships. PET-C diverges somewhat from Bowen's theory in the level of attention PET-C gives to the emotional states that promote secure emotional attachments. Interpretations of Bowen usually emphasize the negative role that automatic emotional (fight–flight) reactions can play in a person's functioning, giving less attention to the indispensable positive role of the automatic emotional systems. Bowen asserts that automatic emotionally driven responses account for the most destructive elements in human relationships. PET-C agrees, but adds that emotionally driven responses account for the most positive, life-giving elements in human relationships as well. In PET-C, we not only help clients short-circuit emotional states that fuel interpersonal strife, we attempt to help clients to activate emotional states that fuel intimacy. Further, the PET-C method diverges from Bowen method in its emphasis on a partnership between rationality and emotion. Following Freud, Bowen sought to put rationality in charge of emotion. Recent findings about the architecture of the brain suggest that this is a futile endeavor, and suggest that emotions will always be the driving force in organizing human behavior. Our best bet is to form a respectful partnership with our emotions, hoping to redirect them as needed.

Although not as influential in the formation of PET-C as the approaches mentioned above, we find significant parallels with certain aspects of PET-C in Susan Johnson's Emotionally Focused Therapy for Couples (EFTC; Johnson, 1996), and Daniel Wile's Collaborative Couple Therapy (Wile, 2002). Wile's method, "Becoming Each Partner's Spokesperson," is very similar to the PET-C Level I intervention, "Priming the Pump." PET-C is most substantially different from Wile's Collaborative Couple Therapy in PET-C's emphasis on explicit training in the skills of emotional intelligence.

Although the methods she uses are somewhat different from ours, Johnson is masterly at creating the kind of internal shifts described in Chapter 6. Our interactions with Johnson and our observations of her clinical work have enriched our own methods for influencing internal state shifts in clients. Like PET-C, Johnson's emotionally focused therapy for couples emphasizes the importance of emotional states in setting the stage for what happens between intimate partners. PET-C and EFTC also share a special interest in the internal states responsible for creating a secure emotional bond between partners. PET-C diverges from EFTC in its emphasis on explicit training of partners in the skills of emotional intelligence, and in PET-C's explicit attention to factors that predict relationship success.

Some parts of PET-C parallel aspects of two other clinical approaches: Solution-Focused Therapy (de Shazer, 1985; 1992) and the Narrative Therapies (White & Epston, 1990). As mentioned earlier in this chapter ("Objectivism vs. Relativism"), PET-C has been influenced by the postmodern critique of notions of certainty, as have both solution-focused therapy and the narrative therapies. However, both solution-focused therapy and the narrative therapies respond to the postmodern critique by taking more of a relativist turn than does PET-C. Both solution-focused therapy and the narrative therapies want clients to generate their own new ways of interpreting and navigating relationships. PET-C also wants clients to decide for themselves what to believe and how to interact in relationships, but PET-C therapists do not hesitate to suggest specific alternatives for which there is empirical support. PET-C endorses the solution-focused method of getting clients to do more of what is already working whenever possible. However, a PET-C therapist would not hesitate to challenge clients to try something altogether different, even if they had no reference for it in their previous history.

PET-C shares with the narrative therapies an emphasis on changing the dominant (and often culturally prescribed) interpretations or stories that partners have about each other and about their relationships. However, unlike the narrative therapies, PET-C proposes specific alternatives to the pathologizing stories that often govern the lives of distressed partners. In practice, we suspect that the kind of nonpathologizing stories that PET-C therapists propose to clients would be similar to those that most narrative therapists would want their clients to embrace as well. PET-C expands beyond the focus of the narrative therapies in its emphasis on the attitudes and behaviors that predict relationship success, and on constraints that automatically activated internal states can put on one's ability to create and sustain nonpathologizing stories about self and other. Both solution-focused and narrative therapies tend to be exclusively strength-based. In contrast, PET-C focuses both on building strength and remedying dysfunction.

Since the mid-1980s, there have been a number of studies and meta-analyses of outcomes in psychotherapy which suggest that there are common change factors at work in all effective forms of psychotherapy (Sprenkle & Blow, 2004). It has been suggested that these common factors may be more important in producing change than the unique factors of effective models. While many aspects of PET-C are unique, PET-C methods are responsive to these commonly cited change factors as well. For example, PET-C methods are explicitly designed to enhance client motivation, positive client expectations, and a strong therapeutic alliance between therapist and clients, three of the most widely regarded common change factors. Therapist competence is also regarded as an influential common change factor. As described in Chapter 13, training in PET-C involves cultivation of not only technical competence in practitioners, but increased internal awareness, and the ability to access and regulate emotion as well.

CHAPTER 5

PET-C Assessment

T HE FIRST THREE HOURS of time spent with clients in PET-C are typically devoted to the task of obtaining specific information that will be used in the
therapy process. Although some of the information gathered is standard in the
typical mental health assessment process, PET-C assessment investigates the
specific habits of each partner that will later become a target for intervention.
The following information is obtained in the PET-C assessment process:

- The past and current symptoms and present level of emotional stability
  of each partner.
- The extent to which the relationship is characterized by alcohol/drug
  abuse, violence, or infidelity.
- The extent to which each partner is currently engaging in the 10 habits
  that predict relationship success (see Chapter 3).
- The patterns of automatic internal state activation-suppression that char-
  acterize each partner's interaction in the relationship (see Chapter 2).
- The pathologizing interpretations that each partner uses to explain the
  upsetting aspects of his or her partner's thinking or actions.
- The extent to which each partner harbors global contempt for the other.
- The specific issues over which partners are gridlocked.
- The core differences and bigger issues at stake behind each partner's
  position on gridlocked issues.
- Significant past hurtful experiences that each partner has experienced
  in the current or past relationships.

Unless there is a crisis that requires immediate intervention, we normally delay
making suggestions or recommendations to clients until we have gathered
enough information to feel confident that we understand what life is like for

each of them, and how each experiences the relationship. This is usually accomplished in the first three sessions: one conjoint session and one individual session with each partner. In the fourth hour, we meet conjointly and share our observations about strengths and areas that need attention, and we suggest a plan for how to go about making the changes that we believe are needed.

This three-session assessment plan is agreeable to approximately 90% of partners beginning therapy. The most common reason cited by those who do not agree is a crisis that requires immediate attention, such as the discovery of an affair or an incidence of violence. In these situations, we begin interventions directed at helping the partners stabilize as soon as possible. When crisis intervention is necessary, we use the same PET-C methods as we use when a couple is not in a crisis. We simply base our interventions more on our intuitions about what is needed, rather than on detailed assessment data. In these situations, we gather assessment data "on the run," even as we attempt to resolve the current crisis.

Before beginning to assess each partner's relationship habits, we do a brief assessment of the following areas:

- Past and present history of violence.
- Assessment of drug/alcohol use.
- Past and present history of psychiatric medication and/or previous treatment.
- Assessment for severe depression, anxiety, or other psychiatric conditions.
- Assessment for potential harm.
- Past and present history of infidelity.

If there are significant findings in any of the areas listed above, the therapist must make a decision about whether to proceed with the assessment of relationship habits, or delve into the specific area of concern. The therapist may delay the three-session assessment, and shift immediately to crisis intervention, recommend additional therapy or treatment, or recommend evaluation for possible medication.

A medical evaluation is recommended whenever partners meet criteria for mood disorders, anxiety disorders, or other disorders for which there is evidence of the effectiveness of certain medications. We do not recommend medication, but rather an evaluation by a physician to determine the appropriateness of medication. In some cases we have observed that a client's ability to make necessary shifts in internal states is enhanced through appropriate medication. For example, a person who has trouble calming a RAGE state may be better able to do so with the help of medication. In these cases, medication is not considered a substitute for developing the psychological ability to shift internal states. Rather, medication may assist clients in this process.

In some cases, especially where there has been violence, significant drug/alcohol abuse, or a recent affair, the therapist may recommend (or insist on) delaying couples therapy until other forms of treatment have taken place. The presence of any one of these problems does not in itself, however, constitute grounds for delaying couples therapy. In fact, depending upon the situation, couples therapy may be the treatment of choice for any of these problems. The therapist evaluates each situation on a case by case basis.

ASSESSMENT OF THE 10 HABITS

Throughout the assessment process, the therapist asks questions that elicit information about the extent to which partners are evidencing the 10 habits that predict relationship success (described in Chapter 3). To what extent does each partner critically judge the other? How able is each partner to stand up for him- or herself without putting the other down? When upset, is each partner still able to find and acknowledge the understandable reasons for his partner's actions or feelings? Do partners offer assurances, or give equal regard? To what extent is each partner able to understand the bigger things at stake behind seemingly trivial arguments? To what extent does each partner have knowledge of the other's internal world? Are there daily expressions of affection, fondness, or admiration? Do partners seek emotional support from each other? Do they feel that they receive emotional support from each other? To what extent do they function as a team in planning their lives together? Questions such as these guide the therapist's inquiries.

ASSESSMENT OF INTERNAL STATE
ACTIVATION PATTERNS

As partners interact and answer questions, the therapist also comes to understand the internal state activation patterns operating within each partner. The therapist is especially interested in the self-protective states that are activated in each partner when she or he feels mistreated or misunderstood by the other. Under what circumstances does a partner attack or withdraw, signifying the activation of RAGE or FEAR? (see Chapter 1). What are the characteristic thoughts and actions that go along with self-protective state activations for each partner? In addition to gathering information about self-protective state activation patterns, special attention is also given to investigating the extent to which the intimacy states (PLAY, LUST, CARE, PANIC) are active in the couple's day-to-day life with each other (see Chapter 2). When they are not fighting, does each partner experience periods of playfulness with the other? To what extent does each partner experience sexual desire and fulfillment? How often, and in what circumstances does each partner experience genuine tenderness or fondness for the other? To what extent does each partner experience a need for emotional support or affirmation from the other?

ASSESSING AREAS OF GRIDLOCK

Throughout the assessment process, the PET-C therapist assesses content as well as process. That is, in addition to looking for the redundant habits and internal activation patterns that transcend specific conflict situations, the therapist identifies specific issues over which partners have become gridlocked. PET-C begins by going to the heart of the most destructive conflicts. These conflicts typically involve "gridlocked" situations that come up over and over again, but never lead to satisfactory compromises. Gottman (1999) defined an issue as gridlocked when partners

- have come to feel rejected by each other.
- keep talking, but make no headway.
- become entrenched in their own positions and are unwilling to budge.
- end up feeling more frustrated and hurt when they discuss the subject.
- are devoid of humor, amusement, or affection with regard to the issue.
- become even more unbudgeable over time, which leads partners to vilify each other during these conversations.
- become more and more rooted in their positions and polarized, more extreme in their views over time, and less willing to compromise.

In PET-C, we begin therapy by going to the center of the storm, asking partners to discuss a gridlocked issue over which they feel completely dismissed or misunderstood by each other. Predictably, as they begin discussing this issue, each partner will come under the influence of a self-protective internal state, and each will be unable to respond to the other in a way that leads to respectfulness or compromise. The PET-C therapist intervenes, helping each partner shift to another internal state. Once a shift has taken place, the therapist helps each partner think and act in ways that predict relationship success (described in Chapter 3). Before beginning the intervention process, however, it is vital for the therapist to understand each partner's explanations and frustrations related to the gridlocked issue.

An important aspect of the assessment of gridlocked issues pertains to the extent to which each partner feels that the other has become more rigid or extreme in his or her positions over time. This is almost always the case. One of the earliest PET-C interventions will help each client consider that his or her partner has gotten more extreme over time partly in response to feeling dismissed or "written off," rather than because of some inherent propensity for selfishness or negativity. But the therapist must first establish that, indeed, each client feels that his or her partner has become more extreme over time.

ASSESSMENT FOR CONTEMPT

As partners become gridlocked over specific issues, they often begin developing pathologizing explanations for the other's behavior, and begin casting the other in the role of the villain. The general pathologizing story that distressed couples usually enter therapy with is: "My partner acts this way because she or he is a _____ person (fill in the blank: insensitive, selfish, negative, critical, lazy, uncaring, or controlling, malicious, etc.) I didn't see it in the beginning, because she or he put on a good front, or I was blind to it. I see it now. How could I have been so blind?"

Such pathologizing interpretations are the kiss of death to relationships. They contribute to a belief system that spawns expressions of contempt (each partner sees him- or herself as "better," or less to blame, than the other). As noted in Chapter 3, contempt is the single strongest predictor of eventual relationship demise. The early phase of PET-C is devoted to helping partners let go of pathologizing interpretations of each other's behavior and embrace alternative, nonpathologizing ones. In the assessment phase of PET-C, we look for the specific pathologizing explanations that clients have for each other's behavior. We also look for evidence of the extent to which clients have an "I'm better than my partner" attitude. Assessment for contempt includes questions such as:

- Do you think your ideas for solutions are usually better than your partner's? Why?
- Generally speaking, do you think you are more emotionally stable than your partner? Why?
- Overall, do you think you're an easier person to be in a relationship with than your partner? Why?

The therapist makes careful notes on each partner's answers to these questions, because she or he will refer to the client's specific words later, when the intervention process begins.

ASSESSING WHAT IS AT STAKE BEHIND GRIDLOCKED CONFLICTS

Clients develop pathologizing interpretations of their partners' behaviors because they cannot see alternative interpretations that fit. If the therapist is to succeed in helping clients let go of their pathologizing interpretations of their partners' behavior, credible alternative, nonpathologizing explanations must be provided. In the PET-C assessment, the therapist looks for credible, nonpathologizing reasons for each partner's rigid positions on gridlocked issues. In general, the therapist assumes that the reasons why each partner keeps refusing to collaborate run deeper than the particulars of each situation. Partners usually adopt rigid positions because they feel threatened. Each partner is fighting for something very important to him or her, but this something is often not clearly understood or articulated. The job of the PET-C therapist is to locate the hopes, dreams, values, or beliefs that lie beneath each partner's position on gridlocked issues. In the assessment phase of PET-C, the therapist looks for evidence that supports at least one of three compelling alternatives to the typical pathological explanation that each partner has for the other's behavior.

*Alternative 1: Legitimately Different Hopes, Dreams,
Expectations*

*There's more at stake for your partner than just the present situation. Beneath your
partner's seemingly rigid position on this issue lies an important underlying dream
or expectation for how he hoped things would be. There's nothing wrong with his
dream or expectation—it's just different from yours.*

Most partners enter their relationships with deeply held dreams, hopes, or expectations about how things are going to be. Each partner's dreams are personally compelling, often arising from important formative experiences each has
had (Gottman, 1999). The legitimacy of these dreams seems so self-evident that
they tend to assume that the dreams are shared by their partners. The problem is
that there are a variety of different, legitimate dreams for how relationships can
be, and sometimes important dreams come into conflict. This is almost always
the case when couples gridlock on specific issues. For example, I worked with a
couple that was gridlocked in vicious, repetitive arguments over whether or not
it was acceptable for the wife to wear form-fitting or sexy clothing in public. As is
typical when partners gridlock, each partner had adopted an explanation for the
other's behavior that assumed faulty personality characteristics. The husband insisted that this attire was inappropriate for a married woman, and accused his
wife of having an insatiable need for male attention. In return, the wife accused
the husband of having low self-esteem, arguing that if he were more confident,
the way she dressed wouldn't bother him because she had no intention of becoming involved with anyone else. People have different, legitimate expectations on issues such as how to dress in public. Each accused the other of being
out of line, when, in fact, neither of them was out of line. The couple spent
hours arguing about whether or not the wife's bra could really be seen through
her blouse, or the extent to which her pants were so tight that the outline of her
skimpy bikini briefs could be detected. Neither of them was able to understand
what was really at stake for the other. In the assessment process, I was able to uncover this information by assuring each partner that I believed that she or he had
a legitimate point of view on this matter, and by asking questions such as:

- Why do you feel as strongly about this issue as you do?
- What has happened in your life that makes you feel the way you do?
- Do you feel threatened? In what way?
- Beneath it all, what is at stake for you here?
- What would you lose if you gave in to your partner's wishes on this is-
  sue? What bad thing might happen?
- What's the bigger thing that are you worried about?
- Are you worried about where things are headed? What's your fear about
  the future?

- If your partner keeps acting the way he's been acting, what important dream will you lose?

In response to such questions, I was able to discover that the wife spent her childhood feeling like an ugly duckling. She was overweight and dreamed about what it would be like to turn boys' heads. When she got to college, she received positive attention for intellectual abilities, and started feeling better about herself. This boost gave her enough energy to begin working out, and within a year, she'd lost a good deal of weight. For the first time in her life, she began trying to look good, giving attention to clothing and makeup. Predictably, she began turning heads, and it gave her an incredible, positive feeling. She dated several men, each for at least a year, before meeting her husband and marrying him.

In my interview with the husband, I learned that his parents divorced when he was 15 years old. He remembered distinctly how his mother changed during the last two years before the divorce. When he was younger, she had paid little attention to her appearance, but this shifted suddenly when she took a new job. The husband believed that this shift in his mother's appearance communicated to men that she was interested in them, because within a year she had an affair with a coworker.

This husband and wife had dreams that were in conflict due to their different life experiences, but they didn't realize this, and were gridlocked in pointless arguments about the appropriateness of the wife's clothing. In the assessment process, the PET-C therapist unearthed the dreams and stories that fueled each partner's rigid position. As therapy progressed, the therapist helped each partner drop the pathologizing interpretations that each had of the other, and come to understand the different, but legitimate, hopes and dreams that were at stake for each partner behind their seemingly provocative behavior.

Alternative 2: Legitimately Different Ways of Maintaining Emotional Stability

Your partner clings to his position on this issue not because he or she is _____ (rigid, selfish, irresponsible, etc.), but because your partner has legitimately different ways of navigating life. What makes you feel good doesn't necessarily do it for him.

Partners generally try to present logical, compelling arguments for their opinions on gridlocked issues, even backing up their preferences with philosophical or theological propositions. However, most of the time, each partner's positions on gridlocked issues arise from basic personality tendencies. Different people develop radically different, even opposite ways of making their way through life. What works for one person does not necessarily work for another, and the failure to recognize this basic fact fuels many relationship gridlocks.

People do not volunteer for their style of coping with stress. Rather, they usually just discover ways of coping that make them feel more stable. The relationship dreams that each partner holds, and their respective positions on issues over which couples often gridlock, arise from a person's natural mechanisms for maintaining emotional stability. For example, a person who discovers that, for her, life feels most stable when it is predictable, will tend to gravitate toward a philosophy of marriage that emphasizes responsibility, commitment, and discipline. Her relationship dreams will center around the safety and security that comes when two people join forces against the chaos of the world around them. Another person may discover that for him, life feels best when he lives it wide open, taking risks, and treating life like an adventure. This person will gravitate toward a philosophy of marriage that emphasizes spontaneity, and will see his partner as a coadventurer. His life philosophy will center around the benefits of boundless living of having a companion on this adventure called life.

If these two people marry each other and have relationship problems, they are likely to be gridlocked over issues related to predictability versus spontaneity. For example, they might gridlock over parenting issues, such as whether the children should have a firm bedtime or not. The "orderly" person will respond in negative fashion to her spontaneous partner's tendency to ignore the children's bedtime, accusing him of being irresponsible. Conversely, the spontaneous person will judge the orderly partner's insistence on a consistent bedtime, accusing her of being too rigid or controlling. These partners are likely to enter therapy claiming that their own philosophy of parenting is better than their partners', but in fact, each of them is just following a personal coping style. The spontaneous person fights off boredom and the intolerable constricting feeling that comes from too much structure by making life an adventure. He applies this same approach to parenting. If he tried to operate with the level of structure, order, or discipline that his partner thinks he should have, his anxiety would go way up, and life would feel unstable to him. Conversely, the orderly person reduces her anxiety through structuring life and making it predictable, and her position on gridlocked issues will usually reflect this. If she tried to function with the level of spontaneity that her partner thinks she should, her anxiety would go way up, and she would feel unstable. The therapist's job will be to help each partner drop his efforts to prove that the other's position on the issue is inferior, and acknowledge that their differences probably arise from their different, legitimate coping styles.

To successfully intervene in this way, the PET-C therapist looks for each partner's basic styles of coping during the assessment phase. We have identified five basic differences in ways people maintain emotional stability that most frequently lay beneath the gridlocked conflicts that couples come into therapy with.

Independence First vs. Togetherness First

The first of the core difference areas involves the extent to which a person's most basic inclination is to operate independently or to operate side by side with a partner. We rarely encounter clients who want to operate independently all the time, nor do we encounter clients who are unable to function unless their partners are alongside of them. It's more a matter of a person's first inclination. Independence-first people prefer to operate independently a greater portion of the time and togetherness-first people prefer to share tasks and activities together. For example, when they go grocery shopping, independence-first partners often want to divide and conquer (divide the shopping list and each partner accomplish different tasks) so that they will finish sooner and can spend more of the day doing other things they want to do. But for togetherness-first partners, what's the point in going shopping together if you're not going to be together?

When stressed, independence-first people need space in order to be able to think things through. In contrast, togetherness-first people draw immediately toward others, and seek a measure of emotional comfort which then helps them to cope with the stressful event. For such individuals, togetherness serves as a precursor to working independently. Togetherness-first people often get their feelings hurt by independence-first partners when stress arises, because their efforts to connect are often rebuffed by the independence-first partners—not because the independence-first person doesn't want to offer support, but rather because the togetherness threatens this person's own emotional stability. Like each of the other core personality tendencies discussed in this chapter, the togetherness-first and independence-first tendencies are not simply preferences (e.g., "I like chocolate more than vanilla"). They are ways that people maintain emotional stability, and if they are tampered with, anxiety skyrockets. When stress arises, independence-first people don't just want some personal space, they need it, and if they don't get it, they may be emotionally destabilized. The same is true for the togetherness-first people. When stressed, emotional contact with their partners may be a necessary part of their process of emotional stabilization.

Some of the most rigid gridlocks we've seen in our work with couples arise from the different assumptions that independence-first and togetherness-first people have regarding who is responsible for whose needs. Togetherness-first people want relationships in which each partner assumes responsibility for knowing and anticipating the needs of the other, and helps the other shoulder tasks and burdens, whenever possible. They involve themselves in helping their partners without being asked. In contrast, independence-first partners prefer relationships in which each partner mostly assumes responsibility for shouldering their own tasks and burdens. They dislike the idea of having to decipher the complexity of their partners' moods and ever-changing needs, and prefer to rely on direct requests from their partners. They can be heard saying, "If you want something, just ask for it. Please don't expect me to read your mind." When time or energy resources are short, independence-first people are especially annoyed when their partners expect help from them. They want their partners to meet their own needs, and they expect to do the same. Because independence-first partners make requests for support less frequently than their togetherness-first partners, they often feel burdened by the requests of their partners and dream of relationships in which both partners pulls their own weight. They can often be heard accusing their partners of being too dependent or needy. Of course, togetherness-first partners feel offended by the implication that they are overly-dependent. For them, mutual dependency is healthy. In fact, from their perspective it seems barbaric to go through life primarily thinking about oneself. They dream of relationships in which others would care enough about them to volunteer to take their needs into consideration without their having to ask. Togetherness-first people often believe that their independence-first partners are selfish, and can often be heard saying things like, "You never think about anybody but yourself!" or "You are so self centered!" But independence-first people believe that their togetherness-first people are the ones who are truly selfish. They feel that their partners selfishly demand constant attention, and try to make others responsible for meeting needs that they could meet themselves.

Invest in the Future First vs. Live For the Moment First

A second core difference area involves how much people feel they should delay present gratification for the sake of investing in future happiness. Some people function best by delaying enjoyment until they have fulfilled all of their responsibilities. Others function best when they combine work and play. The second group prioritizes enjoyment of each moment more highly than the first group, reasoning that there is always more work to do, and if you wait to enjoy life until all responsibilities are fulfilled, you might miss some of the good parts of life. These people find it difficult to stay focused on work to the exclusion of play, and often gravitate toward careers that enable them to mix the things they love to do with their job requirements.

Invest-in-the-future-first people don't have the same requirement that work be mixed with enjoyable activities. For them, work is work, it doesn't have to be enjoyable, it's simply something that you have to do, like it or not. Unlike live-for-the-moment-first people, invest-in-the-future-first people find it difficult to relax and enjoy themselves while important tasks are looming overhead. They feel more stable when they stay on top of their responsibilities.

Each partner has a legitimate dream about how an ideal relationship should be. The invest-in-the-future-first person dreams of a relationship in which both partners work hard (side-by-side or independently), sacrificing the present for the sake of an anxiety-free future in which responsibilities are fulfilled, and they can relax together. The greatest fear of invest-in-the-future-first people is that life will become unstable because important responsibilities go unmet while the couple is enjoying the present moment. The live-for-the-moment-first person has a dream of a partner who will live in the present moment with them, not forever putting off the good part of life until later. The greatest fear of live-for-the-moment-first people is that life will pass them by while they are preoccupied with monotonous routine.

This core difference area lies behind many gridlocked issues that couples present in therapy. If partners are unable to maintain a "different, but legitimate" view of each other's core tendencies, they will be on a slippery slope toward relationship discord. The invest-in-the-future-first person will begin seeing the live-for-the-moment-first partner as childish, unable to delay gratification. Conversely, the live-for-the-moment-first person will see the invest-in-the-future-first person as dull or boring.

Predictability-First vs. Spontaneity-First

Another core difference that often spawns gridlocked issues involves the extent of predictability or structure desired in daily life. Predictability-first people function best when they are able to minimize chaos, and organize their lives in predictable ways. They like to have all of their ducks in a row, and to know what they can expect. They prepare for life's challenges, leaving little to chance. The very same conditions are threatening to spontaneity-first people. Spontaneity-first individuals thrive on the unexpected, and typically have vigorous neural circuits for PLAY, which are activated easily. The relationship dreams of predictability-first people tend to center around the safety and protection that is possible when two people "circle their wagons" and fight off the forces that threaten their resources or stability. The greatest fear of predictability-first people is that life will become unstable due to a lack of planning that could have prevented the instability. Spontaneity-first people often have a dream of a relationship in which they have a co-adventurer, a cohort in a wide open exploration of life. The greatest fear of spontaneity-first people is that life will become boring, meaningless, and amount to just going through the motions. Monotonous routine can trigger a sense of claustrophobic-type panic in a spontaneity-first person.

Many couples gridlock over these core personality differences. To the predictability-first person, a spontaneity-first partner may seem irresponsible and inefficient. Conversely, a spontaneity-first person may believe that a predictability-first partner is neurotic, up tight, and incapable of relaxing and just going with the flow of things.

Slow to Upset vs. Readily Upset

People differ with regard to how upset they let themselves get about undesirable circumstances. Readily-upset people experience upset feelings frequently and intensely, and use their upset feelings to motivate them to become agents of change. In contrast, slow-to-upset people have internal mechanisms that dampen upset feelings as soon as they occur. They are generally peace loving people and value interpersonal harmony and tolerance. They tend to believe that the world would work a lot better if everybody were more accepting of each other and didn't get so bent out of shape when things didn't go their way. This doesn't mean that slow-to-upset people are always willing to "go with the flow." In fact, many slow-to-upset people are effective change agents who feel that the secret to their success is precisely in their ability to remain calm. In contrast, readily-upset people use emotional intensity as a primary vehicle for change. Their upset feelings provide internal drive, and also motivate others to accommodate them.

Readily-upset people value justice and quality over peace and harmony. If a situation doesn't seem fair to them, or if a situation seems sub-standard in some way, they'll readily sacrifice peace for the sake of shaking things up and creating the possibility of change. Readily-upset people don't mind "rocking the boat" and are usually comfortable with conflict. To them, anger is a normal and necessary part of life. Slow-to-upset people, on the other hand, feel unstable when anger or interpersonal tension arises. They often value having a peaceful existence more than being "right." Even if something doesn't seem fair to them, they'll sometimes give in to keep the peace. To them, it's just not worth the turmoil that may follow if they assert themselves. They often live by the motto, "Don't sweat the small stuff," a philosophy that really isn't relevant to readily-upset people, because unlike slow-to-upset people, they are often able to engage in highly conflictual conversations without breaking a sweat! Getting upset simply isn't that big of a deal to them, and they are often able to maintain an inner calm while appearing outwardly upset. In fact, becoming upset *is* calming to them.

Slow-to-upset people dream of relationships in which partners are accepting of each other's differences and don't freak out when others fail to meet their expectations. They fear that if they were to become more like their readily-upset partners, life would be a never-ending series of upsets. The dreams of readily-upset people center on feeling respected and influential in their relationships. Their greatest fear is that, to be acceptable, they'll have to stifle their feelings, never rock the boat and pretend everything is okay.

Slow-to-upset people are often very critical of their readily-upset partners, seeing them as being like children who throw temper tantrums if they don't get their own way. Slow-to-upset people can be heard saying things like, "Do you have to get upset over every little thing I do?" and "You make a mountain out of a molehill!" Slow-to-upset people often see readily-upset people as negative, unhappy people for whom "nothing is ever good enough." Readily-upset people can be equally critical of slow-to-upset partners, accusing them of covering up their true feelings to avoid conflicts. Readily-upset partners often believe that their slow-to-upset partners are afraid of their emotions, and they sometimes have trouble respecting slow-to-upset partners because they seem wimpy, and won't stand up and fight.

Problem-solving-first vs. Understanding-first

Readily-upset partners must find ways to resolve their upset feelings, because they get upset fairly often. Slow-to-upset people don't get upset as often or as easily as readily-upset people, but they do get upset in some situations and must find ways to resolve these feelings. Further, if they have readily-upset partners, they frequently must find a way to deal with their partners' upset feelings. There are two different ways of resolving upset feelings. Problem-solving-first people don't see much value in dwelling on negative feelings, regardless of whether the feelings are their own or their partners'. Their motto is, "There's no sense in crying over spilled milk," and they rely heavily on problem-solving as a means to feeling better. If they can't do something about the upsetting conditions, they often feel better by making a plan that they can later implement. Once they have done all they can about an upsetting situation, they detach from negative feelings by focusing on other things. They don't spend much time looking for sympathy or validation when they feel bad. Instead, they look for more concrete forms of action on the part of their partners.

Understanding-first people are almost opposite in this regard. They know that their uncomfortable feelings can be soothed by their partners in ways that require little more than a bit of understanding and validation, and they actively seek and expect these forms of emotional support. It's not that they aren't interested in changing the conditions that produce uncomfortable feelings. For them, it's a matter of timing. Understanding and validation come first; formulating a plan of action comes second.

Problem-solving-first people and understanding-first people can become very critical of each other, because their initial ways of handling upset feelings are in direct conflict. Understanding-first people may not be satisfied by their partners' willingness to make changes, and may even reject their partners' practical problem-solving because they are seeking validation and understanding first, not an action plan. To problem-solving-first people, it seems like understanding-first people just want to complain and complain, but not do anything about their upsetting situations. To problem-solving-first people, it can even seem that understanding-first people *want* to be upset, and love wallowing in misery! Of course, this isn't true. Understanding-first people continue to be upset in spite of their problem-solving-first partners' offers to change because they are looking for understanding and validation of their feelings more than offers for change.

Problem-solving-first people assume that understanding each other is nice, but not necessary in order to function as a unit. They feel that people could spend years trying to understand each other and still be no closer to working solutions to life's problems. But understanding-first people just feel that the beauty in intimate relationships is in mutual understanding. They believe that practical problem solving is fine for business partners, but intimate partners should be invested in each other enough to keep engaged in discussion to the point where they really feel understood and valued by each other.

Problem-solving-first people tend to view the apparent refusal of understanding-first partners to engage in problem solving as unwillingness to compromise. This is not necessarily true of understanding-first people, who are often just as willing to meet in the middle, but only after they've exhausted efforts to promote mutual understanding. It's a matter of timing. The problem-solving-first partner wants to solve problems first; the understanding-first partner wants to delay attempts to solve problems until they feel understood. Problem-solving-first people see repetitive attempts to understand each other as amounting to "beating a dead horse," and believe that people are so different that mutual understanding is an unattainable goal.

The dreams of problem-solving-first partners tend to center around relationships in which partners maintain a "can-do" attitude, and tackle their problems head on. Their greatest fear is that life will be consumed with ill-fated attempts to persuade each other on things they will never agree on in the end anyway. In contrast, the dreams of understanding-first partners center on the special feeling that comes when one truly feels understood. They fear that without understanding, life will become a lonely journey.

Summary

Core differences are often experienced by partners as insensitivities or injustices, because each partner's way of maintaining emotional stability interferes with the other's way of maintaining stability. Rather than seeing a partner's behavior as arising from different ways of maintaining emotional stability, each partner interprets the other's behavior from within his or her own framework, and the other person appears as insensitive, selfish, controlling, or uncaring. (e.g., "I would never treat him the way that he treats me!", or "I would never get mad about something as trivial as that!") This is an easy mistake to make. In a sense, each partner is just following the Golden Rule: "Do unto others as you would have them do unto you." The only problem is that there is more than one way to cope effectively with life.

In the PET-C assessment, the therapist looks for these core differences. When successfully located, they provide the foundation for an alternative to the pathologizing explanation that each partner has for the other's behavior. Specifically, the therapist suggests some version of the following: "Your partner wants to do things her way because if she tried to do things your way, it would mess her up, not because there's something wrong with her, but rather because she has a different way of navigating life than you do. It would mess you up, too, if you tried to do things the way that she wants you to. This isn't about right or wrong, it's about differences in the habits you each have for navigating life."

ALTERNATIVE 3: REACTION TO FEELING
DISMISSED

Your partner's extreme, provocative behavior is not because she is inherently _____ (rigid, selfish, irresponsible, etc). Rather, her extreme behavior is in large part a reaction to the feeling that you have given up on her and believe her to be hopeless.

It is often hard for each partner to accept a nonpathologizing explanation for the other's behavior because the other's behavior seems so extreme. Indeed, by the time partners enter therapy, each of them may look extreme or provocative, even to the therapist. However, a person's extreme reactions are usually the result of feeling pathologized by his or her partner. When each partner constantly judges the other by his or her own standard, and the other continually falls short, each partner begins to write the other person off as constitutionally flawed at a basic level (insensitive, selfish, negative, mean-spirited, etc.) When a husband begins believing that his wife is defective, it is almost impossible for her to change, because to change would be like admitting that her husband was right all along. The wife must prove her husband wrong. It is a matter of survival. The last thing she will want to say is, "Oh, I can see what you mean. You're okay, but I'm deficient. Here, let me fix myself for you!" No, what she'll say is some version of, "Screw you! I won't budge an inch because I'm not wrong!" The wife believes (perhaps correctly) that once her husband has developed a view of her as flawed, she will never be able to prove otherwise, even though she may try. This leads her to think, "What's the point in even trying? I might as well just do whatever I want."

In short, the pathological interpretations that partners often have of each other usually begin with a basic, legitimate difference in dreams or coping styles. This difference becomes a source of frustration, but rather than understanding their partner's behavior as different, but legitimate, each partner begins to judge the other as wrong. As each partner comes to realize that they have been summarily written off and dismissed by the other, they each dig into their respective positions and polarize, becoming even more extreme. By the time they reach couples therapy, each of their reactions may look seriously out of balance. Given how extreme each partner looks, it is easy for a therapist to see each of them as neurotic. The PET-C therapist begins with a different assumption: Partners act in extreme ways because they have been written off by each other as fundamentally flawed.

In the PET-C assessment, the therapist looks for concrete indications that each partner has "written the other off" as hopeless. This information will be used to help challenge each client to consider that his or her partner is acting so provocatively not because it is in his or her nature to be this way, but rather in response to feeling judged as hopeless. In the assessment interviews, we are particularly interested in discovering the ways in which each partner may have written the other off as hopeless. We often uncover this information by asking questions such as these:

- Can you remember a specific time or times when your partner said or did, or failed to say or do things that made you think to yourself any of the following type things?
  - Oh my God, what have I gotten myself into?
  - My partner has psychological problems.

- My partner is dysfunctional.
- My partner has a personality defect.
- My partner is not emotionally normal.
- Has this flaw or characteristic of your partner gotten more intense over time? Explain. . . .
- What important things don't you get to have (or what dreams will you never realize) because of the way your spouse is?
- What practical problems or arguments does this aspect of your partner's behavior or personality contribute to?
- In what ways does it seem to you that your partner has come to the conclusion that you are hopelessly flawed?
- What dreams do you think your partner has given up on because s/he is in a relationship with you?

ASSESSMENT FOR PAST
EMOTIONAL INJURIES

As each partner talks about the feeling of being dismissed by the other, particular attention is given to times when one partner felt vulnerable and reached out to the other, but was rejected. To locate critical emotional injuries, the therapist asks each partner questions such as:

- Can you remember a time when your partner did something that was especially hurtful to you?
- Can you remember a time when you first remember thinking to yourself something like:
  - My partner used to think I was special, but I don't think she or he does anymore.
  - My partner used to feel lucky to have me, but I don't think she or he feels that way anymore.
  - Never again will I allow myself to be hurt like that again (to be made a fool like that again, etc.).

We believe that these moments are of special importance, and often lead to emotional injuries, which may constitute a critical point in a couple's relationship demise, unless the injury is re-processed and healing occurs. In the early phases of therapy, the PET-C therapist will help partners revisit such injuries, shift out of defensive states, and interact with each other in ways that are predictive of success.

CONCLUSION

Information on each of the above areas will continue to emerge throughout treatment. However, to begin intervening in Session 4, it is especially important that the therapist have a good understanding of specific relationship events in which at least one partner was critically hurt by the other. These injuries will be the focus of the earliest PET-C interventions. It is also important for the therapist to be aware of the issues over which partners are currently gridlocked, and the pathologizing explanations each partner has for the other's behavior. These gridlocked issues will also be addressed early in therapy. In order to help partners break out of gridlock, the therapist will need to have clear credible, alternatives to the pathologizing explanations that each partner has for the other's behavior. Specifically, the therapist will need to have discovered the underlying dreams in conflict, or the core differences that lie beneath gridlocked issues. The therapist must understand how the partners have interacted unsuccessfully when trying to discuss past hurts or current gridlocked issues, and have clear ideas about the specific kinds of changes that each partner will need to make in order to promote more successful interaction in the future.

Once PET-C therapists are confident that they have solid information about each of the above areas, they proceed to Session 4, in which therapists use their abilities to create the internal shifts necessary to free each partner to think and interact differently with the other over past hurts or current gridlocked issues.

CHAPTER 6

Creating Internal Shifts

WHEN COUPLES BEGIN THERAPY, partners are usually caught in mutually reinforcing patterns of interaction, fueled by the automatic activation of self-
protective internal states in each partner. A state in one partner automatically
activates a predictable state in the other, which triggers or perpetuates a predictable state in the first partner, and so on. Among the most common of these
patterns is an angry attack from one partner, which triggers a defensive state in
the other, which makes the former partner intensify the attack, which makes the
other partner want to withdraw altogether. Needless to say, the internal states
that propel attack–defend escalations are not compatible with the habits that
predict relationship success described in Chapter 3.

In the early sessions of Phase I, the PET-C therapist creates internal shifts in
partners, freeing them from the compulsion to attack, blame, defend, or withdraw. So long as partners remain within the "pull" of the internal states that propel fight or flight, they will be unable to interact in ways that make mutual respect possible. Once the therapist disarms such internal states, however,
successful interaction flows naturally.

In PET-C, we begin therapy by going to the center of the storm, asking partners to discuss an issue over which they feel completely dismissed or misunderstood by each other. Predictably, as they begin discussing this issue, each partner will come under the influence of a self-protective internal state, and each
will be unable to respond to the other in a way that leads to respectfulness or
mutual cooperation. The PET-C therapist intervenes, helping each partner shift
to another internal state. Once a shift has taken place, the therapist helps each
partner think and act in ways that predict relationship success. Creating an internal shift in each partner is no small task, and the methods we use for accomplishing this make up the content of this chapter.

Intervention typically begins in the fourth session, after the therapist has completed the three-session assessment described in Chapter 5. If the assessment has been successful, the therapist should have a good idea about

- at least one major issue over which partners are gridlocked;
- the bigger issues at stake behind each partner's position on gridlocked issues;
- the specific pathologizing explanation that each has for the other's behavior;
- specific times when one partner felt vulnerable and reached out to the other, but was rejected.

Specific moments when one partner was vulnerable and felt rejected when reaching out to the other are critical moments that often define the course of a relationship. When a moment like this has been identified by the therapist during the assessment phase, partners are asked to begin Session 4 by talking about this incident. Once a past hurt has been successfully reprocessed, partners are often able to let go of their rigid positions on current gridlocked issues. Unresolved resentments from the past often lock defensive or bitter states into place, interfering with new ways of interacting. Where no identifiable past emotional injury has been found, therapy begins with a discussion of a current gridlocked issue. Whether partners are discussing an injury from the past or a gridlocked issue in the present, the goals of the PET-C therapist remain the same: Create internal state shifts, then help partners discuss the issues in ways that are predictive of relationship success.

The methods we use for creating internal shifts will be introduced through a description of their application in the therapy of a couple who sought services at our clinic. Katrina and Michael were referred for couples therapy by a local youth service agency. The family therapist who was working with their children believed that the couple's relationship discord was a significant contributor to the problems their two children were having. Michael and Katrina were both in their mid-30s and had blue-collar jobs. They had a history of several failed attempts at couples therapy. Katrina reported that their most recent couples therapist had told her that Michael was constitutionally incapable of empathy, and that she would either have to learn to live with this or leave the relationship.

During the individual assessment sessions, each partner identified a turning point in their relationship that had occurred 11 years earlier, in the hospital immediately after the birth of their first child. The therapist entered Session 4 with the goal of helping Michael and Katrina go back to the hospital incident and talk about it in a different way than they had before. The therapist wanted to promote a conversation that enabled each partner to feel understood and validated, and also supportive and understanding of the other. Such a conversation would happen if Michael and Katrina could talk to the other in the ways that predict relationship success. The therapist knew that when they opened old wounds, each partner would likely become caught in internal states that fueled blaming and defensiveness, and that if Katrina and Michael were to interact differently, the therapist would first need to find a way to help each of them shift internal states.

The therapist set the stage for revisiting the conversation about what happened in the hospital by giving the following explanation:

Here's the general way that usually works best in conversations like the one I'm hoping we'll have today: In a minute, I'll ask you each to begin trying to talk to each other about what happened back then, and I'll stay out of it for a few minutes. As you talk to each other, each of you will probably begin feeling upset and each of you may begin getting off track in the sense that you'll begin communicating in a way that we know (from the studies of relationships I mentioned earlier) generally prevents conversations from being successful. When you're feeling upset, usually there are a lot of different reactions going on inside. You can't get them all out or else you'd be up all night trying, so you end up giving your partner only some reactions. I'll probably step in and help each of you give each other some different reactions that you might be neglecting to give each other. Sometimes this is all that is needed. If this doesn't help you get back on track, no problem. At that point, I'll probably suggest that we stop the conversation, and I'll meet with each of you for a while in order to make sure that I understand you, and to see what we can do to get you back on track. Then, if there is time, we'll get back together and you guys can resume the conversation. I want to warn you that you might find the process frustrating, because I'm more concerned that you each find a way to get back on track in the conversation than that you resolve this issue today. Sometimes, it takes the whole session to get back on track, but I'll want to take as much time as we need in order to get this to happen, because I know that if you continue to try to discuss the issue in a way that doesn't work, it won't do any good anyway. Does that make sense? How does that sound?

Both partners agreed, and the therapist began by encouraging Katrina to talk about what upset her eleven years ago.

W: Well, I don't want to talk about it because it won't do any good. (*Katrina begins to cry, then decides to speak to Michael*). You know that I'm terrified of hospitals, you know that I didn't want to be left alone in the hospital and there I was in labor, and you and your mother went off and left me. You went home and went to bed, and I just sat in the hospital alone.

H: The doctors told me to leave!

W: I don't care if the doctors told you to leave. I didn't want you to.

H: The doctor said you would sleep!

W: I sat in that room for hours and hours and hours. They told you I was going to go to sleep and they were giving me morphine, but I didn't go to sleep.

H: How was I supposed to know that?

W: I was terrified. I hate hospitals and you left me there.

H: The doctors told me to leave, that you were going to sleep.

W: The doctors have told me to leave when you've been in the hospital too, and I didn't go.

H: Yes you did.

W: I didn't go until you told me "I'm kinda tired I'm gonna go to sleep now." I have never left the hospital until you told me you're comfortable and you're ready to sleep.

H: That's not true!

At this point, it is clear that Katrina and Michael are discussing the event in a way that stands little chance of satisfying either of them. None of the habits that predict relationship success are present in the discussion. Katrina is judging Michael for leaving her in the hospital and Michael is judging Katrina's expectations as being unreasonable. Each feels dismissed or put down by the other. Neither is making an effort to find the understandable part of the other's feelings, no assurances are being offered, and neither is attempting to locate the legitimate needs, dreams, or priorities that might lie beneath their partner's actions at the hospital. More importantly, neither Michael nor Katrina seems to be anywhere near a state of mind that would enable them to do any of these things. Katrina is caught in an internal state that perpetuates an angry, accusatory attitude. Michael is under the influence of an internal state that perpetuates a steady diet of defensive reactions.

LEVEL I INTERVENTION: PRIMING THE PUMP

PET-C therapists use three levels of intervention in order to create internal shifts in partners who are upset with each other. The following dialogue will illustrate Level I intervention, in which the therapist attempts to help clients shift internal states by stepping in and speaking for them momentarily. The major components of this intervention are summarized in Table 6.1.

T: (*The therapist scoots closer to Michael, puts his hand on Michael's shoulder. With a soft voice, he speaks slowly to Michael.*) This is a very important thing that she's saying to you here, right? And, I think there's a lot of reactions going on inside of you.

H: Yeah, and I don't know what the hell they are.

TABLE 6.1
Creating Internal Shifts—Level I: Priming the Pump

The therapist speaks for each partner, one at a time.

1. The therapist prepares to speak for a partner by connecting with an internal state in him or her that is similar to the one needed by the partner at that particular moment. Usually, this is a more vulnerable state.
2. The therapist asks permission to speak for partner 1.
3. The therapist speaks to partner 2 as if he were partner 1, communicating in a way that is predictive of success.
4. If partner 2 responds in a way that is not predictive of success, the therapist asks permission to speak for partner 2.
5. The therapist then speaks to partner 1 as if he were partner 2, communicating in a way that is predictive of success.
6. The therapist repeats the process as needed.

T: Okay, let me try to help out. See if this fits, okay? I wonder if what's going on inside you is partly something like this. Let me just say it as if I were you, okay?

H: Go ahead, 'cause I won't say it right!

T: (*Therapist looks at wife and speaks as if he were the husband. The therapist speaks, softly, slowly, and tenderly.*) Katrina, it's really hard for me to hear you say these things. And my first reaction is to get defensive, you know, to try and defend myself because I think you're leveling the worst kind of accusation at me. I mean, if it's really true that you felt abandoned, I feel awful. And, I find myself wanting to just say, you know, it wasn't so! But the fact is, I can see how much that hurt you. And down inside I feel awful about that. (*Therapist turns to Michael.*) Now did I get that right? What part fits how you feel?

With this intervention, the therapist spoke from a place of tenderness emanating from his CARE circuit. With a tone of tenderness, the therapist offered an assurance (one of the 10 predictive habits) on Michael's behalf to Katrina, and acknowledged that her feelings may be understandable (another predictive habit), given the fact that she felt abandoned. Most important, however, is the internal state from which the therapist spoke. Often, as the therapist speaks tenderly on behalf of a client, a similar internal state automatically becomes active inside the client. In Level I intervention, the therapist is taking advantage of the capacity that all humans have to create internal state shifts in others by shifting their own internal states. Recent studies suggest that this happens because of the presence of "mirror neurons" in the brain. Mirror neurons were first identified in monkeys in the early 1990s, and then were identified more recently in humans. Siegel and Hartzell (2003) noted that these specialized neurons enable the triggering of internal states in one subject that resembles the states of others, thereby enabling empathy. When the therapist spoke on Michael's behalf from an internal state of tenderness, there was a good possibility that mirror neurons in Michael's CARE circuit would fire, and Michael would experience a similar internal state.

Notice that the therapist spoke *for* Michael rather than *to* Michael. By speaking for Michael, the therapist allowed Michael to feel the tenderness with which the therapist spoke on his behalf. By offering the assurance from his own internal state of tenderness, the therapist tugged at Michael's own dormant internal CARE state.

H: Well, what you're saying is all right, but . . . I mean, I'm feeling very defensive because I didn't mean for that to happen, I really didn't.

A slight shift in Michael's internal state could be detected in this statement, which enabled Michael to acknowledge his defensiveness.

T: (*The therapist speaks to Katrina for Michael again.*) And, I didn't understand that you would feel abandoned by me like that. If I would've understood that, I really wouldn't have done it the same way. (*Therapist turns to Michael.*) Is that true?
W: (*interrupting*) He knew I didn't want him to leave!
H: All she would've had to have done was asked me not to leave!

With this statement, Michael returned to his previous defensive state.

W: Your mom said that leaving was a good idea, and you listened to her. Remember, she said, "Michael you should go home and get to sleep. You were up all night."
H: I didn't think my mom was being so vicious and attacking you.

Michael continued in his defensive state, and his reactions were beginning to sound predictable.

W: (*exasperated*) I'm not portraying your mother as a vicious person. I'm saying that she was more concerned about your well-being at that time than worried about how I felt. And any signs I was trying to give you about not going like when I said, "Well at least turn on the TV before everybody goes, something, anything, you're leaving me in this room in the dark by myself." You just said, "Oh you'll be asleep," and you all walked away.

H: Well gee don't I feel like a real piece of shit. I mean I thought I was doing the right thing and turns out that I was just being a big jerk 'cause I managed to listen to the doctors.

W: (*angrily*) He's not gonna feel bad that I felt bad. Or acknowledge that maybe there was a possibility that I was trying to make it clear to him that I didn't want to be left alone, but that he didn't want to hear that from me. And that maybe he was wrong in leaving. But because he believes he didn't do anything wrong, I should just get off his back. That I need to let it go . . . there's something wrong with me that I can't let it go.

At this point, the couple was helplessly caught again in the pull of their interlocking anger–defensive states. Undaunted, the therapist decided to see if he could create an internal shift in Katrina. Sensing the unspoken sadness inside of Katrina, the therapist accessed a similar state inside of himself, then proceeded.

T: (*The therapist speaks softly to Katrina.*) I wonder if this is in there too. Let me try and say something for you. And then you tell me if this is right or not. (*The therapist speaks slowly, with a tone of sadness and resignation.*) I know, Michael, that it's hard for you to not feel defensive because it feels to you like I'm saying you did something wrong, right? And not only that, you did something wrong that has caused me so much pain that it was a *big* something wrong. So when you hear me say that, of course it's hard for you to do anything other than feel defensive, but I guess what I'm saying is, right or wrong—maybe I could have communicated it more, maybe you should've been more sensitive—the fact is it devastated me, that's all. (*The therapist turns and asks Katrina.*) Now what part of that do you need to correct?

The therapist had accessed his own internal PANIC circuit, and when he spoke for Katrina, both Michael and Katrina felt the effect of the softer quality of talking that emerged. From this place (*characterized by sorrow*), he spoke to Michael for Katrina, removing the judgmental words from her previous statements.

W: (*Katrina speaks directly to Michael. Her voice is soft, her tone conveying a quality of broken-heartedness.*) I feel like when I needed you most, you weren't there and that scared me . . . because I'm supposed to grow old with you and you need to be there for me and I'm supposed to be there for you and I feel like if I ever really needed you, you're . . . I'm afraid that you're not going to be there for me.

The therapist's internal state successfully evoked a similar state in Katrina, and, with the above statement, she had spoken to Michael from her heart.

T: That's what you're really worried about?

W: Yeah. (*Katrina speaks to Michael.*) I hear you say it all the time that you care about me and you're going to be there for me. I hear those words all the time. But, I don't feel that way.

H: Then I don't know what to do.

T: Let me help. Would it be okay if I talked to Michael just by myself for a few minutes?

This segment of dialogue in the fourth session illustrates the fact that sometimes Level I interventions work and sometimes they don't. The therapist's intervention worked only partially with Michael, and then Michael slipped back into his defensive state. The intervention worked very well with Katrina, however. Her shift from RAGE to SORROW was dramatic, leaving Michael speechless. We generally use Level I interventions first because they are "inexpensive" and efficient. They don't cost the therapist much in terms of the amount of time it takes to deliver the intervention, yet sometimes dramatic shifts follow as the therapist's softened internal state triggers something similar in the client.

When Level I interventions fail to create a state shift in one or both partners, the PET-C therapist moves to the second level of intervention. Katrina experienced a significant internal shift in response to the therapist's initial intervention, but Michael's response was only partial. Thus, the therapist decided to move to Level II intervention with Michael.

LEVEL II: EMBODYING
THE PREDICTIVE HABITS

Level II intervention generally occurs by stopping the conversation and electing to meet with partners individually for a period of time. The therapist creates internal shifts in each of them by embodying the habits that predict relationship success in his or her interactions with the client. Specifically, the therapist:

- Avoids a judgmental attitude.
- Finds the understandable part of the client's feelings.
- Identifies and acknowledges the bigger needs and fears behind the client's reactions.
- Offers assurances.
- Stands up for his or her point of view without putting down the client's point of view.
- Offers equal regard.

The habits that predict relationship success could also be called, "How to get a state shift in another person," because when a person embodies them, they have a soothing effect on others. This is true of all relationships, not just romantic ones. In successful relationships, each partner plays a part in soothing the other, helping him or her to avoid getting caught in defensive or aggressive internal states. The therapist will use his relationship with Michael, and his ability to embody the predictive habits, to soothe Michael and help him shift internal states.

The major moves of Level II intervention are summarized in Table 6.2. The intervention typically progresses in three stages: (Stage 1) The therapist offers strong support and validation. (Stage 2) The therapist issues a strong challenge to the client. (Stage 3) The therapist promotes a respectful dialogue.

The typical flow of Level II interventions can be seen in the following dialogue between Michael and the therapist. Recall that "Priming the Pump" had successfully created a shift in Katrina, but Michael seemed to be caught in an internal struggle. The therapist then asked to speak with Michael individually for a while. Katrina exited the room, leaving Michael and the therapist alone. Michael's jaw and fists were clenched, and he seemed to be avoiding eye contact with the therapist.

T: I want to make sure I understand what's going on inside of you, Michael.

H: (*speaking through clenched teeth*) I don't even know what's going on.

T: Let's take our time then.

H: I don't know what the hell I did wrong in any way, shape, or form. But everything that I was supposed to do, I did it wrong, and this has been the story of the past 11 years.

T: Yes.

H: I've been doing everything wrong since that damn hospital.

T: Yes, that's how it seems.

H: It's been nothing but bad. Everything that I've done has been discounted. It's the same thing over, over, over again.

T: Since that day in the hospital? And you don't really even know what it is that was so wrong about what you did on that day.

H: I don't know what the hell it is.

T: But it changed everything.

H: Yes, it did.

T: You sort of feel screwed in a way. I mean, you don't even know what it is that you were supposed to have done. You were going along just trying to do what you were supposed to do, and it messed her up real bad, and you weren't even trying to mess her up. Do I have that right?

H: Pretty much.

T: So then that gives you the uncertain feeling, like what does that tell you about life? You know, you're just going along trying to do the right thing, and then she shows up and says you've ruined my life. So that's kind of a scary position to be in.

TABLE 6.2
Creating Internal Shifts—Level II: Embodying the Predictive Habits

The therapist meets alone with each client, respectively, and does what the client's partner has difficulty doing: Avoids a judgmental attitude, finds the understandable part, identifies and acknowledges the "bigger" something that is at stake, offers assurances, asks for a change, then responds to resistance or defensiveness by offering more support, understanding, and assurances while continuing to ask for a change.

Stage 1: The Therapist Offers Strong Support and Validation

1. Avoid a judgmental attitude (Predictive Habit 1)
   Make your nonjudgmental attitude clear to the client, offering statements such as
   A. I don't think you did anything that is intrinsically wrong.
   B. Even if it was "wrong," it's not more "wrong" than the things your partner has done.
   C. I don't think you're any less emotionally mature than your partner. Both of you tend to get off track, sometimes in different ways.
   D. I would probably feel the same way if I were in your shoes.
   E. I might react in much the same way as you if I were in your shoes.
2. Find the understandable part (Predictive Habit 3)
   Acknowledge the understandable part of this partner's feelings or actions.
3. Identify and acknowledge the "bigger" something that is at stake for this partner. What is she or he afraid of? (Predictive Habit 6)
4. Offer Assurances (Predictive Habit 5)
   A. I think your feelings (opinions, beliefs, needs, preferences, etc.) are legitimate, and need to be recognized by your partner.
   B. I'm not going to be satisfied until you feel that your feelings (opinions, beliefs, needs, preferences, etc.) are being given equal consideration.

Stage 2: The Therapist Offers a Strong Challenge

5. Ask for a change. (This is the equivalent of predictive habit 2: Standing up for yourself without putting your partner down).
   A. State that although the client's current reactions to his or her partner are understandable, they are preventing the client from getting the cooperation and respect that he or she desires.

(continues)

TABLE 6.2
Creating Internal Shifts—Level II: Embodying the Predictive Habits
(Continued)

Note specifically the beliefs, attitudes, and actions that prevent him or her from getting what is needed from the partner (i.e., judgmental attitude, failing to find the understandable part, failing to identify and acknowledge the important and bigger issues at stake for the partner, failing to offer assurances, failing to offer equal regard).

B. State confidently that you believe that the client can have a powerful positive impact on his or her partner, and that you know how the client can do this. Paint a clear picture of the kind of thinking and action that is needed.

Suggest a nonjudgmental way of looking at the situation that opens possibilities for different ways of interacting.

Give a holistic "feel" for the kind of attitude, internal state, and verbal communication that would increase the client's effectiveness by speaking on the client's behalf to his or her (empty chair) partner about the disputed issue. Your statements are always formulated based on the predictive habits.

Stage 3: The Therapist Promotes a Respectful Dialogue

6. Invite the client to discuss reservations about the perspective or course of action you are suggesting.

7. Avoid judging or dismissing the client's reservations, and avoid arguing with the client. Instead, find the understandable part of the client's reservations, acknowledge the important underlying concerns that may be relevant to the client's resistance, offer assurances, then restate reasons for the requested change.

8. If the client still resists, communicate regard for client's decision. (This is the equivalent to Predictive Habit 4: Giving equal regard).
   - Assure the client that you are not going to try to talk the client into believing or doing anything that the client doesn't feel comfortable with.
   - Explain that you just want the client to think through the whole thing, and then do what makes the most sense to him or her.
   - Assure the client that, if you were the client, in the end you would do what you thought was right in spite of what some therapist might be saying.

9. If the client still resists, invite him or her to talk some more about it after thinking it over.

H: I never know what she's going to be pissed off about next.

T: I want you to know that I can see how frustrating this situation is for you,
       Michael. I'd probably feel the same way if I were you. I don't want you to
       live anticipating being criticized every time this subject comes up. I won't
       be satisfied if this continues to happen. I don't want you to live your life
       waiting for the next criticism to come, okay?

In the dialogue thus far, the therapist has indicated that he finds Michael's frustration and defensiveness understandable (Level II, intervention 2; see Table
6.2), and assured Michael (intervention 4) that he is committed to finding a way
for things to change so that Michael doesn't have to go through his life feeling
criticized. Emotionally supportive statements like these (Level II, interventions
1–4) generally have the effect of disarming defensive states. Michael appeared
to be no exception. At this point in the conversation, Michael's nonverbal behaviors indicated that his defensive state had dissipated. His jaw was no longer
clenched, and he was sitting back in his chair. In the following statement,
Michael seemed to be searching for answers rather than defending himself.

H: I still don't understand what I did wrong. I was there for her, the doctors
       told me that it was going to be at least five or six hours before anything hap-
       pened. And they were going to give her morphine so she could go to sleep.
       I guess the morphine didn't work. They told me to go home. I went in and
       I told her I was gonna go home for a little while and relax, maybe take a
       little nap. I'd be back in a couple of hours. I went home, relaxed, took
       a nap maybe 10 minutes. I was too wired to go to sleep and I was back in a
       couple of hours.

T: Michael, I want to be clear that I don't think you did anything wrong. You
       and Katrina are different, and have different needs. She needed you there,
       but another person might not have. You didn't do anything wrong, but that
       doesn't mean she shouldn't be upset. It's natural to get upset when you're
       disappointed, or when you feel hurt. Do you see what I mean?

Two things have happened here. First, the therapist assured Michael that he
doesn't think Michael did anything that was intrinsically wrong (Level II, intervention 1). Second, the therapist began to ask Michael for a change ("You didn't
do anything wrong, but that doesn't mean she shouldn't be upset"). Specifically,
the therapist asked Michael to change his thinking about Katrina's upset feelings. For 11 years, Michael had been operating under the assumption that Katrina's upset was unwarranted. Michael operated within a paradigm where nobody has the right to be upset unless somebody has screwed up. The therapist
counters with what seems to be a contradiction to Michael: You didn't screw up,
but I don't blame Katrina for being upset. The therapist's statement is confusing
to Michael.

H: I'm trying to understand, but it's not exactly making sense.

T: You did what you thought you should do, and that resulted in her feeling immeasurably hurt and abandoned. Did you do something wrong? Would everyone feel the same way as she did in that situation?

H: No.

T: It doesn't matter. Who cares? I mean, the fact is for whatever reason—maybe she was abandoned too much when she was younger, maybe other people would've just understood without her even saying anything that she needed someone to stay. Maybe someone would've. Maybe someone wouldn't have. Who cares? That's beside the point, Michael. I'm not sure that feels like beside the point to you.

H: I'm trying to soak it in.

So far, Michael's nondefensive attitude is holding. He feels challenged by the therapist's statements, but he is open to trying to understand. The therapist continues to offer assurances that he isn't judging Michael's behavior as inappropriate (Level II, intervention 1).

T: There doesn't have to be a villain here. There doesn't have to be a right guy, a wrong guy, a bad guy, a good guy.

H: Then why do I always feel like the villain?

T: She got hurt. When you get hurt, you usually kick into some kind of a self-protective state. So it's hard to say, "I'm hurting here, I don't know if I should've expected you to be there or not, but the fact is I'm just hurting." It's hard to say that. It's easier to say, "You did this to me!" Right?

For the first time, the therapist introduces an alternative explanation for Katrina's behavior that emphasizes how it was a reaction to feeling hurt or vulnerable. In doing this, the therapist is asking for a change in Michael's way of thinking about Katrina's motivation (Level II, intervention 5).

H: Yeah.

T: Were you watching her when she was talking about this?

H: Yeah. She was furious, red in the face mad.

T: I was watching her. And, I don't know if you were looking at her as closely as I was because I think what tends to happen is you just kind of shut down. But I saw her move back and forth between two places inside of her. One was mad, just like you said. And, another time I looked at her and she looked terrified.

H: Of what?

T: Of the feeling like she's going to have to be alone within this world. That kind of terrified.

H: Why would she be alone?

T: She's afraid that you didn't want to be there. She's afraid that you knew at some level how badly she needed you and you walked away.

H: So, she thinks that I did it on purpose?

T: No, she's afraid that you didn't care enough to think it through and realize that she was going to feel that way.

H: I figured she was going to be sleeping.

T: I know. I know. I'm not saying you did that wrong, Michael. I'm saying that's beside the point. And you know what? I don't think she even needs to hear you say that. I think it's really good enough for you to say, "I guess I don't know. Should I have known? I'm confused about it. I was trying to do the right thing, but I'm worried that I did the wrong thing, but that's all beside the point. The point is, you were over there in a time where you needed me the most and I wasn't there, and that's hurt you so bad that it's as fresh today as it was back then. That's what matters."

Here the therapist begins painting a clear picture (Level II, intervention 5B) of what Michael might say to Katrina that's different from what he usually says. Effective intervention must go beyond simply pointing out that Michael's defensiveness won't work. Often, clients are so caught in their internal reactions that they simply cannot imagine what they might say that would be better. They benefit from concrete examples of what effective communication would look and feel like. The therapist provides this information by stepping in and talking to (an imaginary) Katrina as if he were Michael. This method (speaking *for* Michael) has distinct advantages over speaking *to* Michael about what he might say to Katrina. The most important advantage is that the therapist can give Michael a feel for the attitude and internal state that are required in order to speak the words congruently.

The therapist's words require that Michael adopt a nonjudgmental attitude, assuring her that he doesn't blame her for being upset, and that he cares about the fact that he let her down. Up until now, he's had the attitude that Katrina is overreacting, making a big deal out of nothing, and that she has no right to be so upset. With the above words, the therapist models a different attitude, one in which Michael would disclose his confusion and worry that maybe he should have known better than to leave, and his sadness about having let her down.

The specific words that that PET-C therapists use when they model effective communication for clients are always based on the 10 habits that predict relationship success. When the therapist modeled communication for Michael, he simply translated a nonjudgmental attitude (Predictive Habit 1) into words, then spoke them as if they were coming from Michael. The therapist also then gave an example of how to offer a simple "I care about how you feel" type assurance (Predictive Habit 5), "The point is, you were over there in a time where you needed me the most and I wasn't there and that's hurt you so bad that it's as fresh today as it was back then. That's what matters."

In Phase I of PET-C, therapists generally don't worry about pointing out the connection between the statements they model and the predictive habits, because there is a risk that doing so may actually distract the client from the immediate task at hand (shifting internal states and interacting effectively with his/her partner right now). However, in Phase II of PET-C, therapists encourage clients to give explicit attention to translating the predictive habits into their everyday interactions with their partners.

T: (*After a brief pause to let his words soak in, the therapist continues.*) You have to be able to see her anger for what it is, Michael. She's just sort of protecting herself. She's just hurt. Should you have known what you were supposed to stay? Would I have known? I don't know, maybe I would have, maybe I wouldn't have, but that's really beside the point, Michael. The point is, she doesn't believe that you really care what that was like for her, because you're too busy defending yourself.

In the final words of this statement, the therapist identifies for Michael the habit he has that will need to change (Level II, intervention 5A). PET-C involves candid statements from the therapist regarding habits that need to change as well as what effective alternatives would be. The therapist's words ("you're too busy defending yourself") were a bit too strong for Michael to handle, and had the effect of reactivating a defensive state inside Michael.

H: (*Michael responds defensively.*) I have no way of understanding.

T: She doesn't think that you even *want* to understand.

H: All she had to do was just say "stay here," and I would've stayed. I wouldn't have gone anywhere. The doctors were telling me she was going to be asleep.

T: Yeah.

H: And that's why I left.

T: She wanted you to know.

H: I don't have ESP. I can't read her mind.

T: I understand. I'm certainly not saying you should've known, okay? But, she thinks that you don't really care.

H: And I don't know why.

T: I know why.

H: Why?

T: When she tries to talk about it, you don't say, "Oh my God, I'm so sorry!"

H: Well after you hear her talk about it and you heard the same thing over and over again 10 times, "I'm sorrys" pretty much stop coming. I can only apologize for something so many times. And then it's like, you have a problem! I've apologized for this one hundred thousand times. Then I start getting angry.

T: Yeah. So you couldn't say that to her tonight.

H: Apologize again?

T: She's heard your apologies as sort of like, "Can we just get this over with?" rather than, "I really want to understand what that was like for you. I did something that I didn't mean to do. I need to understand."

H: This is just one thing that she's upset about! There are hundreds of other ones she'll expect apologies for.

   With these words, Michael's defensiveness continues. The activation of a defensive internal state is a normal and usually necessary part of the Level II process. Level II intervention typically involves the following sequence: therapist disarms self-protective state; therapist challenges client's normal way of thinking/acting; client becomes defensive; therapist disarms the defensive internal state again.

   One of the PET-C mottos often recited at the Couples Research Institute is, "If the client doesn't become defensive, your challenge isn't strong enough." Therapists who are inexperienced with PET-C often try to avoid activating defensive states in clients, and feel they have blown it if a client becomes argumentative or resists accepting the challenges they offer. These therapists often tiptoe around delicate issues, and sugarcoat their words. In their attempts to avoid triggering defensiveness, they water down the impact of the challenge that their clients need to hear from them.

   Experienced PET-C therapists understand that activating a defensive state is an integral part of the trust-building process. In any relationship, people usually feel more comfortable and more trusting of each other once they've gotten through their first fight. PET-C therapists take advantage of the same relationship principle that applies to all intimate couple relationships: You can afford to risk offending each other if you know how to repair (see Chapter 3). Clients trust a therapist more if they feel that the therapist will be direct with them, and that they don't have to worry about what the therapist *really* thinks of them. Most clients can tell when a therapist is wording things carefully, and this is often taken as an indication that the therapist is being strategic and can't be trusted. Level II intervention usually involves the therapist saying things that make the client upset with the therapist, followed by the therapist soothing the client's upset feelings, not by rescinding the challenge but rather by validating the client's upset feelings, by becoming more vulnerable, by refraining from judging the client, by offering assurances, and by affirming the client's need to do what she or he thinks should be done, not what the therapist thinks should be done (Level II, intervention 8) . This process usually disarms the client's defensive state, and allows him or her to become receptive to the therapist's challenge. Watch now as the therapist responds to the newly reactivated defensive state in Michael by validating, assuring, then reinstating the challenge.

T: I'm not sure I understand. You're worried that if you open the floodgates, you'll never hear the end of it? If you give her an inch, she'll take a mile?

A vital part of Level II intervention is eliciting the client's reservations about the way of thinking or course of action the therapist is proposing (Level II, intervention 6). Here the therapist elicits Michael's reservations about letting Katrina know he feels bad about what happened.

H: Yep.

T: Well, I think that's a legitimate concern, Michael. I don't want you to spend the rest of your life apologizing. I don't think you'll have to, and I'll tell you why in just a minute. But let me say in advance that if my opinions don't feel right to you, I don't think you should do it. It's you who has to call the moves in your life, not me. If I was you, and I didn't agree with my therapist, I'd tell him to back off. I'll drop this if you want me to, Michael. I'll respect your right to make your own decision. I'm just hoping that you'll talk this thing through with me. Is it okay if we keep talking?

Therapists often feel that they need to challenge the "irrational" reservations clients have about changing. The PET-C therapist takes a different approach, devoting time to hearing the reservations out, then validating the understandable aspects of them (Level II, intervention 7). The therapist also assures Michael that he's not going to try to talk him into doing something that doesn't feel right to him. This is a regular part of Level II intervention.

H: Yes.

T: I want you to understand that I really don't believe that you'll need to keep apologizing hundreds of times once she feels that you really care about what happened in the hospital. Once you learn how to let her know that you care how she feels, and that you want to understand it, she'll shift. You seem to get stuck with your need to defend yourself and you never get to the point of allowing yourself to feel bad that she feels bad, or if you do feel bad, you don't communicate it to her. That habit doesn't work well for anyone, Michael. It doesn't work well for me when I do it either, and believe me; I've done it plenty of times in my own life. If you can learn to do this differently, she will respond differently. (*The therapist pauses, and then proceeds.*) You don't believe me, do you?

Only after validating and offering assurances has the therapist offered information that might satisfy Michael's reservations (Level II, intervention 7).

H: It's hard to believe.

T: I respect that. I'm willing to let this thing go. You have to decide. (The therapist pauses five seconds) What do you think you should do?

Again, the therapist assures Michael that he's not going to push him into doing anything that Michael's not comfortable with.

H: I haven't got a clue. (*Michael pauses momentarily, then proceeds.*) You're probably right. She doesn't think I care.

T: She thinks you're incapable of just caring about how she feels. She thinks that when she says, "I feel bad," that you hear, "You're a bad boy!" She thinks that all you care about is whether you're innocent or guilty. I think she's wrong about that.

H: I know I sound like a broken record. I keep insisting that I didn't do anything wrong because I don't know what else to say.

T: Well, it would sound something like this, Michael: "Katrina, I don't know. I'm confused. I'm afraid that maybe I was a bad person. I don't understand it, okay? And that's honest. I was trying to do the right thing, but that's beside the point. The fact is you sat there feeling devastated, like when you needed me the most, I wasn't there. Now, right or wrong, should you have wanted that, should I have been there? Hell, I don't know. All I know is you went through some of the worst moments of your life at that point and I wasn't there. And that isn't okay with me. And I'm scared it might happen again." (*speaking to Michael*) That's all it takes. It has to come from the heart you know. There's a place inside you that's not defensive.

For the second time, the therapist paints a clear picture of what a successful conversation would look and feel like (Level II, intervention 5B). Again, the therapist does this by stepping in and speaking *for* Michael rather than speaking *to* Michael about how he should speak to Katrina. In doing so, the therapist reminds Michael that the success of the communication hinges on his ability to speak to Katrina from a nondefensive place inside.

H: I don't know where it is . . . I've been on the defensive for so long.

T: I know, but I hear it in between the cracks. There's a place where there's only tenderness.

H: I try to give it to her all the time.

T: Well, she needs it now.

H: I tell her I love her every day. Most of the time, she just turns around and walks away.

T: She has not healed from this. We have to go to this. It'll change your life, Michael.

H: I don't know if I can say it like you did.

T: No, you have to say it in your own words, and you have to speak from your heart.

H: It might sound like a rehearsed speech.

T: Well you certainly wouldn't want to be bullshitting on this one, Michael.

H: No. I'm trying to figure out a way to put it that it'd sound more like me.

T: Sure, that's what you need to do. But more important than the words are where it's coming from in there. You know what I mean?

H: I think so.

At this point, the therapist felt that Michael's state had shifted sufficiently to end the conversation. He encouraged Michael to think these things over in the waiting room while he spoke with Katrina for a while. The therapist then met with Katrina and used Level II interventions to solidify a state shift in her. The couple was then reunited and continued the conversation. This time, however, each partner is approaching the conversation from a different place inside.

H: (*Michael makes eye contact with Katrina, then speaks softly.*) I didn't mean to abandon you in the hospital, and if I knew it was going to make you feel that bad I would have never left.

W: I don't know if it was because of my past, the things that have happened . . . maybe I over-react on things . . . it might not have bothered somebody else as much. Maybe you didn't see that it would upset me so much and it wasn't clear to you what I needed at that time. But it did really hurt me. I need you, though. I need you to be part of my life, and I want you to be there with me, and I don't want to lose that. I don't want to lose you Michael, especially because we don't communicate right, you know?

H: We could start communicating a little better.

T: What happened inside of you when she was saying that? What were you feeling?

H: It made me feel good that she still wants me in her life.

T: I wonder if you can try to tell her that.

H: (*Michael pats the seat next him, motioning Katrina to scoot over.*) I'll meet you in the middle. (*They each scoot toward each other and they embrace. Katrina hugs Michael around the neck and cries. Michael kisses her neck softly.*) Sorry.

Michael had, of course, said "sorry" many times before, but this time it came from a different place inside of him. His CARE circuit was firing, and Katrina felt the difference in his manner. There was tenderness in his tone and words. For the first time, she believed that Michael cared about how she had felt alone in the hospital 11 years before. The therapist continued by asking Katrina to explain more fully to Michael what it was like for her, but she declined. The issue that had clouded 11 years of their marriage suddenly didn't feel like such a big deal to her.

This session illustrates how profoundly a couple's communication can be influenced by their internal states, and how radically the communication can shift once a shift in internal states occurs. At the beginning of the conversation, each partner had difficulty responding to the other in ways that soothed the other's internal state. In fact, their responses tended to trigger more defensiveness in each other. The therapist shifted each partner's internal state by interacting with each partner himself, using the habits that predict relationship success.

Level II movements reflect the process by which all people get increased cooperation and receptivity from others. The moves are relatively simple, but few partners in conflict use them effectively. The moves require that one be able to influence one's own internal states effectively in the face of a resistant or defensive stance on the part of another person. We believe that most successful therapists intuitively use Level II methods to influence their clients positively.

The effectiveness of Level II intervention hinges on the extent that clients experience both profound emotional support, as well as a powerful challenge to their current way of thinking or interacting. The therapist combines radical support with radical challenge. This is only possible when the therapist is able to deliver challenges from a state of tenderness (CARE). If the support isn't there, partners will often continue to be caught in overly self-protective states. If the challenge isn't there, partners will often continue with assumptions and habits that doom their relationships to failure. If the therapist is combative or critical, partners will not experience internal state shifts. In Level II intervention, the therapist takes a straightforward, pull-no-punches approach with clients, but does so from an internal state of tenderness. To do this, the therapist must be highly skilled at influencing his or her own internal states throughout therapy, a topic that will be discussed more fully in Chapter 13.

Stage 3 of Level II intervention (promoting a respectful dialogue) is particularly critical. When the client resists the therapist's request for change, the therapist avoids arguing or attempting to persuade, and instead acknowledges the understandable aspects of this resistance, affirming the need the client has to decide for him- or herself what belief or course of action needs to be taken. The therapist continues by asking if it would be okay to just continue talking things through, so that she or he can better understand the client. When the client continues to articulate his or her reservations, the therapist acknowledges the importance of the reservations, offers information and assurances relevent to the reservations, then makes another request for change. The therapist repeats the whole process as many times as is needed. Although there is often a general flow of steps as depicted in Table 6.2, the steps are flexible, and need not occur in the stated order. Nor do all of them necessarily need to happen in order for an internal state shift to occur.

LEVEL III: INTERACTING DIRECTLY WITH AN INTERFERING STATE

Using Level I and II methods, the PET-C therapist can create needed internal shifts in most situations; however, some still will not shift. In these situations, the therapist either applies Level III methods, or moves on to "Getting Each Partner on Board" (see Chapters 7 and 8). Level III intervention methods are particularly suited to situations in which the client acknowledges the value of the course of action the therapist is suggesting, but simply can't muster the motivation to do it. The client is caught in an interfering internal state, but has awareness that he or she is caught, and that this really isn't working well.

With Level III methods, the therapist helps the client interact directly with the internal state in a way that helps it shift. The therapist accomplishes this by directing the client's attention in a way that strengthens activation of the prefrontal cortex, the part of the brain that is largely responsible for creating internal shifts during normal, everyday life (Davidson, 2001a; Seigel, 1999). As described in Chapter 1, when clients get hijacked by internal states that prevent them from interacting with their partners in needed ways, the entire brain becomes organized by the preprogrammed goals of the internal states. Level III intervention helps clients free up a part of the brain from the tyranny of such hijackings, and use this (prefrontal) area to interact with the hijacked areas in a way that short-circuits the strength of the hijacking.

In Level III intervention, the therapist begins by directing the client's attention to the fact that she or he is "under the influence" of an internal state that has an agenda of its own. The therapist helps the client pay attention to the internal cues that signal the state's presence. The client is encouraged to avoid trying to make the state go away and instead to simply study the internal state without trying to control it. The client becomes more aware of the thoughts, feelings, and urges that characterize the state. Then, the therapist helps the client conduct internal experiments with the state, noticing how "it" reacts to various thoughts, or proposed courses of action. As the client interacts with the internal state, the state shifts. A summary of the individual steps of Level III intervention can be found in Table 6.3. As with Level II interventions, Level III steps need not occur in the order listed, and all of the steps are not necessary in order for a shift to occur. Many of our Level III intervention steps have been inspired by the work of Gendlin (1981) and Schwartz (1995).

The following dialogue between a PET-C therapist and a husband illustrates Level III interventions. This dialogue occurred in the fifth session of therapy. The husband, Stuart, had come to couples therapy with his wife, Samantha.

TABLE 6.3
Creating Internal Shifts—Level III: Interacting Directly
With an Interfering State

The therapist helps the client experience an internal shift by sustaining attention on the internal state, attributing agency to the state, assuming a welcoming, respectful non-controlling attitude toward the state, and by engaging in a dialogue with the internal state.

1. **Get "Alongside" of It**
   A. Attributing agency to the internal state
      - "Something inside of you resists? Something says, No, I don't feel like doing that?"
      - "So, when your partner acts like she or he just did, you have an automatic reaction. . . . You think things like. . . . You feel . . ., and you want to. . . . Right?"
   B. Personalizing the internal state
      - "So, when this happens (or when you think of doing this), some part of you objects, and says something like, _____ Right?"
      - "So, it's like you're having several reactions at once? One part of you agrees, but another part hesitates?"

2. **Shift from External to Internal Focus**
   A. Requesting permission to focus on this internal state
      - "Can we pay attention to this part of you for a minute? I have a feeling that this is real important. Would that be okay?"
   B. Inviting the client to slow down
      - "For a few minutes, let's pay especially close attention to this part of you. In order to do this best, we'll have to slow the conversation down somewhat, so that you have time to listen to yourself more carefully than you usually have time to do during regular life."
   C. Using language that invites reflection
      - "See if you can sense how this part of you feels about . . ."
      - "Take a minute and check with this part of you, and ask it . . ."
      - "See if you can get a feel for how this part of you would respond to the question . . ."
   D. Exploring the internal state
      - "What kind of thoughts are going through your head right now?"
      - "What is the internal feeling you are having? What is the physical feeling? Where do you feel it most strongly?"
      - "What do you feel like saying or doing right now?"

(continues)

TABLE 6.3
(Continued)

3. **Assume a Welcoming Attitude**
   - "See if you can allow this part of you to stay for a few moments. Let's just try to keep him [or her] company for a while. Lets roll out the red carpet . . . give him [or her] the seat of honor."
   - "I'd like for you to give this part of you a message from me. Let that part know that I have a lot of respect for him [or her], because he [or she] has taken care of you through some very difficult times."
   - "Let this part of you understand that I know she [or he] must be very tired . . . I have a lot of respect for the dedication to you that part has."
   - "Let this part of you know that I'd like to be able to help take some of the burden off of his [or her] shoulders. I think that part could use a vacation! But I won't do anything unless it's okay with him [or her]."

4. **Interact With the Internal State**
   A. After making any comment or observation, ask the client to check and see how this part of him reacted to it.
   B. Ask the state to consider different ways of looking at the situation or different courses of action.
   C. Elicit the reservations, objections, worries or fears that fuel the assumptions of the internal state.
      - "What reservations does this part of you have about the course of action I'm proposing? And what would be the worst thing about that?"
   D. Acknowledge the understandable aspects of the reservations, objections, worries, or fears that fuel the assumptions of the internal state.
      - "That makes sense. Now I see why you feel that way." (Restate the reasons behind the reservation or worry.)
   E. Offer explanations or assurances that address the reservations, objections, worries or fears that fuel the client's internal state:
      - The explanations or assurances you introduce will be based upon what you have learned about the client's fears or worries.
      - Offer the explanation or assurance, then ask the client to check and see how this part of him or her is reacting to your statements. Often this leads to another question or statement on your part, followed by your request for the client to check his or her gut reaction again, and so on. In this way, you create a respectful dialogue with the resisting part. Don't imply that this part of the client should be assured by your assurances.

(continues)

TABLE 6.3
(Continued)

- Validate the reluctance of this part of your client to accept the explanation or assurance.
F. Assure the resisting part of the client that you're not going to try to force it to change.
  - "I'm not going to try to get this part of you to change if it doesn't feel right."
  - "If she [or he] changes, it will be because she [or he] wanted it to, not because of anyone's bullying. Right now we just want to know more about this part of you."
G. Ask what it would take for this part to feel okay about trying something different.
  - "Ask yourself if there is anything that your partner could do or say that would make it easier for this part of you to react differently."
H. Ask if it would be okay to try doing it differently now (If not, listening to why not).
  - "Is the feeling of hesitation still the same? Check with this part of you and see if it would be okay to give it another try."
I. If necessary, affirm the client's unwillingness or inability to make a change at this moment.
  - Suggest that perhaps this part just needs to feel more understood before it could try something different.
  - Suggest that you're happy to have just been able to learn more about what happens inside, and why.

5. Be Persistent

"Let this part of you know that we'll take as long as needed to make a plan for doing things different. If she or he is not okay with doing anything different in the end, we'll respect that. For now, we'll just keep exploring.

During the assessment interviews, it became clear to the therapist that Stuart and Samantha had a core difference on the invest-in-the-future-first versus live-in-the-moment-first dimension (see Chapter 5). The inability of the partners to handle their differences in this area led to gridlock over financial issues. Stuart believed that Samantha's spending was wildly out of control, and Samantha thought that Stuart had a neurotic obsession with saving money for the future.

In the preceding session, the therapist had created a successful shift in each partner that enabled them to compromise on how to approach upcoming Christmas shopping. During the following week, Stuart went out of town on business. When he returned, he found that Samantha had spent more money on her mother's Christmas present than they had agreed to. He was furious and began criticizing Samantha. In turn, she simply refused to talk to him about it. On the way to their therapy session, Stuart tried to initiate discussion again. Samantha still refused to talk.

The first five minutes of the session involved more of the same. The therapist suggested that he speak with each partner separately for a few minutes, meeting with Samantha first. Using Level II methods, the therapist was able to help Samantha move from a defensive to a more receptive state, and she became willing to break her silence and try to talk to Stuart about the issue. The therapist then met with Stuart, one-on-one. The following dialogue then occurred between the therapist and Stuart.

T: How you approach her about this is a big thing. Just like we were talking about last week, your style and your attitude are the most important thing. So, I just want you to check for a minute and see how you are in there.

The therapist begins to direct the client's attention to what is happening inside of him. When partners are upset, this is exactly the opposite of what they usually want to do. Their attention is usually riveted on the details of the perceived injustice, or possibly on how they should respond to the injustice. For an internal state shift to occur, the therapist must shift the client's attention from the external circumstances to his or her internal reactions (Level III, intervention 2A). This kind of self-monitoring requires activation of the prefrontal area of the brain which is centrally involved in creating state shifts.

H: (*looking agitated and angry*) Honestly, I feel like I'm blowing smoke out of my ass. It seems like we're not going anywhere. I try to have a conversation about the spending plan, which she agreed to, but she won't even hear it. She's going to just do what she wants. End of discussion.

T: I see what you mean. I'm sure I'd be pretty upset if I were you, too.

Here the therapist mixes in some Level II intervention process, acknowledging that Stuart's feelings are understandable and assuring him that he's not out of line for feeling this way (Level II, interventions 2 and 4).

H: I'm like, "I want to talk about this and you are giving me the impression that there is nothing to talk about because it isn't what you want."

T: Right. Hey Stuart, let's see if you can get something different from her tonight, okay? I think you can, but first we're going to have to figure out how to get you a little more relaxed, right?

The therapist begins to ask for a change (Level II, intervention 5), making it clear that he believes that Stuart can influence Samantha through his own reactions (Level II, intervention 5B).

H: I know. Right now I'm so mad that I know I'll screw it up if I try to talk to her.

Here is the therapist's clue that Level III intervention may be useful. Stuart is acknowledging that he needs to shift internal states, but implies that he's having trouble shifting.

T: Right. When you're in this mode, you have a one-track mind.

By saying, "when you're in this mode," the therapist introduces to Stuart the idea that his reaction is state-driven (Level III, intervention 1A). By implication, the therapist is communicating the possibility that when Stuart is not in this "mode," he might not react to Samantha the same way.

H: Pretty much.
Th: Okay, and when you get here, in this place where you're at right now. . . .
H: I feel like I have to make her see how out of line she's been.

Again, the therapist introduces language that helps Stuart realize that there are different "places" inside of him from which he reacts, and implies that different places will produce different reactions. Throughout Level III intervention, the PET-C therapist reinforces the notion that the client's reactions are state-driven. The therapist helps clients pay attention to the internal states that drive their reactions, using language like, "When you're in that *place* inside," "When you're in this *state of mind*," or "When you're in this *operating mode*."

T: I think I understand. (*five seconds of silence*) I know this might be difficult for you, but for a few minutes, I'd like to ask you to try to stop thinking about Samantha, and let's try to slow things down and pay closer attention to what's happening inside of you right now. Would it be okay to shift your focus for a while?

The therapist always asks permission to shift the focus of the conversation (Level III, intervention 2A). The therapist also cues Stuart into the fact that, if he is willing, the conversation between them is about to shift in tempo (Level III, intervention 2B). If Stuart resists, the therapist will use Level II methods to validate and respect the resistance, then help Stuart resolve it.

H: Okay. I'm just going around in circles anyway.

T: How does your body feel right now? See what you can notice about how it is in there.

In Level III intervention, the goal of the therapist is to help clients pay attention to the feelings that come up with an internal state, and to the "thoughts that these feelings are having." Clients often have ready-made thoughts or opinions about their partners or about their situations and can deliver them to the therapist at a moment's notice. This is not what the therapist is looking for. For this reason, the therapist uses language that invites Stuart to take a moment and check with his internal state before he answers the question. Rather than asking Stuart, "What is it like in there?" the therapist asks Stuart to "See what you can notice about how it is in there" (Level III, intervention 2C). This statement gives permission for Stuart to do some noticing before he responds. Other similar statements offered by PET-C therapists might be, "Check and see how you feel in there about. . . , " or "See if you can sense what your gut reaction is to . . . , " or "Take a minute and pay attention to your internal reaction when I say. . . ."

In helping clients explore their internal states, the therapist begins the process of increasing and sustaining Stuart's awareness of the internal state that blocks him from interacting successfully with Samantha. The therapist will use a variety of methods for sustaining Stuart's internal awareness. Attention to the physical quality of the internal state is just one of these methods (Level III, intervention 2D). The therapist knows that the longer Stuart is mindful of the internal state, the more likely it is that the state will shift.

H: On the way over here, my stomach, up here, felt like it was in a knot.

T: How about right now?

Stuart reports how he *was* feeling, rather than how he *is* feeling. Internal state shifts usually occur when a client gives attention to the state she or he is feeling right now, not in the past.

H: Right now it feels . . . the only thing I can think of is, I feel . . . (*Stuart lets out a groan. He seems to be struggling to find the right word*).

T: Okay. That (*groan*) sums it up pretty well! (*Both laugh.*) So you're sort of caught . . . you're cycling around and around inside that space. That same space. . . .

Again, the therapist reinforces the idea that Stuart is reacting in a particular way because he's caught in a particular *space* inside. The implication is that if he could move into a different place, he might be able to react differently.

H: Right now, I feel like my mind is just stuck on one thing. I can't let her get away with it this time.

T: All right. So this is a critical moment right now, I would suggest, in your marriage. I've got you right in that space where you tend to get, you're in there, the only thing you can think of really is . . .

H: Why can't she stick to an agreement for once?

T: Right. "I can't let her get away with it."

H: I'm just trying to have a nice conversation with her, and she's like, "This is the way it is, and I don't want to discuss anymore of it, this is what I want."

T: Stuart, I want you to know that I believe you need something different from Samantha, and I know how you can get it. But to get it, you'll need to speak to her from a different place inside. You'll need to find a way to switch gears. Do you know what I mean?

The therapist conveys his belief that Stuart can get something different from Samantha by changing his own reactions to her (Level II, intervention 5B). He also makes it clear that this will require an internal state shift.

H: I know. I just don't know if I can do it. Right now I feel stuck.

T: That's okay. I can help you do it. You just have to recognize the need for it.

H: I know I can't talk to her when I feel like this.

T: Here's how I'm thinking about it, Stuart. You're a complex guy, and there are many different parts of your personality . . . you have many different operating modes. There is one part of you—and he's here right now—who reacts strongly in situations like this one. When Samantha shuts down, he comes up and takes over. And when this happens, he's no longer just a part of you, he consumes all of you. For a few minutes, I'd like for you to try to think of what's happening inside of you this way, okay?

H: (*nods*)

The therapist invites Stuart to think of his internal state as having a mind of its own, as if it were a separate person inside of him (Level III, intervention 1B). This analogy is warranted, given the nature of executive operating systems (EOS), as described in Chapter 2. When a person is under the influence of one EOS, his thoughts, feelings, and motivations will be dramatically different from when he is under the influence of another. When a person thinks of his or her internal state as being like another person who lives inside of him or her, then it enables the person to have a *relationship* with this state, and to influence this state through the relationship. The same principles that apply to interpersonal relationships apply to the internal relationship. Just as a client's reaction to his or her partner can increase or decrease the odds that the partner will become more cooperative, a client's reaction to the "partner" inside of his or her own skin (the uncooperative internal state) can increase or decrease the likelihood that this internal state will become more cooperative. In the following dialogue, watch how the therapist helps Stuart cultivate a relationship with his uncooperative internal state. The therapist will help Stuart pay respectful attention, understand and validate, offer assurances, and listen carefully to the internal state.

T: One thing that helps sometimes is to just make it clear to him (*the internal state*) that you are here, too. This guy that I see come up from time to time, he's one of your boys . . . he's trying to take care of you in there, but he's not all of you. Sometimes, when he comes up, you seem to disappear. But you're here now, both you and him, right? I mean, I'm talking to you, but you can feel him here too. (*Stuart nods.*) So, one thing that helps is just to acknowledge his presence when he arrives. You can do that by simply saying inside, "Oh, you again" or "I know you're here." "I know you're there because I can feel it, and I find myself thinking the thoughts that you specialize in." Do you know what I am saying?

It's a powerful intervention simply for a client to use language to punctuate his internal experience in such a way that enables him to become more mindful of it. By asking Stuart to refer to his internal state as "you" rather than "me," the therapist helps Stuart separate a part of himself from the state, so that he can be in a relationship with it (Level III, intervention 1A).

Therapists who are not experienced in using "parts" language with clients often assume that clients will be uncomfortable thinking of themselves in this way. The most unusual aspect of this way of working is assigning personal pronouns to internal states (referring to the internal state as "him" or "her"). Our experience is that most clients instinctively see the value in using this kind of language, and that those who are uncomfortable initially soon grow more comfortable. All of us have at least some experience that is congruent with this way of looking at ourselves (e.g., we all know the feeling of being torn between two parts of ourselves when making decisions). The degree of comfort attained by clients who are initially uncomfortable seems to depend most heavily upon the therapist's level of comfort with the language. When therapists are confident and comfortable, clients tend to follow. With some clients, it's also important for the therapist to be able to explain in logical terms the validity of conceptualizing internal process this way. When clients understand that this way of thinking about things actually closely parallels what we are learning scientifically about the organization of our minds, they are usually willing to try thinking this way.

H: I never thought about it that way.

T: Do you still feel him here, now?

H: (*Stuart instinctively closes his eyes. He appears to be paying attention to how he feels.*) Yeah.

The therapist will repeatedly draw Stuart's attention back to the internal state, checking to see how the state is reacting. The therapist wants to prevent a strictly intellectual or theoretical conversation from occurring between the therapist's mind and Stuart's mind. Rather, the therapist wants to promote interaction between Stuart and his internal state (Level III, intervention 4).

T: All right. I don't want you to try to make him go away. Instead, let's just try and stay with him for a few minutes. What I mean by that is, uh, he's here, we might as well see if we can keep him good company. One thing you can do is recognize how he feels. Pay attention to that feeling in your stomach, and try to relax the rest of your body around it. (*Stuart still has his eyes closed.*) Just because he is tense doesn't mean that the rest of you has to be. See if you can relax the rest of your body. (*Stuart shifts position and relaxes.*) All right? Just focus on the feeling there. Still feel that knot? How is it going?

H: I feel it.

The therapist helps Stuart take a welcoming attitude toward the internal state (Level III, intervention 3). This is an unusual internal move for most clients to make. When a person realizes that they are in a mood that is interfering with their goals, it is natural to try to make the mood change. However, attempting to control one's mood often sets up a symmetrical struggle between the person and their mood. In PET-C, we encourage clients to seek cooperation from their internal states, not control over them. A healthy internal relationship parallels a healthy interpersonal relationship. People in relationships don't like to be controlled. Rather, they will usually become more cooperative if they are respected and encouraged to make their own decisions. Internal states seem to operate according to the same rules. They are more likely to shift if the client tries to welcome and understand them rather than attempting to take control and make them go away. The therapist helps Stuart separate from the internal state by using language that distinguishes the conscious, observing part of himself from the automatic internal reactions of his internal state by attributing agency to the internal state (Level III, intervention 1A), and by personalizing the state (Level III, intervention 1B). The therapist then encourages the conscious part of Stuart to assume a welcoming, exploratory attitude toward the internal reactions he's having.

T: Is it okay to sit here and pay attention to it? (*Stuart nods.*) Let's try a few things. I'm going to say a few things, and as I say them, I want you to pay close attention to the spontaneous, gut reaction that you have inside. I want to know how this part of you reacts to some things. He'll communicate by gut reactions, and that's different from well-thought out responses, okay?

H: Okay.

The therapist sets the stage for gaining a better understanding of the internal state by asking Stuart to pay close attention to his gut reactions (Level III, intervention 4A). Often, clients are not closely attuned to their automatic, internal reactions, and will report to the therapist what they *think* about the therapist's statements rather than their instantaneous internal responses. For this reason, the therapist asks Stuart to pay close attention ahead of time.

T: First, let him know that you and I agree with him—that Samantha needs to understand that you won't tolerate her breaking agreements she's made. Now, check and see if you felt anything when I said that.

The therapist acknowledges and validates the reasons why this part of Stuart is so upset about things, then asks Stuart to check directly with his internal state for a reaction (Level III, intervention 4A).

H: The tightness backed off a little.

T: Okay. Good. He's listening. Let's see how he reacts to another idea. Let him know that, when you talk to Samantha, I don't think that he's the one who should do the talking. When *he* speaks, Samantha shuts down. She and he have some bad history, and now every time she hears from him, she tunes him out. He's lost his effectiveness with her. I think that the communication needs to come from another part of you. Now, see if you can tell what his reaction is to that.

The therapist asks this part of Stuart to consider a different approach, then elicits the reactions that come up from this part of him (Level III, interventions 4B, and 4C).

H: He thinks that's fine, but somebody needs to make sure that Samantha knows that I'm not going to be taken advantage of any longer. He wants to know if the part of me who does the talking is going to make sure Samantha knows that.

T: Yes, but only if Samantha doesn't come to this realization on her own. I'm going to help you speak from a part of you that will help Samantha feel less threatened and defensive, and more able to care about how you feel. It probably won't even be necessary to take a hard line with her.

With these words, the therapist both offers an assurance (Level III, intervention 4E) and restates his conviction that if Stuart can shift internal states, Samantha will treat him better of her own accord.

H: But I've tried being nice to her many times before, and it doesn't work.

T: Stuart, I'm confident that, if I can help you connect with the right place inside, this time will be different.

In the above exchanges, the therapist continues to elicit the worries and reservations that lie behind Stuart's reluctance (Level III, intervention 4C). In response, the therapist offers explanations and assurances that directly address the concerns of this reluctant part of Stuart (Level III, intervention 4E).

H: He's skeptical.

T: No problem. Let's check and see if there is anything that might help him feel better about trying this out.

This is an example of Level III, intervention 4G. It's ideal if this part of Stuart becomes actively involved in working out a solution, rather than simply accepting the direction set by the therapist.

H: Nothing comes to mind.

T: See if he's willing to make a deal. Tell him that, if he really backs off and allows another part of you to communicate with Samantha, and she still doesn't voluntarily acknowledge the validity of your feelings, he can come in and do things his way.

H: (*Stuart looks at the therapist skeptically.*) Really?

T: Really. (*Therapist pauses.*) But I want to ask him to trust my judgment about when it's truly a lost cause.

H: (*Stuart pauses for about five seconds, then exhales slowly, looking defeated.*) I don't think this will work. I think it *is* a lost cause.

This statement signaled a state shift in Stuart. The above words were spoken with a tone of resignation, not anger.

T: Whoa. I think I lost you there, Stuart. I feel like I just came into direct contact with somebody else inside of you. Who is this? (*Stuart is silent.*) Let's try to stay with this guy for a moment or two, Stuart. I don't think I know him yet. Would that be okay?

H: I just think I need to come to grips with the fact that she is the way she is . . . she's not going to change.

The shift in Stuart's attitude seems fairly dramatic to the therapist. A moment ago, he was in a "I'm going to change her if it's the last thing I do" mode, now he's in a "What's the point—she'll never change" mode.

T   This part of you feels real different to me than other one. The other guy had a lot of fight. This guy seems to feel it's not worth the fight.

H: Yeah, you get to that point after a few years.

T: Hey, give this guy a message from me. I won't blame you if you throw in the towel. If you just can't muster up the motivation to try tonight, I'll understand. There's always another day. I'm serious. I don't walk in your shoes. You have to do what you really believe is best. You're the boss. If you say it's no go, it's no go. No questions asked.

H: No, I'm not going to just give up. I'll try.

The therapist's statement seemed to trigger another state shift in Stuart. Often the most powerful shifts come when the therapist stops pushing for change and assures the client's that she or he will respect the client's decision (Level III, intervention 4F). Clients often seem to resist therapists in order to exert some control over their lives. When the therapist makes it clear that he's not going to try to control Stuart, he shifts.

T: I want you to know that I don't believe it's hopeless, Stuart. Not for a second. You feel like you've tried everything that you know of, and it hasn't worked. But I believe that there are some things that you don't yet know how to do, and I can help you learn. And when you do, Samantha *will* respond to you.

Here the therapist moves in with some strong assurances, and restates his conviction that a change in Stuart will lead to the changes he desires in Samantha (Level II, intervention 5B).

H: I wish I could believe that.
T: I like the sound of that. That's a good wish. Good enough for me. You ready to get started?
H: I don't know how.
T: The first thing is that I need an agreement from the big guy to allow you to operate from a different place in there . . . a place where you are willing to believe that, just possibly, there's still hope. Check and see if he's willing.
H: He'll try.
T: I want you to imagine yourself saying to Samantha the kind of things I'm about to say. As I'm saying the words, try to allow yourself to move to a place inside where you match my attitude as you say them, okay? (*Stuart nods; therapist speaks softly, with tenderness.*) "Samantha, I know that I reacted really strongly when I found out how much you spent on your mom's present, and that probably wasn't good. I just assumed the worst, and I don't think I even asked you why you did that, and I'm sorry about that. Can you try to explain your thinking now, because I'll try to understand." (*speaking to Stuart*) Could you find a place inside where you could say something like that?
H: That would be tough. I don't want to give her the impression that she's off the hook.
T: Right. You don't want her to think that you're okay with the fact that she spent that much, or that she didn't talk it over with you first, if she was wanting to alter the agreement.
H: Absolutely.

T: And you really, really want her to understand that, right?

H: Right.

T: I want her to understand that, too, Stuart. See if this makes sense to the
      big guy. If she feels understood by you, the odds are much better that she
      will try to understand you, right? If she feels threatened, or criticized, she
      might feel defensive, right?

H: I guess.

T: Stuart, I want to assure you that I will personally make sure that you are
      able to let her know exactly how you feel about this before the conversa-
      tion is over. I just want to make sure that she will be able to hear you. No-
      body can really respond well when they feel criticized. You can afford to
      allow yourself to care how she feels. In fact, it doesn't have to cost you any-
      thing. There is no downside here. By allowing yourself to relax, and to care
      about her feelings, you can only increase the odds that she will want to co-
      operate with you. Does that make sense?

H: Okay, I think I'm getting it.

   In the above sequence, the therapist asked Stuart to move to a different place,
and consider saying different things than he normally does to Samantha (Level
III, intervention 4B). A predictable sequence followed: Stuart responded with a
reservation (Level III, 4C), the therapist validated this reservation (Levell III,
4D), then offered explanations and assurances that directly addressed the reservation (4E). Having done this, if Stuart's reservations were to have persisted, the
therapist was prepared to put the decision back into Stuart's hands. As it turned
out, Stuart's reservations were lessening.

T: But you really have to allow yourself to go there inside. You can't fake it.
      The words will be hollow. You literally have to let yourself go to a softer
      place inside.

   PET-C therapists emphasize over and over again the distinction between trying to do the right thing and connecting with the internal state from which the
right thing naturally emerges. Clients need to understand that, when it comes to
intimate relationships, you can't succeed by being a wordsmith or spin doctor.
Partners are attuned to each other's emotional states, and the states are what matter. The right words spoken without sincere feeling will have little effect.

H: I don't know if I can do it.

T: I know that you can, Stuart, if you really want to. Let's try it again. Listen
      to me and see if you can allow yourself to go there. (*Therapist speaks
      slowly, with feeling.*) "Samantha, I know you probably think that I'm think-

ing already that I'm right and you're wrong. But I'm really trying to keep an open mind. I don't understand why you did that. I will really try to understand, though, if you try to explain it." (*speaking to Stuart*) Can you go there?

H: I'm getting closer.

A common mistake among therapists who have difficulty creating internal shifts is simply giving up too soon (see Level III, intervention 5), and accepting a client's statement ("I can't do it") at face value. A skillful therapist knows how to respect and validate this kind of statement, then continue the conversation, communicating hope and optimism until finally, the state shifts.

T: Okay. Listen closely to yourself again. What would help you be able to go there? (*Level III, intervention 4G*)

H: (*Stuart meditates silently for about 10 seconds.*) I just want her to listen to me, too.

T: I will make sure that happens, Stuart. But not right at the beginning. I want you to follow my lead when we go back in there, okay. Not just in the beginning. Let yourself match my attitude as the conversation unfolds. If you do that, she will respond

H: I'll try.

Stuart did try. He initiated the conversation by sincerely assuring Samantha that he really did care how she felt. When Samantha responded with a criticism, Stuart began getting defensive, but allowed himself to be influenced by a Level I ("priming the pump") intervention the therapist offered. Samantha also responded to Level I interventions, and was able to acknowledge the validity of Stuart's feelings, and apologized for failing to consult him about the purchase.

The dialogue between the therapist and Stuart illustrates the implementation of Level III interventions for helping clients make internal shifts. In the process of Level III intervention, the therapist generally incorporates elements of Level I and II interventions as well. However, Level III adds a new dimension: Inviting sustained attention to internal states, attributing agency to the states, assuming a welcoming, respectful noncontrolling attitude toward the states, and engaging in a dialogue with the internal states.

The interventions for creating internal shifts in clients typically unfold in stepwise fashion. The therapist engages in Level I intervention, and only progresses to Level II, if Level I interventions fail to create the needed internal shifts. Likewise, the therapist moves to Level III interventions only if Level II interventions fail to create needed internal shifts. Table 6.4 summarizes the situations in which Level I, Level II or Level III interventions are utilized.

TABLE 6.4
Typical Situations in Which Specific Levels of Intervention are Utilized

Level I: Priming the Pump

- Typically used as a first attempt at helping clients shift.
- Once a client has made an initial shift in response to Level II or Level III interventions, Level I interventions are used to help clients *maintain* receptive internal states.

Level II: Embodying the Predictive Habits

- Typically used when clients are having difficulty accepting the value of the changes proposed by the therapist.
- Used along with Level III interventions, as needed.

Level III: Interacting Directly with An Interfering State

- Typically used when a client acknowledges the value of the changes proposed by the therapist, but can't shift into a state required to implement the changes.

CONCLUSION

A fundamental operating procedure that distinguishes PET-C from many other couple therapies is that PET-C therapists will not attempt to salvage a conversation in which partners are clearly operating from defensive or attacking internal states, unless partners shift fairly quickly through Level I (Priming the pump) type interventions. Instead, a PET-C therapist will stop the discussion, meet individually with each partner, and not commence it again until partners have shifted. Once the conversation resumes, if partners shift again into defensive states, the therapist will stop the conversation again, until partners have shifted into states that support the habits predictive of success. In this way, the therapist avoids tacitly endorsing clients assumptions that they can get what they want from their partners even though they are going about it in a way that is predictive of relationship failure.

Therapists who are learning PET-C often ask questions about why we separate and go one-on-one with each partner when creating internal shifts using Level II and III methods. Why can't the therapist create an internal shift in one partner while the other partner is present? Our answer is that actually, you can. We've tried it both ways over a considerable number of years. Through trial and error, we evolved a preference for creating internal shifts individually with each partner, because we felt that the advantages for doing it individually were greater than the advantages for creating shifts in a conjoint format. There are three main advantages for creating shifts individually. First, internal shifts can often be more easily obtained when the partner is not present. When a client's partner is witnessing the process, the client may become distracted by the reactions of the partner, or the client may be hesitant to disclose important information relevant to the state-shifting process. Second, we've found that sometimes, when an observing partner sees how much resistance the client partner gives the therapist before shifting internal states, the observing partner may become upset about the resistance, and this can interfere with him or her responding to the shifts made by the client. For example, even though the therapist has helped a husband shift from anger to a softer internal state, the wife may be unable to accept the husband's soft response, because she's still thinking of all the things her husband said to the therapist before he finally shifted.

Third, and probably most important, we've found that often, it's difficult for the observing partner to refrain from getting into the client's business. Once she or he knows what the therapist is trying to help his or her partner do, as well as how and why the therapist is helping the partners do it, the temptation to meddle is often just too great. In PET-C, each partner learns to bring out the best in the other by developing more ability to influence their own internal states, not by pointing out what their partner should or shouldn't be doing. Watching a therapist "correct" one's partner is a powerful experience, and tends to stick in the mind of an observing partner. For this reason, PET-C therapists try to avoid correcting partners in front of each other. PET-C therapists usually prefer that each client doesn't even know what she or he is working on with the partner.

As the therapist helps each partner connect with a different internal state, rapid and dramatic changes are often experienced by the couple. For the first time in months (often years), each feels understood, validated, and respected by the other. Partners often feel that the emotional walls have been lowered, and that they have access to softer, more cooperative places inside the other person. This initial positive movement is important, because it gives partners a taste of the kind of connection they can experience from each other if they are able to develop the ability to make the kind of shifts that the therapist has facilitated on their own. However, the initial positive movement can be misleading. Partners may assume that the improvement is an indication that their relationship problems are resolved, even though it is the therapist who has done most of the work in making change happen. Sometimes, the therapist-facilitated initial improvement lasts, but most of the time, it won't unless clients take responsibility for maintaining the changes on their own. When misunderstandings or differences arise in the future, without the therapist present to help partners shift, they often revert back to their conditioned internal state activation patterns. For change to last, partners must go through a process of reconditioning emotional habits that they have often had for many years.

Years ago, I never dreamed that I could motivate partners to become more interested in changing themselves than in changing their partners. I now realize that this was because I didn't know how to access motivational states in each partner that fuel a desire to become more skilled in the art of relationship success. Our methods for accessing client motivation for training in emotional intelligence skills are described in Chapters 7 and 8.

CHAPTER 7

Getting Each Partner On Board

Introduction

I N PHASE I OF PET-C, therapists create internal shifts in the service of two goals (see Figure 7.1). First, therapists create internal shifts in order to help partners interact in ways that are more predictive of relationship success (see box A, Figure 7.1). Through this process (illustrated in the case examples in Chapter 6), couples often experience dramatic improvements. However, these changes are almost entirely dependent on the therapist's active role in creating internal shifts and modeling the predictive habits. Unless clients develop the ability to do this on their own, they will relapse when the therapist isn't there to help them. Throughout Phase I, PET-C therapists also create internal shifts in order to help clients become receptive to the idea that the single most effective thing they can do to get more cooperation or respect from their partners is to learn how to make internal shifts and meet the prerequisites for relationship success without the aid of the therapist (see Box B, Figure 7.1).

In the "Getting Each Partner on Board" intervention, the therapist challenges each client to enter a personalized tutoring program in the skills of emotional intelligence. Changing one's emotional habits is no small task, and clients will not embrace it unless they are convinced that it is necessary. Getting on board interventions aim to do exactly this. The therapist makes a compelling invitation to the partners to take the direction of their relationship into their own hands, summarizing evidence suggesting that the way people respond when they feel misunderstood or mistreated dramatically predicts the extent to which they will be understood or treated better or worse in the fu-

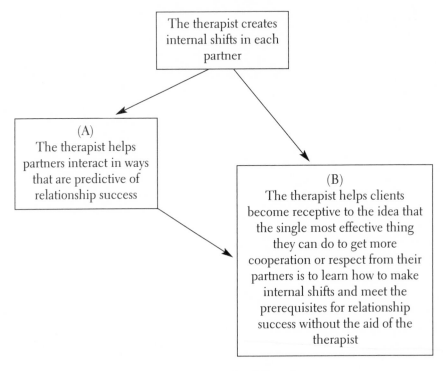

Figure 7.1 Goals of Phase I

ture. In this chapter, we'll look at interventions that help each partner gain confidence that:

- The person can powerfully influence the way he or she is treated by his or her partner.
- It is to the individual's own advantage that he or she makes the first move, rather than waiting for the partner to change.
- The path to getting more respect and cooperation from one's partner is well marked and has been researched and empirically verified by some of the best studies we have in the social sciences.
- The therapist knows this path, and can help the client learn it.
- In general, the path involves developing more ability to shift internal states, then knowing what to do once these shifts have occurred.

It's often hard for clients to believe that their partners will treat them better if they take their focus off changing their partners and put it on changing themselves. In the process of getting each partner on board with a radical commitment to self-change, the therapist must use every inch of his or her ability to create and maintain receptive internal states in each partner.

The getting on board intervention is introduced as early as possible in Phase I. Clients often enter therapy in crisis mode, requiring that the therapist take an active role in creating internal shifts and helping partners resolve the crisis issue. In these situations, getting on board follows crisis resolution. However, with many couples, the therapist can begin implementing the getting on board intervention from the very beginning of therapy.

THE APPEAL TO SELF-INTEREST

A key ingredient in helping partners maintain receptive internal states during the getting on board intervention involves the ability of PET-C therapists to help their clients understand that they want the same thing as their clients do—increased respect, understanding, and cooperation from their partners. Therapists must not only convince clients that they want the same things, but that they know exactly why clients have failed to get these things from their partners, and how clients can get more of them in the days and weeks to come.

This information is usually not what partners expect from the therapist, and they are often confused, even disoriented by it. Most partners come to couples therapy at least somewhat defensive, and wary that the finger is going to be pointed at them. They fear that they will be told that their partners' criticisms are warranted, or that their own complaints about their partners are unwarranted. Instead, the therapist assures them that their complaints about their partners are legitimate, and that the therapist will try to help them positively influence their partners. Rather than criticizing the client's *methods*, the therapist supports the client's *goals*, and offers the client more effective means for pursuing these goals. For example, consider a situation in which the wife is making her most powerful attempt to get her husband to accept influence from her by criticizing him and making him realize how wrong he is. In this situation, the PET-C therapist would help the wife see that she is virtually giving away her power by approaching her husband in this way. Her critical attitude almost guarantees that she won't get the response she truly wants, not because her husband is so pig-headed, but rather because there is evidence that very few people can respond well in the face of criticism. Across the board, people who criticize their partners tend to fail in their relationships. There are much more effective alternatives to criticism. The PET-C therapist will appeal to the wife's self-interest in getting her husband to change. The therapist will *not* say, "You shouldn't criticize your husband because he deserves to be treated more respectfully." The therapist *will* say things like, "I don't blame you for criticizing your husband, but if you could lose your critical attitude, you could be much more powerful in influencing him."

In getting each partner on board, the therapist joins each client in his or her desire to be judged less, attacked less, blamed less, and to be understood, respected, and regarded more. The therapist helps clients realize that the surest way to accomplish this is to learn how to respond effectively when they feel mistreated or misunderstood.

COMPONENTS OF THE GETTING ON
BOARD INTERVENTION

The "Getting on Board" intervention is usually implemented in one-on-one conversations between the therapist and each partner separately. There are many ways that conversations designed to get clients on board can progress. However, we have used a particular sequence (Table 7.1) hundreds of times with remarkable success at the Couples Research Institute. The steps need not occur in the suggested order, and not all of them are always required.

Let's go through each of these components, one at a time.

1. The Therapist Makes Sure He or She is in a
Nurturing State of Mind

Unless the therapist maintains a state of mind that communicates empathy, support, and understanding, it is unlikely that clients will be able to maintain receptive internal states and entertain the idea that it is in their own best interests to focus on changing themselves rather than their partners. This cannot be emphasized enough. A therapist might present a perfect case for why the client should focus on self, but unless the client senses that the therapist genuinely likes him or her, the client will often be unable to feel receptive enough to consider it. When the getting on board intervention is implemented effectively, clients don't feel criticized even though the therapist is critiquing them, because the therapist isn't operating from a critical internal state. Maintaining a nurturing, nonjudgmental attitude with clients who are critical or judgmental is not easy, particularly when these clients become upset with or critical of the therapist. The therapist must be skilled in the art of operating from a nonjudgmental internal state.

2. Help the Client Shift into a Receptive Internal State

Throughout the getting on board intervention, the therapist uses the methods for creating internal shifts described in Chapter 6. In fact, we consider the getting on board intervention to be a specific application of Level II intervention (see Table 6.2), in which the therapist (1) offers strong support and validation, (2) issues a strong challenge, and (3) promotes a respectful dialogue. The therapist begins by offering strong validation and support, empathically summing up the elements of the client's predicament that are painful, frustrating, or infuriating, and indicates that these feelings are understandable given the present circumstances. The therapist offers empathic statements such as: "I think I can understand at least a part of what you are going through . . .;" "You feel like you are constantly walking on eggshells"; "You feel constantly dismissed, as if your thoughts or expectations have no merit at all, or [therapist describes the specific feelings this client is having]." But the therapist goes further than understanding

TABLE 7.1
Getting Each Partner on Board

Getting each partner on board refers to helping each partner develop the belief that it is possible to powerfully influence the extent to which his or her partner tries to understand or cooperate with him or her, and that it is in the client's own best interest that he or she make the first move, rather than waiting for the partner to change. One-on-one, the therapist helps each client shift to a receptive internal state, challenges the client to begin a personalized training program in the skills of emotional intelligence, anticipates defensiveness in response to the challenge, and responds to the client's defensiveness in ways that help the client shift to a receptive internal state again. Some of the steps often included in the getting each partner on board intervention are as follows:

1. Make sure that you are in a nurturing state of mind.
2. Help the client shift into a receptive internal state.
3. Make a case that the client can change his or her partner by changing him- or herself:
   A. Marriage researchers have spent decades looking at how people who are in situations similar to yours cope.
   B. They have found out that people react very differently in these situations, and how they react has a big impact on the future of their relationship.
   C. Your reaction looks pretty normal, but unfortunately, normal will get you divorced or unhappily married these days. People who end up with partners who treat them well don't react normally when their partners do upsetting things. They react in ways that get results.
   D. There's compelling evidence that says if you have the ability to react to your partner in certain ways when you feel mistreated, the odds are very, very good (about 91%) that you'll be treated better in the future. On the other hand, if you don't have these abilities, the odds are slim that you'll get treated well.
   E. The secret to getting your partner to change doesn't involve trying to prevent your partner from doing upsetting things, or trying to convince your partner that he or she is wrong. The secret is in learning how to react effectively when your partner does the upsetting things.
   F. Your partner's reactions to you are no more effective than your reactions to your partner.
   G. The bottom line: If you want to be treated better, you need to learn to think and act like people who almost always get treated better. I can help you learn how to do this.
4. Solicit the client's reactions.

(continues)

TABLE 7.1
(Continued)

---

5. Move back and forth between responding to the client's reservations in a way that reduces defensiveness, and suggest specific ways that the client's reactions to the partner need to change.
6. If the client continues to be defensive and objects to the approach you are suggesting, attempt to work directly with the client's interfering state (Level III, Chapter 6).
7. If the client still persists in a defensive state, discuss your dilemma (wanting to support the client, but knowing that you can't go down a road with the client that you believe is doomed to failure), then suggest that the client take some time to think things over and return for another conversation.
8. If the client is still unwilling or unable to get on board, the therapist respectfully suggests that he or she will not continue therapy with the client.

---

and validation, offering statements that convey a personal quality of caring and commitment:

- I want you to know that I'm sorry you've had to go through this.
- I don't want you to have to live your life feeling this way.
- I won't be satisfied until this is no longer happening, and I feel confident that I know how to get this all to shift.

3. *Make a Case that It's In the Client's Best Interest to Focus on Changing His or Her Own Reactions*

Having taken steps to maximize the possibility that the client will be in a nondefensive, receptive state of mind, the therapist appeals to the client's self-interest, laying out the case for why the single most effective thing that the client can do to get more cooperation and respect from his or her partner is to develop more ability to react effectively to that partner. Reacting more effectively means getting better at the six habits for responding when feeling mistreated or misunderstood (Table 3.1). It is crucial that the therapist be able to present a compelling, coherent, rational case for the necessity of self-focus, that the therapist be in a noncritical internal state when presenting the case, and that the therapist monitors the client's receptivity as the dialogue proceeds, stopping whenever the client shows signs of discomfort or disagreement.

While a reading of Chapter 3 gives therapist trainees most of the information they need to build a case for why the client's best course of action is self-focus, trainees often feel more comfortable "building the case" if they have done more reading about the predictors of relationship success, and our trainees read a number of Gottman's books on the subject (Gottman, 1999, 1994a; Gottman & Silver, 1999; Gottman & DeClaire, 2001). Some of the most important components in making a compelling case to clients that it is in their own best interest to focus on meeting the prerequisites for relationship success are as follows:

A. *Marriage researchers have spent decades looking at how people who are in situations similar to yours cope.* A core component of the studies examining factors that predict relationship success involved examining how partners reacted when they felt misunderstood or mistreated. Distressed partners entering therapy almost always feel misunderstood or mistreated, and the findings of researchers are directly relevant to them.

B. *Marriage researchers have determined that people react very differently in these situations, and how they react has a big impact on the future of their relationship.* The main point here is simply to let the client know that, although it might seem as if one's options are limited for responding when one's partner does provocative or upsetting things, actually there are a wide variety of possible reactions. The therapist lets the client know that some ways of reacting strongly predict that they will continue to be misunderstood or mistreated in the future, but other ways of reacting predict just as strongly that they will be treated better in the future. Researchers have discovered that some people know how to react in ways that elicit respect and motivate their partners to treat them better.

C. *Your reaction looks pretty normal, but unfortunately, normal will get you divorced or unhappily married these days. People who end up with partners who treat them well don't react normally when their partners do upsetting things. They react in ways that get results.* In the previous step, the therapist has offered information that could be interpreted as criticism by the client. If there are some ways of reacting when feeling mistreated that result in receiving better treatment in the future, obviously the client has not figured out how to react this way, because he or she is still feeling mistreated. The therapist quickly lowers the client's defensiveness by assuring the client that his or her reactions are normal. However, the therapist quickly adds that this is not necessarily a good thing, referring to the divorce statistics which suggest that people "normally" either get divorced or remain unhappily married. Doing what is "normal" (i.e., what the majority of people do) will probably get one what most people get—a divorce or an unhappy marriage. The therapist introduces the idea that it takes something extraordinary to succeed in an intimate, long-term relationship. By saying this, the therapist removes the idea that clients' reactions are substandard, and instead challenges clients to be among the few who effect change in their marriages.

D. *There is compelling evidence that says if you have the ability to react to your partner in effective ways when you feel mistreated, the odds are excellent (about 91%) that you'll be treated better in the future. On the other hand, if you don't have these abilities, the odds are slim that your treatment will improve.* The therapist makes two equally important statements here. First, the odds are very good that, if the client is able to do the extraordinary, he or she will get something much better from his or her partner. On its own, however, this powerful, positive statement can create the wrong impression (i.e., that the client has to be a hero in order to deal with the level of provocation he or she is facing from the partner). The therapist counters this notion by stating that actually, anyone who wants to succeed in a relationship must be able to do these things. The therapist isn't asking that the client do anything that's "beyond the call of duty" for those who want to succeed in their relationships.

E. *The secret to getting your partner to change doesn't involve trying to prevent your partner from doing upsetting things, or trying to convince your partner that he or she is wrong. The secret is in learning how to react effectively when your partner does the upsetting things.* Here the therapist begins to introduce the paradigm shift in thinking that clients must grasp if they want their relationships to turn around. Clients think that, in order for their partners to change, they must convince them that their actions are wrong. The therapist presents a radically different notion: Your partner will change if you stop obsessing about how to get him to change and instead focus on yourself. You can change your partner by changing yourself. The therapist insists that, although this might be hard to believe, the evidence on the matter is so compelling that, if the client doesn't think it applies in his or her situation, the burden of proof really lies with the client. In fact, if the client disputes this notion, the therapist might challenge the client to prove him or her wrong:

Show me that you can react consistently to your partner in the ways that predict success. If, after one month, you don't feel treated better by your partner, I'll be willing to consider that you may have one of those rare situations for which the general principles for relationship success don't apply. As it stands, I just don't see anything about your situation that would make me think that the rules don't apply to you.

F. *Your partner's reactions to you aren't any more effective than your reactions to him or her.* Because the therapist is making a strong case for the idea that the relationship will change if the client changes, the client will usually begin to think that the therapist is implying that it is his or her fault that the relationship isn't going well. It is important for the therapist to address this issue, by stating his or her view that both client and partner seem equally off-track when it comes to reactions that predict relationship success. Each of them is acting like someone whose relationship will eventually fail. However, either one of them could turn the relationship around as well. Of course, the client may counter with one of the five most common objections from clients, "Okay, well if either of us could turn it around, let my partner do the work for a change! I'm sick of being the only one who tries!". In response, the therapist makes the case that it is in the best interest of the client to take things into his own hands rather than waiting around for his partner to feel like treating him better. A complete example of this therapist response is given in the case dialogue in Chapter 8.

G. *The bottom line: If you want to get treated better, you need to learn to think and act like people who almost always get treated better. I can help you learn how to do this.* With this statement, the therapist sums up all that he or she has been saying thus far, and makes an offer that will be difficult for the client to refuse: "If you want to get treated better, I can show you precisely how to do it. Researchers have studied it, and I have made it my business to know everything I can about it. It won't require you to do anything unethical. It won't require you to allow yourself to be taken advantage of by your partner. In fact, it will involve you in learning how to exert a more powerful influence on your partner."

4. *Solicit the Client's Reactions*

The therapist stops "selling," and implies that he or she will only continue if the client is interested. This simple question ("Are you interested?") lets the client know that the therapist is not hellbent on convincing the client to adopt his or her viewpoint. At this juncture, a client will react in one of two ways.

A. *The client will be experiencing a defensive or critical internal state, and voice objections to the ideas that the therapist has proposed thus far.* This is a crucial point in the intervention. The therapist must avoid dismissing the client's reservations, or arguing with the client, and instead find the understandable part of the client's reservations, acknowledge the important underlying concerns that may be relevant to the client's resistance, then offer explanations or assurances that directly address the client's reservations (see Chapter 6, Level II, intervention 7).

B. *The client will ask the therapist to explain specifically how the client could better react to his or her partner.* This request may come to the therapist in the form of a sincere question ("Okay, but how am I supposed to react when my partner does these things?") or in the form of an indignant challenge ("How the hell am I supposed to react when she pulls that crap?"). If the client gives a sincere request, the therapist moves on to step 5, and uses specific examples from his experience with this client or the client's partner to describe the kind of changes in reactions the client would need to make in order to increase the odds that his or her partner would respond well (see step 5, Painting a Clear Picture of Needed Changes). If the client's request comes in the form of a skeptical challenge rather than a sincere question, it is usually best to address the client's skepticism, saying to the client something like, "It sounds to me like you're pretty skeptical, which is fine. Is something bugging you about what I'm saying so far?" The client will then voice his or her objections (as in A above), and the therapist will validate and satisfy these general objections before moving on to describe how she or he thinks the client can interact more successfully with his or her partner.

5. Move Back and Forth Between Responding to the Client's Reservations in a Way that Reduces Defensiveness, and Suggesting Specific Ways that the Client's Reactions Need to Change

Almost all clients will have reservations about what the therapist is saying. It's just a matter of when. If a client isn't actively stating them, the PET-C therapist asks anyway, and looks for nonverbal cues that indicate the client's discomfort. As soon as the client shows signs of discomfort, the therapist stops talking and asks the client about the reaction, even if it occurs early in the getting on board intervention process.

Responding to the Client's Reservations. Often, the particular form and timing of the client's expressed reservations will guide when the therapist delivers the various components of step 3. It is unwise for a therapist to keep "selling" if a client is showing signs of discomfort with what the therapist is saying. However, if the client is not looking upset, and expresses no reservations, the therapist will deliver all of the components of step 3 in succession, pausing only at step 4 to solicit reservations or reactions.

As stated in the discussion of step 4, some clients will object to the therapist's proposal that the best thing they can do is focus on changing their own reactions to their partners. Others will not object to this general proposal, but will object when the therapist begins giving specific examples of how the client's reactions need to change. Regardless of when a reservation is expressed, the therapist responds by helping the client shift to a receptive internal state, using the Level II methods discussed in Chapter 6. The therapist patiently acknowledges the understandable part of the reservations, validates the important "something" the client is afraid of losing if he or she adopts the perspective the therapist is suggesting, offers assurances that this perspective wouldn't be suggested if the therapist believed it would lead to the feared situation, and invites further reservations to be expressed. The therapist then offers explanations or assurances that directly address the objections or reservations expressed by the client. Explanations and assurances are always delivered along with interventions that help clients shift to (and maintain) receptive internal states. For example, after offering explanations and assurances, the therapist again checks with the client to see how this new information is being received. The therapist invites further reservations to be expressed, and repeats the process of validating, respecting, assuring, explaining, and checking. This cycle is repeated as many times as is necessary, until the client's reservations are satisfied.

Painting a Clear Picture of Needed Changes. In step 5, the therapist moves back and forth between responding to the client's reservations and painting a clear picture of the specific ways that the client's reactions to her partner need to change. Before even beginning the getting on board intervention, the therapist prepares to talk to the client specifically about the ways the client has been observed reacting to his or her partner that predict marital failure. Even more important, the therapist prepares to talk about what the effective alternatives would be. A skilled therapist will have specific examples in mind, taken from his or her experience with the couple thus far. The therapist will talk about how the client reacted in specific situations, and how the client's reaction would need to change in order to meet the prerequisites for relationship success. At this stage, the therapist will explicitly link the changes he or she is proposing to the habits that support the prerequisites for relationship success. At the end of the first getting on board session, the therapist typically sends a summary of the predictive habits home for the client to read between sessions, along with a written description of the rationale for the treatment focus the therapist has suggested. Each of these handouts can be found in the electronic workbook, *Developing Habits for Relationship Success* (Atkinson, 2005), described more fully in Chapters 9 and 10. The therapist typically also assigns homework asking the client to evaluate his or her reactions to each upsetting thing that the partner does during the next week. These homework assignments are further developed in the following weeks (see Chapters 9 and 10).

As the therapist describes in detail the specific ways he has seen the client react ineffectively to his partner, and paints a picture of effective alternatives, most clients become defensive and express more reservations. A skilled therapist helps clients shift back into more receptive states (using Level II methods described in Chapter 6), and offer more explanations and assurances that directly address the clients' reservations or objections (see Table 8.1).

6. If the Client Continues to Be Defensive and Objects to the Approach the Therapist is Suggesting

The therapist should attempt to work directly with the client's interfering state (Level III, Chapter 6). If the client's reservations persist, the therapist asks the client to pay closer attention to the part of her that resists the proposed ideas and courses of action. The therapist might ask, "Is there any part you that sees some sense in what I'm saying, or do you feel 100% opposed?" Usually, clients feel some internal conflict, and the therapist asks if it would be okay to pay special attention to each of these parts of the client, one at a time (the part that agrees at least partly with the therapist, and the part that objects). The therapist works with the objecting part, using Level III interventions (see Chapter 6).

7. If the Client Still Persists in a Defensive State, the Therapist Discusses Her Dilemma

Here, while the therapist wants to support the client, but knows that she can't go down a road with the client that she believes is doomed to failure, it is appropriate to suggest that the client take some time to think things over and return for another conversation.

In this step, the therapist confesses that she feels pulled in two directions. On one hand, the therapist states her belief that the client must make up his own mind, and must do what he honestly feels is right. On the other hand, the therapist confesses that she just can't get with the client's current line of thinking. The therapist invites further discussion ("Would you please try to explain to me again what doesn't make sense to you about what I'm saying?" or "Would you explain again how your current way of handling things will work out better for you?"). At the end of the therapy session, the therapist invites the client to think things over and return for perhaps one more conversation. The therapist gives the client a written description of the rationale for the treatment focus the therapist has suggested as well as a written summary of the reactions of people who get more respect and cooperation from their partners (Atkinson, 2005).

8. If the Client is Still Unwilling or Unable to Get on Board, the Therapist Respectfully Suggests that She Will Not Continue Therapy with the Client

The therapist offers a statement such as the following:

I've tried everything I can think of to explain the way of thinking (or course of action) that I believe will get you what you want, and I hear you saying you just can't get with that way of thinking (or that plan). I respect that. You have to decide this for yourself. But I don't think I can help you with where you want to go. It goes against what I have come to believe about how relationships work. Listen, I know that there are exceptions to every rule, and that if I were you, I wouldn't do anything I didn't believe in. I just think that you're going to have to do this without me. I hope you don't feel like I'm judging you. I wish you the best, I really do.

Some therapists who attend our PET-C workshops are shocked by this. They feel that we are abandoning the client, that we don't love the client unconditionally (e.g., we love the client only if he or she does things our way), or that the client will inevitably feel judged or dismissed by us. Of course, we have thought through these issues carefully, and feel that this step is a vital and necessary part of the getting on board intervention. Approximately 80% of our clients get on board before we reach this final step. However, most of the remaining 20% get on board precisely when the therapist implements this step. Our experience tells us that some clients will resist getting on board until this point, even if they recognize the sense of the proposal the therapist has made earlier. Further, our sense is that many of these clients would likely never have gotten on board if the therapist hadn't respectfully declined to continue therapy with the client. Understandably, many clients find the idea of taking responsibility for their relationship extremely difficult to swallow, and will only do so when all of their other options are closed. In other words, they will attempt to get the therapist to continue a therapy in which they project blame as long as the therapist is willing to keep that door open. The same client may also be persisting in behavior that seems unfair to his or her partner, and will not stop unless the partner draws the line. We believe that the willingness to respectfully withdraw one's participation from a relationship with someone who persists in behavior that seems harmful is necessary for healthy human functioning.

I want to be clear that we do not support the idea of people walking around issuing ultimatums whenever they don't get their own way. But we do support the notion of, after respectful dialogue, withdrawing participation or coopera-tion with someone who is doing things that we believe are harmful. In fact, in Phase II of PET-C, we explicitly help clients develop this ability (predictive habit 2: Standing Up for Yourself Without Putting Your Partner Down). We be-lieve that relationships will not function in a healthy way unless partners are will-ing and able to do this, when necessary.

A critical component of the final step is drawing a line without contempt, without "looking down" on the client for being resistant. Therapists are in a profession that uniquely sets them up to be contemptuous. It is easy for thera-pists to think of themselves as more emotionally mature than their clients. Af-ter all, they've had extensive training in emotional matters. However, I've been part of this profession long enough to know that accomplished therapists often continue to struggle in their own emotional lives. The healthiest among those who make progress with their own emotional habits retain a certain kind of humility, recognizing that on a good day they can function well, but on any given day, the distinction between their functioning and that of their clients may be imperceptible, possibly even reversed. Divorce rates are no lower for therapists than they are for the general public. The humility of the therapist must be genuinely present when refusing to continue therapy with a client. I recently witnessed a PET-C therapist embody this humility when she told a client:

Look, I'm just somebody trying to make my way through life, just like you. I look for answers, just like you. When things make sense to me, I grab onto them. When they don't I reject them. I think we all have to do this. What else can you do? It doesn't work very well to do things you really don't believe in. I've had more oppor-tunity than the average person to study the evidence on how relationships work, but that doesn't mean that I have all the answers. I know that there are other li-censed marriage counselors who might give you different advice than me. The bot-tom line is, you and me, all of us, we have to make our own call. I'm going to re-spect your need to do that. I hope you can respect me for not feeling I can support you in the direction you're going. I do support you in making a decision that feels right to you, though.

This statement from the therapist was the turning point in the client's therapy. Immediately after the therapist uttered these words, the client shifted, got on board, and entered Phase II of treatment.

CHAPTER 8

Getting Each Partner On Board

Case Example

T HE FOLLOWING DIALOGUE took place between a PET-C therapist and a wife who had come for therapy with her husband three weeks earlier. Both partners were in their late 50s, and each had grown children from previous marriages. The wife, Julie, came to therapy "at the end of her rope," ready to contact an attorney. She complained that her husband, Harvey, was emotionally underdeveloped, because he was unable to speak to her when she became upset with him. Harvey agreed with Julie's assessment of him, saying that communication had never been his strong suit. Julie claimed that Harvey was insensitive and selfish, living in his own little world, rarely thinking about anybody but himself. Assessment sessions revealed that Julie was constantly critical of Harvey, rarely found anything understandable about his feelings or actions, claimed that Harvey's ideas or preferences were usually misguided or somehow inferior to hers, and rarely showed equal regard or offered assurances to Harvey. During conjoint sessions, Harvey listened to Julie attentively and pointed out the understandable aspects of her feelings and opinions. However, in his individual sessions with the therapist, it became clear that Harvey was inwardly contemptuous toward Julie, seeing her as childish in her demands and in her need to have everything her own way. Harvey rarely stood his ground with her. Rather, he placated her, and had withdrawn from her emotionally more and more in the months preceding therapy.

In the first few sessions, the therapist had been able to create internal shifts in Julie and Harvey using the methods described in Chapter 6. In fact, in the previous session, Julie had made a dramatic shift from an angry, critical state to a vulnerable state from which she apologized to Harvey for her aggressiveness, and told him how lonely she felt. Harvey responded with tenderness. When the couple returned the following week and sat in stony silence as the therapy began, the therapist decided it was time to get each partner on board. The therapist met for an hour with Julie, and scheduled another meeting later the same week for Harvey. Excerpts from the therapist's dialogue with Julie reveal various steps of the getting on board intervention.

Before beginning the intervention, the therapist spent a few minutes allowing himself to move into an internal state from where he felt fondness and tenderness toward Julie (Table 7.1, step 1). A neutral mood is usually not sufficient to successfully implement the intervention. In order to maintain receptiveness to the challenges that will be delivered by the therapist, Julie must feel a strong connection with the therapist. She must feel that he really understands and cares about how bad life feels to her.

W: I can't take much more of this. He hasn't spoken to me for two days. I decided, damn it, this time I'm not going to be the one to try to make everything better.

T: What do you mean, Julie?

W: He just turns off. He won't even acknowledge my presence. At least he could give me the courtesy of telling me off, but he acts like I'm not even there . . .

T: . . . just like before you guys came for therapy.

W: Yep.

T: I agree, Julie. You can't go on like this, living with someone who has given up on you to the point that that he won't even talk. I'd probably feel the same way as you do if I were in your shoes.

In making strong supportive statements like this one, the PET-C therapist runs the risk that the client may come to feel that the therapist is on her side, and that the therapist is implying that her partner is to blame. However, strong statements like this one often have a dramatic, calming effect on clients, and experienced PET-C therapists use them liberally. The therapist can afford to risk misinterpretation, because he knows that clarification is just a few moments away. The client's "the therapist is on my side" feeling will be balanced shortly with a "the therapist thinks I'm the one at fault" feeling. Before the session ends, the therapist will have plenty of chance to clarify that he's "on the side" of both partners, and that neither of them is more at fault than the other.

W: He's afraid of me. He can't handle emotion. He thinks I should never be angry. I should be this calm, collected person all the time. He really thinks I'm some kind of a monster. Well, I'm not! It's pretty normal to be angry under the present circumstances.

T: It's like he's afraid of a little emotion.

W: I'm not a monster.

T: No, you're not, Julie. Actually, I like your emotional intensity.

W: (*chuckles*) Well, I do go over the top sometimes.

T: Sure. But I don't think we should try to change your intensity. That's part of what makes you special. Spirited, that's how I'd describe you!

W: Well, that's a nice way of putting it.

T: Julie, I'm really sorry about all of the pain you've had this week. And I want you to know that I don't want you to have to live your life feeling this way. And I won't be satisfied until things have changed so that you don't have to feel this way any more. I believe that things are going to change, and tonight can be a big piece of progress.

Throughout the getting on board intervention, the therapist uses the methods for creating internal shifts described in Chapter 6. Here, the therapist offers a personal, supportive statement (Table 6.2, step 1)

W: I'm not so sure.

T: I want to tell you why I feel this way. Do you think you're in a frame of mind to listen to me for a couple of minutes?

The therapist helps create receptivity by asking permission to give the client some information. If a client asks for the information, she will generally be more able to be receptive to it than if the information is thrust upon her.

W: I probably need to listen, because I'm all out of things to say.

T: Okay, I haven't talked to you about this yet. But I think you're ready now. I think you need to know that the position you're in with Harvey—you know, trying to figure out how to deal with somebody who tends to live in his own world, and just shuts down when things get intense—there are a lot of wives who find themselves in a similar position of having to deal with this kind of thing.

With this statement, the therapist begins step 3 of the intervention (Table 7.1). The therapist will now proceed to make a case that it's in Julie's own best interest to focus on changing her own reactions to Harvey.

W: Oh I'm sure I'm not the only one.

T: Nope. In fact, people in your type of situation have been the subjects of some pretty intensive studies in the last 20 years. Some really well-known researchers have spent a lot of time studying how people cope with situations like this (*Table 7.1, step* 3A). They've followed couples over long periods of time, and they found out some things that I think you should know about.

The amount of information given to the client about these studies varies from client to client. Many clients will want to know a good deal of the information about the studies (summarized in Chapter 3). Here, the therapist felt that Julie would want him to get to the point as soon as possible, so he gave her only what he thought she needed in order to become interested. More information can always be given at a later time.

T: Are you ready?

Again, the therapist enhances Julie's receptivity setting things up so that she asks for him to continue.

W: Go on.

T: Here's what they found. First of all, they found out that with people in your situation, different ones handle the situation very differently. And they found that some ways of handling the situation resulted in things changing for the better, and some ways of reacting seemed to lock the situation down so that it never changed (*Table 7.1, step 3B*). The first thing you should know is that your reaction is pretty normal (*Table 7.1, step 3C*). Most people tend to react in ways that are pretty much like yours. If I were in your situation, I might very well be handling it like you are, too. And it wouldn't be working any better for me than it does you.

The therapist continues to help Julie maintain a receptive internal state by assuring her that she's normal. This "normalizing" step of the intervention seems to be so effective that we almost always include it in step 3.

W: (*smiling*) Oooh. That's harsh!

T: Well, here's the thing. "Normal," these days, will get you divorced, or unhappily married. Up to half of all first marriages end in divorce, and among the other half who stay married, what percentage do you think are really happily married?

W: Probably not very many.

T: How many happily married people do you know?

W: (*Wife thinks for a few seconds*) Most of our friends are divorced.

T: Of those who haven't, are there any who seem happy with each other?

W: This isn't making me feel better.

T: Yeah, but let's face the facts, Julie. Minimally, three quarters of the people in our country are headed for relationship trouble. What that means is that you really can't take how the majority of people act in their relationships as an acceptable standard for how to act. If you measure your own reactions based on what's normal, you'll end up just like people normally end up! You know what I'm saying?

W: I thought you said this was good news.

T: Okay, so the good news is that you're normal, you know, there's nothing weird or anything about how you've been reacting to Harvey. It's just that, well, it won't work. But the really good news is that these studies have pinpointed what people do that *does* work. In fact, it *almost* always works—like 91% of the time.

For the first time, the therapist has introduced a theme that will now become the centerpiece of the rest of the intervention: There are certain ways of reacting when feeling mistreated or misunderstood that greatly increase the odds that you will be treated better in the future (Table 7.1, step 3D).

W: What do you mean? What works?

T: It's a very specific combination of things, and hard to sum up in a few sentences. But it's not that hard to understand, if you really sit down and try. I'm hoping that in the coming weeks, you'll make it your business to become an expert on them. When we're done today, if you're interested, I'll give you something to read about them, and give you some exercises to help you begin taking a look at your reactions to Harvey, and compare them with these things that really work well.

W: (*looking suddenly defensive*) I don't think my reactions are unreasonable, given the shit that I'm dealing with.

T: I'm not saying they're unreasonable, I'm saying that they're *ineffective*. When you react to Harvey, sometimes I cringe, because I see you giving away the potential power you have to influence him. It's like I see the power draining right out of you.

W: What are you talking about?

T: Well, for example, whenever you criticize Harvey—when you talk to him with an attitude that says, "What the hell is your problem?" or "You are out of line!" or "You shouldn't have done that!" it's 100% predictable that Harvey will become defensive and eventually shut down. It's not just Harvey who reacts this way, Julie. It's true for most all of us.

Versions of this last statement are made over and over again in the getting on board intervention. Throughout the intervention, the therapist continually reminds the client that there is information available for anyone who really wants to know about how relationships work. We know the habits that make them work, and we know the habits (like criticism) that make them fail. It's not just Harvey who has a difficult time responding to criticism. Most people do.

W: Well how the hell am I supposed to react when he pulls one like he did Monday?

On Monday, Julie had spent most of the day at work, thinking about some new drapes that she and Harvey had discussed getting for the living room. She assumed that she and Harvey would go to the store that evening and pick some out. While he was at work, however, a friend invited him and some others to get together and watch Monday Night Football. He called from work and left Julie a voice-mail message, saying he was going to go straight to the friend's house after work. Julie sat at home all evening, fuming. When he came home, Julie was furious and raged at Harvey while he, of course, stonewalled.

T: Do you really want to know?

W: (*sounding irritated*) I have the feeling that you're gonna tell me.

T: Not necessarily. Julie, I'm not trying to talk you into doing anything. I just thought you would want to know how you could get something different from Harvey.

Julie's question ("How the hell am I supposed to react?") sounded more like a statement ("There's no good way to respond to something as provocative as that!") than a sincere request for information. The therapist responds by refusing to give the information unless Julie really wants to know. If she already has her mind made up (as it seems), there's no point in the therapist explaining. By questioning the sincerity of her request instead of continuing to make his case, the therapist avoids the beginning of what could turn into an argument. Throughout the intervention, the therapist will only proceed if the client seems to be interested and open to hearing what he has to say. The therapist isn't interested in ramming anything down the client's throat. Clients pick up on this attitude, and feel respected by it, thus helping them retain receptive internal states.

W: Not if it means I'm supposed to put up with his crap!

T: Julie, I don't think you have any idea about the kinds of things I'm gonna talk to you about, or you wouldn't say that. No. It doesn't involve you taking his crap. Quite the opposite, really. I don't think you're hearing me. I'd like for you to get more cooperation from Harvey, not less.

Throughout the intervention, the therapist continually appeals to Julie's self-interest. He isn't suggesting that she change her reactions because Harvey deserves to be treated better. The therapist is making the suggestion because it's in her own best interest for her to change her reactions (Table 7.1, step 3G).

W: (*looking mad and confused*) Okay, so are you going to tell me? (*This is Julie's way of making a request while saving face at the same time.*)

T: Would you stop looking at me like I'm the enemy? (*Not satisfied, the therapist withholds a bit longer.*)

W: Well you're sitting there telling me all of this is my fault. It doesn't feel exactly like you're on my side.

This is the first in a series of objections that Julie offers in response to the case the therapist is making for her to focus on changing herself. It's one of the five most common objections that clients have when presented with this information (See Table 8.1, Objection 5: Are you saying it's my fault that my partner is treating me badly?). As part of his preparation for delivering the getting on board intervention, the PET-C therapist anticipates each of the objections, and considers how he might respond to them with this particular client. In the following, the therapist gives Julie a response that is effective with most clients who voice this objection.

T: All right. Let's get a few things straight. I hope you know me well enough by now to know that I'm not going to blow sunshine up your ass just to make you feel better.

W: Obviously not.

T: Julie, Harvey's reactions to you are no more effective than your reactions to him. He's just as off-track as you are. (*Table 7.1, step 3F*) He could have so much more of what he wants from you if he could just react differently to you when you're upset. You know that, right?

W: (*sarcastically*) Yeah, for starters, he might consider *talking* to me.

T: All I'm saying is that this principle applies both ways. You could get something very different from him, too, if you could change the way you react to him when you're upset with him. (*Table 7.1, step 3G*)

W: Easy for you to say.

T: Easy for anybody to say, hard for anybody to do. The fact that you haven't been effective is hardly a reason to issue a warrant for your arrest, Julie. These things are hard for all of us to do. You know, join the club. But I do know one thing. If you develop the ability to do these things, you'll get the kind of love and respect from Harvey that you want to have. What I'm trying to figure out is if you are up for this or not.

Julie is still feeling criticized, and she's defensive. The therapist helps her shift by assuring her of his noncritical attitude toward her, and assuring her that her difficulty doing these things is normal (Table 7.1, step 5).

W: (Julie sits quietly for a few seconds) You know, I've been working my ass off on our relationship for years, and I'm just fucking tired. I don't know if I have it in me to try one more thing until I see something different from him. Let him do the trying for once. You just said that he could turn things around, too. Right?

In this statement, Julie embeds another of the most common objections clients have to the therapist's getting on board proposal (see Table 8.1, Objection 4: Why should I be the one to change?) Again, this objection is legitimate, and predictable. The therapist is prepared to respond to it.

T: Well, he could, but I think that would put you in a weak position, Julie, not having learned a damned thing about how to exert your influence in this relationship. If he makes the changes, it'll be fine as long as he seems to be able to keep going, but as soon as he begins to slip, you'll have no more idea about how to effectively influence him than you do now. Don't get me wrong, Julie. I'm going to be talking to him next. And I'm going to try to help him stop sabotaging himself, too. But the best situation is where each of you are making progress in changing your reactions to each other.

W: (*Wife sits quietly for about 10 seconds, and appears to be thinking.*)

T: (*sensing her resistance*) Okay, Julie. I hear you. I haven't walked in your shoes. I believe you when you say you've put so much into this relationship, and if you say you're not making any more moves until he does, I'll respect that.

The therapist helps Julie shift by using Level II intervention for creating internal shifts (Table 6.2, step 8: Communicating regard for the client's resistance).

W: You know, I've just spent too much time chasing after him, trying to make him talk to me.

T: I know. Actually, I hope that you're ready to stop chasing, because that's one of the things that doesn't usually work anyway.

W: Okay, I'm having some problems with this idea that my reactions are the problem. I mean, I know I'm not perfect, but I didn't make him this way. He was like this before I even came into the picture. He has always shut down when people around him get emotional. He avoids conflict like the plague, and pretends that everything's okay. He did that in his last marriage, too. His mother says he was like this even when he was a kid.

Here, Julie voices another common objection to the getting on board proposal (See Table 8.1, objection 2: My partner was like this long before he met me.)

T: I don't doubt that for a minute, Julie. But what you have to realize is that there has always been someone in his life doing the exact same thing to him that you are doing now. You're just the most recent in a long line of people who have the tendency to criticize when they get upset. You told me yourself what a condescending bitch his ex-wife is. We really don't know what Harvey's personality would look like if he lived with a person who knew how to react effectively when he shuts down, because so far as I can tell, he's never been in a situation where someone knew how to react effectively. I think you owe it to yourself to find out how he would be.

Here, the therapist uses one of the most effective responses we have found to this objection (see Table 8.1, objection 2).

W: Don't you have this thing turned around? I mean, you're putting all of this emphasis on my reactions to him, and it seems like you're excusing him. I'm sure that I could react better but that's not the real problem. The real problem is what I'm reacting to! I wouldn't be reacting this way unless Harvey wasn't so selfish in the first place. We wouldn't even need to be having this discussion. It seems like you're letting him off the hook.

In the above, Julie has voiced yet another of the most common objections to the "Getting on Board" proposal (see Table 8.1, objection 1). As with the other objections, the therapist will respond by directly addressing the objection (Table 7.1, step 5).

T: There are two kinds of things that people do that sink relationships. One is being selfish, or inconsiderate, or having to have their own way. The other thing has to do with a certain way that people react when they feel their partners are being selfish, or inconsiderate, or insist on having their own way. They react by criticizing, judging, and thinking of themselves as somehow better than their partners. They think they're right and their partners are wrong. They think they are more emotionally mature. They think they are better at being in relationships. Research studies indicate that, of these two things that sink relationships, one is clearly more toxic than the other. Guess which one?

W: I don't like where you're going here.

T: It's the reactions where one partner puts him- or herself on a higher plane. Researchers have discovered that this thing, by far, is the most toxic thing that people do in relationships. Of course, you're not the only one who does this in your relationship. Harvey is critical of you, too.

W: Oh, is he ever!

T: Harvey thinks you act selfishly too, Julie.

W: Oh, I'm sure.

T: And I'm not going to help him get through to you, or help him convince you to stop doing the things that upset him. I'm going to help him change his reactions to you when you do things that upset him.

In the above exchanges, the therapist helps Julie see the validity of the premise, "You can change your partner by changing yourself," by noting how it applies to Harvey as well as her. Most clients can readily see how the premise applies to their partners. Julie has no problem believing the idea that if Harvey changed his reactions to her, he would get a softer side of her in return. Once she makes this connection in her head, it will be easier to consider the reverse, "If I change my reactions to Harvey, I will get something different from him."

W: Exactly.

T: If you're really going to turn things around, you'll have to develop a whole new understanding about how relationships work, Julie. The evidence tells us that people who get their partners to change—they understand that the secret to getting their partners to change isn't in trying to stop them from doing upsetting things or to convince them that they are wrong. No, the secret is in learning how to react effectively when their partners do the upsetting things. (*Table 7.1, step 3E*) You'll need to become more interested in your reactions to Harvey than the upsetting things that he does. Here's how you can make me a very happy man. Next week, you'll come in here and plop down and say something like, "Harvey has done the unthinkable again this week, but forget about that. Let's talk about me. Let's talk about how I reacted to that, because I know that my reactions are the key to getting something different from him."

With the above statement, the therapist emphasizes that Julie won't be able to make sense of what he's suggesting using her old framework for thinking about relationships. The therapist makes it clear that he's challenging her paradigm, not just her reactions.

W: Okay, how am I supposed to react when he does something like that?

This is the question the therapist has been waiting for. Before beginning the getting on board intervention, an effective PET-C therapist prepares to respond in great detail to this question. Notice that the therapist hasn't offered a single statement up to this point about what the alternative to Julie's typical reactions would look like. This is intentional. It's a mistake to throw out your advice before the client wants to hear it. In the getting on board intervention, the therapist first builds a case for the validity of what he will eventually suggest to the client. Then, when the therapist senses that the client is giving a good hearing, he describes the alternative.

T: The Monday Night Football thing?

W: Yeah. I was sitting there waiting for him all night!

T: Well, I can tell you how people who are good at this do it. It starts with how they think about things. First, they might be as upset as you were. I think I would be. So, it's not like they don't get upset. But they would avoid jumping to the conclusion that Harvey did something wrong. It seems like you tend to assume that there is some universal standard for how people should act in relationships, but most of the time, there really isn't. Some people prefer to operate on a basis where they don't have to check in with each other before making independent plans, other people hate that.

In the above and following statements, the therapist goes to considerable length to describe exactly what an alternative to judgmental thinking might be. In doing so, he moves into step 5 of the intervention, moving back and forth between responding to Julie's questions and reservations in a way that reduces defensiveness, and suggesting specific ways that her reactions can change. It's not enough to tell clients that they shouldn't be so critical. They need therapists to "put their money where their mouth is" and show them what an alternative would look like. One of the best, most generally applicable alternatives to "my partner is wrong" is "we have legitimately different expectations."

W: So you're saying I shouldn't have been so upset.

T: No, I do think you had a right to be upset, but not because Harvey did something wrong, but simply because he did something that's really different from the way you want things to be. It's normal to be upset when someone doesn't meet your expectations.

The alternative reactions that the therapist describes are all simply translations of the habits that predict relationship success. Here, the therapist is talking about ways to avoid judgmental thinking (predictive habit 1).

W: I don't think there's anything wrong with my expectations.

T: Me either, but that doesn't make Harvey's wrong, just because they're different from yours or mine. Anytime you go so far as to imply that somebody is wrong, you just lowered your chances of getting more cooperation from that person by about 50%. People really don't like that.

Notice that the therapist has shifted his language so that he's no longer talking specifically about Julie and Harvey, he's talking about general principles of relationship functioning. He wants Julie to understand that the suggestions he's making are all based on compelling evidence about what works in relationships, and what doesn't.

W: Well, if the shoe fits . . .

T: Julie, you've got to decide for yourself. I'm telling you that putting yourself in the position of judge of the rightness or wrongness of your partner's behavior is one of the most self-defeating things that you can do. It almost never has the effect that people want it to have. You're perfectly entitled to it, and if you ask me, there's no reason on God's green earth why you should consider doing it differently, except that it's one of those things that strongly predicts that you'll never get from Harvey what you really want.

W: So what in the hell am I supposed to do, just act like everything is fine when he walks in the door?

T: I wish it was that easy. No, you'd have to actually find a way to shift to a different place inside, where you could be open to some different ways of thinking, something different from, "He is so out of line!" For example, you might think, "Maybe there's more going on here than meets the eye . . ." or "Maybe there's something I don't know that will help explain why this happened," or, "Maybe he just has really different expectations for how he wants things to be."

Here the therapist is orienting Julie to an idea that will be emphasized throughout Phase II: Behavior change isn't enough. Nothing short of a change of attitude will due.

W: Yeah, really selfish expectations!

T: (*smiling*) Right. That would be a good example of what these people would try to avoid thinking.

W: You're saying what he did wasn't selfish?

T: Yes, that's what I'm saying, but that doesn't mean you don't have a right to ask him to change. (*Julie looks confused.*) Let me explain. I'm pretty sure that if Harvey had his preference, he'd like to have things be where you guys cut each other a lot of slack. If you forget something you said you were going to do, or if he forgets something he said he was going to do, he'd like it to not be that big of a deal. You think it should be a big deal, though, right?

W: If you say you're going to do something, you should follow through.

T: Well, I prefer that type of relationship, too. But there are people who are different from you and me on that, Julie—good people, who have good marriages. When both of them are the "cut each other a lot of slack" types, things work out just fine. When they are the "accountability" types, things work out fine, too.

W: So you're saying that I should cut him more slack.

T: No. I'm saying a couple of things: First, things would work better if you could get out of the habit of assuming that if you're upset, he did something wrong. If you could assume by default when he upsets you that this might be one of those areas where nobody is necessarily wrong, but that this might be one of those areas where you want really different things.

Second, instead of criticizing him, you'd just ask him to move over and make room for your expectations, too.

W: Yeah, but when I ask him for what I need, he thinks I have too many requirements.

T: But that's probably because he also is hearing you say that he should meet your requirements. He's not hearing you say, "Will you work with me on this one?" He's hearing you say, "You screwed up, and this is the way things need to be."

W: Maybe.

T: There's more. I'm just giving you the tip of the iceberg, but what I'm saying is that we know precisely how successful people move in their relationships. It's teachable, it's learnable, and if you can do these things, you'll get what you want from Harvey. What I'm asking for is a commitment from you to let me teach you, step by step, the skills involved in getting what you want and need from Harvey. What do you think?

W: Okay, I'm taking your word for it.

T: You won't be sorry. Here, I'm going to give you some things to read (*Atkinson, 2005*). It'll give you some ideas, but I suggest that you hold off doing anything different for now. There's a whole package of things that you have to be able to do together, and if you only do part of it, it can actually make things worse.

W: (*laughs*) Do not try this at home!

T: Right! I feel hopeful, Julie. One of the things that makes me feel best is that you're not afraid to tell me your reactions to things, and you are the type of person who won't do anything that doesn't feel right. As we go through this, you'll have all kinds of reactions, and questions about what you're learning. Every week, there will be something about it you don't like. Just ask me. I believe I'll have good answers to any question you have. But if at any point it doesn't make sense to you, you follow your own sense of what is right for you, not mine, okay?

W: Well, I'm not sure I trust myself anymore.

T: I trust you, Julie.

The therapist met with Harvey the following day for an individual appointment. Using the same methods, the therapist was also able to get Harvey on board, and the couple entered Phase II of their therapy.

CRITICAL COMPONENTS

The success of the getting on board intervention is largely determined by the ability of the therapist to help clients shift from defensive to receptive internal states as the intervention unfolds. Level II and III interventions for creating internal shifts, as described in Chapter 6, are used throughout the getting on board process. If therapists cannot successfully cultivate receptivity on the part of clients, the intervention will fail. Of course, even the most skilled therapist will not be able to cultivate receptivity in every client. However, sometimes the intervention fails due to therapist factors. In recent years at the Couples Research Institute, we have increased the percentage of clients who respond positively to this intervention by studying carefully each situation in which the intervention failed. We have identified a variety of components that seem to be critical to the success of the intervention. In this section, several of the most prominent of these components are discussed.

Strong Personal Connection

The getting on board intervention involves a direct confrontation of the client with the fact that he or she has failed to meet the prerequisites for relationship success. For most clients, this is not exactly welcome news, and a defensive reaction is the rule rather than the exception. Therapists who are successful in helping clients become more receptive to the getting on board proposal share a common characteristic: They create a connection with the client that is personal. During interviews about their experience in therapy, clients who respond positively to the intervention report things like this:

- My therapist really likes me.
- I don't feel like just another case to her.
- My therapist really cares about how I feel.
- My therapist really understands what I'm going through.
- My therapist really believes in me.
- My therapist sees the good in me.
- My therapist doesn't think he's better than me.

The PET-C therapist influences clients through his or her relationship with them. A crucial part of this relationship involves the therapist saying things that make the client mad or upset at the therapist, followed by the therapist responding by affirming, respecting, and validating the client, which results in emotional soothing. Effective therapists know this and don't hesitate to be direct and pointed in their challenges to clients. There is a back and forth movement between confronting and soothing, and this process solidifies trust and bonding between therapist and client. It is our observation that therapists who are reluctant to be direct with clients about the ways in which their reactions are off-track are less successful in getting people on board. Clients seem to benefit from full, compelling, and direct challenges from a therapist who seems to honestly like them and have their best interest at heart.

Refusal to Allow the Focus to Slide

A fundamental operating procedure that distinguishes PET-C from many other couples therapies is that PET-C therapists will not allow conjoint sessions to continue if each partner is not interested or willing to maintain a primary focus on increasing his or her ability to respond to the partner in ways that are necessary for relationship success. As discussed in the commentary on step 8 in Chapter 7, if a client repeatedly refuses to get on board, the therapist respectfully declines to continue therapy with this client. If the partner of such a client gets on board, the therapist encourages the partner to continue therapy. In such a situation, the therapist makes it clear to both partners that the therapist is recommending that the on board partner continue therapy. We have had many cases over the years in which one partner refused to get on board. Therapy with this partner ceased, the therapist worked successfully with the other partner, then the former partner returned to therapy as a result of the changes in the partner who had remained in therapy. With only one partner in therapy, little changes in the therapist's approach. This partner develops more skill in influencing internal states, and becomes better able to interact with the nontherapy partner in ways that predict relationship success. The only disadvantage is that the therapist cannot coach the client in "live" interaction with the partner; rather, the therapist must rely on reports of interactions given by the client. If this client makes progress in developing the abilities that predict relationship success, our experience is that relationship outcomes are just as good as when both partners remain in therapy.

Getting a client on board rarely happens in a single session. It's a very common occurrence for a client to seemingly understand and agree with the therapist's getting on board proposal one week, then come in the next week and act as if the getting on board conversation had never occurred. In spite of good intentions, the focus of clients will gravitate toward what their partners should be doing and away from a focus on how they themselves are reacting to their partners. In the first two months of therapy, the therapist must be prepared to refocus each client over and over again. If a client refuses to get back on board even after the therapist has patiently implemented steps 5 to 7 of the getting on board intervention (Table 7.1), the therapist will not hesitate to respectfully suggest stopping therapy with this client. We believe that to continue therapy with such a client may very well amount to inadvertently reinforcing the client's premise that the relationship problems are mainly a result of the partner's failings, and that his or her relationship can improve even if he or she fails to meet the prerequisites himself.

Most of the time, when a skillful PET-C therapist respectfully requires that partners remain on board in order for therapy to continue, partners will stay on board. If the therapist is willing to allow each partner's self-focus to slide, the therapy will slide. We feel that we have the best results when we maintain a strict requirement that a client remain on board in order to qualify for continuing therapy. In recent years, as staff members of the Couples Research Institute have given PET-C workshops across the country to experienced therapists, the methods most frequently cited by conference participants as most helpful have to do with how we maintain each partner's focus on his or her own reactions. Some therapists feel pressure to keep partners in therapy until they want to end. We believe that this is unfortunate. The willingness of the therapist to end therapy if a client refuses to get on board is among the most powerful of our methods for helping clients maintain self-focus.

Presenting a Compelling Case

Another critical component of the getting on board intervention involves the ability of the therapist to present a compelling case for why it is in the client's best interest to shift the focus from trying to change the partner to changing him- or herself. Most partners entering therapy will not be thinking this way, and the therapist must present a logical, compelling case for this new way of thinking. We frequently find that when clients fail to get on board, one of the main reasons is that the therapist's point of view just didn't make logical sense to them. To make a compelling case, the therapist must be intimately familiar with the prerequisites for relationship success and the PET-C habits that enable clients to meet these prerequisites. The therapist must also be familiar with the research studies that have identified these prerequisites, and be able to talk to the client about them in as much detail as seems helpful.

Identifying and Addressing the Client's Reservations

A crucial stage of the getting on board intervention involves the therapist asking the client to share his or her reservations or objections (Chapter 7, step 4) to the proposal the therapist is making. Many clients won't wait for the therapist to invite objections. They will begin voicing objections to what the therapist is saying while the therapist is making the case for why it is in the client's best interest to shift the focus from trying to change the partner to changing him- or herself. The therapist must be prepared to respond to the client's objections in two ways. First, the therapist must be able to help the client move from a defensive to a receptive internal state, using methods described in Chapter 6. Second, the therapist must provide intellectually satisfying answers to the client's objections. It's imperative to recognize that giving intellectually satisfying answers alone will not suffice if the client is operating from a defensive state. Even the most compelling answers will "bounce off" the client, unless the client is first helped to shift into a more receptive state. However, intellectually satisfying answers play an important role in helping the client feel assured, and thus contribute to a state shift in the client. When clients fail to get on board, we find that a frequent reason is that the therapist has failed to provide compelling answers to the objections clients voice. These objections can be anticipated in advance. The five mostly commonly voiced objections are summarized in Table 8.1. Beneath each reservation are samples of some of the most useful and widely applicable responses that have been formulated and delivered by PET-C therapists to date.

In each of the sample responses given in Table 8.1, the therapist challenges the client to look at things in a different way. Unless the therapist is able to be supportive and maintain a noncritical attitude, he or she will trigger a defensive state in the client. Of course, there is a good chance that even if the therapist delivers the above statements with a nonjudgmental attitude, the client will become defensive anyway. That shouldn't stop the therapist from delivering the comments. It just means that he will need to stop each time the client becomes defensive, and help the client shift back (see Chapter 6). Sometimes, this shift happens several times in the course of one session.

The getting on board intervention can fail not only when objections voiced by clients are insufficiently answered. Sometimes, clients will not voice their reservations in words, and the therapist must pick them up by looking for nonverbal signs of resistance, or by what the client is saying between the lines. In general, it's best for the therapist to address perceived resistance whenever it is sensed. A skilled therapist will not settle for a client who is reluctantly on board, and will continue inviting discussion of reservations in spite of a client's verbal agreement to give the therapist's proposal a try. The therapist will not take yes for an answer if the client's nonverbals are saying maybe. A skilled therapist knows that a reluctant client won't be likely to engage fully enough in the process to make a difference.

Consider the following dialogue, which occurred between a therapist and husband at the end of an initial getting on board session. Much of the session had been spent with the therapist helping the husband (Brad) maintain receptivity, and with the therapist responding to each of the Brad's reservations. Near the end of the session, Brad reluctantly agreed to give the therapist's proposal a try. However, his manner and tone indicated to the therapist that there might be further, unexpressed reservations. The following dialogue demonstrates how the therapist persists in eliciting and addressing reservations until the client's hesitations seem to be gone.

T: Okay, so you've been hearing me say that I know a path that can get you to another place with Trish. I believe that you hold the key that can unlock something different inside of her. So, what I'm looking for is for you to become determined, desperate to get that key, and I'm not experiencing you that way right now, because I think you're thinking, "Key, schmee. I don't believe it."

H: I'm already desperate. So if I think it will work, then I'm going grab it. (*Here the client has made a verbal agreement, but the therapist senses his reluctance and continues.*)

TABLE 8.1.
Common Objections

1. I shouldn't have to react better because she shouldn't be doing these things in the first place!

   This objection is voiced in several ways, but the core of it is, "Sure, I know that I could react better, and I'll work on that, but that's not the real problem. The real problem is what I'm reacting to! I wouldn't be reacting this way unless my partner was doing that bad thing in the first place, and we wouldn't even need to have this discussion. By focusing on me, you're excusing the very thing in my partner that leads me to react this way! I shouldn't have to go to such heroic lengths to make up for my partner's emotional immaturities! If I agree to focus on my reactions, that will take my partner off the hook.

   Sample Responses:

   A. All people in lasting relationships feel that, at least from time to time, their partners do things that are selfish (inconsiderate, demanding, etc.). Your partner feels that you've acted selfishly, too. And if you were married to someone else, sooner or later you'd also feel that that person was being selfish. And if your partner was married to someone else, sooner or later, your partner would feel that this person was being selfish. Selfishness happens. We're not going to stop it. Relationships don't fail because people act selfishly. They fail because the selfishness continues, because those who bear the brunt of the selfishness don't know how to handle the selfishness effectively when it happens. Not everybody reacts the way you do when they feel mistreated. It's likely that, if we could waive a magic wand and put another person in your shoes (a person who knows how to handle selfishness effectively), this person would have your partner acting differently within a week or two. I'm not asking you to do anything that's beyond what we all must do if we want to be the kind of people who are very likely to be treated well by our partners.

   B. There are two things that people do that sink relationships. One kind is obvious. It involves being selfish, ignoring the needs of others, bold-faced lying, cheating, manipulating, stuff like that. The other thing has to do with a certain way that people react when they feel their partners are being selfish, or inconsiderate, or having to have their own way. They react by criticizing, judging, and thinking of themselves as somehow better than their partners. They think they're right and their partners are wrong. They think they are more emotionally mature. They think they are better at being in relationships. Research studies indicate that, of these two things that sink relationships, the second is clearly more toxic than the first.

(continues)

TABLE 8.1.
(Continued)

2. My partner was like this long before we even met!

    With this objection, the client counters the implication of the therapist that the partner's objectionable behavior is linked to his interactions with her. As evidence, the client cites the fact that the partner's objectionable habits predate their relationship.

Sample Responses:

A. There's probably some truth to that, but please realize that there was someone else in your partner's life back then doing the exact same thing to him or her that you are doing now (critical judgment). You are just the most recent in a long line of critical people your partner has been in relationships with. We don't know what your partner's personality would look like if he or she didn't live in a climate of critical judgment, because there's never been a situation in which he or she didn't feel constantly criticized or judged. You owe it to yourself to find out what she would be like.

B. You were like this long before your partner met you, too. Just like your partner, you weren't as extreme in the beginning of your relationship. But I know that your partner felt your critical judgment very early on, and began reacting to your subtle criticisms back then, becoming more defensive and extreme in his or her own reactions to you. You guys began to feed off of each other's reactions, each feeling more justified as you went, because the other's reactions were becoming more extreme.

3. I already tried what you're suggesting. It didn't work.

    This objection generally comes only after the therapist has begun painting a clear picture of what it would look and sound like if the client were to react more effectively (step 5).

Sample Responses:

A. I can tell from the way you're talking to me that you haven't been able to stay on track with the kind of things I've been talking about. Keep in mind that the most important predictors are not related to what you actually say to your partner; it's what you are saying to yourself. Researchers tell us that the outcome of an argument can pretty well be determined before either partner even opens their mouths! The way you think about your partner reveals your attitude, and your attitude determines the odds that your partner will be defensive or cooperative. I can tell from the way you have been talking to me that your attitude isn't the one that elicits cooperativeness. Quite the opposite. Even in very provocative situations, people who will eventually get more respect and cooperation from their partners find a way to avoid a judgmental attitude.

(continues)

TABLE 8.1.
(Continued)

B. You may have been on track for some periods of time in the past, but I can tell that somewhere along the line, you got off-track. If you had been able to stay on track, your partner would be more respectful or cooperative by now, unless you are among that 9% of people for whom the rule doesn't apply. But honestly, I see nothing about you guys that would lead me to believe that you're different from the rest of us.

C. Yes, the good news is that I think that some of the things you have done in the past meet some of the criteria for effective responding. The problem is that there are a number of components that have to be in place. The whole thing must be implemented as a kind of package response. We'll build from what you are already doing well.

4. Why should I be the one to have to change? Let my partner do the work for a change.

Sample Response

There's no reason on God's green earth why you should do anything different, unless you think it's to your own benefit to do so. I'm suggesting that it is. Why wait around for your partner to feel like treating you better when you can take the matter into your own hands? If you rely on your partner to change, that will put you in a weak position, not having learned anything about how to better exert your influence in this relationship. If your partner takes the lead and changes, it'll be fine as long as he or she seems to be able to keep going, but as soon as your partner begins to slip, you'll have no more idea about how to effectively influence your partner than you do now. If he or she is the one who changes, you'll live with the worry that the old ways could return at any moment. But if you know that your partner has changed because you developed the ability to be a positive influence, you'll never worry in the same way again. If she slips back into old patterns, you will know how to get her to shift again. Of course, the best situation is where both of you are learning how to bring out the best in each other.

5. Are you saying it's my fault that my partner is treating me badly?

Sample Responses:

A. No. And I'm not saying it's your partner's fault when you treat him or her poorly, either. Each of you has free will to direct your own actions. However, it would be pretty naïve for your partner to think that his or her interactions with you have no bearing on how you react, don't you think? The same is true for you. You don't make your partner treat you poorly, but you can have a huge impact on the likelihood that he or she will treat you better or worse. That's all I'm saying.

(continues)

TABLE 8.1.
(Continued)

B. Don't get me wrong. So far as I can tell, your partner isn't doing any better than you at these things. He or she feels provoked by you, too, and your partner's reactions to you usually only make you want to be less cooperative too, right? Of course, I'll be talking to your partner about that. But I don't want you to wait around, wishing and hoping that your partner will change, when you could take things into your own hands.

T: Okay, so what's keeping you from beating down my door here, so to speak? You know, because I know that it's not going to work for you to just sort of take a few half-hearted shots at this thing. If it's gonna work, you'll have to really decide to get fully on board. Check and see if there's anything keeping you . . . from like . . .

H: . . . from banging down your door? I know what it is, but I can't put it into words. I'm scared it won't work. I guess that would be the best way to put it.

T: Um-hum.

H: I'd love to try it, but I'd be too scared it won't work.

T: What would be the worst about it not working?

H: I move out.

T: Like, how's that different from what's probably going to happen anyway?

H: I move out with a little less pain.

Brad has finally identified one reason that keeps him sitting on the fence. He hasn't resolved the issue of whether it's worth it to risk more pain. This ambivalence probably would have gone unaddressed if the therapist had accepted his verbal "yes" a minute earlier.

T: It's more painful to have tried and failed. . . .

H: . . . than it is to just cut and run.

T: Yeah

H: I don't want to cut and run, so I have to try, I have to try, not fail. I have to make it work.

Here the client agrees again to give the therapist's proposal a try, but instead of taking it and running with it, the therapist patiently validates the fear that Brad just dismissed.

T: But there is that fear that it's not going to work, and then you kind of open yourself in a way. I could see why you would hesitate to do it for that reason.

H: I've already been hurt quite a bit. Even though I don't think she thinks I have. Am I going to go for it? I know I don't seem too enthusiastic. I'm . . . I guess I'm still a little skeptical.

T: Yeah. It's a hard journey. It really will require a lot of work. And so, if you don't resolve those hesitations in the beginning, then I think we should take however much time we need to try and resolve them. And that's why I ask, seriously, you know, what are the main things that stand in the way of you going for it?

H: If we can, like, practice here . . .

T: You mean like me and you?

H: Like between you and me and the fictional character that sits over there, then I can kind of starting working it in at home.

T: Good.

H: But if she's here, I'm going to shut right off.

T: Good.

H: What I'm saying is if she knows what I'm doing, she might not respond at all, because she'll be expecting it.

T: Um, hm.

H: Then she'll sit there and say you're only doing this because he told you to do this.

Brad has now identified a second source of his lack of enthusiasm. His wife has dismissed previous efforts that Brad has made in response to previous therapists' suggestions, saying that Brad was only making the changes because the therapist told him to. The good news is that Brad makes a proposal to the therapist: Can we practice these things without my wife here? (Brad didn't know that this would be part of the therapist's plan, anyway.)

T: Good. Then we'll start with just you and me, okay? (Husband nods) So, lets see if there's anything else . . .

H: . . . that's scaring me to death?

T: Um, hmmm, because we've gone through a number of things here. And we don't have to go much longer tonight, but I just wanted to try to resolve whatever we can so that next time I see you, you're like, "Boom, boom, boom, let's go. Let's go!" (*Husband laughs.*)

T: Let's see. How about this one? Well, in order to do it, you're going to be getting critical feedback from me—constructive criticism—but there's always a risk it won't feel so constructive, that I am pointing out your faults, or something like that.

In spite of the fact that Brad's nonverbals now indicate much less ambivalence, the therapist insists on spending even more time checking for any small sign of resistance. When Brad can't come up with any more, the therapist suggests another reason. This might seem like buying trouble, but this intervention usually has a powerful, positive effect. It communicates to the client that the therapist is in no rush, and really means it when he says that he wants to resolve every possible source of ambivalence before attempting to proceed.

H: Oh yeah, that happens to me all the time.

T: (*laughter; sarcastically*) It's wonderful isn't it?

H: I don't even care anymore. I mean, she points out so many faults I'm like, "Yeah, yeah, yeah, whatever."

T: Right. So then maybe part of the reluctance could be just the process of me and you doing this could be uncomfortable. If I'm having to stop and say "That wasn't good. You know, try it this way," or something. That can be a little rough on you. It's rough on anybody. Nobody likes to set themselves up to be criticized. Do you think that's part of this?

H: How else, how else am I going learn?

T: Well that's the counterargument.

H: You have to learn from your mistakes.

T: Right.

Notice that Brad now counters the therapist's proposed reservation. Brad is now selling the therapist on the idea that he's on board. The effect of this five-minute conversation was very important. The therapist was unwilling to accept yes for an answer, and proceeded to encourage Brad to dig for more reservations. Once Brad identified and voiced them, he was able to get more fully on board.

Avoiding Arguing with the Client

A final requirement for effective implementation of the getting on board intervention is for the therapist to avoid arguing with the client. The idea of avoiding arguments is somewhat confusing to new PET-C trainees, because part of the intervention involves the therapist providing powerful counterpoints to the client's objections. Isn't a point–counterpoint debate a form of arguing? Technically, it might be, but the problematic part of the argument isn't the point–counterpoint aspect of it. Problems come when the client senses that the therapist is trying to control the client. When therapists become determined that they must convince clients to think or act in particular ways, the intervention fails. A skilled therapist is hopeful that the client will become convinced, but places higher priority on responding respectfully to the client's resistance than on persuading the client.

Arguments begin after the client has voiced an objection, the therapist has provided information intended to resolve the objection, and the client still objects. At this point, the therapist either engages in, or avoids, an argument (see Figure 8.1). To avoid an argument, the therapist must stop trying to make his or her point, and instead validate the understandable aspects of the client's objection, offer assurances (e.g., "I don't want to try to talk you into anything that doesn't make sense to you"), then wait for the client to show more interest before proceeding.

To avoid arguing, therapists must be skilled at shifting out of any defensive or critical internal states that get triggered by the client's defensiveness. Chapter 13 discusses various ways that this skill is cultivated in PET-C training for therapists. PET-C therapists minimize resistance if they enter a session with a non-argumentative mindset: The following thoughts characterize this mindset:

- It's my job to just explain things to the client as well as I can, not to make the client buy into what I'm saying.
- In the end, if the client refuses to get on board, that doesn't mean I've failed.
- In the end, if the client refuses to get on board, I'm not stuck in a non-productive situation. I don't have to keep providing therapy.
- Almost all clients must feel defensive at some point. It cannot be

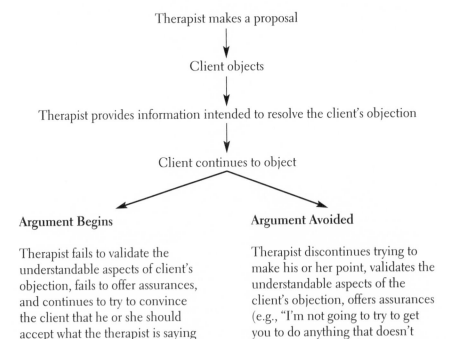

Figure 8.1   Avoiding An Argument

avoided. It doesn't mean things are going poorly. It's a necessary part of the process.

- The definition of a good session: One in which the client became defensive and I responded patiently, taking as much time as needed to address the client's concerns.
- Not the definition of a good session: One in which I successfully persuaded the client into accepting what I was saying.

CONCLUSION

Successful implementation of the Phase I interventions requires that the therapist embody the same relationship principle that he or she is proposing to the client: If you want the other person to become more receptive to you, you must respond respectfully when he or she is not being receptive to you. The key to helping clients become receptive to the therapist's ideas is for the therapist to respond respectfully when they resist getting on board. The skilled therapist awaits and welcomes moments of resistance, knowing that how he or she reacts to the client at these times will dramatically influence the course of the therapy. Responding respectfully to resistance becomes the highest priority, outranking the goal of persuading the client. In following this process, the therapist models the most basic relationship process involved in successful relationships. The process of dropping one's intent to persuade long enough to respond respectfully to resistance is precisely the process that predicts success in relationships. Like the therapist, each client is trying to persuade another person (partner) to consider the merits of his or her point of view. Like the therapist who encounters resistance from the client, the client encounters resistance from the partner. In the same way as the successful therapist lets go of his agenda to persuade long enough to react respectfully to the client's resistance, the client must let go of his agenda long enough to respond respectfully to the partner's resistance. In short, through the client's relationship with the therapist in Phase I, the client experiences what it is like to be influenced by someone who knows how to succeed in a relationship. The client will draw upon this experiential knowledge throughout the remainder of therapy.

CHAPTER 9

Retrospective Review and Prospective Planning

A S EACH PARTNER GETS on board with the focus of improving his or her own ability to meet the prerequisites, the therapy enters Phase II. In this phase of treatment, each partner receives personalized tutoring in the skills of emotional intelligence, using his or her own relationship as a workshop for practicing these skills. This is an exciting phase of therapy in which motivated clients learn a new way of navigating their relationships. Clients become expert in how to respond effectively in any upsetting situation that occurs with their partners. Prior to Phase II, clients often recount incidents of their partners upsetting actions, then ask, "Now how am I supposed to respond to that?" Half of these people are already convinced that there is no good answer to this question. In Phase II, clients learn that, indeed, there are compelling answers to this question. In fact, these same clients become expert on the question within a matter of weeks. At the end of Phase II, clients are able to take any real or hypothetical situation and discuss in detail what the components of more or less effective reactions would be.

Clients generally enter Phase II faintly aware of the extent to which their interactions with their partners are governed by the automatic patterning of internal state activations inside of them. In the course of Phase II, each partner becomes more aware of what is happening internally in the midst of interactions with the partner. Clients learn to recognize cues that signify the activation of certain internal states, and they become more adept at recognizing the triggers for these mood states. Through repetitive practice, they recondition their automatic internal reactions, enabling more flexible interactions with their partners.

The format for Phase II involves individual sessions in which partners work on developing the abilities necessary for relationship success and conjoint sessions in which partners test their abilities to react to each other effectively, under the "live" supervision of the therapist. Between sessions, each partner completes exercises designed to increase awareness of her own reactions in upsetting situations, increase her ability to understand how she can apply the habits that predict relationship success to her own relationship, and increase her abilities to change the automatic internal state activation patterns that have previously constrained her flexibility.

There are three main types of activity involved in Phase II: retrospective reviewing, prospective planning, and reconditioning internal states.

Retrospective Reviewing

Each partner reviews upsetting situations that have recently occurred between the two of them and:

- Identifies specifically the ways that his or her reactions diverged from those that predict relationship success.
- Understands specifically how his or her reactions would have been different had he or she been more able to implement the habits that predict relationship success.
- Identifies the qualities of the internal state that propelled him or her toward nonproductive reactions, or prevented the person from being able to react more fully in ways that are predictive of relationship success.
- Identifies the specific features of the upsetting situation that "triggered" the internal state that propelled him or her toward nonproductive reactions or prevented him or her from being able to react more effectively.

Prospective Planning

Each client identifies specific issues that are personally upsetting (or upsetting to the partner), then plans to have a successful conversation, by:

- Deciding when a good time might be to have the conversation.
- Developing a nonjudgmental way of looking at the partner's thinking and actions related to the issue.
- Becoming determined to find the at least partly legitimate logic behind the partner's thinking and actions on the issue.
- Thinking about how he or she can stand up for his or her position on the issue without putting down the partner.
- Being ready to assure the partner of his or her willingness to give equal regard to the partner's feelings or opinions on the issue.
- Identifying and preparing to explain bigger issues that lie beneath his or her feelings about the specific situation at hand.
- Anticipating less than desirable responses from the partner, and developing a plan for staying on track in spite of them.
- Being aware of the internal state that usually gets triggered in conversations about the issue, and avoiding activation of this state in the next

conversation, or becoming aware when it is activated and shifting out of it, or preparing to take a break from the conversation.

Reconditioning Internal States

Ordinarily, when a client becomes upset with a partner, a repetitive, predictable network of thoughts, feelings, and action tendencies arise at once in the client. The client finds him- or herself in a certain frame of mind, characterized by a specific attitude, and predictable feelings and motivations. This automatically activated internal state often interferes with the client's ability to react to the partner in ways that predict relationship success. Through repetitive practice, the client reconditions this internal state for more flexibility, enabling the client to think and act differently when he or she is upset.

Retrospective reviewing and prospective planning usually take place in individual sessions with each partner, and through homework exercises completed by each partner. Reconditioning internal states occurs in both individual and conjoint formats, and also through structured practice at home. Often, conjoint and individual segments occur in a single session. Phase II typically begins with a combination of retrospective reviewing and prospective planning, but as soon as possible, all three types of activity become incorporated into therapy sessions and homework assignments.

Although the specific upsetting situations that a client examines during each retrospective review will vary, the client will discover that his or her reactions are usually quite consistent and predictable across different types of upsetting situations. Therefore, the 20/20 hindsight that a client gleans during one retrospective review session will apply more generally to many upsetting situations the client faces. In retrospective reviewing, clients learn from their mistakes, then think about how they can apply this learning to future situations. Thus, retrospective reviewing leads naturally into prospective planning.

Retrospective reviewing and prospective planning are a critical part of Phase II, but are only part of the Phase II program, and not sufficient to accomplish the goals of Phase II. Most clients will also need repetitive practice designed to recondition automatic reactions in order to become free to interact more flexibly with his or her partner. However, awareness is the first step, and the retrospective reviewing/prospective planning process is a vehicle for increasing awareness. If a client cannot, in theory, understand the kind of reactions he or she needs to develop, he or she will stand little chance of applying them when the rubber hits the road.

DUAL FOCUS

Through retrospective reviewing, the client becomes more aware of both the automatic internal reactions that happen inside of him or her in upsetting situations, and the predictable external reactions that he or she engages in with his or her partner.

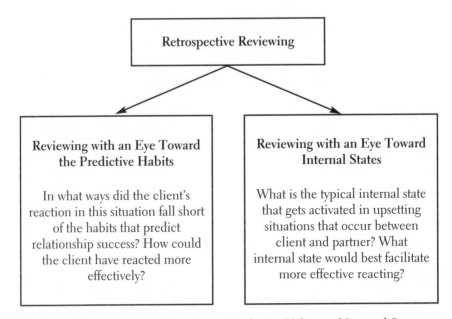

Figure 9.1 Retrospective Reviewing: Predictive Habits and Internal States

Reviewing with an Eye Toward the Predictive Habits

As the client describes the upsetting thing that the partner did (or failed to do), the therapist probes for detailed information about how the client reacted. The therapist looks for the relative presence or absence of the prerequisite abilities for successfully managing conflicts, and the habits that enable clients to meet these prerequisites (summarized in Table 3.1). If the client hasn't already received it, the therapist gives the client a user-friendly summary of the predictive habits from the workbook, *Developing Habits for Relationship Success* (Atkinson, 2005).

As the client describes his or her reactions, the therapist engages the client in a discussion of how the predictive habits could be applied in this situation. Because the therapist is giving the client critical feedback, the client will likely become defensive, and the therapist must apply the methods for cultivating client receptivity described in Chapters 6–8. Sometimes clients can easily understand how their reactions diverged from those that predict relationship success. Other times, clients will have difficulty understanding how their reactions were off-track. For example, a client may insist that he didn't have a judgmental attitude toward his partner because he held his tongue and didn't criticize her. This client doesn't understand that "avoiding a judgmental attitude" refers to what he is *thinking* about his partner, not what he *says* to her. In early retrospective review sessions, the therapist patiently clarifies what the predictive habits actually mean. Success depends upon the therapist's ability to paint a clear picture of how the client can react more effectively in the upsetting situations, and how this contrasts with how the client usually reacts. The therapist attempts to make the predictive habits as clear and concrete as possible.

Reviewing with an Eye Toward Internal States

As a client begins getting a clear picture of the kinds of changes needed in his or her reactions, it becomes obvious that many of the habits for relationship success do not come naturally to that person. The therapist helps each client understand that often, when he or she is upset, an internal response program gets triggered that carries the client's thinking and actions in unhelpful directions. The therapist explains to the client in simple language that each of our brains is equipped with conditioned brain circuits that are preprogrammed so that, once triggered, they unfold as if they had a mind of their own, producing a predictable pattern of thoughts, feelings, and behaviors. These internal response programs are known as "executive operating systems," but we don't have a single word in our everyday vocabulary that captures the essence of these internal states. Terms such as *attitudes, operating modes,* or *mood states* come closest. These automatically activated attitudes or mood states dramatically affect our motivations. In the reviewing/planning process the therapist suggests to the client that, for him or her to become more able to think and act effectively in upsetting situations, the client will first need to become very familiar with the specific internal operating modes that get triggered during upsetting situations, and will need to learn how to shift to operating modes that are more compatible with the kind of thinking and action that is needed.

As a general method for increasing awareness of the client's mood states, the therapist asks the client to describe a recent upsetting incident in vivid detail. If the client's description is vivid enough, the same internal state that was active in the upsetting incident will again become active when describing it to the therapist. When this happens, the therapist helps the client pause and study the qualities of the state (e.g., the physical feeling, the attitude and type of motivation that arises with it). Vivid recall will not always activate a similar state in the pres-ent moment. When it doesn't, the therapist asks the client to try to remember what happened internally when the upsetting situation was actually taking place.

Once clients become aware of the internal states that govern their interactions, they may be able to use this awareness to shift out of the states. However, many times clients need to engage in repetitive practices that recondition automatic internal state activations before they can change their usual reactions. Methods for these practices are described in Chapter 11.

OVERALL STRUCTURE OF THE
REVIEWING/PLANNING PROCESS

Early in the retrospective reviewing process, a decision is made on whether to review recent events, or historical events. This decision is based on the extent to which a client appears to be harboring feelings of resentment, contempt or superiority from the past. When feelings such as these exist, they must be resolved before clients will be successful in responding more effectively to their partners in the present. Methods for addressing lingering feelings of resentment, contempt or superiority from the past are described in Chapter 10 in the section, Global Judgments. Such methods are needed with approximately 60% of clients presenting for couples therapy at our clinic. Once such feelings are resolved, the focus shifts to helping these clients review week-to-week interactions. Not all clients need to resolve lingering feelings from the past, but all clients do need to work on changing their present emotional habits. The retrospective reviewing methods described in this chapter assume that clients have resolved resentments from the past.

In the reviewing/planning process, discussion about the predictive habits and internal states flow naturally from the client's description of an upsetting incident. In general, the therapist uses the following sequence: (1) Client describes the upsetting situation (2) Therapist gives compelling examples of the kinds of reactions that would likely be more effective in situations like this one (3) Client expresses objections or reservations (4) Therapist addresses reservations and makes sure client is still "on board" (5) Therapist discusses how the suggestions he or she has made are specific applications of the general predictive habits (6) Therapist gives handouts, or helps client complete worksheets designed to increase self-awareness of reactions, or to help better focus on needed changes (Atkinson, 2005).

To illustrate various aspects of retrospective reviewing and prospective planning, we will follow the progress of a couple through several sessions of their therapy. The descriptions are of Michael and Katrina, the couple introduced in Chapter 6. Katrina and Michael had come to therapy 11 years after an incident that occurred in the hospital with the birth of their first child had created a rift in their relationship. Early in therapy, the therapist helped Katrina and Michael shift internal states, then revisit the incident in a way that promoted healing between them. The couple felt immediate relief after that session, and dropped out of therapy for two months. When they returned, each partner had reverted back to their typical positions: Katrina was angry and critical of Michael; Michael was defensive and dismissive of Katrina's complaints. The therapist proceeded to conduct individual sessions with Michael and Katrina for the goal of getting each partner on board. These sessions were successful, and the therapy entered Phase II, beginning with individual retrospective reviewing with each partner. Each session began with the client reviewing a recent upsetting situation.

Early in the reviewing/planning process, Katrina recounted an incident in which Michael had agreed to help the children do their homework before supper. Michael typically got off work early, whereas Katrina didn't usually get home until 6 P.M. On the day of the incident, Michael had allowed the children to delay doing their homework because it was an unusually warm Illinois day in November, and he thought that this situation warranted an exception. Upon hearing about this, Katrina was very upset. She immediately assumed that Michael had forgotten his promise to her, and began criticizing him, neglecting to ask him why he had broken his agreement. In short, she engaged in a classic "harsh startup." In response, Michael shut down; refusing to talk to Katrina, then left the house. In an individual session a few days later, Katrina described the situation to the therapist. The following conversation then occurred:

T: I can certainly see why you were upset, and frankly, I think I would have been, too, if I were in your shoes. But Michael didn't understand?

W: He gets that look on his face that says, "Get off my back, bitch!"

T: Right! And that's the thing that's got to change.

W: It seems hopeless.

T: Katrina, here's the thing. It's way too early to tell if it's hopeless or not. You have been so off-track in your approach to him that it's impossible to tell how much his defensive reactions are due to the way he is, or how it's simply a reaction to you being off-track in your approach to him.

W: I'm sure my approach could be better.

T: Well, it's like I suggested before, Katrina. Let's see if we can get you thinking and operating like people who usually get respect and cooperation from their partners, and then see if Michael operates differently, okay?

W: I guess.

T: You don't seem so sure.

Throughout the reviewing/planning process, the therapist pauses whenever the client seems less than enthusiastic about the process or direction the therapist is suggesting. The therapist checks to be sure that the client is on board and revisits getting on board interventions described in Chapters 7 and 8 as needed.

W: It's just that when you talk like that, it makes it seem like it's all my fault.

T: I'm glad you said that, because I need to remember to keep making myself clear. I mean it seems so clear to me that he's just as off-track as you are, and that if he could get more on-track in his reactions to you, you'd treat him the way he wants to be treated, too. In my meeting with him yesterday, I told him the same thing as I'm telling you right now. Is Katrina inherently a negative person? I told him there's no way to know how much of her negativity is an ingrained part of her personality, or just a reaction to you being off-track yourself. Both of you have been way off-track, Katrina. Either one of you could single-handedly sink this ship, but if either of you really got on track, you'd get what you need from the other.

W: Okay, it's worth a try.

T: Are you sure, because I don't want to be headed down a road you really don't want to travel.

W: No, you're probably right. I need to get more on track myself. Then I'll decide what to do.

T: Okay, now I'm getting a little bit excited.

W: Don't get carried away!

T: Right. One step at a time. Let's take it slow.

W: Okay.

T: So let's talk for a minute about how people who are really good at getting what they need from their partners go about doing it. Researchers have been able to identify at least six things they do differently when they initially approach their partners with a complaint. These things are in your workbook, and I'll show you where in just a minute, but for now, let's just talk about how they might react in a situation like the one you just described.

The workbook the therapist is referring to is *Developing Habits for Relationship Success* (Atkinson, 2005), which contains approximately 40 handout/exercises used in Phases II and III of PET-C. There are two versions of the workbook, one for people who have male partners and another for people who have female partners. (The content of the workbooks is the same, except for male and female pronouns.) These workbooks are available in CD-Rom format for therapists to use with their clients. Digital technology allows each partner's name to be inserted into the handouts/exercises. A personalized workbook is printed for each client that refers to his/her partner's name over 350 times throughout the exercises in the workbook. Excerpts from Katrina's workbook are included as appendices at the end of this book. Appendix A shows a chart from Katrina's workbook called, The Sequence: Knowing How and When to Implement Each Predictive Habit When Upsets Occur. Notice that Katrina's chart is customized so that Michael's name is inserted into it in various places. The Sequence is a step-by-step process for combining the predictive habits into powerful movements that elicit respectfulness from one's partner. As partners progress through PET-C, they not only learn the 10 predictive habits described in Chapter 3, but they also learn *when* particular habits are needed, and *how* to use them effectively. When upsetting situations arise, the Sequence helps clients know which habits to use, and in what order they should be used. The Sequence is divided into two sections. Using The First Steps clients make it easy for their partners to interact respectfully and cooperatively with them. Using the second group of steps (7–12) clients require that their partners treat them respectfully, if they haven't already begun doing so in response to the client's "first steps." Steps 7–12 provide a powerful, positive series of moves that enable clients to stand up for themselves without putting their partners down. The therapist's suggestions throughout each retrospective review session are guided by his or her knowledge of the Sequence.

T: The first thing that people who are able to get what they need from their partners do involves their attitude. They avoid jumping to conclusions, and give their partners the benefit of the doubt. In your situation, it would involve keeping an open mind, and rather than deciding that Michael did something wrong, it would involve assuming that there must be some at least partly legitimate reason for Michael's actions.

The therapist's suggestion is an example of the application of step 2 of the Sequence, Giving the Benefit of the Doubt (Appendix A). People who fail in their relationships tend to assume that their partners' upsetting actions are due to misguided reasoning, priorities, motivations, intentions, or faulty personality characteristics. In contrast, people destined to succeed assume that beneath even seemingly provocative behavior, there is a legitimate something that their partners are going after.

W: But what if there isn't any legitimate reason for what he did? What if he just screwed up? He promised me that he'd have them do homework before they went out to play!

The PET-C therapist assumes that, more often than not, the client will have reservations or objections to the proposed changes, and is prepared to offer assurances or clarifications, then check to be sure that the client is still on board.

T: Well, if you were able to operate like one of these highly successful people, you might come to this conclusion in the end, but you wouldn't start out assuming that he screwed up. You'd give him the benefit of the doubt, and just ask him why he did what he did.

W: He'd still react defensively.

T: Probably. But people who are good at getting what they need from their partners anticipate that their partners might think they are accusing, even when they aren't, and so they're ready to assure their partners that this is not the case. You might have to say, "Michael, this isn't a trick question! I'm assuming that there's probably some reason why you did this, and I'm just asking you what your thinking was."

The therapist's suggestion is an example of step 5 of the Sequence, Offering Assurance (Appendix A) Although the sequential ordering of the "first steps" of the Sequence (steps 1–6) is often useful, as can be seen in this example, the first steps can be implemented flexibly, and the order need not be adhered to strictly. A successful person realizes that when a partner responds defensively even when he or she isn't being critical or demanding, he or she just needs to be reassured rather than blamed for assuming the worst. After all, many times in the past, the partner would have been correct in his or her assumptions. People destined for relationship failure, however, tend to respond to false accusations by becoming indignant and critical of their partners.

Of course, the problem in this situation was that Katrina *was* being critical of Michael's after-school decision. A person can't offer assurances unless he or she is truly willing to give a partner the benefit of the doubt.

W: I already know why he did it. He just wasn't thinking. He was tired and didn't want the hassle of having to deal with grumpy kids. He always takes the easy way out.

T: Well that might be the case, Katrina. But there's often more than meets the eye. Sometimes, the reasons why people act as they do aren't obvious. People who get what they need from their partners find a way to suspend judgment and exhaust all of their efforts to find the reasons that at first might not be apparent.

The therapist's suggestion is an example of step 3 of the Sequence, Finding the Understandable Part (Appendix A). Many partners are hesitant to acknowledge anything understandable about their partner's point of view, thinking that if they give an inch, their partners will take a mile. People destined to succeed in their relationships don't worry about this, because they know that they can always stand up for their own point of view later. There is no rush. They know that just because they acknowledge something legitimate about their partner's point of view doesn't mean that their own point of view isn't legitimate, too. They are able to do two things in succession: Acknowledge the understandable part of their partner's opinions and then stand up for their own opinions, if needed. In our experience, people who have difficulty acknowledging the understandable part of their partner's feelings often also have difficulty standing up for their own feelings effectively. In couples therapy, partners must often learn to do both of these things at the same time. Partners will only be able to acknowledge the understandable aspects of their partner's feelings if they are confident that they can stand up for their own.

T: In a few minutes, I'll show you a chart in your workbook that might help you consider possible reasons why Michael acts in seemingly selfish ways. I've already had a chance to talk with Michael about this incident, and I know that there is a reason that doesn't seem to have occurred to you.

The therapist refrains from showing Katrina the worksheet at the moment, because he doesn't want to interrupt the flow of the conversation. He will return to it at the end of the session. In future weeks, Katrina was able to use this worksheet, titled, Finding the Understandable Part: Common Hidden Reasons (Appendix B) to help her keep an open mind about Michael's actions. The worksheet lists common, but often overlooked, reasons that help explain one's partner's actions.

W: Like what?

T: Like the fact that it was an unusually nice day outside. Do you remember? Last Tuesday it got up to almost 70 degrees. He felt that this warranted an exception.

W: That's not a good enough reason! You don't understand. With Michael, there's always some excuse.

T: Listen to me, Katrina. That might not be a good enough excuse so far as you're concerned, but not everybody feels the way that you do about these things. For you, there are probably very few things that would warrant an exception for the after-school rule. But I know plenty of good people who would make an exception with weather like last Tuesday's.

Here, the therapist is referencing one of the common, but often overlooked, reasons that can help explain one's partner's seemingly objectionable actions:

Maybe your partner just has really different priorities or expectations than you do. Maybe he was acting perfectly consistently with his priorities. You just don't like it because they are different than yours, but that doesn't make them wrong.

W: Well I wouldn't! I don't want my kids to get into bad habits.
T: And your feelings need to count here, Katrina. I'm not disputing that. All I'm saying is that, if you want to influence Michael, you've got to be willing to work with him and his priorities, too. This doesn't mean you're supposed to just give in and let Michael do things the way he wants. But it does mean that you'll need to find a way to avoid criticizing Michael and instead ask him to try to work with you to find a way of dealing with these types of situations that you can both live with.

The therapist's suggestion is an example of step 6 of the Sequence, Work With Me? (Appendix A). Successful people realize that they don't have to prove that their partners are wrong in order to ask them to change. Rather than criticizing, they say things like, "I think we may have a difference of opinion here.

I'm sure that there's more than one way to look at situations like this. I'm not saying that we have to do things my way, I'm just asking you to work with me to find a solution we can both feel okay about.

T: Once Michael becomes convinced that you're not saying that you're right and he's wrong, and that you're willing to give his viewpoint equal consideration, he'll become more willing to listen to you. Right now, he's not really interested in your point of view because he's feeling criticized. But once he becomes convinced that, when the conversation is over, you'll be willing to "work with him," he'll really listen. And when he does, if you're smart, you'll avoid telling him he's wrong, and instead just try to explain why this issue is so important to you. That's what people who get more cooperation from their partners do, Katrina. But let me make sure that I understand you. Why is it so important to you that the kids always do their homework before going out to play?

W: Because they need to learn how to delay gratification. If you're gonna get ahead in life, you need to learn to work before you play.

T: So you're afraid that they'll turn out to be undisciplined?

Here the therapist is moving Katrina toward step 4 of the Sequence, What's Driving My Upset? (Appendix A). Rather than trying to convince their partners that their own viewpoints are superior, people who succeed in relationships identify the bigger needs, values, worries, or fears that drive their reactions in particular situations, and they attempt to explain these underlying feelings.

W: Yes, and I know what I'm talking about because both of my parents were this way. (*Katrina goes on to explain how each of her parents were "undisciplined" and how she and her siblings suffered because of it.*)

T: So, here's what it might sound like if you were able to approach Michael in a way that would maximize the chances that he would respect your viewpoint. You might say something like, "Michael, I know that not everybody feels as strongly as I do about these things, but, because of how my parents are, I want to pay special attention to making sure that our kids are disciplined. I want them to have fun, too, but it really makes me anxious when I see them blowing off their homework or chores just because they don't want to do them."

Clients often have difficulty identifying the needs or fears that drive their reactions in specific situations, and instead, they get caught in arguing the rightness or wrongness of their partners' actions in particular situations. In our Workbook for clients, we include a worksheet that includes a list of basic needs that often drive clients reactions in important situations (see What's Driving Me?, Appendix C). Because he didn't want to interrupt the flow of the conversation, the therapist didn't show Katrina this form at that point, but rather drew her attention to it at the end of the session. In future weeks, Katrina used this sheet to help her identify what was driving her reactions when she became upset, and to communicate them to Michael.

W: I've told him my feelings about this a hundred times. He doesn't care.

T: Yeah, but Katrina, it seems very likely to me that he was unable to hear you because he was also feeling criticized, or that you were unwilling to respect his viewpoint.

W: I don't think you understand. I could say it in the nicest way, and he'd still just think I was overreacting, or blowing things out of proportion.

T: What do you mean?

W: I mean that if I approached him with a good attitude, which, I admit, I don't do very often, but if I did, and I told him that I was worried that the kids would be undisciplined if they go out and play before finishing their work, he'd just call me neurotic, and tell me that I needed to lighten up, and that I worry too much.

Thus far, the therapist has taken Katrina through each of the first steps of the Sequence summarized in Appendix A. But Katrina is bringing up an important question. What if she does all of the *first steps*, and approaches Michael with a good attitude and he still dismisses her, or refuses to cooperate with her? It is vitally important that Katrina realize that the therapist has a contingency plan for this possibility. While it is possible, and maybe even likely, that Michael would respond differently if Katrina approached him more positively, it's also quite possible that he'd react the same old way. It is unlikely that Katrina will be able to drop her judgmental thinking, look for the understandable reasons for Michael's actions, and explain the needs or fears that drive her feelings unless she's confident that she can stand up effectively for herself if Michael continues to dismiss her point of view.

The first steps generally involve a softening of the person who is initiating a complaint. Such a softening is necessary, but often not sufficient, to motivate increased cooperativeness on the part of the other partner. Many clients have spent years thinking, "If I just love him more, he'll treat me better." Clients must not only have the skills that make it easy for their partners to treat them with respect (i.e., the first steps). Sometimes, they must *require* that they be treated with respect, if needed. They must insist that their partners give their viewpoints equal regard, and become angry if they do not. The second half of the Sequence provides a path for accomplishing this (Appendix A). The effectiveness of the Sequence hinges on the ability of a person to become angry when they are disregarded and stand up firmly for him or herself, without making a big deal of a partner's temporary uncooperativeness.

T: Okay, you might be right. It's possible that even if you bring up an issue
       with a good attitude, Michael won't work with you. For example, you
       might avoid jumping to conclusions and keep an open mind, identify the
       understandable part of his feelings, you might try to explain why the issue
       is important to you, assure him that you're not saying that you're right and
       he's wrong, and avoid criticizing and simply ask him to work with you.
       Michael would still dismiss your feelings. This happens all the time in re-
       lationships. People who are good at getting what they need from their part-
       ners don't panic here, because they know that it's not over.

W: What do you mean?

T: People who end up getting the things they need from their partners antici-
       pate that, even when they have a good attitude, their partners might not
       become cooperative, and they know how to handle this kind of situation.

W: What do they do?

T: Well, the first thing they do is maintain their cool. Then they say some-
       thing like, "Look! I'm not saying that I'm right or that you're wrong, or that
       we have to do things totally my way here. But I don't think that I'm wrong
       and you're right, either. I realize that we may have different points of view
       on this, and I'm trying to work with you here, but it feels like you're shut-
       ting me down! Are you gonna work with me?

   The therapist is suggesting an application of steps 7 and 8 of the
Sequence, Maintain Your Cool and Offer and Ask (Appendix A). In the *offer and
ask* step, the client makes one last effort to promote mutual cooperation by clarifying her offer to work collaboratively, and asking her partner to do the same. We
see the offer and ask step as hugely important, and spend a lot of time discussing
it with clients. When it is implemented well, it usually has the effect of a friendly
warning. The person offering and asking is making one last attempt to elicit respectfulness before breaking off negotiations (temporarily) and returning hostile
fire. It signals a possible transition from cooperativeness to self-defense. The person making the offer and ask move is, in effect, saying something like, "Up to this
point, I've been trying to work with you, but if you're not going to work with me,
then I'm going to stop trying, too." The offer and ask move concludes with the
client "calling the question." Are you willing to work with me or not?

W: And what if he won't budge? He's *really* stubborn.

T: Then you'd need to get angry. At that point, you'd have been really trying
       to be reasonable in spite of your strong feelings, and in spite of this, he is
       completely dismissing you. It would be pretty normal to be angry at this
       point, and that's what we find that successful people do.

   The therapist is beginning to suggest an application of the Stand Up/En-
gage step of the Sequence. This step is only suggested when, in spite of the

first steps and the offer and ask step, the client's partner continues to completely dismiss the client's concerns. In PET-C, we regard the ability to get angry and stand up forcefully in the face of a dismissal to be every bit as important as the ability to calm one's anger and give one's partner equal regard. A partner who continues to try to be cooperative when his or her partner is unwilling will likely doom the relationship to failure. Successful people connect easily with anger when it is needed, then let it go just as easily when it is no longer needed.

W: I'm confused. I thought I wasn't supposed to get angry.

T: It's all a matter of timing. If you come into a conversation angry and critical, you won't get very far with Michael. But if you have made every effort to be respectful, avoid criticizing him, and offer to work with him to find a solution that includes his feelings, and he's still unwilling to cooperate with you, then you'd better become angry, because if you don't, you won't likely get much cooperation from Michael. There's a time for everything. At this point, you'd need to sort of let him have it. You'd say something like, "Who the hell do you think you are? I'm going out of my way to work with you here, even though I feel very strongly about my position. I don't expect you to agree with me, but I do expect you to work with me, buddy. Is this the way it's going to be?

W: If I talk to him like that, he'll just shut down even tighter.

Of course, Michael might not shut down. At any point in the Sequence, he may instead show signs of a willingness to collaborate. Katrina must be able to respond to any sign of cooperativeness by backing off and returning to the first steps. In this conversation, however, the therapist accepts Katrina's assumption that Michael would continue to be uncooperative.

T: Probably, but that doesn't have to be a problem.

W: What on earth are you talking about?

T: This is just the next part of a bigger sequence that people who are powerful in influencing their partners do. Actually, you may need to go even one step further, and reject him for the moment. If he was still unwilling to work with you, you'd probably need to say something like, "You know what? I don't even want to be around you right now!"

W: Actually, I think I'm pretty good at this part!

Katrina is right. This part of the Sequence (Appendix A, step 10, Reject Your Partner) wouldn't be any problem for her. She connects easily with her anger. Her problem is letting go of the anger, and avoiding getting stuck in contemptuous thinking, which the therapist will help her realize in a moment. Different parts of the Sequence are difficult for different people. Michael has a much harder time connecting with and expressing his anger (see the section in Chapter 10, When a Client is Criticized or Attacked).

T: Good. The problem as I see it is that you tend to do this way too early in the conversation when it really isn't needed, and then get stuck in your anger and are unable to do the final two parts of the Sequence.

W: There's more?

T: Yep. If you stop here, things probably won't get any better. The next step is probably the hardest, and it would need to happen when you're all by yourself. To have an impact on Michael, you'd need to let go of your anger and, in your own mind, you'd need to avoid making a big deal of his uncooperative attitude. You'd need to be thinking things like, "It's not a crime that he was being so stubborn. I do that sometimes, too. It's natural enough for Michael to want to have his own way. No biggie. I just needed to make it clear that his attitude won't fly with me, and I did. I stood up for myself and made it clear that life won't be easy for him if he's gonna dismiss me like that. I can let it go now and give him another chance to change his mind later."

    The therapist is suggesting the application of a crucial step in the Sequence, Don't Make a Big Deal of It (Appendix A). Often, clients resent having to stand up for their own viewpoints in their relationships. They believe that their partners should automatically be willing to give them equal regard, and feel that there's something wrong with their partners if they don't. Either verbally or nonverbally, they communicate something like, "You are disgusting for being unwilling to cooperate with me, especially since I have been willing to respect your viewpoint." Of course, this attitude comes across as a put-down to their partners, and usually promotes further negative escalation. Although it's difficult (and perhaps impossible) for a client to avoid this attitude at the moment when he or she is standing up for him- or herself, successful clients let go of this attitude in the moments and hours following an episode in which they needed to stand up for themselves. They develop an attitude that communicates, "I don't blame you for being stubborn. That's natural enough. I've been that way too many times. No problem. You crossed the line. I let you have it. We're even. No problem. We'll try again later."

W: I don't know if I could do that part.

T: You probably couldn't, at least not right away. This is hard for anybody to do. I have a hard time doing it, too. It might take you hours to make the shift in your attitude. But the shift would be absolutely necessary if you wanted to get something different from Michael. You can learn to do this, Katrina, and I can help you learn. But you have to decide that you want it. The Sequence won't have to go this far with any luck. If you approach Michael with a good attitude to begin with, odds are pretty good that he'll be more cooperative without you needing to get angry and reject him. I'm taking you through the whole sequence because I want you to realize that it doesn't matter if he's uncooperative all along the way. If you can stay on track, he will become more cooperative in the future.

Here, the therapist is communicating the idea that it's not a big deal if Michael doesn't respond right away, because there is a clear path of thinking and action that Katrina can take that will lead to much more cooperation from Michael in the future. This path of thinking and action is the Sequence. Later on, the therapist will help solidify The Sequence in Katrina's mind by showing her a chart in her workbook that presents it in graphic form (see Appendix D).

W: I can't see how this will work.

T: Let me finish. There's one more step, and you can't leave this one out. At some point, you'd need to initiate another conversation about the topic. How you do this is really important. You'd need to approach him with a good attitude and say something like, "That didn't go very well, did it? It's not that I don't care about how you feel about this, I was just having a hard time because I felt I was trying and you weren't. But maybe you were just in a bad mood, or maybe I wasn't communicating well. You wanna try talking about it again? I really am willing to try to work together to try to figure out how to deal with situations like this in a way where we both feel that our opinions count."

W: That's it?

T: Yep. You don't demand an apology. You don't try to get him to see how unreasonable his behavior was. You just offer an assurance of your good intentions and open the door to discussing the issue again. Then you approach the conversation with a good attitude, like you did the first time. Of course, this conversation might not go any better. You need to be ready to repeat the whole sequence, and stand up firmly for yourself, if necessary. But chances are that you won't have to, because he'll sense your good attitude, and he'll also remember that if he doesn't respect your viewpoint, you'll let him have it again!

The request (or demand) for an apology usually arises from an attitude in which the requesting partner feels that he or she is somehow more of a victim than the partner. However, the partner usually (rightly) takes the demand for an apology as a put-down, and such requests often spawn endless discussions about who is truly more guilty in the relationship. In our experience, successful partners rarely feel a need for an apology, because they don't feel victimized. They don't feel victimized, because they stood up for themselves forcefully in the moments when it was needed. This is why it's so crucial that clients are able to stand up for themselves when they feel disrespected. It enables them to move on more cleanly, without resentment, in future discussions.

W: I don't think I can do any of this. It's like you're talking a foreign language
        to me.

Each step of the Sequence is crucial, and unlike the First Steps (steps 1–6),
the remaining steps must be implemented in sequential order. If one's partner
continues to be dismissive, every step must be made along the way, or the process
will be ineffective.

T: I know. It will require a lot of effort, but the good thing is that it's almost
        guaranteed to work. People who can do these things get cooperation from
        their partners. It's as simple as that. I've had to work really hard at being
        able to do these things in my own relationships, and I know first-hand how
        effective it can be. But you have to decide that you really want to learn
        how to do this.

W: I don't know where to begin.

T: We begin by having you become a student of your own reactions.

At this point, the therapist directed Katrina to a sheet in her workbook titled
Reviewing My Reactions, and asked her to use it each time she got upset with
Michael in the following week (Appendix E). The sheet provided a structure for
Katrina to review, in retrospect, how she operated when she got upset. The therapist went over the sheet with Katrina in detail, asking her first to rate the extent
to which she believed she implemented each step of the Sequence. After rating
herself, the review sheet asks Katrina to use the back side to answer the following questions:

1. Where did you first get off-track in your reactions to Michael?
2. If you could do the situation over again, what is one change you could
   make in your thinking that would help your attitude or state of mind,
   and allow you to interact with Michael more effectively (i.e., more on-
   track with the Sequence?
3. If you could do the situation over again, what is one change you could
   make in the way you talked or acted toward Michael that would make
   you more effective (i.e., more on-track with the Sequence).

This review process helps clients focus on their own reactions in upsetting
situations, and come to each reviewing/planning session with questions about
how they could more effectively implement the predictive habits. The review
form helps clients keep from slipping into endless complaining about their partners, and we consider it to be an important part of Phase II of PET-C.

During her second retrospective review/prospective planning session, the
therapist helped Katrina focus on her internal reactions in upsetting situations.
Specifically, the therapist helped Katrina realize that, at the moments when

Michael does something that upsets her, she usually kicks into a state of mind that makes it impossible to implement the first steps of the Sequence effectively. The therapist began socializing Katrina to the idea that to get better at the predictive habits, she'd first need to become better at shifting internal states.

To help her become more aware of the internal state that governed her reactions to Michael, the therapist helped her complete a sheet in her workbook, Studying Your State of Mind (see Appendix F). In this worksheet, Katrina was asked to describe the state of mind that gets triggered inside of her in situations like the one involving Michael and the after-school homework. Specifically, this worksheet asked Katrina to describe what this mood state feels like inside, to identify the types of words, nonverbal gestures, actions, or circumstances that tend to trigger this mood state, and to recognize the kind of thoughts that are usually present when the state is active. The worksheet then prompted Katrina to consider what kind of internal state would be needed for her to be able to interact differently with Michael in the future, and to identify the kinds of things she might try to do or say differently once her mood state shifted. Katrina's responses can be found in Appendix F. Completing this form helped Katrina become more aware of the extent that her internal reactions in upsetting situations were automatic, instantaneous, and utterly predictable. As she and the therapist gave attention to the mood state that typically kicked in when she became upset with Michael, the therapist used words that encouraged Katrina to think of this automatic response as coming from a "part" of her that had a mind of her own. The therapist suggested that she could have a relationship with this part of her, and find ways to elicit more cooperativeness from "her," too (methods for accomplishing this were described in Chapter 6; see Table 6.3).

The therapist conducted retrospective reviewing/prospective planning sessions with Michael, too. As the therapist reviewed the after-school incident with Michael, it became clear that, like Katrina, Michael had failed to implement any of the components of successful responding. Specifically, Michael dismissed the validity of Katrina's complaint, assuming that it arose from a neurotic tendency Katrina had for hyperstructuring life. Michael didn't explain to Katrina why he made the weather-related exception, because he assumed that she would reject his reasoning. Michael avoided Katrina, because he lacked the ability to stand up for his own viewpoints. The therapist used the same reviewing/planning process with Michael as he had with Katrina: Michael described the after-school incident, the therapist painted a clear picture of the kinds of reactions that would be more effective in situations like this one, Michael expressed reservations, the therapist addressed these reservations patiently, and checked carefully to be certain that Michael was still on board. The therapist concluded the session by noting how the suggestions he made were specific applications of the Sequence, and he directed Michael to information on the Sequence in his workbook (Atkinson, 2005). The therapist asked Michael to review any upsetting situation in the coming week using the review sheet from his workbook (Reviewing My Reactions, Appendix E).

In the following session, the therapist helped Michael focus on the internal state that was often activated automatically inside of him each time Katrina became upset. The therapist helped Michael realize that, at the moments when Katrina became upset with him, he usually kicked into a state of mind that made it impossible to respond effectively. Michael began to realize that it would do little good to know how to respond effectively if he could not find a way to change this automatically activated internal state. As he had with Katrina, the therapist used a worksheet (Studying Your State of Mind, Atkinson, 2005) to help Michael increase awareness of this interfering internal state.

A common mistake made by inexperienced therapists involves attempting to implement steps 5 or 6 before steps 2 and 3 of the reviewing/planning process. Before trying to teach the general principles of effective relationship functioning or developing a plan for helping the client learn them, a skilled PET-C therapist captures the client's attention by giving him or her a compelling example of how he or she could react more effectively in a specific situation. To do so, the therapist takes the client back into the recent upsetting situation, then gives clear examples of the kinds of thinking and actions that would be effective in responding in this type of situation. Only when the client seems to agree that this way of responding would have been better than his or her original response, does the therapist proceed to explain how this way of responding is an example of the application of the Sequence for effectively implementing the predictive habits (Appendix A). If the therapist starts "teaching" before she or he has captured the client's interest, the session will often take on the feel of a class in which the students are uninterested or bored. Beginning therapists tend to rely too heavily on the worksheets and handouts, failing to give adequate attention to step 2 (giving compelling examples of how the client could better react in the recently upsetting situation). However, when the timing is right, handouts and worksheets play a vital role in the client's learning. Appendix G shows a set of guidelines from Katrina's workbook that she referred to many times between sessions. This set of guidelines (titled, "Understanding the Sequence) helped deepen her understanding of the importance of each step of the Sequence. The reader is encouraged to read these guidelines before proceeding to Chapter 10. A thorough understanding of each of the steps will aid in the assimilation of information in the coming chapters.

CHAPTER 10

Critical Aspects of Reviewing/Planning

THE SEQUENCE THAT PET-C clients use to guide their reactions to each other in upsetting situations (Appendices A and G) relies most heavily on two predictive habits, avoiding a judgmental attitude, and standing up for onself without putting one's partner down. Unless clients have a clear understanding of these predictive habits, they typically have difficulty implementing the Sequence successfully.

AVOIDING A JUDGMENTAL ATTITUDE

A nonjudgmental attitude involves keeping an open mind. It refers to a stance of looking for (not necessarily having found) an understandable reason for one's partner's actions. To avoid judgmental thinking, one must refrain from jumping to negative conclusions. If a person jumps to negative conclusions, it becomes unlikely that he or she will even look for positive ones. Letting go of judgmental assumptions helps clients become open to finding understandable explanations for their partners' actions. Judgmental attitudes can be either situational or global. The global form occurs when, overall, a partner judges himself or herself to be better in some sense (more mature, more rational, etc.) than his or her partner. Situational judgments occur when a client adopts judgmental explanations for a partner's actions or viewpoints in specific situations.

Global Judgments

During the assessment phase, it may become clear to the therapist that one or both partners harbor feelings of resentment, contempt or superiority stemming from their past relationship history. Such lingering feelings are usually an indication that the client has a belief such as one of the following:

- My partner has treated me worse than I've treated him or her.
- My partner is the villain in the story of our relationship.
- My partner is the bad guy.
- In general, my partner has behaved more poorly than I.
- I have more reason to be upset than he or she does.
- I am more emotionally mature than my partner.
- I am a better person to be in a relationship with than my partner is.

During the assessment phase, the therapist explicitly confirms the presence of such beliefs, asking questions such as: "I know you don't like to think about it like this, but it seems to me that down deep inside, you're afraid that you're just more emotionally mature than your partner, right?" Clients who feel superior to their partners don't always put this attitude into words, but their partners feel the client's sense of superiority acutely, and usually develop an impenetrable defensiveness in return. A superior attitude is the kiss of death to a relationship, and a skilled therapist helps clients who feel superior come to recognize this. A successful therapist conducts conversation about the client's superior attitude without the client coming to feel judged by the therapist. The therapist conveys humility and respectfulness, providing support and empathy from the very beginning. However, the therapist avoids sugar coating his or her words or beating around the bush. Skilled therapists combine strong challenge with strong support (see examples in Chapters 6–8). The PET-C therapist challenges the client's sense of superiority, often using a sequence of points similar to the following:

1. I think I can see how it feels to be you in this relationship. You walk on egg shells (You feel constantly dismissed, you feel controlled, etc.).
2. I want you to understand that I won't be satisfied until you feel more respected by your partner.
3. The question is, "Why is your partner like this?"
4. I've heard you say that you think it's because your partner is basically selfish (irresponsible, controlling, emotionally immature, etc.).
5. I've also heard you say that you don't think you treat your partner as poorly as she treats you. It seems to you that you behave more acceptably than your partner does in your relationship. You feel that you have more to complain about than your partner does. Although you don't want to accept it, down deep in there you feel that you're a better person to be in a relationship with than your partner, right?
6. It's not like you want to believe this. You come by your feelings honestly. It just seems like the honest truth, right?

7. I know that if I can't help you find a different way to make sense of the condition of your relationship, it's pretty much "game over." I don't think your relationship will survive. Relationship studies confirm that once people begin believing that their partners are flawed or that their partners are mostly to blame for their relationship problems, it's almost impossible for their partners to change. When you cross over the line from anger to disgust, or from being frustrated by your differences to seeing yourself as better than your partner, you seal the fate of your relationship. If I can't help you come back across that line, it's very unlikely that things will ever get better.

8. Here's why. Once your partner begins sensing that you've written her off, you'll bring out the worst in her. It might not seem like it, but your partner cares very much about what you think of her, and your critical judgment is a huge powerful negative force in your relationship. Once upon a time, your partner felt that you were her biggest fan. When you entered her life, she felt that finally, someone understood and loved her. She felt your loyalty and knew that together, you guys could do anything. She's still reeling from the dramatic shift in your attitude. You went from being her strongest supporter to her harshest critic. It felt to her like you joined the other side. At this point, she's fighting for her life. She knows how much disdain you have for her.

9. It's likely that you're on your high horse because you've believed that you could be more influential from up there. But the evidence overwhelmingly suggests the opposite. People who get on their high horses are notoriously ineffective in getting the kind of respect and cooperation they want from their partners. In fact, each time a person becomes critical, he or she loses a little more of his or her personal power. It's almost impossible for anyone to respect a partner who has a superior attitude.

10. You need to understand that not everybody whose partners behave in seemingly outlandish ways get on their high horses like you do. People who succeed in getting respect and cooperation from their partners know how to stand up for themselves without assuming negative explanations for their partner's actions. We've studied these people very carefully, and we know how they do it. I can teach you, but not as long as you hold on to the story of your relationship that casts your partner in the role of villain.

11. It's very unlikely that your partner will be able to respond to you differently until you release the death grip you've got on her. You'll need to find a way to loosen the choke hold . . . put your weapon back in the holster. Your weapon is your belief that she's more to blame for the condition of your relationship than you are. It's your conclusion that she acts the way she does because she's a controlling person.

12. Of course, if the best explanation for your partner's actions is that she's a controlling person, and if she's really more to blame for your relationship problems than you are, then there's nothing you can do about it. You can't bullshit yourself. It doesn't help to try to put a positive spin on it, or try to sugar coat your own thinking. But if there's another explanation for what's happened in your relationship (other than one that characterizes your partner as flawed and casts her in the role of primary villain) you desperately need it. As far as I can tell, it's your only way out of this mess. People who are influential in their relationships leave no stone unturned in their search for non-judgmental explanations for their partners upsetting actions.

13. Fortunately, I don't think you need to look very far. I believe there are credible alternative explanations for why your partner has been acting this way, and I'll be happy to share them with you, but only if you want me to. And it seems clear to me that you have contributed just as powerfully to your relationship problems as your partner has, and I can tell you why if you want me to. What is your reaction to what I'm saying?

The therapist invites reservations, validates and addresses them patiently, avoids getting into an argument, and maintains a respectful, nurturing attitude toward the client as the client struggles with the challenging information issued by the therapist. Throughout, the therapist draws upon the methods for cultivating a receptive internal state discussed in Chapters 6–8. The therapist moves on only when the client seems to be genuinely interested in hearing more of what the therapist has to say.

At the point where the client becomes interested in hearing more, the therapist must be prepared to do three things: 1) Present a compelling nonjudgmental explanation of the partner's seemingly provocative actions, 2) Help[the client come to understand that he has contributed as powerfully to the condition of the relationship as has his partner, and 3) Begin describing how the client can stand up for himself while letting go of the critical attitude.

The therapist presents a compelling non-judgmental explanation for the partner's seemingly provocative actions. To present a compelling non-judgmental explanation for the partner's seemingly provocative actions, the therapist must have a good understanding of the partners' core differences discussed in Chapter 5 (independence first vs. togetherness first, invest in the future first vs. live for the moment first, predictability first vs. spontaneity first, slow to upset vs. readily upset, problem solving first vs. understanding first).

By the time distressed couples begin therapy, they often have developed the belief that their partners are constitutionally flawed at a basic level. Such clients can often be heard making statements such as, "My husband is self-centered to the core. I didn't see it in the beginning, because he put on a good front. But I see it now. How could I have been so blind?" The therapist proposes to such clients a different explanation for their partner's behaviors: "What began as your partner's normal, healthy, but different tendency for maintaining emotional stability escalated into rigid, exaggerated or extreme behaviors under the weight of your critical judgment."

Relationship problems often begin with the frustrations that arise from partners' legitimately different priorities or ways of navigating life. These core differences are often experienced by each other as insensitivities or injustices, partly because each partner's way of maintaining emotional stability interferes with the other's way of maintaining stability. For example, when stressed, an independence-first person will often need some space to think about things while a togetherness-first person needs closeness to reduce his or her stress. The independence-first partner's way of maintaining emotional stability directly interferes with that of the togetherness-first partner. Likewise, a predictability-first person's need for structure directly interferes with a spontaneity-first partner's way of relieving stress.

Relationships begin spiraling downward when, rather than seeing their partner's behavior as arising from legitimately different priorities or ways of maintaining emotional stability, each partner interprets the other's behavior from within their own framework. From within their own way of looking at things, the other person appears as insensitive, selfish, misguided, irresponsible, lazy, controlling, etc. (e.g., "I would never treat him the way that he treats me!"; "I would never get upset over such a little thing!") This is an easy mistake to make. In a sense, each partner is just following the Golden Rule: "Do unto others as you would have them do unto you." Neither partner is asking the other to do anything that he or she wouldn't do him or herself. The problem with this approach is that partners often want different things. They want their partners to do unto them as they would do to their partners.

As each partner continues to judge the other by his or her own standard, and the other continues to fall short, each partner may begin to write the other person off as constitutionally flawed at a basic level (insensitive, selfish, negative, mean-spirited, etc.). When people realize that their partners have written them off as hopeless, their reactions usually become more rigid and inflexible. Sensing that nothing they can do will change their partners' minds, they begin thinking "What's the point in even trying? I might as well just do whatever I want!"

By the time partners enter therapy, they've often polarized to the point where each of them looks extreme. After months of criticism from his partner, a spontaneity-first person might be acting irresponsible by most anyone's standards. His partner is certain that this is because he is finally revealing his true, irresponsible self. The therapist counters such pathologizing explanations with statements like the following: "You are seeing an extreme or exaggerated version of a basic tendency of your partner which is quite normal, but very different than yours. Your partner's behavior is exaggerated not because of a fundamental personality defect, but in response to feeling threatened by your reactions. Your partner feels that you do not value or understand something very important to him or her. This has been alarming to your partner, and has triggered fairly intense and sometimes extreme behavior on his or her part. Your partner knows that you have interpreted his or her reactions as evidence that s/he is flawed, and this has escalated your partner's behavior even more. Through your failure to recognize and support the legitimate dreams and needs that are critically important to your partner, you have perpetuated the very behavior in your partner that you want to change. Your conclusion that his/her extreme reactions are evidence of a funda- mental personality flaw (rather than a reaction to feeling threatened) has driven your partner to even more extreme behavior. You have brought out the worst in your partner."

The therapist helps the client come to understand that he (she) has contributed as powerfully to the relationship problems as has his (her) partner. The therapist summarizes how the client has consistently failed to meet at least one of the pre- requisites for relationship success. This information is often upsetting to the client, and may trigger defensiveness. The therapist reduces the client's defen- siveness and cultivates receptivity using the methods described in Chapters 6–8. The therapist's goal is to help the client replace an "I'm better than my partner" attitude with an "I'm just as off-track as my partner" attitude. This shift in atti- tude may be the single most powerful movement that takes place in the course of couples therapy. It has the effect of putting partners on a level playing field, sometimes for the first time in the history of their relationship.

Almost without exception, clients who come for couples therapy have histo- ries of reacting with critical judgment when their partners do upsetting things. Some partners verbalize their criticisms while others keep silent, but both types of clients have equally critical thoughts and attitudes. During the assessment phase, the therapist questions clients in detail about the history of the relation- ship. In particular, the therapist asks about how clients responded (what thoughts they had and what actions they took) when their partner did upsetting things. The therapist takes note of the critical explanations clients had for their part- ners' actions early in the relationship, then uses this information as evidence to support a version of the following statement:

> Early in your relationship, when your partner did or said things that upset you, you often assumed that he was wrong, or out-of-line in some way. This tendency is highly predictive of relationship failure. People who succeed in their relationships stand up for themselves, but they do so without becoming critical of their partners. People destined for relationship failure tend to assume that when their partners do upsetting things, it's because their reasoning is screwy, or their priorities are messed up, or that they are selfish or controlling or some other bad personality characteris- tic. In contrast, people who succeed in their relationships assume that, beneath seemingly the most provocative behaviors, their partners are going after legitimate needs or priorities.

The therapist may continue to point out other ways that the client has con- tributed powerfully to the relationship problems. Here's another example of a statement that fits many clients:

> When people who are destined for relationship success feel mistreated or misun-
> derstood by their partners, they stand up firmly for themselves *without making a
> big deal of their partner's selfish or controlling attitude.* Evidence from relationship
> studies suggests that if you don't have this ability, it's unlikely that your relation-
> ship will succeed, regardless of who your partner is. This ability has two parts: 1)
> You must be willing to stand firm and refuse to allow yourself to be disregarded or
> taken advantage of, and 2) You must be able to do this without making a big deal
> of how seemingly bad your partner is behaving. This two-part ability is every bit as
> necessary for relationship success as is the ability to refrain from being selfish or
> controlling. Chances are that if you had enough of this ability, you'd be getting
> much more cooperation and or understanding from your partner by now. Before
> you conclude that your partners attitude or actions are due to inherent personality
> flaws, consider that they may persist at least partly because your partner is in a rela-
> tionship with someone who hasn't developed sufficient ability to stand up for him-
> self without putting her down.

As the therapist delivers such information, he or she argues that this is all good
news—*very* good news. When a client finds credible reasons to release his partner from the role of relationship villain and subsequently drops his attitude of
superiority or resentment, he dramatically raises the odds that his partner will be
able to be more respectful and caring toward him in the future. Each client's
workbook contains a handout (shown in Appendix H) that describes six nonjudgmental explanations, at least one of which fits every partner we've seen at
our clinic. This handout helps clients realize that they have a choice about how
to interpret their partners' upsetting actions.

Clients have the most difficulty seeing their own shortcomings as being as serious as their partners' when their partners have committed actions that are considered particularly abhorrent by societal standards. Examples include having
an affair, becoming violent, abusing drugs or alcohol, or otherwise acting irresponsibly. Almost without exception, we find that partners of those who cheat,
become violent, abuse drugs, or otherwise act irresponsibly are as "off-track" with
regard to the habits that predict relationship success as are those who engage in
these socially unacceptable behaviors. In fact, partners of individuals who com-
mit socially atrocious acts are particularly prone to the most destructive of relationship attitudes—contempt, or thinking of oneself as better than another person. The tendency to see oneself as superior to one's partner is the single most
powerful predictor of relationship failure that has been found in relationship
studies. Amazingly, it seems the most destructive relationship attitude isn't even
on our cultural radar screen as a potent threat. In fact, it is often lauded. Many
of our political and religious leaders spew contempt for others from the platform,
and they are cheered on for it.

We encourage clients to rank order transgressions if they want to, but we
make sure they know that we believe that in doing so, they'll place themselves
squarely in the company of those who are destined to fail in their relationships.
They'll be starting down a steep mountain road with no guardrails, and ques-
tionable brakes. Scientific relationship research provides a serious challenge to

the way we think about relationships. Most of us grew up thinking that lying, cheating, stealing, and so on were the most destructive things that happen in relationships. Scientific studies suggest that actually, our common reactions to those who lie, cheat, steal, and so on. may be far more toxic than the original transgressions.

Needless to day, the therapist's discussion of a client's shortcomings will only be accepted if the client feels valued and respected by the therapist. Drawing on the methods summarized in Chapters 6–8, the therapist discusses the client's shortcomings with due humility and respect. A skilled PET-C therapist communicates value and dignity for the client even while candidly discussing his or her thoughts about the ways in which the client has fallen short of the habits that predict relationship success.

The therapist begins describing how the client can stand up for himself without becoming critical of his partner. Most distressed partners use critical judgment in an attempt to stand up for themselves, and they will not be able to let go of critical judgments until they understand how to stand up for themselves without a critical attitude. How to help clients stand up for themselves effectively will be discussed in detail throughout the remainder of this chapter.

Critical Judgments in Specific Situations

A globalized attitude of superiority represents the most extreme version of a judgmental attitude. Many clients avoid a global attitude of contempt for their partners, but they regularly develop judgmental explanations for their partners' actions on a situation-by-situation basis. These clients don't necessarily think they're more mature than their partners. However, in many situations, they do think that their expectations or priorities are more warranted or legitimate than their partner's. These partners issue critical judgments situationally, rather than globally. Repetitive situational judgments set the stage for eventual globalized contempt. In general, change is easier for clients who have not reached globalized pathologizing conclusions about their partners' defective personalities.

When reviewing specific incidents, the PET-C therapist looks for the relative presence or absence of a judgmental attitude. Asking the client directly, "Do you think you were judgmental?" will often yield misleading results, because most clients will answer no to this question. Few people want to think of themselves as judgmental. Further, they may very well have *said* nothing judgmental to their partners. However, attitude has to do more with what one thinks to oneself than what one actually says to another person. A judgmental attitude is revealed in phrases like, "He is so out of line," "He was only thinking of himself!" or "He shouldn't have done that." These statements represent attempts to judge the person's behavior as inappropriate, based on some globalized notion of right and wrong. As we have seen, most issues over which partners disagree are not areas in which there are universally agreed upon standards, and thus, the person on the receiving end of the critical judgment resents the implication that he or she is wrong.

Sometimes, clients deny judgmental thinking toward their partners, even though their tone and nonverbal gestures are screaming out critical judgment. These are the trickiest situations, but skilled therapists share their views on this situation with such clients. Needless to say, statements from the therapist must be issued with an attitude of humility and nonjudgment in order for the client to be able to receive them. From behind a one-way mirror, I recently witnessed a PET-C therapist accomplish this skillfully, using the following words:

I hear you saying that you don't think what Jamie did was wrong, but I hear something else in the way you talk about it. You seem disgusted, like you think Jamie was way out of line. Do you? If it wasn't out of line, what was it?

With such a client, it is often helpful to suggest that, although he or she isn't a judgmental person, there might be a "part" that can sometimes be judgmental. Clients can accept the idea that "part of me is judgmental" more easily than "I am judgmental."

In the retrospective review process, the therapist seeks to help the client recognize the judgmental explanations that he or she has for the partner's behavior as incidents arise. The therapist delivers strong statements about the toxic effects of critical judgment, and states unequivocally that, if the client wants to be among those who get high levels of respect or cooperation from their partners, the judgmental explanations will have to go. To make the client's judgmental explanations more concrete, the therapist often helps the client "classify" judgmental explanations into one or more of eight major types of judgmental explanations. A sheet in the client's workbook, Attitude Check (Appendix I), lists eight common types of judgmental explanations that people often develop for their partners, and provides suggestions that can help partners release critical judgments.

When Katrina used the worksheet to study her critical thoughts about Michael, she realized that they most often fell into two of the eight categories (e.g., "My partner is selfish/inconsiderate; My partner is foolish/misguided). In contrast, Michael realized that he most often judged Katrina's actions to be overreacting or controlling. Seeing their judgmental thoughts on paper helped Michael and Katrina become more aware of them when they happened in the following weeks.

During the review/planning process with Katrina and Michael, the therapist proposed nonjudgmental explanations that were mainly of the second type: legitimately different priorities. Michael and Katrina's basic priorities were different in four of the five dimensions that were assessed early in therapy (described more fully in Chapter 5).

1. *Togetherness first vs. independence first.* Michael prioritized independent functioning higher than Katrina. When stressed, Michael needed space in order to

be able to cope and think things through. Katrina, on the other hand, wanted assistance from Michael during stressful times. Katrina thought Michael was selfish for his unwillingness to help her. On the other hand, Michael thought Katrina was a control freak, because every time she got stressed, she wanted him to do something about it.

2. *Invest in the future first vs. live for the moment first.* Katrina prioritized building a secure future over enjoyment of the present, whereas Michael prioritized enjoyment of the present moment more highly. Katrina was the type of person who felt least anxious when she worked first and played later. Michael found little virtue in separating work and play, and believed that many of the tasks that people were obsessed with were simply unnecessary. The lawn didn't need to be mowed every week. Dirty dishes could wait until the next morning.

3. *Slow to upset vs. readily upset.* Michael, a slow to upset person, functioned best when he approached life in an easy-come, easy-go fashion, not making a big deal of things that frustrated him. But Katrina felt best when she vented her frustrations. Each partner thought that there was something wrong with the other. Michael saw Katrina as a person who chronically overreacted to life's frustrations, and Katrina thought Michael was afraid of a little anger, and believed that she and their kids suffered from his passive approach to life.

4. *Problem solving first vs. understanding first.* Michael prioritized problem-solving over understanding, whereas Katrina functioned best when she felt understood. Once she felt understood, she was willing to compromise. But if she felt that Michael was dismissing her viewpoints, she would argue to her last breath. Michael believed that understanding each other would be nice, but was not necessary, and quite possibly unattainable. He believed that people could spend days trying to understand each other and still be no closer to developing workable solutions. Michael was always ready to "agree to disagree," split differences, and compromise. Katrina thought that Michael just wanted to sweep things under the carpet and pretend that everything was just fine. Michael thought that Katrina wouldn't be satisfied unless he agreed with her.

In the following dialogues, notice how the therapist refers to Michael and Katrina's core differences to suggest nonjudgmental ways for each partner to look at the other's actions in the after-school homework incident.

Wife

T: Here's how I'm looking at it, Katrina. You and Michael are different people. Both of you are good people, but you have different priorities, and different ways you go about doing things. He's much more relaxed about being organized and getting things done. You're more of the type of person who likes to stay on top of things. You have trouble relaxing when important things are left undone. Michael has no problem with that at all.

W: When you get married, there are certain responsibilities that come with it! I'd like to just blow things off, too, but somebody's got to do the work.

T: I don't think there's anything wrong with your idea of how things should be, Katrina. And I think that you should ask, and require, if necessary, for Michael to make some changes. It's just that I don't think there's anything wrong with the way Michael would like to do things, either.

W: You don't think there's anything wrong with Michael refusing to do *anything* around the house?

T: Yes, I do think there's something wrong with that. But I think that Michael has come to that kind of attitude mostly because he thinks you basically think he's a loser. Few people can react well when they feel totally written off by their partners, and Michael is no exception. He thinks that you think you're better than him, and I think you do, too.

Here, the therapist has suggested another nonjudgmental way for Katrina to make sense of Michael's behavior—the extreme nature of Michael's behavior isn't due to a basic flaw in his character, rather it's a normal reaction to feeling dismissed (alternative 3, Reaction to Feeling Dismissed, Appendix H).

W: I don't think I'm better than him.

T: Okay, you think you're more responsible than him.

W: I am!

T: I don't think so. I think you guys have different definitions about what "responsible enough" means. Michael wants to play it looser than you do, and in doing so, he'll take the consequences that sometimes go with the territory. Sometimes important things will go undone. He won't like the consequences, but overall, he'd still choose to live that way, because it's more important to him to not have to feel pressure about so many things. There are a lot of people like Michael, and his way, their way, is a legitimate way to live life. When two people who are both like Michael marry each other, they get along just fine. Maybe they don't accomplish as much, maybe their kids aren't as disciplined, but they, and their children, often enjoy life very much.

W: Well, I don't want my kids to be undisciplined.

T: And Michael doesn't want your kids to get into the habit of letting some of the good things in life pass by because they're so preoccupied with doing things in the right order.

The therapist went on to help Katrina realize that dropping her judgmental interpretation of Michael wouldn't mean that she needed to just give in and live life Michael's way. It would just mean that she'd need to be willing to try to find a way of doing things that incorporated both of their priorities.

Husband

The therapist referred to the couple's core differences to help Michael develop a nonjudgmental explanation for Katrina's behavior as well.

T: Why do you think she got so upset?

H: Because that's what she does. That's how she is. Katrina is an unhappy person. If she doesn't have anything to be upset about, she'll find something. She's not happy unless she's chewing on my ass.

T: Okay, Michael. That's a good place to start, because that explanation is a good example of one of those things that people do that dramatically decreases the odds that they'll get what they want from their partners.

H: You don't know Katrina.

T: No, but I've known hundreds of people who used to seem a lot like Katrina, whose partners found a way to avoid writing them off as hopelessly negative, and I've seen those hundreds of people change over time once their partners stopped assuming the worst of them.

H: I don't know any other way to look at it. She's unhappy about everything I do. I could do 50 things right and one thing wrong, and she'll harp on that one thing all day.

T: Well I think you desperately need another way of making sense of things, because Michael, if you don't find one, it will be almost impossible for Katrina to become more positive with you, and I'm not just talking about Katrina. This applies to all of us. When a person feels dismissed by their partner, they tend to dig in even further.

H: I feel pretty dismissed by her, too.

T: It makes it pretty damn difficult to change your attitude toward her when she dismisses you, doesn't it? She's wrong about you, Michael, and I hope to help her realize that. But you're wrong about her, too.

H: How am I wrong?

T: Katrina is so negative because she needs for you to understand her. And she's not weird in this way. You don't have as much of a need to feel understood as she does, so it's hard for you to see the legitimate part of how she operates. But many other people are like Katrina. Somebody else, who knew that she needs to feel understood might be living with a whole different Katrina right now—a much happier one. Neither of you are weird or anything. It's just that you have really different ways of dealing with conflicts. You tend to cut right to the bottom line and want to solve the problem. She wants to be understood. When she doesn't feel understood, she can't compromise, so she keeps on arguing.

H: I understand her, I just don't agree.

T: I don't think she feels understood by you, Michael. Take the after-school homework situation. She thinks that you don't understand why she reacted that way.

H: I understand how she feels.

T: But do you find how she feels understandable? You see the difference?

H: Yeah. (*Michael pauses for a moment.*) Honestly, I don't find her reaction understandable. I find it rigid.

T: Well I find it understandable, Michael. And I find the fact that you let the kids go out and play understandable, too. I think that this is related to another one of your differences in personalities. You prefer things looser, she likes it more structured. There isn't anything wrong with either of you. There are plenty of "loose" people in the world who get along just fine, and there are "structured" people who get along just fine, too. She's not really too rigid, Michael, and you're not really too loose. You just have to find a way to meet in the middle.

H: I guess.

T: I think that Katrina would be a different person if you could drop your negative interpretation of her, and instead figure out a way to be able to honestly say something to her like, "There's nothing wrong with your expectation that the kids do their homework before play, Katrina. In the same situation, plenty of other people would feel the way you do. And you guys are all good people. I just felt the situation warranted an exception, and I don't think there's anything wrong with that, either. I think we have to find a way to work with each other on these things, because we're probably going to tend to prioritize things differently."

Michael had a hard time imagining himself saying something like this, but he conceded that things probably would have gone a lot better if he'd been able to say something similar.

In PET-C, we believe that critical judgments lie at the heart of destructive interactions, and we make it clear to clients that they have a choice about how to interpret their partners' actions. There are always nonjudgmental interpretations that fit the data as well as judgmental ones, and it's always to the client's own advantage to choose the nonjudgmental ones. Generally, clients will be unable to drop their judgmental interpretations of each other unless they get a clear view of credible, nonjudgmental alternatives. They generally won't be able to come up with nonjudgmental alternatives on their own. Before attempting to intervene in a client's judgmental attitude, the therapist must have a clear idea about the couple's core differences, and be able to present credible, nonjudgmental interpretations that draw on these core differences. Clients are often helped by a sheet in their workbooks called Core Differences in Ways of Maintaining Emotional Stability (Appendix J). This worksheet helps clients understand that the differences that drive their arguments are common, and that there is nothing wrong with either of them.

Most clients believe that, to get their partners to change, they must get their partners to realize that they are wrong. They use critical judgments to attempt to influence their partners. Before they are willing to let go of the critical judgments, they must understand that there is a more powerful path of influence: Standing up for oneself without putting one's partner down.

STANDING UP FOR ONESELF WITHOUT
PUTTING ONE'S PARTNER DOWN

Clients often cling to judgmental attitudes because they have the idea that, unless their partners did something wrong, they don't have the right ask their partners to change. When a therapist suggests to a client that a partner didn't do anything wrong, the client will tend to assume that the therapist is implying that there is no reason to be upset, or that the partner's behavior should just be accepted. A skilled therapist anticipates this confusion, and is ready to assure the client that he or she has a right to be upset, and to ask the partner to change, even though the partner didn't do anything that was intrinsically wrong. The therapist clarifies that just because there might not be anything intrinsically wrong with a partners' expectations doesn't mean there is something wrong with the client's own expectations. Similarly, just because there is something legitimate about a partner's viewpoint, doesn't mean that there isn't something legitimate about the client's viewpoint.

Many people use critical judgment as their primary vehicle for self-assertion. In fact, critical judgment and asserting oneself are often seen as the same thing. Most clients need to understand that critical judgment actually undermines one's ability to effectively assert oneself. We use a worksheet to help clients understand that the extent to which one stands up for oneself and the extent to which one criticizes or judges one's partner are entirely independent variables (Katrina's worksheet is shown in Appendix K). It is possible to stand up for oneself without criticizing or judging one's partner, and this is exactly what successful partners do. The sheet in their workbooks helps clients consider which of four quadrants their typical reactions in upsetting situations most often fall into. For example, it's possible for a client to (1) Refrain from criticism, but fail to stand up for oneself; (2) criticize, but fail to stand up for oneself; (3) attempt to stand up for oneself by criticizing; (4) refrain from criticism while standing up for oneself. Michael felt that his reactions to Katrina most often fell into the Critical—Not Standing Up quadrant. Inside, he was usually critical of Katrina, but externally, he often gave in and did what she wanted in order to keep the peace. On the other hand, Katrina felt that her reactions fell into the Critical, Standing Up quadrant. Katrina was both outwardly critical and inwardly judgmental toward Michael. Seeing how their quadrants differed from the "effective" quadrant (Not Critical, Standing Up) helped each partner understand conceptually the changes that he or she needed to make. Michael would need to find a way to drop his internal judgments, and rather than capitulating to Katrina, he'd need to require that his viewpoints be given equal consideration. Katrina would need to find a way to stop relying on critical judgments as a means of asserting herself, and find more effective ways to stand up for herself.

How and When to Stand Up for Oneself Without Putting One's Partner Down

The definition of *standing up for oneself* that we use in PET-C is: "Requiring that your partner give your priorities, viewpoints, or preferences equal regard." Put another way, people who stand up for themselves require that their partners be willing to work with them to find solutions that are mutually acceptable. Standing up for oneself does not mean requiring that one's partner give in and do things the way one thinks they should be done. Rather it means requiring that one's partner meet one in the middle. But before *requiring* that their partners give their feelings equal consideration, successful people *ask* that their partners give their feelings equal consideration. And before they *ask* that their partners give their feelings equal consideration, they go through the first steps of the Sequence (Appendices A and G).

The first steps of the Sequence provide the soil from which increased respectfulness and cooperativeness from one's partner will emerge. Many arguments can be avoided through the first steps alone. However, there are also times in the course of most relationships when further measures are necessary. Steps 7 to 12 of the Sequence provide a powerful combination of steps that can be used to stand up effectively for oneself. Steps 7 to 12 are needed in two situations: when a client's viewpoint is disregarded, and when a client is criticized or verbally attacked.

When a Client's Viewpoint is Disregarded

People who succeed in their relationships refrain from criticizing their partners or trying to prove them wrong and instead simply ask their partners to work with them to find solutions that take both of their opinions into account. Most of the time, when partners feel respected, they will be willing to compromise. However, there are situations in which clients avoid criticizing their partners and instead ask them to move over and make room for both of their viewpoints or preferences, but the partners won't move over! These are situations where, in spite of a client's most sincere attempts to explain his or her point of view without criticism or contempt, recognize and acknowledge the reasonable part of the partner's argument, listen non-defensively, and assure the partner that the client is not as rigid as it may seem on the issue, the partner isn't willing to return the same respectful attitude. The client has skillfully implemented the first steps of the Sequence, but the partner has temporarily refused to give an inch. In such

situations, a PET-C therapist will help the client stand up for him or herself
forcefully.

In the following dialogue, Michael is resisting the idea of telling Katrina that
he thinks she has a legitimate point of view, because he's convinced she'll just
turn around and use it against him. He thinks that she'll dismiss his point of view
regardless of his good attitude. In the dialogue below, the therapist draws from
steps 7 to 12 of the Sequence to help Michael understand how to stand up for
himself without putting Katrina down.

H: If I told her that I thought her point of view was reasonable [wanting the kids
       to stay in until their homework was done, even on a nice day], then she'd
       just turn around and say, "Then why in the hell did you let them out?"

T: Good.

H: No, bad! I'd be right back on the hot seat!

T: Not necessarily. You'd probably just need to say something like, "Wait a
       minute, Katrina. I said I think your point of view is reasonable, I didn't say
       mine isn't! I think that there are legitimate reasons for making an excep-
       tion to the after school rule. I understand that they're debatable. I mean,
       people smarter than you and me have probably disagreed about these kind
       of things. We see things differently, and I'm not saying that we should just
       do things the way I want. I just want to have a vote here, too." (*This sugges-
       tion is an application of step 8 of the Sequence, Offer and Ask.*)

H: She'd probably say, "No way. Kids need discipline. End of discussion."

T: Then you'd probably need to say, "Look, Katrina. I'm trying to work with
       you here. Will you try to work with me on this one?"

H: It still wouldn't work. She'd probably just say I need more discipline, too.

T: Then you'd need to get mad.

H: I already did!

T: Yeah, but you didn't lay the groundwork. This time, you'd have avoided
       thinking negatively about her, and offered to work toward a compromise.

H: Then it's okay to get mad?

T: Then you'd *better* get mad, if you want to have any say in things like this
       (*the Sequence, step 9, Stand Up—Engage*).

H: (smiling) Are you sure you're a therapist?

T: Hang on, I'm not done yet.

H: Okay.

T: Then you'd probably need to storm off (*the Sequence, step 10, Reject Your
       Partner*) and cool down, but while you were cooling down you'd need to
       avoid feeling all indignant and making a big deal about the fact that she
       refused to cooperate with you. You'd need to practice saying things to your-

self like "I don't blame her for trying to get her way on this one. I know she feels strongly about it. But so do I. She simply has to work with me on this one." (*See the Sequence, step 11, Don't Make a Big Deal of it.*)

H: I've never said anything remotely like that to her.

T: I know this isn't what usually happens, Michael, but let me finish painting the whole picture, okay?

H: Sure.

T: Then after you'd cooled down, you'd need to be the one to go back and initiate more conversation about it, saying something like, "That didn't go very well, did it? I know I was pretty mad back then. You want to try to talk about it again?"

H: What if she is just as stubborn when we talk again?

T: Then you'd repeat the whole process over again.

The therapist spent the rest of the session talking to Michael about when it's a good idea to throw a temper tantrum and when it's not. He explained that people who succeed in relationships don't throw temper tantrums and storm off when they don't get their own way. But they do throw temper tantrums when, in spite of their good attitude, their partners are dismissing their views altogether. This is a distinction of huge importance. Many clients come to therapy assuming that they need to be nicer to their partners. Most of the time this is true. But there are also situations that warrant anger, and successful partners know when to allow and express their anger.

When a Client is Criticized or Verbally Attacked

When people voice upset feelings, they either complain or criticize. A complaint is a simple statement about something a person doesn't like, or something a person would like to see changed, and an explanation as to why the person feels this way. A critical person goes beyond complaining and implies that the viewpoints or actions of others are wrong, and his or hers are right, or the person will imply that others have behaved badly. As a general rule, in response to a complaint, the most effective reactions involve the First Steps of the Sequence (Appendices A and G). However, when criticized, responding with "the first steps" may actually be counterproductive. Criticism is a form of attack. Critical people often seem disgusted, and show no interest in hearing the viewpoints of others. If a client responds in an understanding way when his or her partner is in "attack mode," it is likely that the partner will continue attacking in the future. It does no good to persist in attempts to be reasonable with someone who isn't willing or able to be reasonable in return. In PET-C, we encourage clients to skip the First Steps temporarily when they feel criticized, and move directly to steps 7–12 listed in the section When, in Spite of My Good Attitude, My Partner Disregards my Viewpoint or Criticizes Me (see Appendices A and G). We encourage clients to return to the First Steps only when their partners stop criticizing them.

One of Michael's biggest complaints when he entered couples therapy was his contention that Katrina was verbally abusive to him. According to Michael, Katrina would often become utterly disgusted, explode at him, and call him derogatory names. Michael was at a total loss as to how to handle Katrina's explosions, and he usually just fell silent, battened down the hatches, and hoped the storm would blow over. Although the therapist was working with Katrina in helping her find more effective alternatives than putting Michael down, like many people, Katrina had difficulty making this change until Michael did a more effective job of standing up for himself. With Michael, the therapist moved back and forth between helping him allow his anger to emerge when berated by Katrina, and becoming more aware of what an effective reaction to Katrina's putdowns would be.

During Katrina's explosions, Michael typically fell silent, but inside, he was utterly contemptuous toward her, thinking things like, "She's a sick, abusive person." This judgmental thinking would often intensify in the hours that followed, accompanied by anger. In effect, Michael was doing the opposite of what effective reacting requires. He was failing to stand up for himself at the "scene of the crime," and then engaging in judgmental thinking later. The therapist helped Michael realize that he would need to reverse each of these habits. He would need to find ways to stand up for himself at the moments when Katrina was putting him down, then later, he'd need to avoid judgmental thinking about her.

The therapist began describing steps 7 to 12 of the Sequence (Appendices A and G). Specifically, he discussed with Michael how to Maintain His Cool, then Offer and Ask. Together, the therapist and Michael found words for accomplishing this, such as, "Hey Katrina. I'm listening. You don't have to yell!" or "I'm trying to listen to you, Katrina, but I'm having a hard time. Could you just slow it down a little?" Michael insisted that these words would have little impact on Katrina. The therapist went on to describe how, if this were the case, Michael might need to stand up firmly for himself. The following is an excerpt from the conversation between the therapist and Michael.

H: What do you mean? How am I supposed to stand up for myself when she's going off at me?

T: What happens inside of you when she's putting you down?

H: I usually feel kind of scared, like things could very easily get out of control if I do or say the wrong thing.

T: Okay, the first thing we'll need to work on is to see if we can get you to a different place inside at those moments. Do you ever feel angry?

H: Sure, all the time.

T: But you don't show it?

H: No. Mostly I'm just trying to avoid making things worse.

T: I understand. Well, let me tell you what I think you'll need to do, and then we'll begin working on how you can do it. Knowing what to do is one thing, doing it is another. But it helps to have a clear picture. You'll need to find a way to release your anger earlier—while she is attacking you.

H: How would I do that?

T: The first move is inside. Somehow, you've got to lose the fear of what will happen. We'll talk a lot more about that in a few minutes, but let me give you the whole picture first. When she gets furious with you, she's not worried about what will happen, but you are, right?

H: Right. She could care less at that moment about anything but reaming me a new one.

T: Um-hm. You'll need to be able to get to that same attitude. As long as you are more invested in keeping things under control than she is, she won't become concerned about it.

H: Somebody's got to be rational!

T: I'm not saying you should get crazy, or go off the deep end, or that you should put her down, or anything. And you shouldn't ever get close to the point where you'd get physical with her. I'm just talking about good clean anger. For example, you might say (therapist speaks with strong anger) "Don't you fucking talk to me like that!" (*Here, the therapist is discussing step 9 of the Sequence with Michael, Stand-Up–Engage.*)

H: Wow.

T: Could you see yourself saying that?

H: Actually, I've come close on a few occasions.

T: Good. You'll simply need to allow it to flow.

H: So what good is that? Instead of one crazy person, now there's two.

T: Two is much better than one, because now you have created the possibility for her to become concerned about how things are going to go, too. Up to this point, she doesn't need to be, because she knows how hard you're working on it.

H: It sounds like how to deal with a bully in elementary school.

T: Yes, in the sense that, if you stand up to a bully he might stop bullying you, it is similar. But there are some important differences, too. Let me explain. After you say something like, "Don't you fucking talk to me like that!" she'll probably escalate. What do you think she'd do?

H: She'll say something like, "I'll talk to you however I Goddam well please!"

T: Well, and then you'd probably need to say something like, "Well you can just knock it off. I'm tired of this crap!"

H: Ouch. The sparks would fly!

T: The main thing at this point in your reaction is to change the dynamic where you're more afraid than she is, or you're more invested in things getting calm.

H: She'll stay mad for days.

T: Let's talk about that, and fill out the rest of the picture. At a certain point in the argument, if she doesn't start talking more respectfully to you, you'll probably need to say something like, "Get away from me!" and then leave her presence, at least for the moment. She needs to feel you rejecting her. That never happens. *She* criticizes *you. She* rejects *you. (The therapist is suggesting step 10 of the Sequence, Reject Your Partner.)* Now you're going to square up and reject her, just temporarily. Then, and this is absolutely critical, when you're by yourself, you'll need to cool down, let go of your anger, and avoid making a big deal out of what she did. Instead of thinking things like, "She's a freak" or "I shouldn't have to put up with this crap," you'll need to be able to think things like, "She only does this because I haven't known how to handle it up til now." "It's not a crime that she gets this way," and "I did what I needed to do to stand up for myself—I don't need to carry a grudge." *(The therapist is suggesting step 11 of the Sequence, Don't Make a Big Deal of It.)* Later, you'd need to try talking to her again, saying something like, "Hey, I was pretty mad back there, but I'm feeling calmer now. You wanna try to talk about it again?" *(See step 12 of the Sequence.)* If she tries to explain it to you, you'll use the components of effective responding we've already talked about *(i.e., the first steps).* You know, give her the benefit of the doubt, look for the understandable part, and so on. But the first few times you do this, she may start attacking you again, and you'll need to repeat the whole process of standing up firmly for yourself. You mustn't be any more invested in avoiding an escalation this time than you were the last time. But over time, if you can really do this, along with the other things we've been talking about, I think you'll see a big change in Katrina.

Each component of the therapist's suggestion required a major change for Michael. He couldn't think of a single time when, after an argument, *he* had ever initiated discussion about the topic of the argument again. His normal procedure was to hope that the thing would just blow over and that she wouldn't bring it up again. The therapist urged Michael to take the bull by the horns and face things head on.

In a session like this one, the therapist usually cautions the client against using the therapist to justify his actions. If Michael carried out some of the "standing up" components, and then Katrina got really mad, Michael might get scared and say, "The therapist told me to do it!" This would, of course, completely undermine the strength that Katrina needs to feel coming from him. Because Michael's new way of responding would be so radically different from the past, Katrina might come to her next session demanding to know, "What did you tell Michael?" In this situation, the therapist would pull no punches, and tell

Katrina that he told Michael the same thing that he would tell her if she complained about Michael putting her down. The therapist would discuss with her any situations in which she felt put down by Michael, just as he had discussed with Michael. Even more important, the therapist would discuss the situations in which she puts Michael down, and discuss ways that she could get more of what she really wanted by dropping the put-downs and instead, standing up for herself.

When Anger is Needed

At certain points in the standing up process, clients are encouraged to express anger toward their partners. This is a move seldom discussed in the couple therapy literature, and was certainly not part of the training that those of us who have developed PET-C received earlier in our careers. Most of the time, couples therapies are designed to help clients shift out of angry places and into softer ones, and PET-C is no exception. However, we have come to believe that the ability to connect with and express anger is just as important as the ability to shift out of angry modes, and the inability of a partner to experience and powerfully express anger when dismissed, criticized harshly, or put down is every bit as responsible for relationship failure as is the inability to calm oneself and approach one's partner with understanding. Angry attacks on the part of one partner and the inability to effectively stand up on the part of the other partner usually go hand in hand. We see them as complementary parts of one process, and believe that "attacking" partners are no more to blame than partners who fail to deal with the attacks head on.

John Gottman (1999) has pointed out that there is an unfortunate bias against anger in the psychotherapy fields. In fact, in our culture, anger is generally though of as a greater "sin" in relationships than detachment, or silently contemptuous attitudes. However, research on successful couples suggests that anger itself is not a dangerous emotion. Many highly successful couples regularly blow up at each other. Blow-ups are not destructive. Getting stuck in anger that fuels disgust is destructive. The secret is in effective repair. Healthy partners quickly become angry when they feel disregarded. However, they let go of the anger as easily as they connect with it, and refrain from looking down on their partners for doing the things that made them angry. They are willing to try failed discussions again, and continue to give their partners new opportunities to cooperate. In our work with couples, we've found that this ability (connecting with anger, then letting it go and avoiding getting caught in disgust for one's partner) can be cultivated, and we work as diligently with partners on this ability as we do on helping them soften with each other. We encourage softening first. But when a soft response is disregarded, anger is often needed, followed by measures to avoid getting stuck in a contemptuous attitude.

When a person fails to get angry and stand up forcefully when feeling disregarded or criticized harshly, they almost always harbor resentment and an internal attitude of contempt. Often, we hear clients say that they won't engage in an angry exchange, because they don't want to "stoop to their partner's level." They think of themselves as "better" in some sense than their partners. This attitude is a perfect example of contempt, the single most toxic thing identified by relationship researchers. It's almost impossible for a person to avoid contempt in the face of an attack, unless they become angry and defend themselves at the moment of the attack. We find that those who can angrily defend themselves are much more able to assume noncontemptuous attitudes in the aftermath of a verbal scuffle than those who disengage when attacked. This finding is confirmed by our interviews of people who easily kick into attack mode. These people generally report that it feels much more like a slap in the face when their partners stonewall than when their partners return the anger. Stonewalling is often heard as "I'm not even going to waste my time trying to talk with you. You are too disgusting or scary or irrational to even deal with."

Relationships that have been stuck for years in an attack/withdraw pattern change dramatically when the disengaging partner loses his or her fear and develops the ability to square off with a partner, provided that he or she can avoid making a big deal out of how awful the partner was for "picking a fight." When faced with an attack, the most effective response is to engage the attacker forcefully during the attack, then refrain from harboring contempt, and instead return to a willingness to try again.

Of course, we spend a lot of time helping partners who easily kick into attack mode develop the ability to soften and approach their partners differently, and we refuse to support the philosophy of "I could be much less angry if my partner would just engage or listen to me." It's in the best interest of such people to develop the ability to shift from attack mode, and we will not continue therapy with a partner who cannot see that their attacks prevent them from getting what they truly need from their partners. However, we will also refuse to support a philosophy that says, "I cannot do anything different as long as my partner keeps attacking me." Often, the work of one partner involves developing more ability to shift from anger, and the work of the other partner involves more ability to connect with anger when it is needed.

When a Partner is Clearly Wrong

Most of the time, arguments that partners have are based on differences of opinion on matters for which there is no generally accepted standard. However, sometimes people do things that almost anybody would agree are wrong: examples include infidelity, bold-faced lying, or violence. When a partner's behavior is clearly wrong, few people will be comfortable with the definition of "standing up for yourself," given in the previous section (i.e., requiring that one's partner give equal consideration to one's opinions or preferences). If you think your partner's actions are wrong, or harmful, you're not going to feel satisfied by negotiating a compromise. For example, what if your partner's opinion is he should have several lovers, and yours is that he should have sex with nobody but you? How can you work toward a mutually satisfying solution? What would a compromise be? Would you ask your partner to have only one lover rather than several? Most people wouldn't accept such a compromise. There are some issues over which most people will be unable or unwilling to compromise.

In situations where people believe that the actions of their partners are wrong or harmful, successful people stand up for themselves by asking their partners to stop doing the harmful or objectionable behavior. Among those who make this request, the difference between those who do it more or less successfully involves the extent to which they are able to do it without getting stuck in an attitude of superiority. They might get on their "high horse" temporarily, but they don't stay there.

Two months into therapy, Katrina discovered one week that Michael had lied to her. Michael had called her during the day, saying he had the opportunity to work a double shift that day. She agreed that he should, because they needed the money. But Michael didn't work the second shift. Instead, he went to play poker with some friends. Katrina found out inadvertently while talking on the phone to one of Michael's friend's wives. Upon finding out, Katrina exploded at Michael in disgust, saying he was just like his father (a chronic liar), calling him a loser, and letting him know that she was too good for him. She screamed at him, insisting that he leave the house. Michael spent the night at a friend's house. The next day, the couple was scheduled for a therapy session. As they began talking about the incident, the couple enacted their usual pattern: Katrina harshly criticized Michael, and Michael fell silent. The therapist suggested a break, then met with each partner individually.

With Katrina, the therapist spent a good deal of time validating her anger. The therapist admitted that if he were in her position, he'd have been furious, too. As Katrina's anger subsided, the therapist encouraged her to consider what she could do to maximize the odds that Michael wouldn't do this again. When she was ready to hear it, the therapist helped Katrina realize that, even though this was a situation in which Michael was clearly wrong, she could stand up more strongly for herself if she could avoid putting herself on a higher plane than him. They discussed the various ways Katrina could combine a firm stand with a nonjudgmental attitude. When the couple resumed conversation, Katrina began with the following statement:

W: I've never been so mad at you in my life, Michael. I'm not sure I can forgive you for straight-out lying to me. I need to understand why you did it. I really mean it. I'll try to understand. I've done things I'm not proud of before too, but there were usually reasons. We've got to get to the bottom of this, because I know I can't live with you if you're going to lie to me.

Of course, Katrina couldn't have made a statement like this without first shift-ing from her angry mode to a softer place inside. However, once she allowed herself to feel some of the pain and insecurity she had inside over the issue, it was a tremendous help for her to hear clear descriptions from the therapist as to how she could stand up strongly for herself without assuming an attitude of superiority. After the session, the therapist directed Katrina to a sheet in her workbook titled, When My Partner is Clearly Wrong, which helped her main-tain the stance she had cultivated in the session. Katrina's worksheet is shown in Appendix L.

Taking a Firm Stand

Most of the time, individuals who develop the ability to soften and progress fully through the Sequence when needed find that their partners become more coop-erative and willing to listen over time. There are some occasions, however, when clients demonstrate a good ability to stay on track with the Sequence but their partners persist in their unwillingness to take the client's priorities, or viewpoints into account. These are situations in which clients have made substantial progress in explaining their points of view without criticism or contempt, recog-nizing and acknowledging the reasonable part of their partners' points of view, listening nondefensively, assuring their partners that they are not as rigid as they may seem on the issue, and standing up for themselves without putting their partners down. But in spite of all of this, their partners consistently refuse to budge on certain issues, conversation after conversation. In these situations, suc-cessful partners take "standing up for themselves" to another level. Specifically, they tell their mates that they are unwilling to continue "business as usual" as long as their mates are unwilling to show regard for the person's priorities or viewpoints. If people are able to do this without becoming disgusted or con-temptuous toward their partners, the odds are good that their partners will even-tually become more cooperative or respectful.

The best way of taking a firm stand will vary from situation to situation, and the therapist makes careful plans with clients who need to implement this move, referring them to a detailed description in their workbooks (Taking a Firm Stand, Appendix M). The degree of refusing to conduct business as usual may vary from situation to situation in terms of how much and how long. In one situ-ation, it might involve just refusing to do things a client normally does for the partner, until the partner is willing to give equal regard. In a more serious situa-tion, it might involve separating from one's partner until he or she decides to get some assistance to change abusive or addictive behavior. Those who are most successful in eventually getting cooperation from their formerly noncooperative partners share one characteristic: They draw the line with their partners without criticizing, blaming, judging, or putting them down.

Clients are encouraged to take a firm stand only after they have fully and successfully implemented the Sequence on many different occasions, and their partners still show no regard for their feelings. Taking a Firm Stand is illustrated beautifully in many of the stories told by Harriet Goldhor Lerner (1989, 1985). Her books are required reading for PET-C trainees, and we frequently recommend them to clients who find themselves in the position of needing to take a firm stand with their partners.

Clients are understandably reluctant to make this move, because their actions will undoubtedly evoke strong reactions from their partners. However, our experience tells us that sometimes, situations in which clients feel taken advantage of may persist indefinitely if they do not take a firm stand on their own behalf. On the other hand, those who do take a firm stand, and do it skillfully, often experience dramatic changes in their partners.

Many clients feel that they are at this crossroads before they really are, and the therapist helps them judge when the time is right. Specifically, the therapist helps them develop the ability to successfully implement the standing up sequence (i.e., maintain your cool, ask and offer, stand up/engage, reject your partner, don't make a big deal of it, try again later), and implement the sequence many times, before concluding that their only option is taking a firm stand with their partners. When, in the therapist's opinion, the client has done everything else possible to elicit cooperation from the partner, and the partner still stubbornly refuses cooperation, the therapist provides specific guidance. The key to success in such situations involves the client's ability to maintain a nonjudgmental attitude while taking a firm stand. I recently witnessed one of my clients embody this combination of abilities in a conversation with her husband. In spite of his promises to end an affair, the wife discovered that he was still cheating on her. In the following therapy session, she said:

Jim, I don't think you're a bad person. I don't think I'm better than you. I can't imagine that I'd ever cheat on you, but I don't think you could have imagined you'd do this either. I just know I'm not one of those types of people who can keep going on like this. I'm going to miss you terribly (wife's lip quivers, heartfelt tears roll down her cheeks, she then pulls herself back together), but I won't tolerate this any longer. I want a divorce.

This wife initiated a separation, which was very disorienting for the husband. He dropped out of therapy, but during their period apart, he realized how much he missed his wife, and broke off the affair, this time for good. The couple resumed therapy three months later.

Another example of the ability to maintain a nonjudgmental attitude while taking a firm stand recently occurred in a conversation between a client (Ron) and his male partner:

I believe that when you drink, your personality changes, Scott. It's affecting our re-lationship, and I think it's also keeping you from getting promoted. I know you don't think so, and I know that you need to do what makes sense to you. But I can't go down this road with you any longer. If you continue drinking, I'd like to sepa-rate, at least for now.

A person doesn't have to be ready to leave a relationship in order to take a firm stand. Consider the following statement, made by a stay-at-home mom to her husband. In spite of the wife's impressive progress in implementing the compo-nents of effective responding over the course of three months of therapy, her husband insisted on controlling the checkbook. He made expensive purchases without consulting her, and decided how much spending money she should have. With the therapist's help, the wife finally implemented a firm stand, using the following words:

Stan, I know that you think that you should be in charge of our money because you've always made good financial decisions, and I made some poor ones before we were married. I don't dispute that. But it's become clear to me that I feel dis-respected by your unwillingness to have me as an equal partner in the decision-making process. I know that not all relationships work the way I want ours to. But I've come to realize that I'm not ever going to feel right about our relationship un-til I feel I have equal say in financial decisions. I'm not going to pretend that things are okay anymore. So far, I've been too embarrassed, but I'm going to start talking to my friends and family about my dissatisfaction. I need for somebody to understand me. Also, I've been thinking that I don't want to go places as a couple anymore, I don't want to socialize with other couples. I need to do more things with my friends, and maybe you should do more things with your friends, too. I know you're not trying to be mean to me, and you're doing what you honestly think is best. I'm not going to walk around all pissed at you, but I am taking a step back from you emotionally, and I want you to know why.

This wife is a good example of someone who had given careful thought to how she wanted to take a firm stand. She implemented it without hostility, and weath-ered her husband's anger in reaction to her moves. He still refused to let go of fi-nancial control, even refusing to pay for babysitters when she wanted to go out with her friends. The wife had anticipated this, however, and made arrange-ments with her family members to care for the children. Her parents even agreed to give her money to socialize with her friends. Eventually, the husband felt the impact of her emotional distance, and began initiating some changes. At first, these changes involved just attempting to give her more spending money. The wife impressively refused this gesture, telling him again what her bottom line was: To be partners in decision making. It took six months, during which time the husband dropped out of therapy, but the wife came in for her therapy one day reporting that she was now jointly on all of their financial accounts. This was a symbolic victory for her. The real rewards came as she and her husband became true partners for the first time.

Often, by the time a client is ready to take a stand, they have become so angry and bitter, that they do so with utter contempt, saying things like, "You're disgusting and I'm not going to take it any longer." In such situations, their efforts to stand up for themselves will yield few positive results. Clients who are most influential require that they be treated with respect, and make it very easy for their partners to treat them with respect at the same time. Even as they are taking a firm stand, they are endearing themselves to their partners.

Not all partners respond to an effective taking a stand intervention by becoming more cooperative. The odds are lower in situations where addictions are involved, or when there has been an affair. However, even in these situations, we believe that taking a stand is the single most effective thing a client can do to create the possibility for change.

All partners have some days, or some situations, in which, for whatever reason, they are unwilling to work collaboratively toward mutually acceptable solutions. A partner's temporary unresponsiveness to a client's efforts to be collaborative on a few occasions is normal, and not an indication that taking a firm stand is necessary. In PET-C, clients are encouraged to take a firm stand only after they have successfully responded to their partners' temporary unresponsiveness on many occasions, and their partners *still* refuse to collaborate. Successful responding to a partner's temporary unresponsiveness is a crucial skill, and often becomes a focus of discussion in the reviewing/planning process. A client knows if the partner's unresponsiveness is temporary by responding effectively (i.e., with the Sequence) when the partner is initially unresponsive and then seeing if the unresponsiveness persists.

As clients progress in their skills, they become better at the initial moves in conversations. For example, it was quite an accomplishment for Katrina to simply refrain from jumping to negative conclusions about Michael's upsetting behavior, and ask him why he did what he did. When a client makes this sort of change, it's deflating when the partner doesn't recognize his or her efforts, and responds in the same old way. Clients frequently want to take a firm stand at such moments.

Remember that when the therapist first described how Katrina could have reacted more effectively in the after-school homework incident (described earlier in this chapter), Katrina claimed that it wouldn't have mattered how she approached Michael, he would have dismissed her complaint anyway. Katrina was beginning to believe that she had only two choices at this point, to let Michael control her, or to take a firm stand, as described in the above paragraphs. The therapist helped her see that it was way to early to implement the take a firm stand moves, because she hadn't yet implemented all of the Sequence even once. The therapist asked Katrina to develop the ability to stand up well for herself (using steps 7–12 of the Sequence) on at least four different occasions. The therapist conceded that, if she did this successfully, and Michael's attitude still didn't change, then she might need to implement the taking a firm stand approach.

CONCLUSION

Retrospective reviewing and prospective planning will only be helpful to clients who are more concerned about developing their own abilities to respond effectively than they are about convincing their partners that they must change. Throughout the reviewing/planning process, when a client's focus begins to slip over to the partner, the therapist must help the client refocus and get back on board. Skilled PET-C therapists do not allow the client's focus to slide, and are unwilling to proceed if the client persists in focusing on the partner's inadequacies. The methods for getting clients on board are also used to keep clients on board as needed throughout Phase II.

The assumptions behind Phase II of PET-C depart radically from many other approaches to couples therapy. Rather than helping partners gradually build upon each other's increasing cooperativeness, the PET-C therapist helps each partner develop the ability to respond effectively when his or her partner is being the most uncooperative. Partners learn the skills of eliciting cooperativeness. Gradually, each partner does become more cooperative with the other, but not because his or her partner made the first move. In PET-C, each client learns to make the first move, developing confidence that he or she can influence the partner's level of cooperativeness through his or her own way of responding.

The methods described in this chapter help increase partners' awareness of their typical reactions in upsetting situations, and provide clear descriptions to clients of what more effective responding would look like. However, in spite of an increase in knowledge, clients may be unable to react differently to their partners due to the automatic internal state activations that govern their reactions.

CHAPTER 11

Rewiring Internal States

THROUGH RETROSPECTIVE REVIEWING and prospective planning, each client becomes more aware of the specific ways her thinking and actions need to change in order to interact more successfully with her partner. However, awareness is often not sufficient to promote lasting change, because at the moments when a client needs to use this awareness, she is often caught in a frame of mind that carries her thoughts in a different direction. It is one thing for a client to know, when she's calmly thinking things over, how she can best respond in upsetting situations. It is another thing to apply this knowledge when the rubber hits the road, and the client is actually feeling upset. The neural response programs that guide a client's reactions when she is upset are usually activated automatically, and are not under the client's conscious control. Even when a client becomes aware in the present moment that she is under the influence of an automatic internal response program, she may be unable to resist the same old modes of thinking and action, because the response state is conditioned to unfold in particular ways. Once activated, a neural response program has a momentum of its own.

In order to engage in different thinking and action when it is needed, the client must develop the ability to recognize when an interfering internal state has been activated inside of her, and the client must think and act differently in the moments when the state is active. In PET-C, clients accomplish this through repetitive practice designed to recondition automatic internal reactions. Specifically, clients rewire interfering internal states for more flexibility, making it possible for them to think and act in ways that are predictive of relationship success.[1]

---

[1] With clients, we use a variety of terms to refer to the brain's executive operating systems, such as *frame of mind, state of mind, mood state, mood, neural response state, preprogrammed response mode, operating mode, internal state,* and *attitude*. Different clients seem to feel more comfortable with different terms, and different situations demand terms with the right fit. In this chapter, these terms will be used interchangeably to refer to the brain's executive operating systems.

Each client's brain has become conditioned to respond in specific ways due to repetitive experiences the client has had, beginning early in life. New insights or experiences in the therapy room may fade if they are not sufficiently wired into the client's neural circuits. Weekly sessions simply do not provide enough opportunity for changes to become integrated into the brain's neural patterns (Atkinson, 2004). One of the most enduring concepts in the field of neuroscience is called Hebb's Law, which states that brain processes that occur together over and over again tend to become grafted together, so that they are more likely to occur in conjunction in the future (Hebb, 1949). For the clients to respond differently, they need to retrain their brains, and this retraining occurs through repetitive practice.

Ordinarily, when clients become upset with their partners, a predictable network of thoughts, feelings, and action tendencies arise at once. Clients find themselves in certain frames of mind, characterized by specific attitudes, and predictable feelings and motivations. When these states of mind carry clients in unproductive directions, we refer to them as *interfering states*. In the repetitive practice process, each partner becomes more aware of interfering states, and then practices pairing new thoughts and behaviors with activations of interfering internal states, over and over again, until the new thoughts and behaviors become grafted to the internal states. Once this grafting takes place, the new thoughts and behaviors arise automatically each time an interfering state is activated.

THE NECESSITY OF
REPETITIVE PRACTICE

Most clients understand intuitively that learning physical skills, like playing the piano, requires repetitive practice. However, clients often assume that psychological learning, like applying the ability to think differently, shouldn't require practice. They assume that, once they understand a situation differently, they should be able to apply this insight and think or act differently each time a similar situation arises. Such clients may not realize that psychological learning *is* physical learning, requiring physical changes in the brain just as surely as learning to play the piano. The therapist emphasizes the essential similarity between practicing the external moves necessary to acquire the ability to play a musical instrument, or to acquire an athletic skill, and practicing the internal moves necessary for acquiring state-shifting skills.

The process of helping clients set up repetitive practices to recondition their internal states begins with some education about the brain. Explanations about the brain are best kept simple and to the point. The following explanation includes the most important components that clients need to know:

The prerequisites for relationship success are easy to understand and learn, but can be very difficult to do, because, at key moments, you may find yourself in a state of mind that isn't compatible with the needed behavior or attitude. In order to change your thinking or behaviors, you must learn how to get into the right frame of mind for the task. For example, marriage researchers have noticed that, when a marriage is distressed, each partner generally reacts to the other during arguments in highly predictable and patterned ways. Thanks to some very helpful brain research since the early 1990s, we now know that this is because, across our lives, each of our brains gets conditioned to produce highly specific response programs. These are conditioned brain circuits that are preprogrammed so that, once triggered, they unfold as if they had a mind of their own, producing a predictable pattern of thoughts, feelings, and behaviors. Brain researchers call these brain states executive operating systems *or* intrinsic motivational circuits. *The common names are* states of mind *or* moods. *The important thing is not what they are called, but to recognize that these internal response programs can dramatically dictate how you interact with your partner.*

Most of the time, it's an advantage to have these automatic, prepackaged response circuits in our brains, because when they are activated, we automatically experience motivation to learn, to love, to be close to others, to be playful, and to defend and protect ourselves when needed. But when relationships are distressed, researchers have found that these automatic response circuits are often to blame. Often, the wrong circuits get activated at critical moments, and the needed circuits remain dormant. To improve your relationship, you will need to become familiar with the specific response state patterns that happen inside of you during key intimate situations. Your best shot at acting differently comes when you practice the ability to shift internal states when needed.

CULTIVATING MOTIVATION

Most clients do not like to practice reconditioning their internal state activations. Those who find the motivation to practice typically do so by developing a clear vision of how much better their relationships will be once they have mastered the ability to change aspects of their internal states. The PET-C therapist helps clients develop a vision of how much better their lives will be once they have reconditioned the automatic internal habits that have limited them from getting from their partners the things they want the most. The role of the therapist in imparting hope and belief in the client's potential cannot be overemphasized. Because clients can only know what life has been like for them so far, they usually have a hard time developing a vision of how different life could be if they could break out of the habits that constrain their potential. The therapist must be a visionary, seeing clearly what the client's life could be like, and imparting this vision to the client. Most importantly, the therapist must convey hope and confidence that the vision is within reach, that in fact, it's just around the corner. If clients will faithfully practice the daily reconditioning exercises for just a few weeks, life will begin to change dramatically for them. It's a relatively small investment to make for such huge gain, and clients must be helped to realize this.

Changing one's automatic habits of reacting to others is arguably the single most important change a person will ever make. We all know people who tend to be, for example, overly defensive, or overly sensitive. Many people like this go through their entire lives automatically enacting these same patterns over and over again. A defensive person at age 20 often continues to be a defensive person at age 70, sometimes even more so. What a waste! An automatic habit such as defensiveness can be reconditioned within weeks, but few people take the time to go through the reconditioning process. The PET-C therapist allows herself to become openly excited about what the client is about to do and marks the coming weeks as the most important period in the client's life. The following dialogue between the therapist and Katrina illustrates how desire can be cultivated in a client.

T: Today is a big day, Katrina. Everything we've been doing leads up to today. We're going to get you started on some practices that will change the whole feel of your relationship. I've been excited all day, just thinking about it.

W: You crack me up!

T: I'm serious, Katrina. If you'll let me help you, today we'll set up some practices for you to do that will enable you to break out of the habits we've been talking about. I know it can happen. I've seen it hundreds of times. I *love* this part!

W: Don't get too excited. I might not be able to do it.

T: Katrina, you can do it. It won't be easy. But I'm not going to let you fail. There's too much at stake here. It will change your life so much. You were *born* to do this—and I get to be part of it!

W: (*shaking her head, trying not to smile, but unable to resist*) Don't set me up like this.

T: I can't help it. You are going to look back on today and remember it. Today was the day when you began something that made the difference, man!

Every therapist has her own style of conveying enthusiasm and belief in the client. The way that hope and encouragement are delivered will vary according to therapist style, but one way or another, the client must feel the therapist's belief and investment in her, and feel the therapist's confidence that life-altering changes are possible through these reconditioning practices.

Of course, unless clients are on board, they will be unwilling to practice shifting their own internal states. Sometimes, clients will say that they are on board, but when the therapist proposes daily practices designed to help them develop the ability to shift, they balk. A new barrage of objections may arise. The therapist is prepared for this, and welcomes the client's objections. Generally, objections must arise, and are seen as a normal, even essential part of the process of helping a client stay on board. The therapist patiently responds to the client's objections by avoiding arguments, and applying the other methods described in Chapters 6 and 8.

SHIFT OR REWIRE?

Reconditioning practices can impact a client's internal states in one of two ways. They can help clients shift from one state to another, or they can help rewire an existing state for more flexibility.

Shifting Internal States

Through repetitive practice, a client can develop the ability to shift from one internal state to another. Some internal states naturally foster specific attitudes and actions that are predictive of relationship success. For example, internal states that produce feelings such as sadness, loneliness, loss, grief, and the longing for emotional contact, will help clients disclose the underlying worries and fears that often explain their reactions in certain situations (predictive habit 6: understanding and explaining what is at stake). In a similar way, internal states that produces feelings of tenderness and empathy, are ideally suited for finding the understandable part, giving equal regard, offering assurances, and understanding what is at stake (predictive habits 3–6). On the other hand, feelings of anger are often needed for clients to stand up for themselves effectively (predictive habit 2). States such as these do not necessarily arise automatically in situations where they are needed, but through repetitive practice clients can develop the ability to shift into these states.

Rewiring a State for More Flexibility

Developing the ability to shift from an automatically activated internal state to a state that is not naturally activated in upsetting situations is not an easy task. Fortunately, it is often unnecessary. If a client can make even one small change in the way an automatically activated state unfolds, the small change can set off a cascade of positive reactions back and forth between partners. For example, if a client can simply develop the ability to become aware in the present moment that her typical interfering state has become triggered, and say something like, "Okay, I'm just getting mad now. I'm not in a very good frame of mind to talk about this," a destructive escalation can be avoided. Later, when the client is calmer, she can often discuss the same topic much more effectively. Developing the ability to implement even a small change such as this one usually requires repetitive practice. The client must train her brain to function differently when the usual interfering state is up and running.

Most of the repetitive practicing that PET-C clients do involves rewiring an automatically activated state rather than shifting to another state. For example, many of the thoughts and behaviors that predict relationship success can be implemented while one is angry or frustrated. The problem is not the state of anger or frustration. The problem is the thinking and actions that typically go along with these feelings. For many clients, judging and criticizing always go along with frustration or anger. Fortunately, judging and criticizing are not hardwired components of the neural state. Rather, people who judge and criticize when they are angry or frustrated have become conditioned to judge and criticize when they become angry. The good news is that they can rewire their brains to loosen this connection. The rewiring process involves the client pairing new thoughts and behaviors with activations of the interfering internal state, over and over again, until the new thoughts and behaviors become grafted to the internal state. Once this grafting takes place, the new thoughts and behaviors arise each time the internal state is activated.

IDENTIFYING INTERNAL SHIFTS NEEDED
AT CRITICAL JUNCTURES

Early in the reviewing and planning process (described in Chapters 9 and 10), the therapist helps each partner identify where she tends to first get off-track in arguments with regard to the steps needed to positively influence her partner. Figure 11.1 identifies the four places in the Sequence (Appendices A and G) where clients most frequently need to give attention to shifting or rewiring internal states in order to carry out the moves they may need to make in order to respond effectively. We like to think of these places as "stations," because they serve as checkpoints where clients may need to "change trains" (i.e., shift internal states) or perhaps shift to a different track (rewire the same internal state, so that they can move in a different direction), in order to navigate the portion of the journey that lies immediately ahead.

Station 1

In order to accomplish the first steps when they become upset (give the benefit of the doubt, find the understandable part, explain what's driving their feelings or actions, offer assurance, and ask for equal regard—see Appendix A), clients often need to find ways to calm their anger. A client who is furious or indignant will be unable to engage in any form of soft startup or accept influence. At station 1, clients must calm such feelings enough to be able to keep an open mind while they are interacting with their partners, or shift into other softer states from which they can express their fears or needs, without criticism.

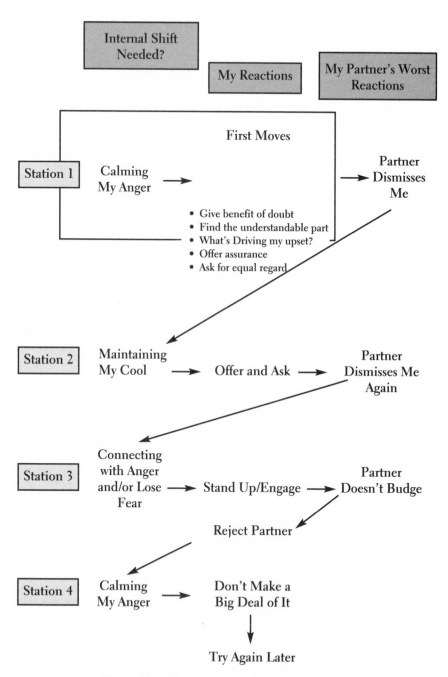

Figure 11.1 Identifying Needed Internal Shifts

Station 2

For some clients, station 1 is the only checkpoint they need to navigate, because once they develop the ability to implement their first moves with a good attitude, their partners immediately become more cooperative and respectful. These are the lucky ones. Most clients need to work minimally at stations 1 and 2. If the client navigates station 1 successfully, she has managed to respond to her partner with a good attitude and engaged in the first steps effectively. However, in spite of the client's good attitude, her partner may show disregard for the client's feelings or viewpoint on the issue at hand. When the client has gone to some lengths to maintain a good attitude and react to her partner in an understanding way, it often feels like a slap in the face when her partner doesn't seem willing to do the same, and this is what makes the station 2 transition difficult. The client must maintain her cool, and implement the offer and ask step (clarify her offer to work toward a solution that they both can live with, and ask her partner to do the same). When implemented well, the offer and ask step has the tone of a "friendly warning," but when a client bypasses station 2, the friendly tone is missing from the warning, and her partner experiences the offer and ask step as an insult. She hears the client's attitude as something like, "This is so typical of you to be unwilling to work with me even after I've worked really hard to try to understand you're warped way of thinking!" Station 2 requires that the client continue to give her partner the benefit of the doubt, and assume that maybe her partner simply needs to be reminded that the client needs something different from him or her.

Station 3

At station 3, clients make a very different kind of transition. Here, clients connect with their anger and express it forcefully. If a client arrives successfully at station 3, she will have managed to find her way to an internal state that allows her to respond initially to her partner's upsetting behavior with a good attitude. In spite of this, her partner will have dismissed her feelings. At station 2, the client will have maintained her cool and calmly clarified her offer to work cooperatively with her partner, and asked that her partner do the same. In spite of all of this, her partner may continue to disregard the client's feelings. At this point, the client must allow her anger to surface. For most clients, feeling anger is a natural response to their partner's dismissal, and many clients will have little difficulty expressing it. However, other clients will experience automatic mechanisms that shut down a forceful expression of anger. For these clients, station 3 work involves letting go of the fear that holds their anger in check. In order to stand up and engage the dismissing partner, clients must have no more fear of conflict than their partners, and this is no small task for many clients.

Station 4

Station 4 is similar to station 1, in that it typically involves letting go of anger and preparing to approach or respond to one's partner with a good attitude. However, because of its positioning in the overall sequence, it will have an even more powerful impact on her partner, if navigated successfully. If a client has taken the steps needed at the previous stations, she will have given her partner every reasonable chance to collaborate, and yet the partner may refuse to do so. When the client makes the needed internal shift at station 4, and then approaches the partner again without resentment or disgust, the partner's motivation to collaborate will typically be higher. However, if the client cannot resolve resentful feelings at station 4, all of her previous work at stations 1 to 3 may be wasted, and be of little positive impact. At station 4, the client not only lets go of resentment, but also prepares to engage her partner in a conversation about the topic again. The client lets her anger go, but not her determination to have her viewpoint on the topic be equally regarded by her partner. Rather, she engages her partner again on the same topic, prepared to initiate the first steps skillfully again, and gets ready to move through the entire sequence again, if necessary.

PRACTICING UNDER "GAME CONDITIONS"

When clients are caught in neural operating programs that propel self-defeating habits, it is as if parts of their brains shut off. Whey they are calm, they often know very well how irrationally they think and act when they become upset. But when they become upset, the part of their brains that knows this shuts off. The neural networks involved when they are thinking clearly are rarely active when the neural processes that generate their self-defeating habits are active. Successful therapy sessions are probably effective because we help clients activate the neural processes involved in clear thinking precisely when their old neural response programs are up and running. In these moments, clients change because they are able to use more of their brains. But when we aren't there to help them, they often revert back to their old neural habits. The question is, "How can clients learn to think clearly when they are in the grips of emotional states that seem to preclude clear thinking? Following Hebb's law, it seems that our clients need to practice new ways of thinking while they are upset, over and over again. If the neural networks involved in new thinking are active when the old neural response programs that drove their ineffective reactions are activated, and this happened enough times, eventually these two distinct neural processes will bond, so that whenever the old neural response programs become active, new thinking will arise automatically.

Clients need some way to practice thinking differently at the moments when they are actually upset. Practicing new thinking alone will not do the trick.

Learning the dance moves is of little value unless they are practiced when the music is playing. Clients need to practice new thinking under "game conditions," that is, when they are actually upset, and least able to apply new ways of thinking. But how can they do this? When they get upset, they seem completely unable to think differently unless we are there to help them. As we pondered this question over the years, an idea hit us which has completely transformed the way we work with couples: Maybe we could go home with them so that we could remind them to think differently when they became upset. Of course, this idea is absurd. It would be impossible to actually go home with our clients. However, maybe our *voices* could go home with them. We began making audiotapes for our clients to listen to at home whenever they became upset. Clients didn't need to remember new ways of thinking when they were upset, they just needed to remember to turn on the tape recorder, and our voices directed them through a new thinking process. We reasoned that it might not matter that it was our voices that prompted clear thinking rather than theirs. What mattered is that the neural networks involved in new thinking were activated at the same time that the "emotional takeover" neural networks were active, and that this happened over and over again.

The following is a transcript of such an audiotape that was made for Katrina to listen to whenever she became upset with Michael. The tape was made during a session in which only Katrina and the therapist were present.

Hey Katrina, it's me, Brent. First of all let me say that I'm impressed that you're listening to this tape, cause I have a feeling that it's not something that you really want to do right now. But I'm glad you're listening because you and I have talked about this many times. When you get upset, you tend to automatically react in a way that chases away from you what you really want. And what you really want, I think, is for Michael to care about how you feel and really listen to you and be willing to make some changes. And you want him to stop being so defensive too, right? So that's what we're doing here, Katrina. We're gonna try and see if we can get you into a frame of mind that would allow that to happen, OK? And let me say right off the bat that I know there are some situations that are so frustrating, and seem to you so basic that you shouldn't have to do anything other than let him know how out of line he is, or how insensitive he's been. And he should just be able to recognize that and adjust his attitude and make some changes. But whether you or I like it or not, the evidence suggests that this approach rarely works. We influence our partners more by endearing ourselves to them than by criticizing them.

At this point, you might be thinking, "How can I not be critical when he does something like this? It's just not right!" Katrina, if indeed Michael has done something that really is selfish, or inappropriate, or out of line in some way, I agree that you should call it what it is. But I know that the odds are good that there's another possibility, and that Michael's thinking or actions aren't wrong, but rather arise from different standards or priorities. You remember those relationship studies I told you about? Researchers found out that the vast majority of the time, when partners are upset with each other, nobody has done anything that's intrinsically wrong. Most upsets arise over different expectations or priorities for which there are no universally agreed upon standards. Evidence from these studies suggests that there are many different, equally workable ways to do relationships.

I'm not saying that there are no areas of right and wrong in relationships. I'm just saying that I know you, Katrina, and you often want to lump more into the "wrong" category than really fits there. And when you do, you weaken your potential to influence Michael. You lower your credibility by overshooting your goal. Of course, this may be a situation where Michael really did do something wrong, and if you think so, I suggest that you take some time to read the section of your workbook titled, When My Partner is Clearly Wrong. But the odds are that this isn't really one of those situations, but rather one where you guys have legitimately different expectations. And if it is one of those situations, you'll shoot yourself in the foot by taking the attitude that Michael is wrong.

At this point, the therapist stopped speaking into the tape recorder, hit the pause button, and asked Katrina what her reaction was to what he recorded on the tape thus far. Katrina said it made sense, but she still didn't know if she could do it, because it seemed like if she dropped the idea that he was wrong, she'd be letting him off the hook, and Michael would feel that he could do whatever he wanted. The therapist validated her reservation, then explained why he wasn't worried about it. His ideas made sense to Katrina, so he added them when he continued recording.

As you're listening to this, you might be thinking, "If I drop the idea that he's wrong, then that would be like letting him off the hook. Why should he change then, if he's not wrong?" The answer is, because if you need to, you'll insist that he change. But you won't insist because he's wrong, you'll insist because he's married to someone who has different feelings and priorities, and he needs to be willing to respect your feelings if he wants to be married to you. This doesn't mean that he needs to just give in and do things your way, but neither does it mean that he can just do whatever he wants. He needs to be willing to work with you—not because his way is necessarily wrong, but because your way isn't wrong either. Both of you deserve to have your feelings and priorities respected.

Let me put it another way: If you imply that Michael needs to change because he's out-of-line, he won't change, or if he does, he'll feel coerced and feel silently resentful. But if you ask him to work with you to try to find a way of doing things that takes both of your feelings into account, the odds are dramatically greater that he will be willing to make some changes, and he'll do it with a good attitude.

Remember that you have just as much right to have your feelings honored as he does. It's just that you don't have more right than he, and if you believe that your standards are more correct or sound than his, Michael will feel disrespected by you, and it's likely that he'll be less cooperative and caring toward you in return. If it feels to you that by dropping the idea that he's wrong is gonna make you less powerful or less influential, think about it again. That's just not the way it works. Each time you criticize Michael, you actually get a little bit smaller. It's like you're pissing away your personal power. On the other hand, if you can drop the critical attitude and keep an open mind, and approach him with a willingness to try to value his perspective too, you become more powerful.

Of course, if you're like me, sometimes the idea of compromising doesn't sound very good to you. You probably just want him to think and act the way you want him to think and act. Well, there's nothing wrong with that. It's just that relationships don't work that way. You have to ask yourself, "Is it good enough if he's willing to try to find a way to respect my feelings as much as his own?" I know there are some situations where compromising just won't be good enough, because you feel so strongly about it. But here's the thing, Katrina. If I know Michael, I think he's very willing to be flexible, and willing to accommodate you, and do things even more your way than he would naturally do it if he just didn't feel criticized by you. When he feels that attitude coming off of you, you know how it goes. He just shuts down. And he's not weird in that way. Most of us are like that. If we're feeling that the other person is saying that we're wrong, or that we're out of line in some way, usually that just creates defensiveness right from the beginning.

Katrina, I want you to know that if you just can't figure out how to change your attitude, I certainly don't want you to fake it. This might be one of those situations where you're gonna need to just go ahead and let it fly and let the chips fall where they will. There are plenty of times when I've plowed ahead with my own critical attitude. It never really works very well for me, and I don't think it will work well for you either, but I understand. Sometimes you've got to do what you've got to do. There's a time and a place for everything, and maybe this just isn't the time for you to change your attitude. Believe me, I'll accept whatever you need to do in this situation. We can talk about it in a few days from now. OK, Katrina, just remember, I'm with you. I'm thinking about you, OK?

Katrina promised to listen to this tape each time she got upset, and it was a great help to her. In her third week of using the tape, Katrina told her therapist that she began to spontaneously hear his voice inside her head every time she got upset. When the therapist heard these words, he knew that Hebb's Law had taken effect, and a new neural integration had occurred in Katrina's head. The neurons activated by his voice had been paired with the neurons active when Katrina got upset enough times so that they were now automatically activated when Katrina became upset.

Here's a transcript of a tape the therapist made for Michael to listen to when he found himself shutting down in the face of Katrina's anger. The therapist made the tape during a session with Michael present.

Hello Michael. It's me, Brent! If you're listening to this tape, it probably means that you're back in that familiar position. Katrina has criticized you, or dismissed your point of view or your feelings, and you shut down. And if I know you, you have an incredible urge to be a million miles away from her. If she was in the room, you wouldn't be able to make eye contact. You'd just want to escape, right?

Let me remind you that I'm not going to be satisfied until you're feeling less criticized, and you're feeling more like Katrina is willing to recognize your feelings and your priorities, OK? So that's what we're doing here. That's the purpose of this tape. So here you are. This is the moment we've been planning for—the one that separates the men from the boys, psychologically speaking. Michael, if you can shift your attitude at times like these, you will begin to get more respectful treatment from Katrina.

Michael, when you hear a critical tone in Katrina's voice, it seems clear to me that a feeling usually comes up inside of you that says, "Oh my god, here we go again! This woman is never satisfied! She's always gotta find something to pick at." This is probably what you're feeling right now. And if you are, that's the first thing that we need to see if we can get to change. Like we've talked about many times before, I'm pretty convinced that Katrina would already be much more cooperative and less critical if she didn't sense that attitude from you—the one that says to her that here complaint is an overreaction—that it's unwarranted. I've seen that attitude come over you many times, Michael. And each time it does, it's clear to me that you begin losing your power. This is the attitude of people who never get the kind of respect and cooperation they want from their partners. The next time you talk to Katrina, I want you to be more powerful, and I know that if this is going to happen, you'll need to find a way to shift your attitude first.

The attitude that works is one where you assume two things at once. First, you assume that Katrina's expectations are valid. Second, you assume that your expectations are valid, too, even though they may be different than hers. If you're honest with yourself, you'll probably recognize that this isn't exactly what you're feeling right now. You believe your actions or expectations are justified and hers are unreasonable, right? You feel that she's too demanding or controlling, and she should just get off your back, right? I don't blame you for feeling this way. I just don't want you to bullshit yourself. This attitude will take you down. Believe me, I know, because I've been there. It's deceptive, because a critical attitude can make a person feel stronger. Trust me; this feeling is an illusion, Mike. Powerful people don't become critical of their partners. What they do instead is recognize that both perspectives are probably legitimate. Rather than dismissing their partners' expectations as unreasonable, they ask their partners to work with them to try to figure out how both of their feelings or priorities can be respected.

At this point, the therapist paused the recording process and asked Michael what he was thinking. Michael responded. "OK, I can try that, but it won't work. It doesn't matter what attitude I have. Once she gets her mind set on somethjing, she won't back down no matter what!" The therapist spent 10 minutes validating and addressing Michael's reservation. When Michael seemed satisfied, the therapist incorporated their discussion in the next words he recorded.

You might be thinking that this is all well and good, but once Katrina gets something in her mind, she's inflexible. She'll keep hammering away until she gets her way. Right? You believe it really doesn't matter what attitude you have. Don't be so sure about that Michael, because I can't think of one time when, without my assistance, you were able to respond to her criticism with a non-judgmental attitude. You can't really know what will happen until you do something different yourself. But let's just say for the sake of argument that you're right. Let's say that no matter what your attitude is, Katrina continues to attack you or dismiss your point of view. This is not a problem. In fact, I hope she does! That way you'll have a chance to practice steps 7–12 of the Sequence, which you need to be able to do sooner or later if your relationship is going to turn around. These are things that we all must be able to do if we want our relationships to succeed. You might want to review the Sequence before you try talking to Katrina again. These steps will take you where you want to go, Michael. Studies have proven beyond any reasonable doubt the effectiveness of these steps.

I don't know if my words are making any difference to you right now, Michael, and you know what? I know that sometimes when I'm really shut down, I don't know that any words would make a difference to me, so if they aren't making a difference, that's OK. Let's just talk about it at our next meeting. But if you can, relax and give it a chance, and get to that place inside where you can do the things I'm talking about, Then give it a shot. Alright, my man? Either way, I'll talk to you later. May the force be with you.

Clients often can't describe how they get attitude shifts to happen. The theme seems to be some sort of "letting go" of control, and a momentary surrender to the fact you can't make life go exactly according to your wishes. It usually is accompanied by a kind of physical relaxation, and a release from obsessive thinking about what isn't going according to plan. The client returns to the present moment, and is able to respond based on what actually happens rather than on their fear of what is going to happen. Our experience with clients is that when they decide they want to make an attitude shift, they are usually able to do it. It might take a while, but the most important ingredient is desire. The problem of normal life is that, when emotional takeovers occur, clients simply forget that they want to shift attitudes. The tapes serve as reminders at the precise moments when the reminders are needed.

It was only after we began making these tapes that we realized that clients had actually been asking for them for years. Clients have often said things to us like, "I wish we could remember the things you were saying in our last session," or "The way you said that was so good. It really got me thinking, but I lost it as the week went on," or "I wish you could have been there to tap me on the shoulder and remind me to keep my cool." Once we started making these tapes, some clients reported just carrying the tapes with them made a difference. Once they'd listened to the tapes a few times, simply glancing at them often activated a reflective process that resulted in an attitude shift.

Clients report that attitude-shifting has something in common with many repetitive religious practices—from praying "Thy will be done" to practicing mindfulness, kissing a St. Christopher medal before going up to bat, or making a list each night of things one is grateful for. All of these approaches help people create enough of a pause to free them from the grip of intense rage or fear and to generate states of generosity, acceptance, and trust. Like them, our audiotapes allow the body and brain to calm down, and they serve as timely reminders that it's in the client's best interest to try to shift.

DAILY PRACTICE THROUGH
AUDIO-GUIDED REEXPERIENCING

One of the most powerful procedures that we use in PET-C to help clients rewire their brains for more flexibility involves a daily practice routine in which clients revisit upsetting situations in their minds. Clients recall the situations vividly enough so that they can actually feel the usual internal state beginning to kick in. In their mind's eye, clients watch the scene unfolding, and feel anger or frustration beginning to build as they are recalling the situation. Clients visualize themselves beginning to react as they did in the situation. However, as the scenario unfolds, the clients picture themselves becoming aware that they are reacting ineffectively, and picture themselves proposing self-reminders that have the effect of helping them shift internal states. After visualizing themselves relaxing and issuing self-reminders, they picture themselves interacting with their partners in ways that are predictive of success.

When this simple visualization procedure is done repeatedly, it has a powerful effect. If a client is going to be able to implement the new ways of thinking and acting she is learning about, she'll need to integrate them with the internal states that are usually activated when she gets upset. Hours of insightful discussion in therapy will have little effect when the client shifts to a state that is different from the one in which the client's learning took place. In this daily practice procedure, the client pairs new thinking and action with the activation of the old internal state, over and over again. After a while, the client finds the new thoughts she's practiced popping up whenever the old internal state becomes active. When this happens, the old internal state has been rewired, so that the new thoughts are now part of the automatic cascade that unfolds when the state is active.

Of course, the problem is that nobody likes to practice, especially if the practice involves getting upset. Most clients feel it to be a strange experience sitting down and deliberately trying to conjure upsetting feelings. In fact, most of them simply won't do it on their own, at least not in the beginning. The therapist must assist with this process, by guiding the client, step by step, through the procedure.

Before a successful visualization can take place, the therapist must have a clear idea about the kinds of thoughts that will help the client make an internal shift. Early in the session, the therapist poses the following question to the client: "If a situation like this one were to come up again, can you think of anything, that, if you could remember to think about it at the moment when you first get upset, could help you get into a frame of mind that would make it more likely that you could react more effectively?"

The therapist and client brainstorm answers to this question together, generating a number of ideas, then deciding together which ones will become a part of the practice scenario. Once they decide which self-reminders would be most effective, the therapist takes the client through a practice visualization in which the client travels back through time, and sees herself in the upsetting situation as if she were a third, invisible person. To make it as vivid as possible, the therapist helps the client recall specific details, such as the look on her partner's face, the exact words exchanged, the flushed feeling in the client's face as she reacted. The therapist helps the client recall the situation vividly enough so that she can actually feel the usual internal state beginning to kick in. The therapist then helps the client see herself proposing reminders to herself, and reacting differently.

As the therapist is taking the client through the visualization, he records it on an audiotape. The client is asked to listen to this audiotape at least once a day during the next week. Most audiotapes are just two or three minutes long. The client finds a time each day when she can give her undivided attention to the audio-guided recall, plugs in the tape, and simply follows the therapist's voice, picturing herself back in the upsetting situation, shifting internal states, and interacting differently with her partner. Again, the important thing is that the client is able to recall the situation vividly enough to experience at least a mild activation of the typical interfering internal state. Otherwise, the process becomes simply a mental exercise, rather than an emotional reconditioning exercise. The client must experience an internal shift each time she engages in this practice.

Ideally, from the time of the first visualization, not a single day goes by without the client working on rewiring the internal state that typically interferes with her reacting effectively in upsetting situations. As the weeks pass and different upsetting situations occur, new guided-visualization tapes are made to help the client reexperience different upsetting situations.

There are often a number of internal shifts that a client may need to make in order to fully implement the Sequence. Each time a new visualization is constructed, the therapist focuses on the specific part of the sequence where the client first got off track. Was the client unable to get into the right frame of mind to initiate the "first steps" (station 1)? Did the client initiate the first steps well, but get angry and fail to implement the offer and ask step when dismissed (station 2)? Did the client stay on track all the way through the offer and ask step, but then fail to express anger, stand up, and engage, when the client's partner continued to disregard her (station 3)? Or, did the client do all of the above, but fail to shift, let go of her anger, and try the conversation again with a good attitude (station 4)? The therapist and client focus on the place where the client first got off-track, and begin discussing the kinds of self-reminders that might have helped the client stay on track, had she possessed the presence of mind to remember them.

Example of a Guided Visualization at Station 1

Early in therapy, the most common internal shift that clients need to make is at station 1. This was the case with Katrina. Recall from Chapter 9 that, in the after-school incident, Katrina was unable to implement the first steps, because her anger at station 1 took her in the direction of critical judgment. The therapist helped Katrina pinpoint the exact moment when she became upset with Michael, and reviewed with her what a more effective reaction might be in a situation like this one. The following dialogue then occurred:

T: What you need is somehow to be able to apply the way you're thinking now, when you're calm, to when you're actually upset, "at the scene of the crime," so to speak. I mean, you can sit here and say to yourself, "I'm going to react differently next time," but when you get upset, the same old reactions take over. Your brain needs to be trained to remember the way you're thinking right now when you get upset. What we need is a way to get you upset everyday, and then have you practice thinking this new way, over and over again.

W: (*sarcastically*) Sounds great! And how do you propose that I get upset? I'm sure Michael would be happy to help out!

T: I'm sure that he could get you good and pissed, but I don't want you getting *that* upset. It's better if you can just get mildly upset. If you get too upset, at least for now, you'll have a hard time remembering to think or act differently.

W: How do I do that?

T: By remembering a recent situation that upset you, like the one we've just been talking about. Here's the plan.

The therapist goes on to explain the audio-guided daily reconditioning practice, and together, they brainstorm answers to the question, "If a situation like this one were to come up again, can you think of anything that, if you could remember to think about it at the moment when you first get upset, could help you get into a frame of mind that would make it more likely that you could do these things?" When they had generated some ideas that Katrina felt might work, the therapist guided Katrina through the following visualization, recording it on an audiotape as he proceeded.

Okay, Katrina. You're traveling back in time to the day when the after-school incident happened. You remember? You got off work early that day. Picture yourself driving home. You pull in the driveway and see the kids playing in the neighbor's yard, right? You see Michael's truck in the driveway, and that's when it first hit you—they didn't do their homework! You feel a surge of anger, like you could explode! Are you feeling a bit of that anger right now? You have a look of disgust on your face as the thought goes through your mind, "He did it again! That lying sack of shit!" Can you see yourself? You fumble for the handle of the door. But just then (therapist slows his voice) *a different thought occurs to you. You say to yourself, "Hold on, Katrina. Maybe things aren't as they appear. It won't hurt to just do a bit of investigating before you get all upset." You sit there for a minute, behind the wheel, and you're actually relaxing your body, wondering what explanation there might be. Try to relax right now, Katrina, as you're listening to my voice.*

Now put yourself back in the situation. You're back there, looking at the front door. You can't think of any possible explanation that might legitimate, but you become determined to approach Michael with an open mind. You remind yourself that you can always become upset later, if you need to. But for now, you find Michael sitting in front of the TV. Remember? He's surprised to see you. The thought races through your mind, "He looks guilty. He didn't expect to be caught!" But you relax and decide it won't hurt to give him the benefit of the doubt. You relax and calmly ask him, "Hey, how come the kids are outside playing? Did they finish their homework already?" You're feeling good about yourself at this point, Katrina, because you just passed through the first station successfully. You calmed yourself down, gave Michael the benefit of the doubt, and approached him determined to try to understand why he acted the way he did. These are some of the moves that people who get cooperation from their partners do. If you have time, you can review them in your workbook (Appendix A).

The therapist stopped the tape here, although he could have gone on. During the following week, the therapist wanted Katrina to focus on her *first* reactions. If she could change this much alone, it would likely make a big difference.

In early visualizations, the therapist speaks on the audiotape, but as Phase II progresses, the client often makes his or her own tapes. There are advantages both ways, but in the beginning, we feel that the advantages to a therapist-generated tape are greater. First, the sound of the therapist's voice alone often has a calming effect on the client. Second, the therapist's voice often cues the client to think about the things recently discussed in therapy sessions. There seems to be some value for the client in having his or her therapist's voice in her head daily, especially early in therapy. Third, the therapist often makes a better quality tape. When clients make the tapes, they tend to rush over the details and just tell themselves what to do. Because the therapist has experience with guided imagery, he or she knows how to use pacing and detail to let the visualization unfold slowly and vividly. Vivid reexperiencing is necessary if the client is to experience an activation of the same internal state that was present in the original situation.

In Michael's sessions, the therapist constructed similar guided visualizations. As the weeks progressed, new visualizations were repeatedly constructed, helping both Michael and Katrina to reexperience a variety of situations, guiding them in navigating through each of the four stations. The particular station serving as the focus of any particular visualization depended upon where the client got off-track in the most prominent upsetting situation of the week. Audiotape-guided visualizations continued throughout Phase II of the therapy. However, as the weeks passed, the therapist encouraged each partner to construct her own visualizations after each upsetting situation occurred. A sheet summarizing how to do these visualizations is included in each client's workbook.

PRACTICING WITH AUDIOTAPED COMPLAINTS

Another method used in helping clients rewire their internal states for more flexibility involves helping clients practice thinking and acting differently when their typical interfering states are activated by listening to audiotaped complaints, recorded ahead of time by their partners. During individual sessions, the therapist and client study the internal reactions that arise in the client as she is listening to audiotaped complaints. In those moments, the therapist helps the client engage in thinking and responding in ways that help her shift internal states.

The first part of the process involves the therapist asking the client's partner to record some complaints. Partners are asked to record each complaint twice. The first time, the partner is to complain harshly, and the second time the partner is to complain using steps from the Sequence. Instructions are written up in the partner's workbook sheets (see Complaints on Tape, Atkinson, 2005).

The therapist asked Katrina to tape some complaints, and met with her to review the complaints before meeting with Michael. He could have met with Michael first, but that would have required Michael to bring the audiotapes. The therapist wanted to avoid this situation, because the temptation for Michael to listen to the tapes before his session may have been too great to resist. Generally, the therapist wants to be present for the first listening of the tapes, so that he can assist the client in studying and working with his or her reactions to it. When clients listen to the tapes ahead of time, they often fail to use the complaints as an opportunity to study their reactions and instead become upset about the content of the complaints.

In his session with Katrina, the therapist helped her realize that, although her complaints on the second audiotape were less harsh than those on the first tape, the complaints on the second tape were still ineffective, and failed to reflect some of the first steps of the Sequence. The therapist helped Katrina shift her attitude and come up with statements that she could make to Michael when she actually delivered the complaints that would be more effective. This process was eye-opening for Katrina, because she had thought that her complaints on the second tape were pretty good. The "Practicing with Audiotaped Complaints" exercise often helps the complaining partner as much as the partner who practices listening to the audiotaped complaints, because it forces him or her to think carefully about the attitude that lies beneath his or her complaints.

When he met with Michael, the therapist had already heard the audiotaped complaints in his session with Katrina, and knew the reactions that would likely be triggered in Michael when he listened to the complaints. Here are some sections of the transcript of the therapist's session with Michael. The therapist chose to use the harsher of the two versions of the complaints that Katrina had made. In the following dialogue, the therapist helps Michael make a shift at station 2, then take an Offer and Ask step.

T: Okay, Michael. You've got the plan, right? I want you to try to do two things at once. Listen to the content of her complaint, and at the same time, notice the automatic reactions you are having to what she's saying. That includes the feelings that get stirred in you, and the thoughts that run through your head.

H: Right. (*Michael looks apprehensive.*)

T: Are you nervous?

H: Yes!

T: Okay. Just try to relax. She's not actually here.

H: Yes she is. (*pointing to the portable cassette player*) She's in that little box! (*Both laugh, then the therapist turns on the cassette.*)

(Voice of Katrina on audiotape): *Michael, the bottom line is, I don't think you want to be married. I mean, I don't think you're ready for the commitment, or the responsibilities that go along with being a married man. You and your buddies are a bunch of adolescents. Take this weekend, for example. You arranged things so that you could be all day Sunday at the Cubs game, and I was stuck home with the kids. First of all, you had your friends ask me if you could go. I would have looked like a bitch if I'd said "no." You were afraid to ask me yourself, because you know it was a selfish thing to leave me with the kids all day. And you guys didn't have to be gone all day and night. The game started at 3:00 P.M. This is so typical of you! You don't think of anyone but yourself. (*The therapist stops the audiotape.*)*

T: Okay, Michael. What's going on inside of you right now?

H: Welcome to the world of Michael. I get this treatment constantly.

T: Okay. So that's the thought that goes through your head first?

H: I didn't plan to have my friends ask her, and we weren't gone all day, either.

T: So that's the thing that crosses your mind? You think of the errors in her thinking, or the exaggerations.

H: They aren't hard to find.

T: What would you say to her if you guys were at home and she said these things?

H: I'd probably just say what I was thinking.

T: You'd defend yourself against her criticisms, and let her know that this is just another example of her finding something to complain about, and exaggerating?

H: I guess so. That's probably not good, right?

T: That's okay. Right now I'm just trying to get a clear picture of what happens inside of you. What is the feeling like?

H: I feel defensive, and irritated. I'm so tired of her nagging at me all the time.

T: Physically, what's the feeling like, in your body?

H: I feel sort of agitated.

T: Good. It's a familiar feeling?

H: Oh yes.

T: Okay. We're gonna see if we can get that feeling to let up a bit.

H: I don't know how.

T: Let's try a few things. First, try to relax, physically. You look kind of tense.

H: I am tense!

T: I don't blame you. But if you're going to get Katrina to treat you differently, you'll need to learn to stay relaxed when she's criticizing you, at least in the beginning. Sit back, take a few slow breaths, and try repeating a few things to yourself. You don't have to say them out loud, just inside: (*the therapist speaks slowly*) "I'm gonna stay cool and calm, and I'm gonna handle this situation effectively. If I get upset, I won't be as effective. She's criticizing me. No biggie. I can handle this" (*Here, the therapist prompts Michael to take step 7 of the Sequence: Maintain Your Cool.*) How are you doing?

H: I'm trying.

T: Okay, now picture yourself saying this to her, calmly: "Katrina, obviously you're upset, and I'm interested in understanding how you feel. I honestly am. But I'm having a hard time because it feels like you're criticizing me. Could you slow down a bit, and try to just tell me how you feel?" (*This is an example of step 8: Offer and Ask.*)

H: She'll just say, "Well, you've been a jerk, and I'm upset about it!"

T: No problem. Everything is still on track, Michael. You can afford to stay relaxed. Everything is still cool. Picture yourself saying, "I'm not saying you shouldn't be upset, Katrina, and I'm willing to talk about it. It's just hard when it seems that you've already made up your mind. Can we just talk it over?"

H: But what if she just keeps hounding away at me?

T: Be open to the possibility that she might not just keep hounding you, Michael. Think about it. Have you ever really stayed calm and talked to her like this?

H: Maybe a long time ago. Actually, probably not. (*Michael thinks silently for a moment.*) I don't think I can remember what you said.

T: That's okay. In a minute, we'll make a practice tape for you.

The therapist then talked Michael through the rest of the Sequence, clarifying when it would be good to connect with his anger, stand up for himself, not make a big deal of her having continued to criticize him, then helping him visualize getting into a frame of mind in which he could initiate the conversation again with a good attitude.

T: But your *first* reactions are critical, Michael. If you can't react effectively in the beginning, then your attempts to stand up for yourself won't have any impact. Let's go back to the beginning. I'm going to rewind the tape, and let's try it again. This time, as you listen, notice that irritated feeling building, and notice those thoughts that automatically go though your head. But as you do, remember to stay relaxed, and try saying those things to yourself we talked about. Then picture yourself responding differently to Katrina.

The therapist played the tape again, stopping at the same place.

T: All right. What's going on inside, Michael.

H: I'm staying relaxed, but I can't remember what I'm supposed to say to myself.

The therapist repeated the words he had suggested the first time, while Michael sat with his eyes closed, looking relaxed.

T: Okay, are you still feeling irritated?

H: Not so much.

T: Good, now what are you going to say to Katrina? Just say it out loud.

H: "I can see that you're upset, and I'm feeling kind of defensive, but I'll try to listen. Just try not to criticize me, okay, because it's harder for me to listen."

T: Great! Fantastic, even! How does it feel?

H: She'll look at me like, "Is this my husband?"

T: It will be pretty different, won't it?

The therapist and Michael proceeded to listen to another complaint, and Michael practiced the same internal moves, this time with much more success, right from the beginning. The second complaint involved Katrina accusing Michael of reckless spending. Michael was able to listen, stay calm, and do the Offer and Ask move, just as he had done with the first complaint. This time, the therapist suggested that he visualize Katrina responding to his request by calming down a bit, and simply explaining her worry about their financial situation. The therapist helped Michael visualize acknowledging the legitimate feelings that were driving Katrina's complaint, assuring her that he didn't want her to have to feel this way, and offering his willingness to try to find a way of handling their finances that they could both feel okay about. The therapist also helped Michael visualize how he could explain his own feelings on the issue without invalidating hers.

Before the session was over, the therapist took Michael back to the first complaint and recorded an audio-guided visualization. Just as he had done with Michael earlier in the session, the therapist took him through the stages of hearing Katrina's complaint (focusing on her tone), paying attention to the feeling and thoughts arising inside of him, relaxing and saying self-soothing things to himself, then doing the Offer and Ask step. Michael promised he would listen to the tape several times on the way home from the session.

There's often time for a client to practice with two or three audiotaped complaints in a single session. The close proximity of practice opportunities (multiple complaints in one session), and the evocative nature of the complaining partner's voice and tone on the audiotapes, makes this method powerful, and different from the audio-guided visualizations discussed earlier. As was the case in Michael's session, audiotaped complaints often serve as a basis for an audio-guided visualization that the client uses for practice during the following week.

Throughout the process of responding to the audiotaped complaints and constructing audio-guided visualizations, the therapist checks constantly with the client to be sure that he is able to make the internal shifts in attitude that are needed in order to respond effectively to her partner's complaints. It will do the client little good to say the right words if his attitude doesn't match them. The most important thing is that the client is able to say things to himself that have the effect of cultivating the needed attitude.

"LIVE" ASSISTANCE IN STATE SHIFTING

Another vital component of the process of helping clients rewire automatically activated internal states involves conjoint sessions in which the therapist gives each partner "live" assistance in state shifting. It is one thing to respond to an audiotaped complaint by shifting states and visualizing effective responses to one's partner. It is another thing to be able to do this when one's partner is actually present. Throughout Phase II of PET-C, the therapy alternates between individual and conjoint sessions.

The main purpose of conjoint sessions is to give each partner a chance to practice the abilities they've been developing. A secondary goal is to help partners resolve specific issues. Since partners often have reverse expectations for conjoint sessions, the PET-C therapist clarifies the goal of conjoint sessions, and the process that typically unfolds during conjoint sessions, before actually beginning the sessions.

Conjoint sessions alone will not likely be sufficient for clients to rewire internal states, because, compared to practices clients can implement at home, conjoint sessions occur with relative infrequence. Unless conjoint sessions are accompanied by the "at home" practices described in this chapter, they will not usually be sufficient to help partners rewire their automatic internal activations. However, conjoint sessions are a vital part of the overall Phase II process. They are implemented early in Phase II, and are alternated with individual sessions throughout this phase of PET-C. In addition to providing partners with the opportunity to practice the abilities they have been developing under the "live" supervision of the therapist, conjoint sessions provide the therapist with an opportunity to witness the progress of each partner in implementing these abilities. In the beginning of Phase II, clients often don't realize when they are getting off-track in their reactions to their partners. Individual sessions are limited by the client's self-reports. In conjoint sessions, the therapist is able to witness partners in action, clarifying for them the specific ways in which they each got off-track, and assisting them in shifting as needed.

During each conjoint session (typically scheduled for 90 minutes), the therapist encourages partners to discuss an issue that one of them is upset about. As they discuss these issues, the old internal states frequently get triggered in each of them, and the therapist asks them to take a break, asking them to go into separate rooms. In the following moments, each partner attempts to make a state shift. When they are able to do this, partners are then reunited to continue their discussion.

When things go well during each partner's break, the couple is reunited to continue their discussion. Often, the second round of the conversation goes much better than the first. However, sometimes, partners get "triggered" a second time, and the therapist again suggests another break so that each partner can try to shift again. If either partner fails to make the needed internal shift during a break, the therapist refrains from reuniting the couple for further discussion. If needed, the therapist will spend the remainder of the therapy session with one partner, working toward a shift. If a shift has not occurred by the end of the session, the therapist schedules individual appointments with each partner soon after, during which the therapist continues to help each partner move toward the attitude that is needed for continuing a successful conversation about the issue.

These conjoint sessions are commenced early in, and continue throughout therapy. Early in therapy, the therapist plays an active role in helping partners shift internal states during session "breaks," using Level II and III interventions described in Chapter 6 (Embodying the Predictive Habits and Interacting Di-

rectly with an Interfering State). As clients get on board and begin individual-
ized training in the skills of emotional intelligence, the therapist becomes much
less involved during these breaks. In fact, near the end of Phase II, the assistance
of the therapist is often not needed during breaks. Instead, each partner listens
to one of the audiotapes the therapist has previously made for them (see the section Practicing under Game Conditions). After each partner has had time to listen to his or her audiotape, the therapist enters the room with each partner, respectively, checking to see if this partner has been able to shift into an attitude
that would enable a productive discussion with the partner. If the client has not
been able to shift, the therapist helps him or her make the internal shift needed.
But if therapy has been progressing well, the tapes often do the trick, and clients
are ready to be reunited to continue their conversation.

Sometimes, especially early in therapy, partners don't like the process of taking breaks, and want to get back into conversations quickly in order to try to get
their points across to their partners. The therapist supports the client's desire to
be heard and respected by the partner, but helps the client understand that the
client's desire to continue the conversation with her partner at this point cannot
be supported by the therapist. The therapist reminds the client that he or she
will not likely be heard and respected unless he or she is able to produce a shift
in attitude. The therapist encourages the client, and communicates optimism
that if the client is able to shift, he or she will indeed be heard and respected.
The therapist helps the client become receptive to what is being said, using the
methods for creating internal shifts described in Chapter 6. An effective therapist is gentle, noncritical, supportive, and avoids arguing with the client. Instead,
she patiently encourages the client to express her reservations, validates the desires or worries that fuel them, and offers assurances and explanations that help
the client become receptive.

Skilled PET-C therapists hold fast here. Inexperienced therapists will often
relinquish to the requests of clients to resume conversations before their attitudes have sufficiently shifted. Predictably, these conversations fail. The therapist communicates the theme that drives this therapy: If you want increased respect and cooperation from your partner, you'll need to find a way to think and
act like people who usually get respect and cooperation from their partners. The
therapist makes her priorities clear. The main goal is not the resolution of the
particular issue being discussed. The goal is for each partner to develop the ability to interact effectively in the conversation. When this happens, issues will be
easily resolved. While partners have previously agreed, in theory, with this approach, they may change their minds once they are upset and a live issue is on
the table. Throughout Phase II, the therapist anticipates the reemerging of the
client's objections and reservations to focusing on her own reactions (see Table
8.1 for a summary of the most common objections). Each time, the therapist patiently fields the client's objections, validates his or her feelings, and helps the
client realize that the best way to resolve the issue is to develop the ability to react effectively with the partner.

Eliciting and resolving the client's reservations is an indispensable part of this process. A skilled therapist is happy when clients express reservations. Almost all clients have them at various points in Phase II. The therapist looks for nonverbal expressions of reservations as well as verbal ones, and actively encourages clients to verbalize them. Unless clients express their reservations or frustrations with the process, there is a risk that they may comply with the process outwardly, but be inwardly resistant. To an inexperienced therapist, a client's reservations can be frustrating, and often trigger an internal state in the therapist that can hinder her effectiveness. A therapist may find herself thinking, "Oh come on! Haven't we covered this before?" Often, therapists must rewire their own internal reactions to these situations, using the same methods they have helped clients learn to rewire their reactions. The application of these rewiring methods to the therapist's own internal states is described more fully in Chapter 13.

A skilled PET-C therapist will suggest a break early in a couple's argument, soon after it is clear that the partners are caught in their usual reactions to each other. Inexperienced therapists often wait too long, hoping that partners will somehow be able to shift into more productive conversations. This rarely happens, and valuable time is wasted that could be used by each partner during breaks. Further, if the therapist waits too long, she runs the risk of inadvertently reinforcing the client's hope that she can get what she wants from her partner, while going about it in a way that predicts relationship failure.

Throughout Phase II of PET-C, clients are asked to bring their audiotapes to each therapy session. However, sometimes clients forget to do this, and situations may arise in which clients don't have personalized audiotapes to listen to during a break in a conjoint session. When this happens, the therapist asks clients to review sheets in their workbooks (Atkinson, 2005) during breaks which take them through some moves that are generally helpful in getting internal states to shift. One page of the workbook, "When I'm Upset," can be used as a worksheet in which clients write down their thoughts in a way that often enhances state shifting (see Appendix N).

Most of the time, clients can shift internal states if they want to. The therapist must simply assist clients in remembering that it is in their own best interests to try to shift. However, there are occasions in which a client appears to sincerely want to shift, but can't. Some part of the client resists, even though the rest of him or her is willing. Simple reminders to clients that it is in their own best interests to shift aren't enough. On these occasions, the therapist must help the client suspend efforts to talk him- or herself into shifting, and instead explore the internal resistance. To accomplish this, the therapist uses Level III methods described in Chapter 6 ("Interacting Directly with an Interfering State"). The reader is encouraged to review the guidelines given in Chapter 6. In a Level III intervention, the therapist begins by directing the client's attention to the fact that he or she is "under the influence" of an internal state that has an agenda of its own. The therapist helps the client pay attention to the internal cues that signal the state's presence. The client is encouraged to avoid trying to make the state go away and instead simply study the internal state without trying to control it. The client becomes more aware of the thoughts, feelings, and urges that characterize the state. Then, the therapist helps the client conduct internal experiments with the state, noticing how "it" reacts to various thoughts, or proposed courses of action. As the client interacts with the internal state, it shifts.

CONCLUSION

When clients faithfully engage in the practices described in this chapter, their internal states become rewired for more flexibility, and clients are released from the constraints that previously restricted them. In designing practice tapes for any particular client, the therapist draws heavily on his or her previous successful experiences in helping this client make state shifts. Different words, ideas or metaphors will be helpful to different clients. For example, one client may respond to a reminder that she can be more powerful if she drops her critical judgments of her partner. Another client may simply need to be reminded that her father was critical, and she really doesn't want to be like him. Often, the words, ideas or metaphors that help clients shift can be discovered by simply asking clients, "If you could remind yourself of one thing when you get upset, what would help you make the attitude shift we've been talking about? What could you say to yourself or think about?" Important self statements or reminders discovered are incorporated into state-shifting practices.

Clients often have trouble believing that such simple practices could result in such powerful changes, but those who resolve their skepticism and actually do the exercises change in profound ways. In the seminars our faculty members give on PET-C around the country, audiences are often amazed to see videotapes of clients with significant histories of trauma and abuse become transformed as they engage in repetitive exercises. Mental health professionals tend to believe that clients like these cannot become more functional without extensive, long-term psychotherapy. However, when the internal states that have constrained their interactions are tracked, targeted, and rewired through repetitive practice, even clients with traumatic injuries become transformed into effective agents of change in their relationships. Sometimes, the answers to life's most seemingly impenetrable problems are so simple that they are overlooked. The simple answer involves repetitive exercises designed to help clients rewire their automatically activated internal states. Almost without exception, when therapy fails, it is because the clients did not engage in the exercises. When clients do them, they change. It's that simple.

For many therapists, the idea of repetitive practice conjures up images of thought-stopping or communication skills training in which clients practice stopping irrational thoughts or making "I statements." The problem is that we all know that these methods can promote changes that are less than heart-felt. We've watched clients trying to make "I feel sad" statements while inside, they're thinking "You're a jerk!" and we're uncomfortable with the "fake it 'til you make it," philosophy behind the cognitive/behavioral rehearsal approach. But let's not throw out the baby with the bathwater. Isn't it possible to practice changing the condition of one's heart? Sacred traditions have always understood the necessity of repetition and ritual in cultivating attitudes of the heart. Devotees often get together week after week to soften their hearts by reminding themselves of what they have to be grateful for, acknowledging their shortcomings, asking for forgiveness, and seeking the attitudes of love and compassion. As clients progress through therapy and release judgmental attitudes over and over again, they experience transformations of the heart that seem similar to those that have been experienced by spiritual pilgrims throughout the ages who have sought to be released from the hatred, bitterness, resentment and contempt they found in their hearts. It is perhaps ironic that most advanced scientific discoveries about the brain may end up supporting the concepts of routine and ritual, largely ignored by modern psychotherapists, but intuitively known and practiced by our spiritual traditions since the beginning of time.

CHAPTER 12

Accessing the Intimacy States

W HEN PHASE II OF PET-C is successful, partners have become able to recondition the automatic internal reactions that formerly propelled them into gridlock, and they begin experiencing increased respect and cooperativeness. Critical as these changes may be, they will not be enough to ensure a couple's lasting happiness. Long-term studies on relationships suggest that the absence of fighting alone is not sufficient to predict good relationship outcomes. Couples who succeed don't just stop fighting, they form powerful positive emotional bonds. They become best friends, experiencing warmth, fondness and admiration toward each other on a daily basis.

In Phase III, the therapist helps partners increase friendship-enhancing thoughts and interactions. Compared to Phase II, Phase III is relatively stress-free, as the focus shifts from eliminating the negative to increasing the positive. In this phase of therapy, partners are less guarded with each other, and with the therapist's encouragement, they experiment with different ways of connecting during and between sessions.

As in Phase II, the pragmatic/experiential method is used in Phase III to promote change. We begin by talking with partners about the studies identifying the types of processes used by partners who succeed to build strong friendships. From these studies, we have identified four friendship-enhancing processes that have become the focus of Phase III: (1) curiosity about your partner's world; (2) keeping sight of the positive; (3) pursuing shared meaning; (4) making and responding to bids for connection.

These abilities are described in detail in Chapter 3 (see Table 3.1), along with six other abilities used in managing conflicts that make up the 10 predictive habits that guide the pragmatic focus of PET-C. The four friendship-enhancing abilities arise naturally when the brain's intimacy-producing internal states are active (see Chapter 2). The nontechnical terms we use in PET-C to discuss these states with clients are *longing, tenderness, playfulness,* and *sexual interest.*

Longing creates a desire for emotional support or contact. Feelings such as sadness, loneliness, inadequacy, or disappointment may propel this desire. When this state is active, a person will experience a need for the interest, support, or attention of others, and look forward to expressions of warmth, admiration, or fondness from them.

Tenderness produces feelings of warmth, tenderness, and generosity toward others. When this state is active, a person will feel empathic toward others, and be naturally motivated to give emotional support.

Playfulness produces the urge to interact with others in spontaneous or playful ways. When it is active, a person feels like teasing, roughhousing, tickling, or getting an unpredictable reaction.

Sexual Interests can be expressed in a variety of ways ranging from fantasy to flirtation, to direct sexual advances. Usually, its activation is accompanied by desire for contact with others, and often occurs in tandem with playfulness.

In Phase III of PET-C, our goal is to increase each partner's access to these four intimacy states, which then produce the motivation to engage in friendship enhancing habits that distinguish people who are destined to succeed in their relationships from those who are destined to fail. As each partner gains greater access to these states, we help partners give meaningful and effective expression to the feelings and motivations that arise with them.

SIMPLE REMINDERS

As partners progress through Phase II, they experience relief from the antagonistic attitudes that have dominated their relationship. When negative feelings decrease, positive ones may arise naturally. However, this is not always the case. Partners have often gotten out of the habit of connecting daily in meaningful, positive ways. With some couples, little more is needed from the therapist in Phase III than to help partners remember to prioritize connecting with each other, and help them develop some habits and rituals for connecting. These partners are able to move freely into intimacy states and the friendship enhancing process, and the only reason they haven't already is that they're just not in the habit of doing it. During their period of marital distress, they organized their lives so that they had minimal contact with each other. As the couple enters Phase III, these isolating habits may be left in place, even though they are no longer necessary.

Friendship-Building Exercises

We have developed a variety of exercises that prompt partners to think about and interact with their partners in ways that are predictive of success (Atkinson,

2005). We've also found a number of helpful exercises in John Gottman's books (Gottman, 1999; Gottman & DeClaire, 2001; Gottman & Silver, 1999). For partners who have good access to their intimacy states, doing the exercises is an easy and fun way to activate these states. For example, when a husband is prompted to think about a recent time when he felt "extra positive" toward his wife, he will reexperience the positive moment again, often connecting with feelings of tenderness or fondness for his wife. When he communicates this extra positive moment to his wife, it may trigger good feelings in her as well. Her expressions of tenderness in return can trigger further good feelings in the husband. In this way, simple exercises can create a positive escalation of good feelings. In addition to the extra positive moments exercise, we use exercises that prompt partners to remember good times, express appreciations, learn about each other's internal worlds, check in with each other about important happenings in their respective lives, and initiate small acts of caring (see Appendices O–S for some exercises from one client's workbook).

Of course, these exercises are minimally helpful unless they actually activate positive feeling states in partners. If a wife talks about a good time that she and her husband had in the past, but doesn't feel good when she's talking, the memory will be of little benefit to either of them. Likewise, if a husband expresses appreciation for his wife's efforts, but doesn't actually feel appreciative, his words will feel hollow to her. For this reason, the therapist asks partners to bring completed exercises to sessions, and goes over what the experience of doing the exercises was like for each partner. The therapist monitors the level of affect present when clients engage in the practices promoted by these exercises, and notices when clients are failing to connect with the feeling states that fuel their connecting power. When the therapist notices a lack of authentic feeling in a client, he or she helps the client explore the things that may be blocking intimate feelings from flowing, and helps the client resolve them (see below, "Exploring and Resolving Activation Blocks"). However, many times, partners have little problem connecting with the good feelings that these exercises are designed to stir, and they enjoy doing them.

Audio-Prompted Reminders

Researchers have discovered that the first few minutes when couples are reunited after being apart for periods of time are particularly important in a relationship (Gottman, 1999). The success or failure of a relationship can be powerfully predicted by how partners interact at these times. We have found that if partners spend just a small bit of time preparing themselves mentally for these reunion moments, these small efforts yield big rewards in terms of the positive feelings that follow. For example, when a husband remembers on the way home from work that his wife was to have a stressful conversation with her boss that day, and he remembers to ask his wife about it as soon as he walks in the door, she feels cared about, and is more likely to experience tender feelings toward her husband.

We have found that many partners benefit from listening to audiotapes in the moments before they reunite at the end of the day, designed by the therapist to help them shift gears and connect with positive feelings toward their partners. Clients frequently listen to tapes like this while commuting home from work, but partners who stay at home during the day listen to these tapes too, stopping whatever they are doing 10 to 15 minutes before they anticipate the arrival of their partners, and running the tape. Here's an example of an audiotape that a PET-C therapist recently made for a husband to listen to during his commute home from work each day. The therapist recorded this tape when he was in a playful mood. We have found that the tone in the therapist's voice often activates a similar mood in the client. If the therapist is personal, playful, and free when making these tapes, clients often shift to similar states when listening, and are often still in these states when they see their partners.

Hi Tony! It's me again. Just when you thought you were rid of me for a week. Ha! How are ya doin today, buddy? Are you up for this? Let's get started! First, take a minute and mentally review your day. See if you can identify the high and low point. You know, what made you feel good today, and what made you feel bad. Go ahead. Stop the tape for a minute. I'll wait for you.

Here, the therapist is prompting Tony to engage in thinking that will help him share information about his emotional world with his wife. Knowledge of each other's worlds is one of the things that distinguishes partners who are destined to succeed in their relationships from those who are destined to fail. Partners who succeed share significant emotional experiences with each other such as their "highs" and "lows."

Okay, try to remember to tell Mary these things some time this evening. Now we're gonna see if you can shift gears and leave work at work. Do whatever you need to in order to make this happen. Empty your mind. Maybe jot down a note to yourself if you need to, or scream really loud. I know what you're thinking. Hey, you're in the car, right? Nobody will hear you! Don't knock it until you've tried it, dude! Turn the tape off if you need to. Just do whatever it takes to get your mind off your work.

The therapist is helping Tony realize that he needs to shift internal states. When he reunites with Mary, he needs to be able to focus on her and leave work behind.

Okay, have you got it all out of your system yet? Good. Now, let's start thinking about Mary. Do you remember anything about what she was going to be doing today? What kind of a mood was she in the last time you spoke with her? What's one thing about her day that you want to remember to ask her about? Stop the tape if you need a minute to think about it.

Here, the therapist has prompted Tony to be prepared not only to share emotionally significant information about himself with Mary, but to connect with his curiosity about her, too.

Don't forget to ask her about these things, okay? She'll really appreciate that. Now, take a minute to think about what's happened between you two since the last time you listened to this tape. Try to think of one thing that she's done that you really appreciate. Stop the tape if you need a minute to think. Take a minute and let yourself really feel appreciative of that, okay? And be sure you remember to tell her you appreciated it, okay?

Now, take a minute and think of a moment that happened lately when you felt a little bit extra positive about Mary. It doesn't have to be anything big. Maybe she just looked extra good at one point yesterday, or maybe you liked how excited she got about something. Let yourself relax for a moment and have that good feeling again. Stop the tape for a minute to think of when this moment was.

Here, the therapist is helping Tony connect with feelings of fondness that emerge when he connects with the internal state we call *tenderness*, the intimacy state that fuels the predictive habit *keeping sight of the positive*.

Now I'd like for you to think of one small thing that you could do for her this evening or tomorrow that would make her feel cared about. Again, it doesn't have to be anything big. Maybe just leave her a little note, or pick up her favorite candy bar on the way home, or something. Maybe remember to make a call and take care of some planning that needs to be done, so that she won't have to do it. Stop the tape if you need a moment to think. Be sure you come up with something, because I'm gonna ask you about these things when I see you next. I don't want to have to kick your butt! (The therapist is encouraging Tony to think of something he can do for Mary that will activate tenderness in her, too.)

Now, prepare to be in a good frame of mind when you walk in the door. Maybe imagine how good it will feel to get a good hug from her. Hey, I know what you're thinking, but leave the sexual thoughts for later! Okay, maybe a little is okay, but you have to keep in mind that she might not exactly be feeling sexy when you see her, right? There's a time and a place for everything!

What's one small, unexpected, intimate thing you can do when you see her? Put your hand on her cheek? Give her buns a squeeze? Smack her butt with whatever object you find laying around? Blow in her ear? Tickle her? Tackle her? Pick her up off her feet when you hug her? Echo every word she says until you drive her crazy? Do you have any playfulness in you today, Tony? Let's come up with something besides the standard peck on the cheek, okay?

The therapist is helping Tony connect with another of the intimacy states, playfulness. A playful internal state propels partners to make and respond to bids for connection, another of the predictive habits.

Okay. Now turn off the tape and think over some of the things you've thought about while listening to it. Try to get into a good mood. Good luck, Tony. This is probably the most important part of your day. May the force be with you!

When we describe this audiotape procedure at our seminars for therapists, audience members sometimes ask us how we find time to make all of these tapes for our clients. We have two answers. The first is that it really isn't as time consuming as you might think. Once a therapist becomes accustomed to making these tapes, it doesn't take any advance planning. I often make these tapes while I'm commuting around during the day. The second answer is that once you see how effective these tapes are, you'll *want* to find the time to make them. Clients are often very willing to do the things on these tapes. They often just don't remember to do them, unless prompted. The beauty of this procedure is that all the client has to do is to remember to plug in the tape. They are then prompted to engage in some valuable thinking and state shifting. Clients can often shift internal states very easily if they can just remember to take the time. These tapes really make a difference. When partners are reunited, they actually look at each other and interact in personal ways.

ACTIVATING DORMANT LONGINGS FOR
EMOTIONAL CONNECTION

Another important aspect of Phase III involves connecting clients with the internal state we call *longing*. Partners usually enter marriage with an abundance of longing. They frequently share with each other important dreams and expectations about how cool things will be as they make their way through life together. When conflicts arise, partners often give up on the expectation that their partners will care about their hopes and dreams. Often, they feel it would be a major accomplishment if their partners would just stop criticizing them. As Phase II progresses, partners do stop criticizing and judging each other. A truce emerges, and they are often relieved. Partners could begin talking about what they really want the most from each other, but are often reluctant to press their luck. It's one thing for partners to tolerate each other, but quite another thing to think that partners could once again become supportive of each other's dreams. In successful relationships, partners champion each other's dreams, and make every effort possible for each other to realize their deepest hopes and longings. This process is central to *creating shared meaning*, one of the relationship-enhancing predictive habits.

Some clients enter relationships with very low expectations for emotional connection. We often hear husbands say things like, "My only dissatisfaction is that she is so dissatisfied. If she just wouldn't get so upset about everything, I'd be happy as a pig in mud." For some such individuals, this attitude is a result of lowered expectations due to the relationship distress they've experienced. However, people do vary with regard to how much need they experience for emotional connection, independent of how much conflict is present in the relationship. For example, Jack (Chapter 2) was a person who had limited access to the brain state that produces longing, or the need for emotional support. As a child, Jack had learned that he couldn't rely on others to help soothe his stressful or upset feelings, and had stopped looking to others for emotional support. Chapter 2 describes how he learned to reconnect with his need for Loretta's support, and learned how to accept the emotional support she offered.

Regardless of whether clients have lowered expectations for emotional support due to their relationship distress, or whether they just never had many hopes or expectations for support to begin with, Phase III seeks to help partners awaken dormant longings for emotional support. This process begins with the therapist asking each partner to think about what they really want from each other, regardless of whether or not they think they can realistically have it or not. Some clients have no problems coming up with an extensive "wish" list. In fact, it's often the case that the longing circuit of at least one partner has been overactive. Such individuals experience keenly the need for the other's emotional support. In fact, the partners of such individuals are often overwhelmed by the level of expectation placed on them to provide support.

Other partners have a very difficult time coming up with a list of things they want from their partners. Such individuals often generate items like, "I want my partner to be able to meet her own needs more," or "I want my partner to become less upset with me." Such clients are often reluctant to even try to connect with a need for emotional support, because they have been trying to model self-sufficiency to their partners for years. If they ask for emotional support, they fear it will open the floodgates for their partners, who will then feel increased justification for making their own requests. Other clients simply do not feel much need for emotional connection. These are the difficult ones. These individuals often have a relationship philosophy that supports their relative lack of emotional need. They believe that relationships function best when acceptance of the other person is high, and demands and expectations are low. Predictably, the partners of such individuals don't feel needed. Indeed, they may not be needed.

People with limited access to a need for emotional contact often have difficulty developing emotional bonds in their relationships. Since they don't make as many requests for emotional support, they are often not as attached to their partners as their partners are to them. They don't need their partners as much. They don't ask for much, and they don't want their partners to ask for much, either. Often, these people form relationships with partners who have an abundance of emotional need. A pattern may develop where the partner with greater emotional longing makes continual requests, and the partner with less emotional longings become more detached over time. The detaching partner begins seeing his mate as a burden, and stops looking forward to time together. The relationship becomes a chore for such individuals, who see the only answer to their problems as involving their partners becoming less needy. They often see themselves as more emotionally stable, and think of themselves as being better relationship partners because they don't place too many demands on their mates.

In PET-C, we see two, equally compelling problems arise: (1) when a partner has an overly active longing circuit, or a limited capacity to self-soothe; (2) when a partner's longing circuit is dormant, and this person experiences minimal need for emotional support and comfort. Each problem feeds the other in recursive fashion. One partner's emotional detachment creates elevated emotional need in the other, who then increases the intensity of her requests for emotional contact, which overwhelms the partner with limited emotional longings, and so on. In Phase III, we seek to help the partner with limited emotional need awaken his or her longing circuit, and we help the partner with greater emotional need develop the ability to temporarily satisfy this need partly by providing increased emotional support to his/her partner. Each person must learn to do the opposite of what they are naturally inclined to do. The partner with more naturally activated longing must seek less emotional support and instead focus on giving it. The partner who has wanted his mate to learn how to become less needy must learn to be more needy. Of course, not all partners are as polarized as this. Therapy is easier with less polarized partners.

The first steps in depolarizing have generally occurred in Phase II, as each partner drops judgmental interpretations of the other. Rather than seeing her partner as "emotionally detached," the partner with greater emotional longing comes to recognize that her partner simply has a different level of emotional need. Further, she comes to understand that her partner's emotional distance is partly due to her criticism of him. On the other hand, the partner with less emotional longing learns to drop his judgment that his partner is "too needy," and recognizes instead that another person who is more in touch with his own emotional needs might not see her as overly needy at all. This partner comes to recognize that his mate's emotional neediness is partly due to the fact that he has so few emotional needs of his own.

As each partner drops critical judgments of the other, the stage is set for Phase III, in which one partner connects with more emotional need, and the other partner temporarily satisfies a portion of her emotional need by providing increased emotional support. By the end of Phase III, the more emotionally needy partner also receives direct emotional support. However, we have found that before her partner is able to provide genuine, heart-felt emotional support, he must be in touch with his own emotional need, and know how good emotional support can feel. Sometimes, clients have experienced so little emotional support in their lives that they have no frame of reference for what emotional connection feels like.

Making and Responding to Bids for Connection

This part of Phase III begins with a discussion about the importance of emotional need in successful intimate relationships. The therapist summarizes research findings on the subject, which suggest that, in successful relationships, each partner has an abundance of longing for the emotional support of his or her mate, and easily gives emotional support as well. The therapist then asks each client to think of some things that the partner could do that would really make the client feel cared about. The types of emotional support desired vary from person to person, and the therapist validates each partner's wishes, helping his or her mate stay open to the possibility of giving the type of emotional support that is desired. Even after years of marriage, partners often don't realize that there are some relatively simple things that they could do that would have a huge impact on their partners' feelings. Partners often make the mistake of assuming that the same things that make them feel cared about will also make their mates feel cared about. Sometimes, the exact opposite is true. For example, a wife may feel cared about if her husband would spend a leisurely Saturday morning in bed with her, whereas a husband would feel more cared about if his wife would sacrifice some "together" time and support his desire to play golf on Saturday mornings. Often, partners fall into a pattern of arguing about these conflicting desires, neither feeling supported by the other. The therapist helps partners develop a new approach to such issues, encouraging each partner to realize how much positive feeling comes between partners when each feels supported by the other. As a practical strategy, the therapist might suggest that the couple alternate Saturday morning activities, but the most important shift the therapist promotes happens inside of each partner. For example, the therapist might make an audiotape for the husband to listen to on the way to the golf course, helping the husband dwell on the good feelings he has about his wife's support of his desire to play golf, and reminding him to tell her how much it makes him feel cared about. The therapist might also make a tape for the wife to listen to when she gets up on Saturday morning, congratulating her for being wise enough to know the importance of trying to support her husband's desires, reminding her of the occasions when her husband has done the same for her recently, and helping her dwell on how good he feels when she supports him in this kind of way. Audio-guided support is used throughout Phase III of PET-C (see Table 12.1).

An important part of Phase III involves helping extend the process of making and responding to bids for connection into their sexual relationship. There are many benefits to couples who develop robust and exciting sex lives (see Chapter 2). One of the brain's intimacy states produces sexual desire, and the neurochemical processes produced during sexual activity can solidify feelings of emotional bonding. Couples sometimes go years without ever having a single conversation about their sexual relationship. In Phase III, the therapist encourages conversation about sexual desires even if partners report a satisfying sexual relationship. Such conversations provide the opportunity for partners to benefit from the positive feelings that arise as partners talk about what they like about sex with their partner. The therapist promotes a relaxed, accepting atmosphere where the feelings and desires of each partner are explored. Partners not only discuss their desires, but also discuss why they have the desires, or what they would like about a particular way of sexual relating. The therapist explores and helps resolve any blocks that stand in the way of each partner's sexual desire (see Jack and Loretta's story, Chapter 2).

TABLE 12.1
Audio-Guided Support

During Phase III, the therapist enters each session with the goal of making a new audiotape for each client, helping him or her go through some important reminders, remember to do something for his or her partner, or just dwell on a good feeling resulting from some positive relationship event. Clients often listen to more than one tape per week. For example, a husband may listen to the same tape everyday on his commute home from work (such as the one described earlier in this chapter), and he might also listen to a tape designed for the therapist for specific occasion, such as the Saturday morning golf outing. One therapist recently made a tape for a husband to listen to on the mornings after he and his wife made love, to help this husband dwell on the positive feelings he had, and remind him to tell his wife about them or leave her a note. As a rule of thumb, when partners agree to attempt to meet each other's requests for support in specific ways, the therapist makes a tape for partners to listen to as they go about implementing or receiving the special caring behaviors.

Direct Physiological Soothing

We have found that some of the most powerful forms of emotional support involve direct physiological soothing. In these situations, one partner is experiencing stress, and is comforted by the other. Typically, the stressed partner is upset about a difficult situation encountered at work, or with extended family members, or with a task he's been trying to finish, or due to some other situation that may only indirectly impact his partner. We often set the stage for helping partners increase direct soothing interactions by assigning "high/low" conversations. In these conversations, partners take turns talking about the high and low points of their respective days. When speaking, partners are encouraged to talk about, and allow themselves to experience, the feelings they had (and often still are having) about the stressful or happy situations they are speaking about. When listening, partners are encouraged to refrain from trying to solve their partner's problems, and instead just give emotional support. Guidelines for these conversations are included in their workbooks (Atkinson, 2005).

Sometimes, partners are able to engage in these emotionally supportive conversations with little guidance needed from the therapist. However, partners may have difficulty accessing the internal states of longing and tenderness that make these conversations emotionally soothing to each partner. A partner's access to these states may be blocked for some reason, and the therapist must help this client identify and resolve the blocks. An excellent way to help a client explore internal reactions that may keep him from connecting with a needed intimacy state involves a procedure where partners have a series of high/low conversations at home while an audio recorder is running. Each partner then brings a tape of one of these conversations in and listens to it with the therapist.

As they listen to the tape, the therapist stops periodically to ask the client the thoughts and feelings he was having during the conversation. This format allows a level of relaxed exploration that is difficult to achieve during conjoint sessions, because without the partner present, the client does not need to worry about his partner's reactions to the thoughts and feelings he is exploring. Sometimes partners are reluctant to disclose to each other the fact that they have been "faking" caring feelings to a degree. The individual review format allows partners to explore their thoughts and feelings more freely.

At first, the presence of the tape recorder may interfere with genuine conversations at home, but after recording a few conversations, partners often forget about the tape recorder, and the conversations captured on tape really reflect each partner's capacity to give and receive support. Instructions for the recording of these conversations are included in each partner's workbook (Atkinson, 2005).

After partners have completed a high/low conversation at home, each of them is asked to reflect on how the conversation went, using two questionnaires from their workbooks called, High-Low Review: Your Experience Speaking, and High-Low Review: Your Experience Listening (see Appendices T and U for questionnaires from one client's workbook). These questionnaires begin the process of helping clients pay attention to the extent to which they engaged in a conversation with genuine feeling. The questionnaires also help them think about the reasons why they may not have participated in a more heartfelt way. Partners often have high/low conversations sometime during the evening, then each of them completes the forms before going to bed.

In the individual sessions that follow, the therapist and client listen to audiotapes of the high/low conversations, and the therapist helps the client pay close attention to the feelings he was having as the conversation unfolded. Often, clients learn to say the right things in these conversations, but the therapist is able to help them realize that they weren't really "feeling" the conversation. For example, a husband may make sympathetic remarks to his wife, but the words sound hollow. In these situations, the therapist helps the client listen carefully to his internal reactions, identifying thoughts, or attitudes that are likely to be keeping him from connecting with feelings that would make his words meaningful.

EXPLORING AND RESOLVING ACTIVATION BLOCKS

Throughout Phase III, the therapist applies the pragmatic/experiential method to help partners change. Recall that in the pragmatic/experiential method, the therapist paints a clear picture of the kinds of thinking and action that predict relationship success, and asks partners to move in the direction of these ways of thinking and acting. The therapist then closely monitors the presence or absence of automatic internal state activations that enhance or inhibit these ways of thinking and acting, and then helps partners develop the ability to influence internal states in needed ways. In Phase III, we use this method to help partners identify and resolve things that block them from access to the intimacy states.

For example, we might ask a client to listen in a supportive way to her partner describing some stressful circumstances in his or her life. As her partner talks, we help the client notice the extent to which she feels sympathy or tenderness toward her partner. If these feelings don't naturally arise, we help the client pay close attention to the part of her that resists, and try to identify the reasons why she might not feel supportive toward her partner. As she identifies the reasons, the therapist helps her resolve them, and unblock the natural activation of the intimacy states. The blocks that each client has to accessing intimacy states are very important, and must be treated with utmost respect. A skilled PET-C therapist avoids forcing a resolution, and instead gently helps the client explore possible ways to resolve these blocks.

This process happened in Phase III of PET-C with George, who held a doctorate in physics, and worked in a nearby nuclear testing facility, and his wife, Natalie, who worked at home raising the kids. George and Natalie progressed through the first two phases of PET-C in a period of four months, each making considerable progress in developing the ability to react to each other differently in upsetting situations. As the therapy moved into Phase III, the therapist asked the couple to record some high/low conversations. The therapist then met with each partner separately to review these tapes. Below are excerpts from a session the therapist had with Natalie. In this session, the therapist and Natalie listened to a high/low conversation in which George was talking to Natalie about the frustration he had with his supervisor, who had assigned him an important task that he couldn't complete within the specified time. Here's the dialogue that followed.

W: (*speaking to her husband*) Did you tell him (*the supervisor*) that his expectations were unrealistic?

H: No.

W: (*sounding frustrated*) Why not?

H: It wouldn't have done any good. You don't understand this guy. He'd just put it back on me.

W: (*exasperated*) George, you've got to say something!

H: (*silent*)

W: He takes advantage of you all the time, and you just sit there and take it! I know that Paul (*a coworker*) would have said something if he were in your shoes.

H: Yeah, and Paul will never get promoted. You know that.

W: Well at least he speaks up!

H: Maybe I'm not describing it right. It really wasn't that bad. It'll be okay if I turn the report in tomorrow. I think he (*the supervisor*) will understand. Sometimes he just says things and doesn't mean it.

At this point, George tried to change the topic, and asked Natalie to talk about her day. This type of exchange was typical of those that occurred when George tried to talk to Natalie about his stress, and we see it frequently in couples in which one partner is more emotionally expressive (Natalie), and the other is more reserved (George). When the more reserved partner begins to speak, the more expressive partner sometimes reacts strongly to the information he offers. Instead of being a conversation where the reserved partner feels soothed by the expressive partner, the reserved partner becomes worried about the intensity of the expressive partner's reactions, and the roles reverse. He ends up trying to calm her down.

The therapist stopped the tape and the following exchange took place between him and the wife:

T: Okay, Natalie. It seems like something happened inside of you that kept you from responding as supportively as I'd like to see.

W: (*looking guilty*) I know. I should have just kept my big mouth shut. He didn't like it when I started questioning him. It's just really frustrating.

T: I think I understand. If you were in his situation, you would have handled it differently.

W: He can't stand up for himself. He hates confrontation.

T: So, when he talks about things like this, some part of you wants to help him see what he needs to do.

W: Right! But I know that's not what I'm supposed to do.

T: Yeah, but that's okay. You can't do anything different unless we can figure out some way to help that part of you feel that it would be okay.

W: That's a tough one. I mean, it's a strong reaction I get.

T: I know, and it's not bad. But it does have the effect of shutting him down. Did you notice that? He sort of stopped talking to you. I don't think he felt supported.

W: How can I support him when I'm feeling that he blew it?

T: You can't, and I don't want you to.

W: What do you mean? I thought I was supposed to.

T: Yes, but only if you can get that feeling to shift. Otherwise, it would be better not to try.

W: Well, I want to try!

T: Okay. Well, we just need to see if there's something that you could do to calm that part of you that makes you feel like you want to tell him what to do.

W: I know.

T: Can you think of anything that you might be able to say to yourself in situations like this that might help you shift out of that "I've got to get him to realize he's doing it wrong" state of mind?

W: I don't know. I feel that way a lot when he tells me things.

T: I have an idea. What if you made it a habit of assuring yourself that you'll talk to him about it, but not until later?

W: Well, maybe. But I'm afraid I'd still have that nagging feeling.

T: Right, you'd have to really decide that this was a worthwhile thing to do.

W: It is a worthwhile thing, but, something inside of me wants to hold on.

T: Okay. Let's listen to this part of you, because she's the boss here. She has to be satisfied that it would be okay. See if you can sense what her reservations are to the idea of giving your advice later.

W: I really don't know what I'd have to lose.

T: I want to suggest something, then have you pay attention to your first reaction when I say it. Have you ever considered that one of the reasons why he may not speak up more for himself is that he feels your disapproval?

W: I don't get it. If he doesn't like my disapproval, why wouldn't he try to do the things I want, in order to get my approval?

T: Two reasons. One, because your disapproval makes him feel bad about himself, and when he feels bad about himself, it's less likely that he'll be able to move with as much confidence in life. He's not unique in that. We're all sort of like that.

W: I guess I don't think he cares that much about my disapproval.

T: I see something very different, Natalie. But let me finish. The second reason is not because of the disapproval as much as what *doesn't* happen instead. What doesn't happen is a feeling of support, a feeling of being nurtured. He might move with less confidence because he doesn't feel you behind him. He doesn't think you care about how he feels, he just thinks you want him to do what you think he should do. People who feel that their partners care about what they feel tend to move more confidently in life.

W: (*laughs*) He doesn't seem like he wants to be nurtured.

T: Don't be fooled, Natalie. He needs your tenderness very much. I see it in his eyes.

W: (*Natalie's eyes moisten*) Really? (*Natalie sits silently for a moment.*) Now that you mention it, sometimes I think I see it too, but just for a split second, and then he usually changes the subject. It's sort of like a child who wants approval, but is afraid to ask. But then I think to myself that maybe I'm just imagining it.

T: No, Natalie. I see it too. He *is* afraid to ask. Somewhere in there, I think he got the idea that he's supposed to handle the world alone.

W: That's really sad. I know it's true. You should meet his parents.

T: Right. There's a place inside of him where he feels alone, and just wants to know that you care how he feels, regardless of whether he's doing things right or not.

W: I guess I know that . . . I just forget about it.

T: That's because there's another part of him who quickly comes in and shuts him down from staying with his need for your approval. He sort of gives up on it and changes the subject.

W: I make him do that?

T: At this point, the process is already set in motion. You just feed it, unintentionally.

W: I guess I do.

T: Okay, so is that part of you who often wants to change him listening to this conversation?

W: (*thoughtful for a moment, then replies*) She is.

T: And how is she feeling about things now?

W: It's a whole different way of thinking about it. I think I feel different.

T: Okay, well let's see if we can set something up so that you hold onto this way of looking at things.

The therapist went on to make an audiotape like the ones described in the section, "Daily Practice Through Audio-Guided ReExperiencing,"in Chapter 11. In this tape, the therapist had Natalie mentally revisit the conversation she'd had with George, imagining herself beginning to feel her frustration with George in the conversation, then remembering some of the things she'd thought about in this session. Specifically, Natalie pictured herself remembering the look in George's eye that she recognized as childlike, and reminding herself that he needed her tenderness. As she projected herself back into the conversations, she saw herself remembering that he'd probably move more confidently and be able to solve his own problems if he felt support instead of criticism. Finally, she pictured herself relaxing, softening, and touching George on the cheek as he spoke. Before she left the session, she listened to the tape once more. When the therapist saw Natalie's eyes moisten while she was listening, he knew it would work for her.

The block that Natalie had was her assumption that George didn't want, or need emotional support from her. Once she realized that, not only did he need it, but that his confidence was affected by the lack of it, she was able to shift. Natalie's conversations with George began to change, and she reported to the therapist that often, as conversations progressed, George came around to telling her about his own plans to handle situations more aggressively. She had a hard time believing that this could be because of the increased level of support that she was giving to him, but the therapist reminded her of how little of this kind of support he'd experienced in his life, and stated confidently that her love was changing George.

While Natalie was working on connecting with feelings of tenderness and empathy for George, his therapy was focused on removing the blocks that kept him from connecting with and expressing his need for Natalie's support. Let us take a look at George's first audio review of a high/low conversation with the therapist. George wanted to review the section of the audiotape in which he attempted to listen to and support Natalie. Having listened to the same conversation with Natalie, however, the therapist asked if George would mind listening to the portion where he talked to Natalie. The following dialogue occurred:

T: When I listened to you on the tape, I couldn't tell what you were feeling when you were talking.

H: I'm not too good at expressing my feelings.

T: Right now, I'm not so much interested in how you were expressing yourself. I'm more interested in how you were actually feeling.

H: I don't know really. I guess I was a bit apprehensive.

T: How come?

H: It doesn't usually go very well when I talk about work. Natalie usually just gets upset with me.

T: Like she did this time?

H: Yes.

T: Let me tell you what I'm thinking, George. I don't think that she knew what you were looking for in this conversation. I mean, I don't think she could feel what you were looking for. Actually, I couldn't feel it either.

H: Like I said, I'm not too good at getting my feelings across.

T: Yes, but my point is that I'm not really sure that you were feeling like you wanted, or expected anything from Natalie. It's not that you didn't communicate your feeling. It seems like you didn't have it in the first place. Did you?

H: What feeling are you talking about?

T: The feeling that you were wanting something from Natalie in this conversation, other than for her to not get upset.

H: I guess that's the only thing that was on my mind. I was waiting for her to get upset, hoping that she wouldn't.

T: Dude. You have really low expectations.

H: I think that things work out better that way.

T: I think I understand. If you're not going to expect something, then you won't get as upset if it doesn't happen.

H: Exactly.

T: Here's the problem, as I see it. Your solution works for some things, but it rules out others. It works for keeping her from getting upset, but it pretty much shuts down the possibility of you guys getting into the kind of friendship that I think you'd like to have.

H: How's that?

T: Well, when researchers look at couples who really enjoy each other the most, they find that partners have a high expectation that the other person really cares how they feel. Conversations go kind of like in those sheets in your workbook. They look forward to talking to each other about their stresses, and know that they'll feel better afterward. You know, they know they'll feel understood and supported.

H: You're right. I don't think that happens very much.

T: Right. And I get the feeling that you think it's because of the way Natalie is.

H: No. I don't think I'm very good at being supportive either.

T: Yes, but that's probably because you're not used to looking for support. I get the idea that you've spent most of your life handling stress on your own.

H: That's true. I think I've always been that way.

T: Are you open to changing that?

H: Yeah, but you'll have to tell me what to do.

T: Okay. The first thing you'll probably need to do is shift to a place inside where you feel like you want Natalie's support.

H: What do you mean by support?

T: I mean a conversation where you're talking about something that bothers you, and she seems interested in knowing how you're doing, and she acts kindly toward you, kind of the equivalent of when a child skins his knee and his mom scoops him up and holds him for a few minutes, in a soothing way.

H: (*kidding*) You want me to sit in her lap?

T: (*laughs*) Well, I wouldn't rule that out! But we might just start with wanting to hear tenderness in her voice as she listens to you.

H: That would be kind of weird.

T: It's not weird for everybody, George. It might feel kind of weird because you're not used to it.

H: But I don't see how I can get that to happen. Wouldn't that depend on her?

T: Only partly. The way things are right now, she can't tell that you're looking for any TLC from her. She can't feel you reaching out for it.

H: I'm sure she can't.

T: That's because I don't think you're expecting it. I don't think you *allow* yourself to want it. And that's probably because, up until now, you've had the idea that it wouldn't be a good thing to want it.

H: I see. Is there something wrong with me?

T: (*laughs*) Hardly. A lot of people have the same idea. A few years back, I did, too. I've had to practice the same thing that I'm hoping you will.

H: What do you mean, practice?

T: I think you'll have to practice letting yourself want to get some tenderness from Natalie when you're feeling bad. When you do, she'll feel it in your voice, and then I think you'll be surprised at what you get from her. Right now, when you talk to her, you're kind of matter of fact.

The block that kept George from allowing himself to want tenderness and soothing support from Natalie was his assumption that the relationship would go better if he didn't need it. Further, he hadn't realized that she didn't give it partly because he didn't seem to want it. Gradually, George found his way to the place inside where he really wanted tenderness from Natalie when he was stressed, and she began to feel this desire in him. Once she felt it, she was able to respond in a nurturing way.

CONCLUSION

The therapist begins Phase III interventions as soon as the hostility or resentment that partners bring in to therapy subsides. Skilled PET-C therapists are careful to avoid attempting to get partners to interact more positively with each other until they are feeling more positively. If the therapist assigns partners the task of expressing appreciations to each other during a week in which they are embroiled in critical judgments toward each other, there's a risk that they might "fake" the appreciations, or that an expression of appreciation may be taken as a criticism (a husband may hear his wife's expression of appreciation for changing the cat litter as "It's about time you did the cat litter!" even if she intended it as a compliment). Or, a partner may deliver a criticism along with an expression of appreciation (as when a husband says, "I appreciate you finally writing those thank you notes.") Such failed attempts may contaminate the "appreciation" intervention, making it more difficult for partners to trust each other later. Throughout PET-C, the therapist encourages her clients to avoid trying to act differently toward each other if they don't feel like it. Instead, the therapist helps each partner identify the reasons why they don't feel like it, resolve these feelings, and then interact in positive, congruent ways.

CHAPTER 13

Becoming a Skilled
PET-C Practitioner

A S THE PET-C MODEL has taken form since the mid-1990s, we have begun offering seminars and courses in PET-C. Through these training sessions, we have identified a number of factors that contribute to the success of individuals becoming skilled PET-C practitioners. Training has occurred primarily in three different contexts. First, at the Couples Research Institute in Geneva, Illinois, we have offered externships to licensed mental health professionals who have wanted to develop skills in implementing PET-C. For the most part, these trainees have been seasoned professionals, the majority having many years of clinical experience working with couples. We have also provided training to individuals on the other end of the experience continuum, through courses and practice for first and second year graduate students in marriage and family therapy at Northern Illinois University. These individuals had often never provided any type of mental health counseling before, and PET-C was one of the first treatment models they explored. Third, we have provided ongoing training and supervision for staff members of various agencies and clinics in the Chicago area. Regardless of the training context, several factors seem to be crucial in the training of therapists. One class of factors has to do with the extent to which trainees develop confidence in the assumptions of PET-C. A second involves the extent to which trainees develop certain crucial abilities in conducting the treatment process.

CONFIDENCE IN THE
ASSUMPTIONS OF PET-C

For many practitioners and graduate students, PET-C requires a revision or modification of some basic assumptions they have had about how relationships work, how people change, or how one can best help people change. To be effective, a practitioner's attitudes and actions must be congruent with the assumptions of PET-C. As his confidence in the PET-C assumptions increases, so does his effectiveness. Trainees sometimes have difficulty fully embracing certain PET-C assumptions. This section highlights these difficulties, and discusses some of the processes employed in supervision to help trainees develop more confidence with the assumptions.

One Partner Can Transform a Relationship

A crucial aspect of PET-C involves helping clients develop confidence that they can dramatically influence the odds that they will receive increased cooperation and respect from their partners if they develop more ability to implement ten habits that predict relationship success, summarized in Table 3.1. Sometimes, PET-C trainees have a hard time believing this. Many of them were taught, "It takes two to make a relationship work. If both partners aren't motivated to work on the relationship, it won't survive." This is probably true enough, but it doesn't mean that both partners must begin with equal levels of motivation, or maintain equal levels of motivation at all times. We have found that, most of the time, when a motivated partner learns to interact more effectively with his less motivated partner, the less motivated partner becomes more motivated. Convincing a client who has an unmotivated partner to operate under this assumption is no small task, and a therapist who is anything less than fully convinced of the legitimacy of the assumption will not likely succeed with the client.

In our experience, the best way to build a trainee's confidence is for him to experience first hand the effectiveness of the predictive habits of his own relationships. From the beginning of training, we facilitate opportunities for PET-C trainees to discuss their attempts to develop the predictive habits and apply them in their own lives. Often, many of our trainees are struggling with their own relationships. Divorce rates among mental health professionals are consistent with those for the general public. We therapists are often in need of developing these abilities as much as our clients.

Trainees who are at least somewhat dissatisfied in their own intimate relationships are often reluctant to embrace the assumption that one partner can transform a relationship, because they have developed a belief that their own relationship dissatisfactions are rooted in the limited capacity of their partners to interact in healthy ways. They have often concluded that they made a poor choice in their mate, and now they are stuck with this person. PET-C assumptions ask them to consider that they are equal contributors to the relationship trouble, and if they were more able to meet the prerequisites for relationship success, their partners would likely be treating them in more satisfying ways. Our experience is that therapists tend to weight the predictive habits selectively, considering the habits they are most skilled in to be more important to the success of relationships than those in which they have limited proficiency. For example, the single most powerful negative predictor in relationships is the tendency to consider oneself as "better" than one's partner. Therapists are particularly vulnerable to developing this view of their relationships, because, after all, they are professionally trained in the dynamics of relationships. They often think that they are better at "doing" relationships than their partners. Although they may have enough sense to avoid saying as much to their partners, inwardly they have this view, and their partners generally know it. Therapists are often good at "soft startups," and "accepting influence," but when their partners don't do the same, rather than standing up effectively for themselves without making a big deal of their partners' uncooperativeness, they look down their professional noses at their partners, seeing them as deficient. This contemptuous attitude undermines their effectiveness in getting the things they need from their partners. Of course, this is a generalization, and doesn't apply to all therapists. However, we find that it does apply to many therapists. Those who are able to see this, and find ways to change it often see their relationships transformed. This transformation gives them the conviction they need to help their clients believe that they can transform their own relationships by more fully meeting the prerequisites for relationship success.

Small supervision groups are an ideal forum for trainees to examine their own relationship habits. In these groups, supervisees agree to discuss their attempts to apply the PET-C methods in their own lives. These groups are led by experienced PET-C supervisors, who candidly discuss the struggles and successes they have had in implementing the predictive habits in their own lives. The openness of the supervisors helps trainees realize that almost all of us have difficulty implementing the predictive habits, and makes it acceptable for them to disclose their struggles. It also assures trainees that supervisors won't assume an attitude of superiority when they learn the ways that trainees fail to meet the prerequisites in their own lives.

Partners are Equal Contributors to Relationship Problems

A related assumption that many PET-C trainees struggle with is that when relationships are distressed, both partners are equally off-track. Trainees often have difficulty because the shortcomings of one partner will be more obvious than the shortcomings of the other. Some shortcomings are more glaring, and more socially unacceptable than others. For example, a trainee may find himself sympathizing more with a partner who is often on the receiving end of vicious attacks, and find himself thinking that the attacking partner is more at fault. The trainee may focus most of his efforts toward getting the attacking partner to stop criticizing, and fail to realize that the tendency of the other, "calmer" partner to placate, while inwardly despising his partner, is an equally toxic factor in this relationship. Trainees must learn to look at each partner's attitude and actions as complementary parts of the same process. Either partner can transform the relationship by changing their attitudes and actions.

Contempt Stands Alone

At the beginning of each PET-C training course, we ask trainees to write down what they consider to be the things that people do that are most destructive to relationships. Trainees typically give answers such as "dishonesty," "cheating," and "self-centeredness." More seldom do trainees mention "self-righteousness," "superiority," "judgmentalism," or other words designating contempt. Marital studies suggest that the tendency to see oneself as better than one's partner is the greatest destructive force in relationships, but it often doesn't even make it on to a trainee's list of "relationship sins." Incredibly, many therapists are relatively blind to the process studies that identify it as the single most toxic force in relationships (Gottman, 1999). While lying, cheating, and selfishness all have ill effects, the subtly contemptuous reactions of the partners of those who lie, cheat, and act selfishly may be far more destructive to the relationship than the lying, cheating, and selfishness. At present, neither the public, nor the mental health professions have fully digested this research finding.

Contempt is not only excused in our society, it is encouraged. The speeches of our country's leaders are frequently loaded with sneering, mockery, disgust, and a sense of superiority as they talk about how much better they are than their competitors. The attitude could be heard in a televised speech given by the president of the United States, as he spoke with disdain toward those who engaged in terrorist activities against the United States, calling them evil and morally bereft. Clearly, he was encouraging the people of the United States to put themselves on a higher moral plane, and look down their noses at their fellow humans. Research on the toxic effects of contempt raises questions about this socially acceptable rhetoric. If the data from relationship studies holds true of international relationships, expressions of contempt may contribute as powerfully to international strife as the combative actions that countries initiate against each other. Intimate partners often feel terrorized by each other, each feeling like an innocent victim of the other's offenses. Yet, it is not their aggressive behaviors toward each other that contribute most powerfully to their relationship dysfunction. It is their contemptuous attitudes that drive these acts, and characterize individuals' reactions to these acts.

The perspective embraced by PET-C is that contempt is the most potent virus attacking the fabric of relationships today. Contempt spawns an infinite variety of toxic narratives, in which a person casts himself as a superior in one way or another. It is the mother of all toxins, and it was the basis of Hitler's extermination of millions of Jews, yet its toxic effects continue to be ignored, even within the helping professions. I had the privilege of sitting on a panel at an international conference several years ago with a prominent theoretician who has inspired one of the most respected forms of psychotherapy. I remember my surprise when he said, "I try to stay as far from those radical behaviorists as I can." What caught my attention was not so much the words he used, but the attitude beneath them. It seemed clear that he saw himself as considerably more enlightened than the radical behaviorists. No doubt, this prominent theoretician was unaware that his attitude of superiority was a problem. He made no attempt to hide his feelings. He is not alone. I have sat through dozens of seminars given by leading figures in the field of mental health, and listened to them scoff at those who disagree with them, seemingly proud of their arrogance. In our culture, contempt is part and parcel of the way people attempt to stand up for themselves.

Unlike other egregious acts that are dramatic, verifiable, and public (e.g., getting caught having an affair), contempt can be elusive and subtle, and be communicated without words. Its effects aren't subtle. When a wife gets the feeling that her husband is morally superior because she cheated and he didn't, something slams shut inside of her. She can handle his anger, and she can understand his need to end their relationship, but when he begins to assume moral superiority, she feels attacked at her core, and feels compelled to retaliate. Over and over, we find that it is the attitude, not the actions, that have the most inflammatory effect in relationships. Partners who are able to stand up for themselves without getting caught in contempt are the ones who get what they need most in their relationships.

Because of its central place in the PET-C model, our training courses are filled with ongoing discussions about contempt, and how it can be avoided. We encourage dialogue about pivotal issues surrounding contempt, such as reflected in the question, "Is it possible for a person to believe that his viewpoint is better than another person's without assuming an attitude of contempt? If so, how?" This particular question is of great importance, because most people do believe that the viewpoints, values, and standards they use to guide their lives are the best alternatives, and often believe that these values, standards, and viewpoints are universally applicable. It is less common to find a person who believes that his or her values and beliefs are best for him- or herself alone. Since the beginning of history, philosophers, theologians, and now social scientists, have attempted to formulate general principles for successful living that are believed to be widely (if not universally) applicable. Similarly, clients who hold the viewpoint that sex outside the marriage is wrong generally believe that this principle applies not only to themselves, but to everybody. Can this person avoid a contemptuous attitude toward someone who engages in extramarital relationships?

I remember first seriously grappling with questions like this in my early 20s, when I was pursuing the study of world religion in a seminary setting. I noticed that the professors seemed to hold their beliefs about God with different attitudes. For all of these professors, beliefs about God were of major significance, organizing their entire lives in meaningful ways. Each of them seemed confident in the legitimacy of his views, yet some of them held their views with more humility than others. The more respectful professors would say things like, "Here are my views about God. They are the ones that make the most sense to me, and I live by them. I'll try to convince you that they make the most sense, too. However, I'm just one person, making my way through life, trying to make sense of things. I don't have all the answers, and I recognize that I could be biased.

I know that there are other people who might even be smarter, or more spiritually sensitive than me, who hold different views. How can I know for sure that I am right and they are wrong? I can't. All I can say is that their views don't make as much sense to me. They've got to make up their own minds, and I respect that."

In contrast, other professors seemed to be saying, "God has revealed himself to us in compelling ways, and the truth about God is there for us all to discover. I've examined the evidence, and know the truth about God. If you are spiritually sensitive, you'll come to these views too, sooner or later. For your sake, I hope it's sooner."

I found myself drawn toward the first group of professors, and I felt disrespected and talked down to by the second group. These professors often didn't get along with each other, each looking down their noses at each other's theology. This attitude of superiority didn't depend on how conservative or liberal the professor was. One of the most liberal professors held the view, "The truth is that there is no truth about God, and any intelligent person must come to this conclusion." Such liberal professors seemed equally as offensive as conservative professors who insisted that their more precisely defined views about God were the correct ones. The offensiveness wasn't in the views they held, it was in the attitude with which they were held.

It would be two decades before research on the toxic effects of contempt emerged, which helped me pinpoint my discomfort with these professors. Studies on intimate relationships suggest that the same attitude of superiority that created animosity between my seminary professors can be seen tearing away at the fabric of intimate partnerships (Gottman, 1999). This same principle probably applies to all relationships. When I switched from the study of philosophy and theology to the social sciences, I found the same tendencies toward contempt. Well-intended social activists are often just as caught by the pull of contempt as are those whose oppressive practices they speak out against. I have come to believe that contempt for the oppressor seriously undermines the effectiveness of social advocacy. Advocates often see themselves as more enlightened, and set about to correct the less enlightened leaders who hold power. There seems to be a societal assumption that if one truly feels oppressed, then contempt is not only warranted, it is integral to one's ability to stand up for oneself.

PET-C embraces the assumption that an attitude of respectfulness must be the cornerstone upon which social advocacy stands. All PET-C therapists are social advocates, seeking to intervene in the oppressive practices that characterize distressed relationships. However, when a therapist begins subtly looking down on partners who perpetuate oppressive acts, he perpetuates the same virus that he seeks to help partners elude.

PET-C supervisors help trainees recognize the often unrecognized forms of contempt that creep into their own interactions with clients. For example, one trainee recently found himself disgusted with a partner who continued to assume moral superiority in spite of the sincere apologies of the partner who had an affair. This trainee wanted to convince this "morally superior" partner how wrong his attitude was. The trainee didn't recognize that he was assuming the same attitude toward the client that the client was assuming toward his partner. Before this trainee could be helpful to the client, he had to realize that he was looking down on this client, and find a way to shift his attitude. Skilled supervisors avoid judging such trainees (we've all been there!), and instead help trainees develop the ability to shift internal states. This is a point of major importance. The tendency for therapists to see themselves as somehow "better" than their clients, and for supervisors to see themselves as "better" than their supervisees, is a widespread problem in the field of psychotherapy. Effective PET-C therapists recognize that they often get just as off-track in their relationships as do their clients. When PET-C therapy and supervision go well, both trainees and supervisors proceed with an attitude of humility.

When trainees embrace the PET-C perspective on the toxic effects of contempt, a new type of problem emerges. A trainee may become overly zealous in an attempt to eradicate contempt from the face of the earth. We don't believe this is possible, nor is it necessary. Contempt is a natural response to feeling threatened, and all of us experience it at one time or another in our partnerships. In PET-C, eradication of contempt is not the goal. Skilled PET-C therapists don't scold partners who deliver contemptuous expressions to their mates. Rather, they try to help these clients keep from getting *stuck* in contempt. Expressions of disgust occur regularly between distressed partners in the moments when upsets occur. We find that partners can tolerate such expressions from their mates as long as their mates don't hold onto the contempt. We try to help partners shift from contemptuous states in the moments and hours following an emotional argument, then approach their mates with a different attitude, repairing the damage that occurred. When partners are able to do this, their relationships heal and expressions of contempt diminish, even during emotional arguments. We encourage trainees to adopt the goal not of eradicating contempt, but rather preventing contempt from getting a foothold.

As PET-C enthusiasts, we endeavor to go one step further, remaining open to the possibility that our views on the toxicity of contempt could be misguided or off-base. The studies suggesting the powerful negative effects of contempt could be skewed or biased. In our training programs, we attempt to convey our conviction about the role of contempt without assuming that we have a corner on the truth. We recognize that there are other competent practitioners and supervisors who do not share these views, and we encourage both clients and trainees to decide for themselves. The viewpoint we have adopted on contempt is simply the one that makes most sense to us. PET-C is founded upon it. However, trainees who do not share this view often have difficulty implementing PET-C effectively.

The Necessity of Anger

A core assumption in PET-C is that anger is not a dangerous emotion. In fact, it is a natural and necessary part of healthy relationships. Those who have difficulty allowing their anger may limit the success of their relationships as surely as those who are constantly caught in their anger (see Chapter 10). Many trainees have difficulty with this assumption. Often, they enter the helping professions because of their desire to promote peaceful human relationships, not angry ones. Many times, peace can be promoted without anger, but we believe that many times, peace will not occur unless partners stand up forcefully for themselves, and require that they be treated with respect.

In our training programs, we help each trainee look carefully at his level of comfort with anger. Chances are that a trainee who is uncomfortable with anger will be having difficulties in his or her own relationships. The best way for this trainee to become more effective with clients is to work on expressing anger when needed in his or her own life. Once a PET-C trainee recognizes that he or she has a problem connecting with (or expressing) anger when it is needed, we help this trainee develop practices to rewire his internal reactions, using the methods described in Chapter 11.

The Importance of Repetitive Practice

Most PET-C trainees begin our training programs because they resonate with the assumption that couples act as they do because they are caught in automatic internal states that propel them into unproductive interactions. However, when their clients are unable to shift these internal states, they often assume that they must help these clients build ego strength, or gain greater insight into why they act as they do, or that they need to reprocess traumatic injuries. As described in Chapter 11, the PET-C perspective is that this may be unnecessary, and clients can often break out of their habits by simple, focused, repetitive practices designed to help them rewire their internal states. Many trainees cannot believe that it could be that simple. Until they can fully embrace this assumption, these trainees will be limited in their ability to conduct the PET-C treatment model.

These trainees gain greater confidence as they experiment with repetitive practices to rewire their own internal states. Trainees develop personalized practices in the "personal application" supervision groups described above, and also in the ongoing supervision of their cases. During their therapy sessions with couples, trainees often experience automatic activation of internal states that limit their effectiveness. The PET-C supervision helps them develop repetitive practices that result in an increase in their ability to interact more effectively with clients (an example can be found in the section below, "Maintaining Awareness of, and Shifting One's Own Internal States as Needed"). As they experience success in changing their own internal reactions through repetitive practice, they develop greater confidence that clients can change through these methods as well.

Respect for the Client's Decisions

As trainees become enthusiastic about PET-C, they embrace the role of social change agent. In this role, however, astute trainees maintain respect for the integrity of each client. Our job as PET-C therapists is not to make people change. Our job is to present new information for clients to consider, and to interact with them in a way that helps them to remain open to the perspectives that we suggest. Each client must decide for himself whether the way of navigating relationships that we propose feels right to him. We believe that it is more destructive for a client to adopt the therapist's viewpoint because he feels pressured than it is for the client to continue along a path that the therapist believes will be destructive. When the therapist has a respectful attitude, clients don't feel pressure, and they feel free to raise objections. The therapist values these objections. When a client is unable or unwilling to adopt the perspective on relationships suggested by the therapist, an experienced therapist will respect this decision. PET-C therapists adopt the perspective that they cannot know for sure what any client needs to do at any time. The PET-C therapist encourages the client to operate on his or her own convictions, not (those of) the therapist. The therapist offers a specific way of navigating relationships to the client that has worked for many people. However, if the client doesn't believe that this way is applicable for him, the therapist supports the client's decision, while at the same time helping the client realize that the therapist won't be able to help the client along this other path. If the therapist believes that the path the client is traveling will result in continued distress, the therapist respectfully declines to participate, while acknowledging at the same time that the therapist could be mistaken.

There are two kinds of difficulties that PET-C trainees have with this process. First, a trainee may have difficulty encouraging a client according to his own convictions, if they are different from those of the therapist. Such trainees communicate subtle forms of disapproval to a client when they express reservations. This is a serious impediment to the therapy process, and therapy usually fails unless the therapist is able to shift his or her attitude. Second, trainees sometimes have difficulties parting ways with a client whose convictions prevent him or her from getting on board with the PET-C assumptions. These trainees are willing to continue therapy with a client who is headed down a path that the trainees believe is destructive. In our experience, this is a prescription for disaster. Trainees inevitably communicate disapproval toward the client as the weeks go by, and it is much better to respectfully part ways.

In his or her relationship with the client, a skilled PET-C therapist implements the same relationship moves that the therapist is trying to help the client make in his intimate relationship. When a client believes that his partner's behavior is destructive, the therapist helps the client pursue a respectful dialogue with his partner, listening carefully to the partner's reasons, finding the understandable parts of these reasons. The therapist also helps the client develop the ability to explain why the client thinks the partner's behavior is destructive, and acknowledge that his perspective could be mistaken. If the partner persists in what the client feels is destructive behavior, the therapist will help the client respectfully withdraw cooperation from the partner (see "Taking a Firm Stand," Chapter 10). In his or her relationship with the client, a skilled therapist follows the same path. If he or she feels that the client is headed in a destructive direction, the therapist will engage the client in a respectful dialogue, encouraging the client to express his or her reservations, becoming determined to understand the logic behind these reservations, validating the fears or needs that drive them, acknowledging that the therapist could be wrong, and supporting the client's need to operate according to his or her own convictions. However, if the therapist still feels that the client is headed in a direction that is destructive, he or she will respectfully refuse to go down that road with the client. Unless a trainee is comfortable with this process, he or she will be limited in the ability to conduct PET-C effectively.

KEY ABILITIES

PET-C is an ambitious therapy, aiming at a rewiring of neural structures that have often been in place for decades. The process of conducting successful therapy requires much of the practitioner, who must be competent with cognitive, behavioral, and experiential interventions, and maintain a high level of awareness of his or her own internal states during the therapy process. In this section, we review the abilities that a PET-C practitioner must have in order to be effective, as well as some of the methods we use for helping trainees acquire these abilities.

Conceptualizing the Whole Process of Treatment

Successful PET-C trainees develop a good understanding of the entire treatment process, and have a feel for which interventions are needed at particular points in therapy. Inexperienced trainees sometimes try to implement specific interventions before they have adequately laid the groundwork for them. For example, a common mistake made by some trainees is to attempt to tutor a client in the skills of emotional intelligence before the client is fully on board. Inexperienced trainees tend to forge ahead with a client, neglecting to pick up on signs of resistance, or failing to encourage the expressions of them. Another mistake trainees commonly make involves trying to implement Phase III interventions when the level of resentment or hostility in the relationship is still too high. For example, the trainee may encourage partners to become more vulnerable with each other and engage in emotionally supportive conversations before they are ready. These interventions backfire because of the interference of the partners' hostility. One partner may take a risk and make himself vulnerable, then experience his mate's hostility as a slap in the face, resulting in a regression of the therapy. Table 13.1 is used to help trainees understand the overall sequence of PET-C interventions.

Presenting a Compelling Case

Skilled PET-C therapists acquire the ability to present a compelling case for the idea that it is in the client's own best interest to focus on changing his or her own habits. At the Couples Research Institute, we have spent years developing specific sequences of logic, words, and phrases that have proven effective in helping convince clients of the wisdom of self-focus. After years of hearing trainees say to us, "I wish I could remember the way you said that," we adopted the practice of asking trainees to literally memorize specific phrases such as those spelled out in Table 7.1, step 3. Of course, these are only a sample of possible phrases and sequences that can be used in presenting a compelling case, and trainees often find ways to add, subtract, or modify them. However, they usually find it helpful to have something in their heads to work from. We also suggest that trainees memorize the most common reservations that come up during the getting on board process, and the effective responses summarized in Table 8.1.

Finding and Presenting Credible, Nonjudgmental Ways of Making Sense of the Client's Behavior

The success of PET-C often hinges on the ability of the therapist to find credible, nonjudgmental ways of making sense of each partner's attitudes and actions. Often, each partner enters therapy with an explanation for why their relationship is in distress that casts his or her partner as the culprit. Clients often will not drop their critical judgments until they can see alternatives that truly make sense to them. Supervision includes helping each trainee understand how to take the information he or she has about each couple the trainee is working with, and formulate a new story of the couple's relationship. Whereas clients often explain their partners' objectionable actions in pathological terms, the therapist helps them see that their partners' actions are rooted in legitimately different hopes, dreams, expectations, or priorities, and that their partners actions are so extreme or rigid because they feel judged.

Each trainee becomes intimately familiar with core differences in each partner's priorities, or ways of maintaining emotional stability (see Chapter 5), as these differences often underlie gridlocked issues that clients enter therapy upset about. In the early phases of therapy, a skilled PET-C therapist picks up on clues about these differences, and gathers more information about them. Successful PET-C trainees maintain a focus on these differences, and use them to help partners drop their judgmental interpretations and develop new ways of understanding each other's positions.

TABLE 13.1
Overview of PET-C

Phase of Therapy	Goals	Interventions & Methods
Assessment	The therapist gathers information about: • The past and current symptoms, and present level of emotional stability of each partner. • The extent to which the relationship is characterized by alcohol/drug abuse, violence, or infidelity. • The extent to which each partner is currently engaging in the 10 habits that predict relationship success. • The patterns of automatic internal state activation/ suppression that characterize each partner's interaction in the relationship. • The pathologizing interpretations that each partner uses to explain the upsetting aspects of his or her partner's thinking or actions. • The extent to which each partner harbors global contempt for the other. • The specific issues over which partners are gridlocked. • The core differences and bigger issues at stake behind each partner's position on gridlocked issues.	The therapist typically begins with a conjoint session, then conducts an individual session with each partner.

(*continues*)

TABLE 13.1
(Continued)

Phase of Therapy	Goals	Interventions & Methods

Assessment (*continued*)

- Significant past hurtful experiences that each partner has experienced in the current and/or past relationships

Phase I

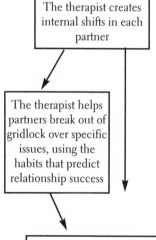

The therapist creates internal shifts in each partner

The therapist helps partners break out of gridlock over specific issues, using the habits that predict relationship success

The therapist gets each partner on board (committed to focusing on increasing his or her own ability to shift internal states and meet the prerequisites for relationship success)

The therapist uses three levels of intervention to get clients to shift internal states:

Level I: Priming the Pump

The therapist speaks for each partner by connecting with an internal state in him or herself that is similar to the one needed by the partner at that particular moment.

- Typically used as a first attempt at helping clients shift.
- Once a client has made an initial shift in response to Level II or Level III interventions, Level I interventions are used to help clients maintain receptive internal states.

Level II: Embodying the Predictive Habits

The therapist meets alone with each client, respectively, and does what the client's partner has difficulty doing: Avoid a judgmental attitude, find the understandable part, identify and acknowledge the

(*continues*)

TABLE 13.1
(Continued)

Phase of Therapy	Goals	Interventions & Methods
Phase I (***continued***)		"bigger" something that is driving the client's resistance or defensiveness by offering more support, understanding, and assurances while continuing to ask for a change.
		• Typically used when clients are having difficulty accepting the value of the changes proposed by the therapist.
		• Used along with Level III interventions, as needed
		Level III: Interacting Directly With An Interfering State
		The therapist helps the client experience an internal shift by sustaining attention on the internal state, attributing agency to the state, assuming a welcoming, respectful non-controlling attitude toward the state, and by engaging in a dialogue with the internal state.
		• Typically used when a client acknowledges the value of the changes proposed by the therapist, but can't shift into a state required to implement the changes.
		Once a shift occurs, the therapist
		1. Helps the client interact with his or her partner in ways that are predictive of success, or

(continues)

TABLE 13.1
(Continued)

Phase of Therapy	Goals	Interventions & Methods
Phase I (***continued***)		2. Presents a compelling case that it's in the client's own best interest to develop the ability to meet the prerequisites for relationship success
Phase II	Phase II begins when a client gets on board, and agrees to focus on developing the ability to meet the prerequisites for relationship success.	**Retrospective Reviewing** Each partner reviews upsetting situations that have recently occurred between him- or herself and partner, and <ul><li>identifies specifically the ways that his or her reactions diverged from those that predict relationship success.</li><li>understands specifically how his or her reactions would have been different had he or she been more able to implement the habits that predict relationship success.</li><li>identifies the qualities of the internal state that propelled him or her toward nonproductive reactions, or prevented him or her from being able to react more fully in ways that are predictive of relationship success.</li><li>identifies the specific features of the upsetting situation that "triggered" the internal state that propelled the client toward nonproductive reactions or prevented the client from being able to react more effectively.</li></ul>

(continues)

TABLE 13.1
(Continued)

Phase of Therapy	Goals	Interventions & Methods
Phase II (*continued*)	Each partner receives personalized tutoring in the skills of emotional intelligence, using his or her own relationship as a workshop for practicing these skills.	**Prospective Planning** Each partner identifies specific issues that are upsetting to him or her (or upsetting to the partner), then plans to have a successful conversation, by • deciding when a good time might be to have the conversation; • developing a nonjudgmental way of looking at the partner's thinking and actions related to the issue; • becoming determined to find the at least partly legitimate logic behind the partner's thinking and actions on the issue; • thinking about how he or she can stand up for his or her position on the issue without putting the partner down; • being ready to assure the partner of his or her willingness to give equal regard to the partner's feelings or opinions on the issue; • identifying and preparing to explain bigger issues that lie beneath his or her feelings about the specific situation at hand. • anticipating less-than-desirable responses from the partner, and developing a plan for staying on track in spite of them.

(*continues*)

TABLE 13.1
(Continued)

Phase of Therapy	Goals	Interventions & Methods
Phase II (*continued*)		• being aware of the internal state that usually gets triggered in conversations about the issue, and avoiding activation of this state in the next conversation, or becoming aware when it is activated and shifting out of it, or preparing to take a break from the conversation.
		Rewiring Internal States: Repetitive Practice • Daily Practice Through Audio-Guided Reexperiencing • Practicing under "Game Conditions" • Shifting Before Launching a Complaint: Audio-Guided Practice • Practicing with Audiotaped Complaints • "Live" Assistance in State-Shifting
Phase III	The focus shifts from eliminating the "negative" to increasing the "positive." 1. Increase each partner's ability to • Maintain curiosity about his partner's world • Keep sight of the positive • Pursue shared meaning	**Apply the Pragmatic/ Experiential Method** 1. Start by asking partners to spend more time thinking and interacting in friendship-enhancing ways (i.e., Predictive Habits 7–10, Table 3.1) 2. If partners fail to follow through, or just "go through the motions," explore blocks

TABLE 13.1
(Continued)

Phase of Therapy	Goals	Interventions & Methods

Phase III (***continued***)	• Make and respond to "bids" for connection
	2. Help each partner gain greater access to the brain's intimacy states
	   • Longing
	   • Tenderness
	   • Playfulness
	   • Sexual Interest
		that inhibit the natural activation of the brain's intimacy states.
		
		Simple Reminders
		Homework Exercises
		
		• Knowing My Partner's World
		• Appreciations
		• Extra-Positive Moments
		• Small Acts of Caring
		• What's on My Partner's Mind?
		• Remembering Good Times
		   Activating Desire for
		      Emotional Connection
		   Making and Responding to
		      Bids for Connection
		   Direct Physiological
		      Soothing
		   Exploring and Resolving
		      Activation Blocks

Modeling the Predictive Habits

A skilled PET-C practitioner not only educates partners about the habits that predict relationship success, he shows them how the habits can be applied in the day-to-day issues that come up in their relationship. Week by week, the therapist models the application of these habits, over and over again, showing partners how they can be applied in every situation they encounter. The PET-C practitioner can often be heard saying things like, "If you want your partner's respect and cooperation, you'll need to say something like. . . ." The therapist gives vivid examples of the attitude and words that embody the predictive habits in specific situations.

This process is new to some trainees, and they often stop short of modeling. For example, a trainee might say, "You need to tell your partner what you find understandable about his point of view," but fail to show the client what it might actually look or sound like if he or she were to do this. Many times, clients have never done anything like the predictive habit the trainee is suggesting. They don't have a "feel" for it. Clients often feel foolish asking the trainee for examples, so they don't. They then become frustrated, as the trainee repeatedly corrects their efforts.

In our training programs, we help trainees develop confidence in modeling the predictive habits, using a group supervision format. We have accumulated an extensive collection of videotapes of couples arguing. We play these videotapes in group supervision, stopping the tapes at particular points in the couple's arguments, asking a trainee to step in for one of the partners and speak for the partner in a way that embodies the next move the client would need to make if he or she were going to be more effective in the argument. We do this over and over again, until any trainee can stand in at any point for a client and skillfully make the next needed move. Even after they have studied the predictive habits and the moves extensively, we find that trainees often come up blank when asked to step into real arguments and make statements on behalf of clients. Inexperienced trainees often make simple mistakes, such as continuing to be understanding in the face of a critical attack, rather than implementing an Offer and Ask. Trainees quickly learn the value of this video-guided practice, and are grateful for opportunities to practice.

Waiting Until the Client is Motivated

As trainees gain confidence in the effectiveness of PET-C's 10 predictive habits, they enthusiastically encourage clients to implement them. In their enthusiasm, however, they sometimes overlook signs of resistance or reservation on the client's part, instead encouraging the client to "just do it!" Many clients will not express their reservations directly to the therapist, and if they feel that the therapist isn't interested in the reservations, they'll tell the therapist what he or she wants to hear during sessions, then simply neglect to do what the therapist suggests when the client gets home.

Perhaps the most important aspect of PET-C involves helping clients believe that the single most effective thing they can do to get more respect and cooperation from their partners is to develop more ability to react to the disrespectful or uncooperative actions of their partners in ways that predict relationship success. An experienced PET-C therapist will not encourage clients to practice the predictive habits until they are motivated to do so. In fact, a skilled PET-C therapist won't even tell clients what the predictive habits are unless the client is actively asking for this knowledge. A skilled therapist will drop his or her agenda and attend to client reservations, and not pick it up again until the reservations are resolved.

When Phase II is going well, clients often get more upset about their ineffective reactions to their partner's provocative behavior than they are upset about the provocative behavior itself. Clients destined to succeed take a "first things first" attitude. "First, I'll make sure that I'm reacting like people who usually get respect and cooperation from their partners, then I'll decide what to do if my partner still doesn't change." Unless clients develop this kind of commitment and motivation, it's unlikely that they will do the practicing necessary to make needed changes. Inexperienced therapists frequently try to move forward before the client is sufficiently motivated.

Relentless Focus on Authenticity

In PET-C, clients often know what they "should" do before they have the motivation to do it. This creates the possibility that clients might simply go through the motions, not really meaning what they say or do. While knowledge of the predictive habits often plays a central role in motivating clients to make needed attitude changes and guiding their actions once their attitudes have shifted, clients may also try to use the information strategically. For example, as a client comes to realize that criticizing his partner never works, he may try to get more cooperation from his partner by biting his tongue and pretending he's not critical, while inside he may be stewing with contempt.

Skilled PET-C practitioners anticipate that clients will try to skip over needed attitude shifts, and notice when expressions are inauthentic or incongruent. They help clients realize when they are not in the right frame of mind to do or say the things that are predictive of success. Rather than encouraging clients to say or do the "right" things, experienced therapists help them learn how to make the attitude shifts necessary for new thinking and actions to authentically emerge. Almost all clients try to "go strategic" (say or do things they don't really mean, trying to trick their partners in to changing) to a certain extent before they embrace the much more ambitious task of changing underlying habits of the heart. Seasoned therapists continually direct clients to examine their attitudes and motivations, and help them develop the ability to make genuine attitude or mood shifts. Inexperienced trainees focus too much on getting clients to communicate or interact in ways that are predictive of success, often neglecting the far more important tasks of helping clients learn to recognize when their attitudes or moods need to shift, and develop the mood shifting abilities.

Maintaining Awareness of, and Shifting One's Own Internal States as Needed

Each PET-C intervention described in this book requires that the therapist be in a state of mind that enables him or her to deliver it effectively. Most of the time, an effective PET-C therapist operates from a state in which he or she is focused, goal-directed, organized, and also flexible, and not too intense. Playfulness is often a valuable asset. The clients of skilled PET-C practitioners feel that the therapist genuinely likes them, and enjoys being with them. There are times, however, when the therapist feel impatient, frustrated, or critical. Therapists are governed by automatic internal reactions as surely as clients, and the therapist must maintain awareness of internal states and be able to shift when an interfering internal state is activated.

We believe that the activation of interfering internal states in the therapist is inevitable, and not a sign that something is wrong. Experienced PET-C therapists experience unhelpful internal activations, even after years of working on rewiring their own internal reactions. Certain clients are more challenging than others for certain therapists. What's important is that the therapist is able to recognize when an interfering internal state is active, and is able to shift as needed. PET-C supervisors help trainees recognize unhelpful internal activations, and assist them in developing practices that help rewire these reactions, or help trainees shift when needed. This process happened in a recent supervisory session at the Couples Research Institute. During supervision, a PET-C supervisor and trainee watched a videotape of a recent session the trainee had conducted with a couple. During this session, the wife criticized her husband harshly for what she saw as his excessive involvements that took time away from family life. The husband was heavily involved in community organizations, and also exercised daily at the fitness club after work before coming home. Here's a section of the dialogue that occurred between partners in the opening minutes of the session.

W: I am so fucking tired of being last on your list of priorities. You have time for everything else, and we get the scraps of you that are left over. We get you when you're too tired to even function. Well you know what? You can keep your lousy scraps. We don't need you anymore.

H: What are you talking about? I was home three nights this week. I didn't even go to the meeting at the library that I organized myself. Do you know how embarrassing that was for me? I came home, and you didn't even notice. Nothing is ever good enough for you.

W: Oh, like I'm supposed to praise you because you gave up one night to go to your son's hockey game? Most fathers come home every night!

H: Most fathers don't give a damn about anything except what's on TV tonight. Is that what you want?

W: I want someone who gives a damn about his family.

The supervisor and trainee continued watching the video as the trainee requested a break in the session, and met with each partner separately. The following is an excerpt from the trainee's conversation with the wife.

T: Helen, what were you doing in there?

W: He doesn't have a clue about the kind of sacrifices it takes to have a family!

T: Okay, who made you the judge of the level of sacrifice it takes?

W: (annoyed) You're trying to tell me that it's okay for a father to be gone five nights a week?

T: I'm trying to tell you that you're in no position to be an authority on the subject. People do their lives differently. There are no rules on this.

The supervisor stopped the tape at this point, and stated that he felt a little uncomfortable about how the session was going. He asked the trainee how it felt to him. The trainee explained that the wife was resistant to his comments at first, but that if the supervisor would watch the rest of the tape, he'd see that the wife came around in the end. The supervisor watched the rest of the tape, and saw the therapist continue arguing with the wife until she fell silent, then agreed with the therapist that he was right, and tried another conversation with her husband. In the second conversation, the wife controlled her anger, but her hostility leaked through in the form of sarcastic comments. The trainee remarked that he thought this was progress for her, because at least she had stopped her biting criticism. The following dialogue then occurred between supervisor and trainee.

Superv: I think I'm seeing this somewhat differently. It looked to me like Helen didn't make the internal shift you were looking for. She just ran out of justifications for her critical approach. You sort of backed her into a corner, and she finally just shut up, and went along with you, at least in the way she acted. Part of her probably knew you were right, and she tried to do it differently in the second conversation. But it seemed to me that there was a big part of her that hadn't shifted inside. In the second conversation, she chose her words carefully, but I think that her husband still felt her critical attitude.

Trainee: I guess I didn't pick up on that. She seemed to be trying.

Superv: I agree. She was trying, but I don't think she'd shifted to a noncritical place inside. She was trying to refrain from being critical even though she felt critical.

Trainee: Maybe I just didn't know how to help her drop the critical attitude. What should I have done?

Superv: First, I liked your willingness to be straight with her. You risked her getting pissed with you, and that takes guts. But if a situation like this comes up again, I can think of some things that might make you more effective. It probably starts with what you were feeling when she was attacking her husband. Can we rewind the tape to that point?

They rewound the tape and watched the wife criticizing her husband again. This time, the supervisor stopped the tape and asked the trainee to stop and pay attention to the feeling he had inside. The trainee sat thoughtfully for a moment, then replied:

Trainee: I felt impatient and frustrated with her.

Superv: Good. And what kind of thoughts were going through your head?

Trainee: (*chuckles*) I'm embarrassed to say it, but I guess I was thinking, "Oh come on, Helen! How many times have we been through this?"

Superv: Hey, I've had worse thoughts than that! Really. Sometimes I think things like, "Oh my God! This person is a total idiot!" On my good days, I catch myself slipping into that attitude, and I'm able to shift to a different place inside, but on any other day, I feel critical as hell, and it doesn't work any better for me than it did for your in there (both laugh).

Trainee: I don't know how to stop myself from thinking that way.

Superv: Right. You'll probably have to really practice on this one. Most trainees do. I'll show you how I've practiced with myself. It's really just the same thing we teach our clients to do when we have them re-experience upsetting situations and imagine themselves thinking and acting differently.

Trainee: You mean, by listening to an audiotape?

Superv: Yep.

The trainee and supervisor then proceeded to go through the process described in Chapter 11 (Daily Practice Through Audio-Guided Reexperiencing). First, the supervisor and trainee spent time brainstorming answers to the question, "What kind of thoughts might help you shift internal states in a situation like this one?" The trainee thought it would be useful for him to remind himself of the following things:

- Just relax. I can afford to take my time. Everything is going fine. It's normal for clients to regress, and it doesn't mean that the therapy is off-track.
- I need to help her shift before she can hear anything I say.
- I don't blame her for feeling critical. I get that way too, lots of times.
- She'll probably shift quickly if she feels that I understand her frustration.

The trainee and supervisor then made an audiotape in which the trainee was guided to imagine himself back in this exact situation with the client. The tape helped the trainee remember vividly enough so that he could feel the frustration and impatience beginning to arise inside of him. He then pictured himself remembering to relax and think of the self-reminders he'd come up with. Finally, the trainee pictured himself interacting differently with the client, empathizing with her frustration and gradually helping her shift to a receptive state, using the methods the trainee had already learned. The trainee agreed to listen to this tape every day during the next week.

Supervisory sessions like this one are common in the PET-C training process. Trainees use the same methods to rewire their own automatically activated internal states that they help clients use. These daily practice methods are just as powerful for trainees as they are for clients. This trainee did listen to the audiotape repeatedly, and as he did, he developed the ability to shift his frustration, not only with this client, but with others as well. The trainee made other audiotapes on his own, helping himself develop the ability to shift with particularly challenging clients.

Confronting and Supporting at the Same Time

The ability to be confrontive and supportive at the same time is probably the most crucial ability needed by a PET-C practitioner. Throughout therapy, the therapist helps clients shift from defensive to receptive internal states, then challenge them to move more effectively in their relationships. A skilled PET-C therapist listens patiently to his clients, enthusiastically welcoming any objections or reservations they have, validating their frustrations or reservations, empathizing with them, and making it clear that the therapist believes that they must make their own decisions about what beliefs and courses of action they should take. At the same time, the therapist states directly his observations about where he sees the client getting off-track, and paints a clear picture for the client about the kind of attitudes and actions that he believes will result in the client getting what he needs from his partner.

Therapists who are successful maintain humility and respectfulness throughout therapy, repeatedly acknowledging to clients that the moves the therapist is proposing are difficult to do, and that, if the therapist were in the client's shoes, he might not be any more able to do them than the client has been able. However, the therapist continually communicates hope and confidence that the moves are possible to learn, and the rewards are great for those who are able to increase their abilities to implement them. This hope and confidence arises from the fact that the therapist has experienced their power in his own life.

CONCLUSION

PET-C proposes a way of navigating relationships that arises from years of research on the factors involved in making relationships work, and uses a model of change suggested by new knowledge about how the human mind works. With new information about the inner workings of the brain, we have learned that it's possible for anyone to literally rewire his or her neural circuits for more flexibility. The secret to this process is in repetitive practice. PET-C provides a coherent package that has been useful to hundreds of therapists and thousands of clients over the past decade. However, we recognize that human relationships are vastly complex, and that there are many possible ways for improving them. We encourage trainees to try out the principles and methods we offer, evaluate them critically, and modify them in ways that make sense to them. We offer them to the reader with the goal of furthering dialogue among those of us who seek to understand human relationships, and promote compassionate and respectful interaction. It is my hope that readers will test these methods with their clients and in their own lives, and give us feedback about their utility.

Appendices

The Sequence

Knowing How and When to Implement Each Predictive Habit When Upsets Occur

Knowing How and When to Implement Each Predictive Habit When Upsets Occur

Knowledge of the ten habits that predict relationship success is a critical first step, but people destined to succeed in their relationships also know when particular habits are needed, and how to use them effectively. When upsets occur, successful people combine the predictive habits into powerful movements that elicit respectfulness from their partners. Here's a step-by-step sequence for implementing the predictive habits that has been used by thousands of successful couples (the steps are described more fully on pages 13-19).

The First Steps

1. **Self-Reminder: Do Something Different**
   - ➤ Remind yourself that it's in your <u>own best interest</u> to try to respond differently than you typically do. Your old way of reacting never works for <u>anybody</u>, in <u>any</u> relationship. If you can respond effectively in situations like these, Michael will become more understanding and cooperative.
2. **Give the Benefit of the Doubt**
   - ➤ Avoid jumping to conclusions, and with an open mind, ask him why he acted as he did, or is thinking the way he is.
   - ➤ Assume there is something at-least-partly legitimate about his complaint.
   - ➤ Assume there must be a reason for his thinking or actions that you don't fully understand yet.
   - ➤ Hear Michael out before explaining your point of view or defending yourself.
3. **Find the Understandable Part**
   - ➤ Become determined to find any at-least-partly-understandable reasons for his thinking or actions, and acknowledge them.
4. **What's Driving My Upset?**
   - ➤ Tell Michael <u>why</u> you're upset, or tell Michael why you're having trouble acting or thinking the way he wants… explain the bigger thing that's at stake for you
5. **Offer Assurance**
   - ➤ Assure Michael that you're not saying that you are right and he's wrong, or assure Michael that you're not saying that he shouldn't be upset. Let him know that you're not saying that things have to be entirely your way.
6. **Work With Me?**
   - ➤ Let Michael know that you're willing to make some changes and to work with him to find a mutually acceptable solution.

When, in spite of my good attitude, Michael disregards my viewpoint or criticizes me

7. **Maintain Your Cool:**
   Stay calm, and, in your mind, don't make a big deal of Michael's initial criticism or disregarding of your viewpoint. Remind yourself that maybe he just needs an "offer and ask" reaction from you.
8. **Offer and Ask**
   Assure Michael that you care about how he feels, and you're willing to work with him, but also let him know that you expect that he be willing to work with you, too. (e.g, "Hey, I'm trying to work with you here, but it feels like I'm not getting it back! Will you work with me?")
9. **Stand Up/Engage** (only if Michael keeps criticizing you or dismissing your viewpoint)
   If Michael continues to criticize you or dismiss your viewpoint, let your anger build. Tell Michael that you don't expect to agree with you, but you do expect him to be willing to work with you. Make it clear that his attitude is not OK with you. Don't back down. Stay engaged and demand that Michael explain why he thinks it's OK to dismiss your viewpoint.
10. **Reject Michael** (only if Michael keeps criticizing you or dismissing your viewpoint)
    If Michael continues to criticize or disregard you, tell him something like, "Get away from me!" or "You know what? I don't even want to be around you right now!"
11. **Don't make a big deal of it.**
    When you're by yourself, let go of the anger, feeling good that you stood up well for yourself. Promise yourself that you'll do it again, if needed. Remind yourself that it's natural enough for Michael to want to have his own way. You don't have to make a big deal of his stubborn or selfish behavior. It's not a crime that Michael acted this way. He crossed the line, and you stood up for yourself. No biggie.
12. **Try again later**
    - ➤ "That didn't go very well, did it? You want to try again?
    - ➤ Don't try to get him to see how "wrong" his stubborn behavior was. Don't demand an apology. Go back to "The First Steps" again. Be ready to stand up again, if needed.

Finding the Understandable Part

Common "Hidden" Reasons

This page will help you with Step 3 (Find the Understandable Part)
of the *Sequence*

Because the understandable reasons for Michael's feelings, intentions or motivations will not always be obvious, it's to your advantage to become good at finding the reasons that are sometimes difficult to see at first. Here's a list of possible reasons that might make Michael's thinking or actions more understandable to you:

1. Maybe Michael didn't realize how important the issue is to you.
2. Maybe Michael was having a bad day.
3. Maybe Michael had a lot on his mind.
4. Maybe Michael didn't have all the facts.
5. Maybe Michael was acting this way because he felt mad at you about something else.
6. Maybe Michael was operating on different assumptions or information than you.
7. Maybe Michael was reading something between the lines that you didn't intend to be saying.
8. Maybe you are reading something between the lines that Michael didn't intend to be saying.
9. Maybe the issue was more important to Michael that you previously understood.
10. Maybe Michael wasn't upset so much about this particular situation as he was about where he feared things might be headed.
11. Maybe Michael felt threatened by you in a way that you didn't understand.
12. Maybe Michael was afraid he was going to lose something very important to him if he did things the way you wanted.
13. Michael's actions are crucial to his way of feeling stable. Maybe Michael would feel anxious or unstable if he tried doing things your way. Maybe Michael has a different way of coping in life than you do.
14. Maybe Michael just has really different priorities or expectations than you do. Maybe he was acting perfectly consistently with his priorities. You just don't like it because they are different than yours, but that doesn't make them *wrong*. (See your workbook sheet, *Core Differences in Ways of Maintaining Emotional Stability*)
15. Maybe beneath Michael's seemingly inexplicable or provocative behavior, there's something legitimate that he's going after. There's something bigger at stake for Michael than is immediately apparent. There's a legitimate need, dream or priority that Michael is trying to preserve or obtain (see your workbook sheet, "What's Driving Me?"). This need, priority or dream is probably one that isn't as important to you, but that doesn't make it wrong.
16. Maybe Michael's actions or attitude are a reaction to feeling dismissed or "written off" by you (see your workbook sheet, *Developing Non-Judgmental Explanations for Michael's Attitude or Actions*).
17. Maybe Michael's actions or attitude are partly due to your inability to stand up for yourself without putting him down in the past (see your workbook sheet, *Developing Non-Judgmental Explanations for Michael's Attitude or Actions*).
18. Maybe Michael's uncooperative or critical attitude is partly due to his feelings that you just don't like him very much lately, or his feeling that you don't care about his feelings (see your workbook sheet, *Developing Non-Judgmental Explanations for Michael's Attitude or Actions*).

What's Driving Me?

This page will help you with Step 4 (What's Driving My Upset?) of *The Sequence*

People who are destined to succeed in their relationships realize that the reasons why they feel or act as they do often run deeper than the present situation. Often, it's not the situation so much as what it symbolizes. There's something bigger at stake -- an underlying need, fear, dream, or priority. Examples of underlying needs that often drive the feelings and actions of people in specific situations:

> - To feel competent
> - To feel loved and accepted
> - To feel admired
> - To feel respected.
> - To feel extra special to somebody.
> - To have free time
> - To be able to relax and not have to work so hard
> - To feel taken care of
> - To feel that someone thinks they're fortunate to have me as their friend.
> - To feel secure
> - To feel useful to somebody else
> - To <u>not</u> feel taken advantage of, or taken for granted
> - To feel like I can influence my future.
> - To feel attractive
> - To feel that someone cares enough to make a sacrifice for me
> - To feel free to go with my intuitions
> - To feel like I'm growing
> - To get revenge
> - To enforce justice
> - To feel that life is predictable
> - To feel that life is an adventure
> - To <u>not</u> feel bored
> - To feel creative.
> - To feel well-organized
> - To feel productive
> - To feel able to make my own decisions

People who are destined to succeed in their relationships understand and discuss the underlying needs, fears, dreams and priorities that influence their opinions or actions in specific situations. They also try to understand the needs, dreams and fears of other people involved in their lives. At some point during or after an argument, people destined for success pause and take the conversation to a different level, saying something like, "OK, I think I just figured out why this bothers me so much… I'm worried that…"

APPENDIX D

Flow Chart

Ordering of The Sequence

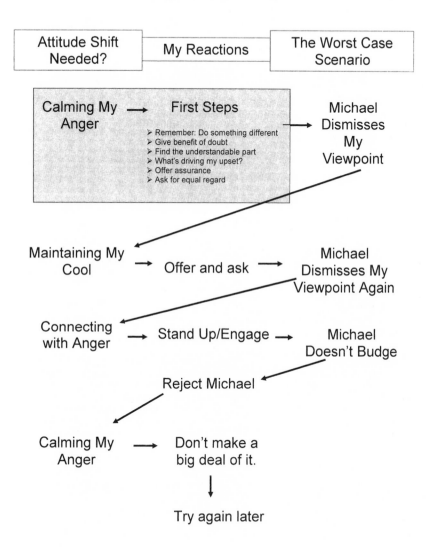

Attitude Shift Needed?	My Reactions	The Worst Case Scenario

Calming My Anger → **First Steps**

➢ Remember: Do something different
➢ Give benefit of doubt
➢ Find the understandable part
➢ What's driving my upset?
➢ Offer assurance
➢ Ask for equal regard

Michael Dismisses My Viewpoint

Maintaining My Cool → Offer and ask → Michael Dismisses My Viewpoint Again

Connecting with Anger → Stand Up/Engage → Michael Doesn't Budge

Reject Michael

Calming My Anger → Don't make a big deal of it.

↓

Try again later

Reviewing My Reactions

What did Michael say or do (or fail to say or do) that upset me?	

On a scale of 1-10, rate (right column) the extent to which you did each of the things described in the left column. 1= not at all; 10 = completely

	The First Steps (see your workbook sheet, The Sequence)	
		Rating (1-10)
1	**Remember: Do Something Different** (Did you remind yourself that it's in your own best interest to try to respond differently than you typically do?)	
2	**Give the Benefit of the Doubt** (Did you avoid jumping to conclusions, and assume there must be some at-least-partly-legitimate reason for Michael's actions or viewpoint?)	
3	**Find the Understandable Part** (Did you become absolutely determined to find an at-least-partly-understandable reason for Michael's actions or viewpoint?	
4	**Explain What's Driving My Upset** (Did you explain to Michael the bigger need or worry that underlies your actions or viewpoint on the issue?)	
5	**Offer Assurance** (Did you assure Michael that you weren't saying he was wrong, or that things have to be entirely your way?)	
6	**"Work with Me?"** (Did you ask Michael to work with you to find a way of proceeding that respects both of your feelings?)	

	In spite of my good attitude, Michael didn't respond well to "The First Steps" (see your workbook sheet, The Sequence)	
		Rating (1-10)
7	**Maintain Your Cool** (Did you say calm and avoid making a big deal of Michael's initial disregard of your point of view?)	
8	**Offer and ask** (Did you assure Michael that you care how he feels and you're willing to work with him, and also let him know that you expect him to be willing to work with you as well?)	
9	**Stand Up/Engage** (only if Michael keeps dismissing your complaint) – (Did you let yourself get angry and make it clear that Michael's attitude is not OK with you?	
10	**Reject Michael** (only if Michael keeps dismissing your complaint) -- (Did you let Michael know that you didn't want to be around him?)	
11	**Don't make a big deal of it.** (In your own mind, did you avoid making a big deal of Michael's stubborn, selfish, or critical behavior?)	
12	**Try again later** (Did you avoid demanding an apology? Did you avoid trying to get Michael to see how selfish, stubborn or inappropriate his behavior was? Did you assure Michael that you care how he feels and are willing to try to talk about it again?)	

On the Back Side

Please use to back of this form to answer the following questions:
1. Where did you first get "off track" in your reactions to Michael,
2. If you could do the situation over again, what is one change you could make in your <u>thinking</u> that would help your attitude or state of mind, and allow you to interact with Michael more effectively (i.e., more "on track" The Sequence)
3. If you could do the situation over again, what is one change you could make in your *actions* to Michael that would make you more effective (i.e., more "on track" with The Sequence)

Studying Your State of Mind

Researchers have discovered that, when intimate partners are upset with one another, each partner generally reacts to the other in highly predictable and patterned ways. Thanks to some very helpful brain research in the past 15 years, we now know that this is because, across our lives, each of our brains gets conditioned to produce highly specific *response programs*. These are conditioned brain circuits that are pre-programmed so that, once triggered, they unfold as if they had a mind of their own, producing a predictable pattern of thoughts, feelings and behaviors. Brain researchers call these brain states "executive operating systems;" or "intrinsic motivational circuits;" ordinary people call them "states of mind" or "emotional states." The important thing is not what they are called, but to recognize that these internal response programs can dramatically dictate how you interact with your partner. To improve your relationship, you will need to become very familiar with the specific response state patterns that happen inside of you during key intimate situations. Your best shot at acting differently comes when you can easily recognize when a response state problem is automatically activated inside of you, and when you develop the ability to shift internal states when needed.

What is the situation(s) that you are hoping to try to react differently in?

When Michael does something that seems selfish

In this situation, what is the internal state or mood like that gets triggered in you? What does this state feel like?

I get angry instantly, like I could explode. If I don't say anything, I'll explode. I feel that I have to make him understand how wrong he is. I have to let him know that he's not going to get away with it.

What are some specific cues (words, nonverbal gestures, actions, circumstances) that trigger this mood state?

- Whenever he does something selfish, or he forgets to do something.
- When he gives some bullshit excuse.

What things do you often think, do or say when you're in this state?

- I can't believe how selfish he is!
- This is so typical of him.
- I have to let him know that he's not going to get away with it.

What is the internal state you're going to practice shifting to?

Calmer, and open-minded (to the possibility that he may have a legitimate point of view)

What can you say to yourself that might help you shift?

I can afford to take the time to listen to him (I can always get mad later!)

Once you shift internal states, what kinds of things do you hope to say or do differently?

- Ask about his point of view
- Avoid criticizing him, and instead ask him to meet me half way.

Understanding The Sequence

The Sequence summarized on the preceding page of your workbook has been used by thousands of partners to elicit more understanding and cooperation from their mates. If you can follow this sequence each time an upset occurs between you and Michael, you'll find that Michael will become more caring and respectful of your feelings within a matter of weeks. Let's take a closer look at each step in the sequence

The First Steps

1. Remember: Do Something Different

When Michael does something that upsets you, the first thing you'll need to do is to remember to focus on making sure that you change your usual reactions, rather than dwelling on how offensive or uncaring Michael's behavior is. Three decades of research on relationships suggests you'll be more effective in getting Michael to understand and care about your feelings if you **focus on your own reactions**. Studies on couples show that how people react when they feel misunderstood or offended strongly predicts whether or not they'll get treated better by their partners in the future. These are the moments that "separate the women from the girls," psychologically speaking. If you learn how to react effectively in the moments when you're upset with Michael, the odds are very, very good that you'll get more cooperation and respect from Michael in the future. Some ways of reacting virtually guarantee relationship failure. Remember that all people in long term relationships feel mistreated or offended at one time or another. Those who know how to react effectively get treated better in the future. If you want to get treated better by Michael, first make sure you're reacting to him like people who almost always get treated better. Then you can decide what to do if Michael doesn't treat you better. However, if you develop the ability to respond effectively when you feel upset or offended, the odds are very, very good that you'll soon feel more respected and understood by Michael. The reminders on your workbook sheet, *Sample Self-Assurances,* might help you remember to give attention to your own reactions before concluding that Michael won't change. When an upset occurs between you and Michael, try to develop the habit of instantly thinking something like,

> ➤ *My usual reactions won't work. They never work for <u>anybody</u> in <u>any</u> relationship.*
> ➤ *The single most effective thing I can do right now to get more of what I want from Michael is to develop the ability to react more effectively when I'm <u>not</u> getting what I want.*
> ➤ *First, I'll make sure I'm thinking and acting like people who usually get respect and cooperation from their partners. Then, if I'm still not getting it, I'll figure out what else I may need to do.*

2. Give the Benefit of the Doubt	*This step draws heavily on Predictive Habit #1: Avoiding a Judgmental Attitude*

Now that you've reminded yourself to do something different, let's focus on what you need to do. How do people who get understanding and cooperation from their partners go about getting it? There's nothing that shuts down a conversation faster than the feeling that the person you're talking to has already decided that you're guilty before even talking to you. People who are good at influencing their partners avoid jumping to negative conclusions, and try to keep an open mind when their partners do things they don't like. They understand that if they assume the worst of their partners, they'll *get* the worst. People destined for relationship success give their partners the benefit of the doubt – that is, they assume that there is an understandable reason for their partner's words or actions, even if they don't know what it is yet. Beneath even seemingly provocative behavior on the part of their partners, they assume that there is a legitimate need, priority or dream that's driving their partner's actions. In contrast, when people who are destined to fail in their relationships are faced with words or actions from their partners that are upsetting to them, they assume that their partners are acting this way because they have misguided, priorities, reasoning, motivations, or intentions, or that their partners have faulty personality characteristics (e.g., "my partner is just lazy, controlling, irresponsible, insensitive, etc."). Use the sheet in your workbook titled, *Attitude Check* to help you identify judgmental explanations you might often have for Michael's actions.

It is totally to your advantage to give the benefit of the doubt. If Michael isn't willing to do the same, you can always stand up for yourself later (see steps 7-12). But if you decide in the beginning that he's done something "wrong," behaved badly, or that his thinking is "off," you'll join the company of those destined to fail in their relationships. Try thinking something like:

> ➤ *There are probably reasons why Michael is thinking or acting this way that I don't yet understand.*
> ➤ *Even if I can't yet find a legitimate reason for his attitude or actions, I'm still going to assume there is one.*
> ➤ *Just because I assume there is a legitimate reason for Michael's thinking or actions doesn't mean that I need to go along with what he wants. My viewpoints and needs are just as legitimate.*

3. Find the Understandable Part	*This step involves putting into action predictive habit #3, Finding the Understandable Part)*

If Michael does something upsetting to you, you might not at first see anything that could be understandable about his feelings or actions. However, if you can find any at-least-partly-understandable reasons for his thinking or actions, you'll dramatically increase the odds that Michael will also be able to understand the reasons for your own feelings or viewpoints as well. People who succeed in their relationships understand that they can increase the odds that they'll get understanding if they give it first. Hence, they become absolutely determined to understand the logic behind their partners' thoughts and actions. Because the understandable reasons for Michael's feelings, intentions or motivations will not always be obvious, it's to your advantage to become good at finding the reasons that are sometimes difficult to see at first. A list of possible reasons that might make Michael's thinking or actions more understandable to you can be found on your workbook sheet, *Finding the Understandable Part: Common Hidden Reasons.* Sometimes the reasons why your partner acts or thinks differently than you may be related to the fact that Michael may have legitimately different priorities or ways of maintaining emotional stability than you do. They're not necessarily better than yours, but neither are they worse. Some of the most common of these core differences are summarized in the section of your workbook titled, *Core Difference in Ways of Maintaining Emotional Stability.*

4. What's Driving My Upset?	*This step provides a way of implementing predictive habit #6: Identifying and Explaining What is at Stake.*

Many times, if you're able to keep an open mind and try to understand the logic behind Michael's thinking or actions, you'll find that you no longer have a problem with what he wants. However, there are other times when you'll still find that you see things differently, or that you have different priorities or expectations. In these situations, you'll need to explain why you feel the way you do. You'll be most effective if you can identify the bigger needs or worries that drive your feelings about the particular situation, then explain them

Arguments often fail because couples argue about the wrong things. People who are destined to succeed in their relationships realize that the reasons they are upset or have trouble doing what their partner wants sometimes run deeper than the present situation. Often, there is something bigger at stake. Your ability to explain the underlying reasons for being upset will help your partner become more cooperative and understanding. At some point during an argument people destined for success pause and take the conversation to a different level, saying something like, "OK, I think I just figured out why this bothers me so much... I'm worried that..." See your workbook sheet, "What's Driving Me?" for a list of underlying needs that often drive the feelings and actions of people in specific situations. Are any of these needs driving your upset feelings in the current situation? Unless you are able to identify what the bigger issues are that lie beneath your reactions in the present situation, you may end up arguing over superficial things and leave the real issues unaddressed. Try asking yourself the following questions:

> ➤ *Why is this such a big deal to me? Underneath it all, what's at stake for me?*
> ➤ *What am I worried about?*
> ➤ *Is this really about the present situation, or is there something bigger at stake?*

5. Offer Assurance	*This step draws upon predictive habit #1 (Avoiding a Judgmental Attitude) and predictive habit #5 (Offering Assurances).*

You may find that when you talk to Michael about a dissatisfaction you have, even though you're not feeling critical of him, he may react defensively – as if you've criticized him. Not realizing that his defensiveness is a reaction to feeling attacked, you might think that he's just being stubborn. There's a simple way to remedy this situation: Begin with the assumption that he's being defensive or dismissive of your feelings because he feels criticized or attacked, not because he's being uncooperative. Don't make a big deal of the fact that he has misinterpreted you -- simply say things to him that will help him understand that you're not feeling critical of him. For example, you might say something like,

> ➤ *I'm not saying that it was wrong for you to do that – It's just different than what I was hoping for (or, I just don't think I understand why you did it)*
> ➤ *I'm not saying that we have to do things the way I think they should be – I think your feelings should count too. I'm just trying to understand them.*
> ➤ *Look, I care about your feelings here too, and I'm going to respect them even if I don't agree.*

People destined for relationship success learn the following general rule:

> *When your partner seems critical or defensive,*
> *don't make a big deal of it – just offer an assurance.*

If Michael accuses you of having a critical "tone" or "attitude" or criticizes the way you're talking to him, resist the urge to debate whether or not his perceptions are valid. Assume that there may be at least some truth in what he's feeling. No big deal. Just start over again, and this time be sure to add assurances that explicitly let him know you're willing to keep an open mind and be cooperative. For example, say something like,

> ➤ *OK, it's certainly possible that there's a part of me that wants to be critical of you, because I am upset, but I'm trying to keep an open mind.*

If you realize that maybe you do feel critical, you can say something like.

> ➤ *OK, maybe I am being critical, but that's not fair. I'm sure there are reasons why you did what you did that I probably just don't understand yet. Will you just talk to me about them?*

If Michael's defensiveness or dismissive attitude continues in spite of assuring him that you're trying to keep an open mind, and you're willing to try to understand and respect his feelings too, you'll need to move on to step #7 below and stand up firmly for yourself. But most of the time you'll likely find that if you avoid getting all indignant about his initial defensiveness and just assure him that you're trying to approach the conversation with an open mind, he'll become more cooperative.

6. Work with Me?	*With this step, you'll begin to implement both predictive habit #4 (Giving Equal Regard) and predictive habit #2 (Standing Up for Yourself Without Putting Your Partner Down).*

Dropping the idea that Michael is wrong doesn't mean that you have to give in. People who are destined to succeed in their relationships believe that their own opinions and expectations are just as important as their partners'. Rather than criticizing or trying to prove their partners wrong, people who are destined to succeed in their relationships simply ask their partners to "move over and make room for me." They ask their partners to meet them half way.

Ideally, when you and Michael have a difference of opinion, you'll refrain from assuming that you're right and he's wrong, keep an open mind, and become determined to understand his viewpoint or the logic behind his actions. If you do this, you might actually find that you agree with Michael. However, if you still feel differently, you'll need to explain the logic behind your feelings, too, and try to help him understand the underlying needs and/or worries that drive your feelings on the issue. In the end, however, the two of you may still have different feelings on the issue. People destined to succeed show regard for their partners feelings, and are willing to work toward solutions that take both of their feelings into account. They simply ask the same of their partners. When people stop criticizing their partners or trying to prove them wrong, and instead simply ask their partners to work toward a compromise, they usually find that their partners are willing.

If, after giving the benefit of the doubt, finding and acknowledging the understandable reasons for Michael's feelings, offering assurances and explaining why you feel the way you do, you find that you and Michael still disagree, try saying something like,

> ➢ *OK, I guess we feel differently about this. Will you work with me? Maybe we can figure out a way of doing things that takes both of our feelings into account.*

When, in spite of my good attitude, Michael disregards my viewpoint or criticizes me

The First Steps (described above) provide the soil from which increased respectfulness and cooperativeness from Michael will emerge. Many arguments can be avoided through the first steps alone. However, there are also times in the course of most relationships that further measures are necessary. Steps 7 and 8, and possibly steps 9-12 are needed in two situations:

A. **When Michael criticizes or attacks you.** When Michael is upset with you, he'll either complain to you, or criticize you. If he complains, he'll simply tell you he's upset or dissatisfied with something, and he'll probably also tell you why, and what he wants. If Michael criticizes you, he'll go beyond complaining and imply that your viewpoint or actions are *wrong*, and his are *right*, or he'll imply that you've behaved badly. As a general rule, when Michael is complaining, your most effective responses will always involve "The First Steps" (See workbook sheet titled, "The Sequence"). However, if Michael is criticizing you, "The First Steps" may actually be counterproductive. If Michael criticizes you, it will feel like an attack. He may seem disgusted, and show no interest in hearing your point of view. If you respond in an understanding way when Michael is in "attack mode," you'll make it more likely that he'll resort to attacking in the future when he gets upset with you. It does no good to persist in attempts to be reasonable with someone who isn't willing or able to be reasonable with you. When you feel attacked, skip over "The First Steps" temporarily and begin with step 7. Return to "The First Steps" only when Michael stops criticizing you and simply begins explaining why he's upset.

B. **When Michael disregards your viewpoint.** These are situations in which you avoid criticizing Michael and instead ask him to move over and make room for you, but he won't! In spite of your most sincere attempts to explain your point of view without criticism or contempt, recognize and acknowledge the reasonable part of Michael's argument, listen non-defensively, and assure him that you are not as rigid as you may seem on the issue, he isn't willing to give your feelings equal consideration.

7. Maintain Your Cool	*This step requires the implementation of predictive habit #1 (Avoiding a judgmental attitude), and confidence that you can*

| | eventually implement predictive habit #2 *(Standing Up for Yourself Without Putting Your Partner Down)* if necessary. |

If you're implementing this step, it's either because Michael is criticizing you, or because he continues to be unwilling to work with you in spite or your non-critical, cooperative attitude. A huge difference between those destined to succeed in their relationships and those destined to fail has to do with how indignant they get about their partner's objectionable behavior. People destined to succeed realize it's still too early to get all bent out of shape. They don't see their partner's temporary attack mode or stubbornness as a big crime, and hence, they don't make a federal case out of it. They realize that all of us can become uncooperative or disrespectful at times, and they know that just because their partners are treating them poorly in the moment doesn't mean that they'll continue to do so. They're confident that if their partners continue to disregard or criticize them, they'll stand up firmly for themselves in just a moment. But first, they'll make it as easy as possible for their partners to shift their attitudes. They do this by avoiding a judgmental attitude (predictive habit #1)

When it feels like Michael is attacking or disregarding you, try saying the following to yourself:

> ➢ *"It's no big deal that Michael is acting this way. It doesn't make him an awful person."* (It <u>will</u> be a big deal if he keeps on acting this way after I do the "Offer and Ask" thing in just a minute, but at this point, it's no big deal).
> ➢ *"Just because he's treating me bad right now doesn't mean that he'll continue to do so."*
> ➢ *"There's no rush. If he continues treating me poorly, I can stand up firmly for myself in a minute. But first I'll make it as easy as possible for him to change his attitude."*

| **8. Offer and Ask** | With this step, you'll implement several predictive habits at the same time. For example, it requires that you maintain a nonjudgmental attitude (predictive habit #1), begin standing up for yourself without putting your partner down (predictive habit #2), give equal regard (predictive habit #4), and offer assurance (predictive habit #5) |

In this step, you ask Michael to become more cooperative and assure him of your willingness to do the same. For example, if he's criticizing you, you might say something like,

> ➢ *"Hey, I'm willing to listen to you, but I'm having a hard time because it feels like you've already decided that I'm wrong. Could you slow down a bit and just tell me why you're upset?"*
> ➢ *"I'm sure that there are valid reasons why you're upset. I'm just having a hard time listening because I feel like you're starting with the assumption that I'm guilty before we even talk!"*

If Michael is putting you down, you might say something like,

> *Hey! You have my attention. You don't have to talk to me like that!*

If Michael is being stubborn or uncooperative in spite of your attempts to cooperate with him, you might say something like,

> *Hey, I'm trying to work with you here, but it feels like I'm not getting it back!*
> *Will you work with me?*

In the "offer and ask" step, you *offer* assurance (I'm willing to listen; I'm not saying that things have to be entirely my way; I'm not saying that I'm right and you're wrong; I care about how you feel too, and I'm willing to work with you, etc.), and you *ask* him to be willing to do the same (Will you work with me? Will you stop criticizing me and just tell me what's bothering you? etc.)

To be effective, the "offer and ask" step must be made calmly, but firmly. Usually, when people take this step, there's some frustration in their voices, but it's also clear that they're still able to be respectful. They make it clear that they're still willing to try to maintain a cooperative attitude, but only if their partners are ready to return cooperativeness. When implemented well, this step has the tone of a "friendly warning shot" fired into the air. It should have the effect of getting Michael's attention, but also making it clear that you're still willing to try to be understanding and work together. With it, you'll communicate something like, "You're beginning to piss me off, but I'll try to stay calm if you can just give me some indication that you're willing to work with me here!"

9. Stand Up/Engage	With this step, you continue to puts predictive habit #2 (Standing Up for Yourself Without Putting Your Partner Down) into action.

Once you've taken the "offer and ask" step, you'll often find that Michael shifts to a less critical or more cooperative attitude. If he does, simply return to "The First Steps" (e.g., explain your point of view without criticism or contempt, recognize and acknowledge the reasonable part of Michael's argument, listen non-defensively, and assure him that you are not as rigid as you may seem on the issue). However, it's possible that, in spite of your good attitude and assurances, Michael will continue to criticize you or refuse to recognize any validity in your feelings. If this is the case, you'll need to allow your anger to surface, and let him know in no uncertain terms that his attitude is not acceptable. If Michael is putting you down, you might say something like,

> *Who do you think you are -- talking to me like that?*
> *I don't care how valid your point is – I'm not going to put up with this crap!*

If Michael is refusing to recognize any validity in your viewpoint, you might say something like,

> *Look, I don't expect you to agree with me, but I do expect you to be willing to work with me. My viewpoint is just as valid as yours here. Who in the hell do you think you are?*

It's really important to note that successful partners "return hostile fire" only when their mates reject their "offer and ask" steps. Many people skip over "offer and ask," and immediately unleash their anger. **This is a huge mistake**. If you blast Michael every time he becomes critical or stubborn without "firing a warning shot," he'll feel unfairly assaulted by you, and he'll probably become even more uncooperative over time. On the other hand, if Michael rejects your good attitude and criticizes you or stubbornly refuses to "work with you," somewhere inside he'll know that your anger is justified, even if he can't recognize or admit it at the moment.

Some people find it confusing when their therapists encourage them to vent their anger at their partners. Don't relationships already have too much anger? Aren't we supposed to become less angry? Yes, too much anger is indeed toxic in relationships. If you become angry at Michael every time you don't like what he does, you'll not likely ever get the kind of understanding and respect from him that you'd like to have. However, there are also times when anger is not only justified -- it's necessary. If you avoid anger at moments that call for anger, your relationship will likely fail. So what is the difference between the moments when anger is needed and when it's counterproductive? The answer is relatively simple:

> *When you've made a good faith effort to assure Michael of your willingness to assume a cooperative attitude, and he just keeps on attacking you or is unwilling to give an inch, you need to get angry. **In most other situations**, your anger will probably do more harm than good.*

Often, we hear clients say that they won't engage in an angry exchange, because they don't want to "stoop" to their partner's level." They think of themselves as "better" in some sense than their partners. The problem is that this attitude (I'm more mature my partner) is the single most toxic thing to relationships identified by researchers thus far. Technically, it's a form of contempt. It's almost impossible for you to avoid contempt in the face of an attack, unless you become angry and defend yourself at the moment of the attack. We find that those who can angrily defend themselves are much more able to assume non-contemptuous attitudes in the aftermath of an attack than those who disengage when attacked. A bit of good old fashioned verbal scuffling is much less damaging than refusing to fight and then looking down on your partner. If you become silent and "stonewall" when you feel criticized or disregarded by Michael, he'll likely hear you saying, "I'm not even going to waste my time trying to talk with you. You are too disgusting or scary or irrational to even deal with."

Relationships that have been stuck for years in an attack/withdraw pattern change dramatically when typically withdrawing partners develop the ability to square off with their mates, provided that they can avoid making a big deal out of how awful their partners are for "picking fights" (see step #11 below).

10. Reject Michael	With this step, you take predictive habit #2 (Standing Up for Yourself Without Putting Your Partner Down) to its most forceful level.

If the anger you unleash has been preceded by good-faith efforts on your part, it may have the effect of "snapping Michael out of it." He may get a grip and begin working more cooperatively with you. However, he might not. He might respond with his own anger. If he does, don't back down. Engage in a heated exchange for a while. Demand to know why on earth he thinks that he could possibly be smarter or better than you. Make it clear that his know-it-all attitude infuriates you. The most effective people in relationships are no more afraid of relationship discord than their partners are, and are able to "pitch a fit" when the situation calls for it. When faced with an attack from Michael, the most effective response is to 1) assure him that you're willing to listen, 2) ask him to stop attacking you, 3) "let him have it" if he continues to attack or disrespect your feelings, 4), refrain from making a big deal of his offensive behavior, and 5) be willing to talk about the subject you were fighting about again with an open mind.

At any point, if his attitude softens even a little, return to the "First Steps." However, if 5 minutes of heated arguing result in no change in his attitude, you'll probably need to say something to him like,

"You know what? I don't even want to be near you right now."
"Get away from me!"

If he won't get away from you, get away from him! Go to another part of the house. Leave temporarily. Remember, rejecting your partner is a strong and provocative move, and should be reserved only for situations in which Michael continues to attack or utterly disregard your feelings in spite of your efforts to collaborate.

11. Don't Make a Big Deal of It	This step requires a strong ability to implement predictive habit #1: Avoiding a Judgmental Attitude.

If you've progressed all the way through step #10, you're pretty angry. Now it's time to calm down. People destined to succeed become angry and stand up firmly for themselves, then they let it go. They don't make a fuss about the fact that they had to stand up. To them, it's not the end of the world when their partners act in ways that required them to get angry and growl back. "Standing up" is all in a day's work. In contrast, in the aftermath of an argument people destined to fail become consumed with thoughts like, "He is a monster!" He's the most selfish person in the world!" He's a control freak!" "He's verbally abusive!"

After a situation in which you got angry and stood up for yourself, try adopting the attitude reflected in the following thoughts:

> ➤ *"It's not a crime that I had to stand up and put him in his place. It doesn't make him a bad person."*
> ➤ *"It's natural enough for him to want to have his own way. I don't blame him."*
> ➤ *"It doesn't have to be a big deal. He stepped over the line – I let him have it. No biggie. I'll do it again if necessary!"*
> ➤ *"He probably only does this as often as he does because I haven't known how to stand up for*

myself without making a big deal of it in the past."	
12. Try again, later.	This step draws most heavily on predictive habits # 1, 4 and 5 ("Avoiding a Judgmental Attitude," "Giving Equal Regard" and "Offering Assurances")

Just because you don't make a big deal of Michael's offensive behavior doesn't mean that you're going to just forget about it and move on. Nope. The issue didn't get resolved. People who succeed in their relationships don't settle for situations in which they don't feel that their feelings are given equal consideration. You'll need to approach Michael again, but do it in a good way. Don't demand an apology. Don't get him to see how awful his offensive behavior was. Instead, just ask him to talk to you about the subject again. Be willing to compromise and ask Michael to do the same.

Often, attempts to re-process arguments get off track because couples end up arguing about how they argued the first time (e.g., "You had no right to talk to me like that!" "You implied that my viewpoint was stupid!" etc). Resist the temptation to do this. Instead, go back to the issue you were arguing about, and try to talk about it again. Use the "First Steps" (explain your point of view without criticism or contempt, recognize and acknowledge the reasonable part of Michael's argument, listen non-defensively, and assure him that you are not as rigid as you may seem on the issue). If Michael reacts defensively, offer assurances. If he continues to be defensive or critical, maintain your cool and go to the "Offer and Ask" step. If necessary, get angry and stand up for yourself all over again, then refrain from making a big deal of it. Try again later. Be willing to go through the whole process as many times as may be necessary. If you develop the ability to stay with this process, Michael will become more understanding and cooperative over time.

Guidelines for Implementing The Sequence:

1. Start with *The First Steps* (1 - 6), and go to steps 7-12 only if Michael disregards or criticizes you.
2. *The First Steps* need not be implemented strictly in the sequence suggested in the chart. However, the suggested sequence is highly effective and a good plan to begin with.
3. If Michael criticizes or dismisses your viewpoint, do not continue with *The First Steps.* Instead, go directly to steps 7 and 8 ("Maintain your cool," and "Offer and Ask"). If Michael still continues to dismiss or criticize you, proceed to steps 9 and 10 ("Stand Up/Engage" and "Reject your Partner").
4. Whenever Michael stops criticizing or dismissing you, return immediately to The *First Steps.*
5. While Steps 9 and 10 ("Stand Up/Engage" and "Reject your Partner") are absolutely essential in situations where, in spite of your good attitude, Michael continues to disregard or criticize you, they can cause more harm than good unless they are followed by steps 11 and 12 ("Don't Make a Big Deal of It" and "Try Again, Later"). *Whenever you implement steps 9 and 10, be sure that you follow through with 11 and 12.*

Developing Non-Judgmental Explanations for Michael's Attitude or Actions

This section will help you with habit 1 (Avoiding a Judgmental Attitude)

If you have thoughts about your partner like the one's listed in the "Attitude Check" sheet on enough occasions, you may begin thinking of Michael's personality in globally negative ways. For example, you may begin thinking things like, "Michael is just a lazy person," or "he's just plain inconsiderate, selfish, controlling, negative, critical," etc. These kind of global negative thoughts about one's partner are the kiss of death to relationships. If you begin thinking about Michael in this way, you'll bring out the absolute worst in him. He'll feel like you've lost faith in him, and that you're no longer on the same team. In fact, you'll have positioned yourself as the enemy.

If you hold negative explanations for Michael's actions, it's probably not because you deliberately set out to think of him this way. It's likely that you have come by these negative explanations honestly. To you, it may simply seem like the facts. Regardless of whether you've begun thinking of Michael in global negative terms or you just find yourself thinking negatively about him on specific occasions, the pathway to getting more respect and understanding from him involves finding a way to lose the judgmental or superior attitude, while standing up for yourself at the same time. There are three ways you can do this. First, you can find the legitimate motivations that drive Michael's upsetting behavior. Second, you can recognize ways in which it's likely that your own attitude and actions have unintentionally fueled the very attitude and actions in Michael that you have found upsetting. Third, you can see that your own contributions to your relationship problems have been as serious as Michael's.

Find the legitimate motivations that drive Michael's thinking or actions.

If you're open to finding them, there are always legitimate motivations that drive Michael's attitudes or actions, even if you don't feel it justifies his actions. You may be reluctant to try to find and acknowledge these motivations, because you're afraid that it will fuel Michael's tendency to think he's right and you're wrong. But the evidence from relationship studies contradicts this assumption. It's the inability or unwillingness to acknowledge the legitimate priorities or motivations of one's partner that fuels defensiveness and stubbornness. People who are most successful in relationships know that if they assume the worst of their partners, they'll get the worst. Instead, they find and acknowledge the legitimate priorities and motivations that drive their partner's attitudes and actions, *and they also stand up for their own.* Influential people in relationships combine a generous attitude toward their partners with an unwillingness to allow their own feelings or priorities to be dismissed. Successful people require that their feelings and opinions be given equal consideration, and they make it very easy for their partners to do so. How? By assuming the best of their partners.

1. **Beneath Michael's seemingly inexplicable or provocative behavior, there's something legitimate that he's going after.** There's something bigger at stake for Michael than is immediately apparent. There's a legitimate need, dream or priority that Michael is trying to preserve or obtain. This need, priority or dream is probably one that isn't as important to you, but that doesn't make it wrong or misguided.

2. **Michael's actions are crucial to his way of feeling stable.** Michael has a different way of coping in life than you do. For example, some people feel better when they operate more independently while others feel better working as a team; some feel better with a work first/play later approach while others feel better if they play along the way; some feel better when life is orderly and predictable, while others feel stifled or suffocated by the same conditions (see the workbook sheet, "Core Differences in Ways of Maintaining Emotional Stability"). Maybe Michael's seemingly provocative or inexplicable behavior is related to one of these legitimate differences that the two of you have.

Recognize the ways that you have unintentionally fueled Michael's upsetting attitude or actions. People who are most successful in influencing their partners recognize that their own shortcomings are as serious as those of their partners. In fact, their own shortcomings often *fuel* those of their partners. Michael's attitude or actions may be part of a vicious circle in which he is reacting to the worst in you as much as you react to the worst in him.

3. **Michael's attitude or actions are partly a reaction to feeling dismissed or "written off" by you.** Has Michael's attitude or actions gotten worse over time? If so, it's likely because he feels that you've "turned" on him and "joined the other team." He knows that you've written him off as hopeless in some ways, and this has made his reactions to you more extreme or provocative. When people get branded by their partners as hopeless, it's almost impossible for them to change, because doing so would feel like admitting that their partners were "right" and they were "wrong" all along.

4. **Michael's attitude or actions are partly due to your inability to stand up for yourself without putting him down.** When people who are destined for relationship success feel mistreated or misunderstood by their partners, they stand up firmly for themselves *without making a big deal of their partner's selfish or controlling attitude*. Evidence from relationship studies suggests that if you don't have this ability, it's unlikely that your relationship will succeed, regardless of who your partner is. This ability has two parts: 1) You must be willing to stand firm and refuse to allow yourself to be disregarded or taken advantage of, and 2) You must be able to do this without making a big deal of how seemingly bad your partner is behaving. This two-part ability is every bit as necessary for relationship success as is the ability to refrain from being selfish or controlling. Chances are that if you had enough of this ability, you'd be getting much more cooperation and or understanding from Michael by now. Before you conclude that Michael's attitude or actions are due to inherent personality flaws, consider that they persist at least partly because he's in a relationship with someone who hasn't developed sufficient ability to stand up for herself without putting him down.

5. **Michael's attitude or actions are partly due to his feeling that you just don't like him very much lately (or his feeling that you don't care about his feelings).**
   If you have become at least somewhat emotionally distant or emotionally reserved toward Michael, he may not feel the kind of tender and connected feelings from you that are normally needed to nourish relationships. His uncooperative or critical attitude may be at least partly due to feeling that you don't like him very much.

Recognize that your own transgressions have been just as detrimental to the relationship as Michael's.

6. **Some of Michael's actions may have been wrong, but no more wrong than some of your own.**
   You may be ranking Michael's transgressions as more serious than your own, particularly if they are more blatant or provocative than your own. But relationship studies suggest that many subtle, non-provocative habits can undermine relationships just as surely as the more blatant ones.

Remember, just because you recognize that your shortcomings may contribute to your relationship problems just as much as Michael's doesn't mean that you must accept his attitude or actions. It just means that you don't have grounds to feel superior, and that he has just as much right to ask you to change as you do to ask him. In the best relationships, partners avoid assuming judgmental attitudes, and instead of criticizing each other, they respect their differences and work toward compromises that take both of their values, priorities or preferences into account.

APPENDIX I

Attitude Check

This page and the next will help you with Step 2 (Giving the Benefit of the Doubt) of *The Sequence*

The attitude that breeds defensiveness and predicts bad things in relationships is *critical*. It happens each time you think something about Michael like "He shouldn't do that." "That's inappropriate (or shortsighted, selfish, controlling, etc.). It's entirely possible to have an "I didn't like that" attitude without the "You shouldn't have done that" attitude, and that's exactly what people do who are most successful in relationships. They know how to stand up for themselves without putting others down. The first step toward being able to do this is to get real honest with yourself about the "put-downs" that automatically arise in your head when Michael does or says something you don't like. Think about the thing you are upset with Michael about right now. Complete one of the following sentences by circling which of the eight descriptions of Michael (below) seem fitting.

"What Michael did was…"
or
"The way Michael was thinking was…"

Selfish / Inconsiderate	Foolish / Misguided	Over-Reacting	Judgmental	Manipulative / Deceptive	Controlling	Defensive	Unfeeling
He acted this way because he is so	□ "I can't believe he can't see how stupid (short-sighted, self-defeating) that was!"	□ "I can't believe how upset he's getting over such a small thing!"	□ "He is so arrogant!"	□ "He is just mean!"	□ He won't be satisfied unless he has his own way.	□ "There's no talking to him!"	□ "I could be sitting over here devastated, and he wouldn't even care."
□ Lazy			□ "What's the point in even talking to	□ "This man is a sociopath!"	□ What's the point in even talking to him?	□ "Why do I even bother? He can't ever admit that he's wrong!"	□ "I feel all the pain, and he feels nothing."
□ Irresponsible	□ "How could he possibly think that way?"	□ "He blows everything out of proportion!"	somebody who thinks he knows everything?"	□ "He has no conscience!"	He's already got his mind made	□ "He is incapable of apologizing!"	□ "He's incapable of feeling bad about hurting me."
□ Undisciplined	□ "That's irrational!"	□ "Does everything have to be such a stinking ordeal?"	□ "He always finds a way to turn things around to look like I'm in the wrong"	□ "He is a cold-hearted, calculating manipulator!"	up.	□ "He's got a rationalization for everything	
□ Insensitive	□ "I'm in a relationship with someone who can't think things through!"	□ "I can't believe that, after all the things I do well, he chooses the one thing I don't and obsesses about it."			□ "He's just a control freak!"	□ "He doesn't even care what the truth is. He has already decided that!"	
□ Inconsiderate			□ "He thinks he's better (smarter) than everybody else!"		□ "He never considers asking me what I'd like. He just plows ahead and makes decisions."		
□ Selfish	□ "He is so shallow!"	□ "He is just a negative person!"	□ "Everything is black and white for him!"				
□ "I would never do that!"	□ "He can't see the bigger picture!"	□ He's not satisfied unless he has something to be upset about!"					
□ "He is incapable of thinking about anyone but himself!"							
□ "He always has to do things his way."							

Core Differences in Ways of Maintaining Emotional Stability

Legitimately Different Ways of Navigating Life

		Independence-First	Togetherness First
1 Independence vs. Togetherness		➢ Often prefer to engage in activities and tasks independently ➢ Each partner mostly assumes responsibility for meeting their own needs and completing their own tasks. ➢ Rather than assuming responsibility for anticipating each other's needs, each partner expects the other to speak up when they need something. ***Dream:*** Not having to worry about inadvertently hurting someone by one's inattentiveness. Not being responsible for someone else's happiness. ***Fear of Accepting Influence:*** I'll spend my whole life meeting my partner's needs, and I'll be neglected. ***Critical Stance:*** You want me to read your mind! You expect too much! You're too needy! You want me to do things for you that you're perfectly capable of doing for yourself!	➢ Often prefer to engage in activities and tasks together. ➢ Each partner counts on help from the other in completing tasks or shouldering burdens. ➢ Each partner anticipates the needs of the other, and attempts to meet them without having to be asked. ***Dream:*** That my partner would take my feelings into consideration without my demanding it. A feeling of companionship. Never having to be alone. ***Fear of Accepting Influence:*** I'll feel like I'm in this world alone. There will be nobody looking out for me but myself. I've got no backup. I'm on my own. ***Critical Stance:*** You live in your own little world! You're self-centered (or selfish)! Any moron would have realized that I needed help. I shouldn't have to ask!
		Invest in the Future First	**Live for the Moment First**
2 Present vs. Future Orientation		Delay gratification. Work first, then play. ***Dream:*** To share a secure future together. ***Fear of Accepting Influence:*** If we goof around along the way, we may invest inadequately in our future happiness. ***Critical Stance:*** You're lazy! You're irresponsible! You're like a child who has to have everything right now!	Invest in the future, but not at the expense of enjoying the present ***Dream:*** To have a life where you enjoy each moment. ***Fear of Accepting Influence:*** Life will be a continual chore. What's the point, if you don't enjoy it along the way? There will always be more work... enjoyment will fade. ***Critical Stance:*** You're anal, neurotic, anxious, etc.
		Predictability First	**Spontaneity First**
3 Degree of Structure		Seek security, predictability and order first, then feel safe to experiment within the safe parameters. ***Dream:*** To have a safety net so that life feels more stable, less anxiety-provoking. ***Fear of Accepting Influence:*** If you don't plan it, it might not happen. Life will be out of control. ***Critical Stance:*** You're reckless!	Seek adventure, creativity, open-endedness first; the rest will fall into place. Be more structured only if a more spontaneous approach fails. ***Dream:*** To avoid boredom. Life as an adventure! ***Fear of Accepting Influence:*** Slowly dying of boredom. Life will be dull and meaningless. ***Critical Stance:*** You're boring! You're a coward!
		Slow to Upset	**Readily Upset**
4 First Reaction to Things You Don't Like		Getting upset doesn't help anything. Don't make a big deal of things. It's not the end of the world if everything doesn't go the way you wanted it to. ***Dream:*** To have a partner who doesn't freak out when I fail to meet his/her expectations. ***Fear of Accepting Influence:*** That life will become a never-ending series of things to be upset about. ***Critical Stance:*** You are never satisfied! You're a negative person. You're not happy unless you have something to be upset about!	It's normal to feel upset when something seems wrong, deficient or less than it should be. If nobody gets upset, nothing ever changes. ***Dream:*** To have a partner who understands that there's nothing wrong with getting upset if something bothers you. ***Fear of Accepting Influence:*** That I'll go through stifling my feelings. I'll feel like a Stepford wife, or hen-pecked husband. ***Critical Stance:*** You're a fake. Underneath it all, you get just as upset as I do. You're just afraid of a little conflict! You're a wimp!
		Problem Solving First	**Understanding First**
5 Resolving Upset Feelings		Feel better by doing something about the upsetting situation. Solve the problem or make a plan and you'll feel better. ***Dream:*** To have a partner who lets by-gones be by-gones --who has a positive attitude toward life. ***Fear of Accepting Influence:*** I don't want to "fuel the fire" by giving his negative feelings too much attention. ***Critical Stance:*** You're a hopelessly negative person, a whiner, a victim. Stop feeling sorry for yourself and get over it. Either do something about it or get over it!	Feel better by feeling understood. ***Dream:*** For someone to understand what its like to be me. To avoid loneliness ***Fear of Accepting Influence:*** If you let go of upset feelings before feeling understood, you will never feel understood. You'll just fix things on the surface. ***Critical Stance:*** You could care less about how I feel. You just want to pretend the whole thing never happened!

Standing Up For Yourself Without Putting Your Partner Down

This page will help you with steps 7-12 of *The Sequence*

People who get respect and cooperation from their partners realize that the extent to which they stand up effectively for themselves and the extent to which their partners feel put down by them are two independent things. These people have the ability to stand up for themselves without feeling critical of their partners. (See the shaded quadrant below).

Did You Stand Up For Yourself?

(Did you require that your feelings or expectations be given as much consideration as Michael's?)

	Yes, I Stood Up for Myself	No, I didn't Stand Up for Myself
YES, I felt critical	***Critical, Standing Up*** ➢ You stood up for yourself, but Michael felt put down by you. ➢ Although you didn't let Michael "win," you made it almost impossible for him to truly respect your feelings and expectations. If Michael feels you putting yourself on a higher plane, he won't respect you in the long run. ➢ Even if Michael "gave in," he is probably feeling resentful toward you, and will try to "make things even" before long. ➢ You were on the right track by attempting to stand up for yourself, but you traded the more lasting satisfaction of increased respect and cooperation from Michael for the more immediate satisfaction of trying to prove him wrong.	***Critical, Not Standing Up*** ➢ You felt disapproving, disgusted or resentful, but didn't believe that it would get you anywhere to try to require equal consideration. It wasn't worth the hassle. ➢ Michael felt put down by you even though you "gave in." ➢ Michael didn't feel grateful for you "giving in." In fact, he may still be angry with you, and even less likely to respect your feelings and opinions in the future. ➢ You have probably begun to distance yourself emotionally from Michael. Unfortunately, this makes it even less likely that he will treat you with more respect in the future.
No, I didn't feel critical	***Not Critical, Standing Up*** ➢ You stood up for yourself without putting Michael down. ➢ You both required that Michael give your feelings equal consideration and made it easy for him to do so. ➢ You minimized Michael's defensiveness. ➢ You reacted like someone who stands a very good chance of getting more respect and cooperation in the future, even if you didn't this time. ➢ Michael may be upset that he didn't get his way, but he feels respected by you, and beneath his anger, he also respects you.	***Not Critical, Not Standing Up*** ➢ You didn't require equal consideration, but you didn't feel upset about it. ➢ You may not have felt that you deserved to be given equal consideration, or if you did deserve it, it wasn't going to happen and it wasn't worth feeling upset about. ➢ Without meaning to, you encouraged Michael to disrespect you. ➢ You may try to ignore or distract yourself from the fact that Michael isn't willing to value your feelings and opinions equally.

Did You Feel Critical of Michael?

(Did you feel disapproving, disgusted or resentful toward Michael, or think "put-downs" about him in your head?)

When My Partner is Clearly Wrong

There may be times when Michael's behavior is so provocative or extreme that it is very difficult to look at it any other way than, "It's just plain wrong!" Examples include if he were to lie to you, cheat on you, or physically restrain or harm you (or threaten to). People who are destined to be treated better in the future respond very differently in these situations than people who are destined to be treated poorly over and over again. In a nutshell, people who are destined to succeed find a way to stand up for themselves without getting stuck in an attitude of superiority. If you communicate disgust or contempt for Michael when you stand up to him, it is unlikely that he will treat you better in the future. If you are feeling indignant or superior, you will cancel out the positive impact that your assertiveness would have had.

How can you avoiding feeling disgusted, indignant or superior if Michael acts in ways that are clearly wrong? Few people can avoid these feelings at such moments. Fortunately, what you do in the minutes and hours following Michael's objectionable words or actions is more important than your immediate reaction. People who are destined to be treated better may react immediately with disgust, but they avoid fueling their feelings of disgust or superiority in the minutes and hours that follow. In fact, they often think of things that help them shift out of these feelings. Examples of such thoughts are:

"My partner is clearly out of line here, and I need to make it clear that this is unacceptable but…"
➤ Even though it doesn't excuse his actions, there are probably reasons why he acted this way that will make it more understandable to me once I know what they are.
➤ I've done plenty of things that were wrong in the past, too. I'm not in a position to act all high and mighty.
➤ "Just because I try to avoid getting on my high horse doesn't mean that I should excuse Michael's behavior, it just means that I don't need to get all superior about it. I just need to make it clear that I won't tolerate it any more than Michael should tolerate me if I get out of line." I need to stand up for myself without making a big deal out of how wrong he is."

One of the most common mistakes that partners who are mistreated make is trying over and over again to explain how "wrong" it was for their partner to treat them that way. Such explaining is self-defeating for two reasons: First, it often substitutes for what really needs to happen… action. Actions speak louder than words. When your partner is doing something wrong, he probably already knows it, but doesn't care. Rather than trying to explain how awful it is, just tell him to stop it! The second reason why explanations are usually self-defeating is that it's almost impossible to point out how wrong your partner is without assuming a superior attitude. Michael won't be able to keep an open mind if he hears a morally superior tone from you.

The refusal to have a "high horse" attitude doesn't lessen the determination that successful people have to stand up for themselves. In fact, the combination of the right action (standing up for yourself) and the right attitude (not making a big deal of how wrong your partner is) is necessary for lasting change to occur. Once the right action and attitude are in place, you will likely find that Michael will become more respectful. As this happens, you will need to try to understand why he treated you poorly in the first place, and assure him that you are willing to work with him to find mutually acceptable solutions. You'll also need to try to explain to Michael your own feelings about the issue(s) over which he became upset. However, your willingness to discuss issues should come only after more respectful treatment from Michael.

Taking a Firm Stand

Most of the time, individuals who develop the ability to do things predictive of success during or after arguments find that their partners become more cooperative and willing to listen. There may come a time, however, when in spite of your most sincere attempts (on many occasions) to interact with your partner with a good attitude (as summarized in the first steps of your workbook sheet, The Sequence"), and respond to your partner's continuing dismissals or criticism by standing up for yourself effectively (as in the bottom section of The Sequence), your partner refuses to work collaboratively with you. In such a situation, you may need to take "standing up for yourself" to another level. You may need to "draw a line in the sand," and refuse to continue "business as usual." This involves taking action on your own behalf to make sure that you do not continue to be taken advantage of or disrespected. If you are able to do this without getting stuck feeling disgusted toward your partner, the odds are good that he will eventually become more cooperative or respectful. Because implementing this skill generally involves doing something that your partner will find upsetting, there is a risk of an escalation when you apply it. For this reason, we strongly recommend that you seek the support and advice of your therapist if you attempt to implement it.

Focusing on what you need to do to be OK rather than focusing on what your partner should be doing (or trying to figure out what's wrong with him)

This skill involves a significant shift in attention. Rather than focusing on (and talking about) what *your partner* is doing that is unfair or selfish, this way involves focusing on what *you* need to do to make sure you do not continue to be mistreated. Rather than ruminating about what your partner should be doing, or trying to figure out why your partner is so clueless, or thinking about how unfair it is that you have to put up with this, you focus on "cutting your loses" and taking action on your own behalf.

Acting <u>for</u> Yourself (rather than <u>against</u> your partner)

Acting for yourself involves regulating your participation and cooperation with your partner, rather than trying to regulate how your partner participates and cooperates with you. Rather than putting your partner down, you simply tell him what you will and will not do. The key word is *action*. Acting for yourself means being willing to withdraw your participation when, after your best attempts to create a respectful dialogue with your partner, you still don't feel you are being treated with respect. People who develop the ability to act for themselves do not walk around issuing ultimatums to their partners, cutting themselves off when their partners don't see things their way. In fact, they explore all possible avenues for mutual understanding and cooperation first, drawing a bottom line only when all else has failed. When they take a stand, it is usually with an attitude of resignation rather than intense anger.

When should I take a firm stand?

First of all, be sure that you have exhausted all other avenues. Have you implemented *The Sequence* summarized earlier in your workbook (including all 12 steps, if necessary) on many previous occasions? Does your therapist agree that you have? If your therapist agrees that you have, and your partner still continues to be unwilling to work with you toward mutually acceptable resolutions to your differences, then you should consider taking a firm stand.

If I need to, how should I take a firm stand?

The best way of withdrawing cooperation will vary from situation to situation, and you should work closely with your therapist in developing a plan for your situation. The degree of withdrawal may vary from situation to situation in terms of "how much" and "how long." In one situation, it might involve just refusing to do things you normally do for your partner. In a more serious situation, it might involve separating from your partner until he decides to get some assistance to change abusive or addictive behavior. Those who are most successful in eventually getting cooperation from their formerly non-cooperative partners share one characteristic: They draw the line with their partners without criticizing, blaming, judging, or putting them down. They avoid implying that they know what their partners should or shouldn't be doing, they just state clearly what is and isn't OK with them.

After a period of withdrawal, try another attempt to explain your point of view without criticism or contempt, recognize and acknowledge the reasonable part of your partner's argument, listen non-defensively, and assure your partner that you are not as rigid as you may seem on the issue. Sometimes stating your intent to withdraw, particularly if it is made in a non-critical, non-blaming way, will trigger a shift in your partner toward more willingness to listen and cooperate, and actual withdrawal may not be necessary. However, if you are withdrawing in an attempt to change your partner (rather than preventing yourself from being taken advantage of), it will most likely fail. In these situations one of life's most profound paradoxes can be seen: Those individuals who genuinely stop trying to get their partners to "see the error of their ways" (and instead focus on changing their own reactions) most often end up with partners who "see the error of their ways."

"Taking a Firm Stand" is a serious move in a relationship, and should be done only with careful planning and consideration, only as a last resort, <u>and should be done in consultation with your therapist</u>. If this move is not implemented skillfully, it will likely result in a worsening of your situation. However, taking a firm stand may be necessary for you to increase the possibility that your partner will treat you with more respect. When attempting to take a firm stand, there are so many ways to get "off-track," that it's always good to have the consultation and support of your therapist as you engage in this process.

When I'm Upset

What am I upset about?	
Date and Time of attempt to shift	

Quick Shift?

1. **Assure Yourself**.
   Remind yourself that it's in your <u>own best interest</u> to change your usual reactions. If you can change your reactions in situations like these, Michael will become more understanding and cooperative.
2. **Shift**: Relax and see if you can shift to a calmer place inside.
3. **Imagine...**
   Now ask yourself:
   1. Can I keep an open mind and look for the at-least partly-legitimate reasons behind Michael's actions or opinions?
   2. Can I let go of my agenda and just listen for a few moments?
4. **If some part of you resists doing these things, proceed to step five below.** If you feel ready to give it a try, review "The First Steps" of The Sequence, then talk to Michael.

When Quick Shifting Doesn't Work

5. **Let it be**. Stop trying to get the feeling to change. Instead, try to just let it occupy your body for a few moments, while you try to listen to it. Sit down somewhere. Try to get into a position to allow your body to relax so that you can sense what you are feeling.

6. **Why not?** Ask this part of you, "Why don't you want to shift?" "What would be bad about getting into a frame of mind that would allow you to
   - keep an open mind and look for the at-least partly-legitimate reasons behind Michael's actions or opinions?
   - let go of your agenda and just listen for a few moments?

   Listen to this part of you for a while, then write down the answer that comes to you.

7. **What's driving me?** Ask this part of you, "What underlying need, fear or priority is driving your feelings or actions in this situation? " Listen to this part of you for a while, then write down the answer that comes to you.

8. What assurances can you offer to this part of yourself?

Check again and see if you can imagine yourself giving Michael the benefit of the doubt, and becoming determined to find and acknowledge the understandable logic behind his words or actions. If you feel ready to give it a try, review the "The First Steps" of The Sequence, then talk to Michael.

9. If some part of you still resists, refrain from talking to your partner about the upsetting issue until your next therapy session.

Knowing Michael's Internal World (Part 1)

This exercise will help you with habit 7, Curiosity About Your Partner's World

Studies suggest that a significant difference between couples destined to succeed versus those destined for failure is how much they know about each other's worlds. To build or refresh your knowledge of each other, take one question at a time. Take a guess at the answer. Don't feel bad if your guess is off the mark... just ask Michael to fill you in. Use each question as a springboard to find out more information about each other. Don't stop once you confirm the answer. Try to guess *why* Michael answered as he did, or ask him.

	Use each question as a springboard to find out more information about each other...
Monday	What is Michael looking forward to the most in the next week? Why?
Tuesday	What has Michael done that he is most proud of lately? Why?
Wednesday	What one thing would Michael like to accomplish most this year? Why?
Thursday	If Michael had more free time, how would he want to use it? Why?
Friday	What has been most disappointing to Michael lately? Why?
Saturday	What possession does Michael most wish he could afford to have? Why?
Sunday	What is one talent that Michael wishes he had more of? Why?

	Use each question as a springboard to find out more information about each other...
Monday	When would Michael say he made the biggest error in the judgment of character? Why?
Tuesday	What is at the top of Michael's wish list for home improvement? Why?
Wednesday	What has Michael been most upset at his parents about? Why?
Thursday	The last time Michael was feeling down, what kinds of things did he say to himself to feel better?
Friday	What compliment has Michael received from a person other than yourself in the past? What was Michael's reaction to the compliment?
Saturday	If Michael could follow his heart right now and do one thing he otherwise wouldn't, what would it be?
Sunday	How would Michael change his job if he were able to make it "ideal." Why?

What's on Michael's Mind?

This exercise will help you with habit 7, Curiosity About Your Partner's World

Studies suggest that a significant difference between couples destined to succeed versus those destined for failure is how much they know about each other's worlds. Do you know the things that are weighing the heaviest on Michael's mind these days? What keeps his from feeling totally carefree? Each day during the next week, set aside a few moments to ask him what three concerns are weighing heaviest on his mind. Encourage him to tell you his thoughts and feelings about these things. Each day, see if he can tell you on a scale of 1 – 10 how stressed he is about each of his concerns. Do his most pressing concerns vary from day to day, or do the same issues tend to weigh on his mind?

Week of _____

How stressed is Michael about this?
1= just a little   10 = totally stressed

The Things that Weigh Heaviest on Michael's Mind	MON	TUE	WED	THU	FRI	SAT	SUN

APPENDIX Q

Appreciations

This exercise will help you with habit 8, Keeping Sight of the Positive, p. 10.

Research studies confirm that one difference between relationships that succeed and relationships that fail is that, in relationships destined for success, partners notice and acknowledge the small, positive things that happen. One powerful way you can improve your relationship that costs you very little is to simply notice the positive things that are already happening. It could be something as small as a kind word or non-verbal gesture. Every day during the next week, make it a point to notice the small, positive things that happen. Then, cut or rip off the section of this paper for that day and slip it to Michael to read sometime.

Day of Week	What is one thing Michael did (or said) yesterday that I appreciated?
Today is _____	
Today is _____	
Today is _____	
Today is _____	
Today is _____	
Today is _____	
Today is _____	

Extra-Positive Moments

This exercise will help you with habit 8, Keeping Sight of the Positive

Another powerful way you can improve your relationship that costs you very little is to simply notice the positive things that are already happening. It could be something as small as a kind word or non-verbal gesture. Every day during the next week, make it a point to notice the small, positive things that happen. Then, cut or rip off the section of this paper for that day and slip it to Michael to read sometime.

Day of Week	Think back over the last the day or two and ask yourself, "When was a moment or moments when I felt the most extra-positive about Michael or about our relationship' Take a minute to remember the details. Write about it briefly.
Today is _____	
Today is _____	
Today is _____	
Today is _____	
Today is _____	
Today is _____	
Today is _____	

Small Acts of Caring

This exercise will help you with predictive habit 9, Making and Responding to Bids for Connection,

Research studies suggest that partners who initiate small acts of caring or connection, delivered without strings attached, are much more likely to end up in happy relationships than partners who neglect such small acts. When intimate partners are upset with one another, they often neglect to initiate these small acts. This is self-defeating, because research studies show that you can dramatically increase the odds that Michael will treat you well if he feels cared about. Because you may be upset with each other, initiating small acts of caring may not come naturally. If you wait until the urge hits you spontaneously, you may initiate very few such acts. The following chart is to help you plan to initiate small acts of caring for Michael. Plan a week in advance. Then, when the day comes, see if you can get yourself into a mood to initiate these acts because of the sense of being cared for that they will bring Michael. Remember, no strings attached. Even if Michael doesn't seem to initiate small caring acts in return, try to not worry. You are now doing a behavior that is strongly predictive of marital success. If you are able to continue, the odds are simply much greater that, in time, you will feel cared for by Michael, too.

Examples of small acts of caring: Something you can do to make Michael's load a little lighter; something you can improve around the house that Michael would appreciate; take initiative to plan something for the two of you; spend time thinking about or learning something about something important to Michael; notice something in your day that you know Michael would be interested in, then remember to tell Michael about it; remember to ask Michael about something specific that you know will be happening in Michael's day; ask Michael to do something with you (bike ride, walk, watch a TV show, etc.); take responsibility for making (or ordering) food for Michael; buy Michael a small something that you know he would like.

	Small acts of caring I can easily do for Michael
Monday	
Tuesday	
Wednesday	
Thursday	
Friday	
Saturday	
Sunday	

High-Low Review

Your Experience Speaking

Tell Michael about the high and low points of your day – when you felt the best and the worst. Later, by yourself, please complete this form.

Name:	Date:

What was high and low point?

How interested did Michael seem in what you were saying?

1 2 3 4 5 6 7 8 9 10
Not interested   Totally
at all   Interested

What do you think kept Michael from being more interested?

How excited or sympathetic did Michael seem?

1 2 3 4 5 6 7 8 9 10
None at All   A Lot

What do you think kept Michael from being more sympathetic or excited?

How much did you really cut loose and talk about your high and low points in detail, with feeling?

1 2 3 4 5 6 7 8 9 10
Not much   Totally

What do you think kept you from cutting loose more and talking about your high and low points in more detail, or with more feeling?

High-Low Review

Your Experience Listening

Ask Michael to sit down and tell you what it was like to be him today. Ask what was the high and low points of the day, when he felt the best and the worst. Later, by yourself, please complete this form.

Name:	Date:
What was the topic that Michael talked about?	

How interested were you in what he was saying?

```
      1   2   3   4   5   6   7   8   9   10
      Not interested                    Totally
      at all                          Interested
```

Why do you think you weren't more interested?

How much sympathy or excitement did you feel for Michael when he was describing the high and low points?

```
           1   2   3   4   5   6   7   8   9   10
           None at All                      A Lot
```

Why do you think you didn't feel more sympathy or excitement?

References

Adolphs, R., Tranel, D., Damasio, H., & Damasio, A. R. (1994). Impaired recognition of emotion in facial expressions following bilateral damage to the human amygdala. *Nature, 22,* 669–672.

Adolphs, R., Tranel, D., Damasio, H., & Damasio, A. R. (1995). Fear and the human amygdala. *Journal of Neuroscience, 15,* 5879–5891.

Aggleton, J. (1992). *The amygdala: Neurobiological aspects of emotion, memory and mental dysfunction.* New York: Wiley-Liss.

Agmo, A., & Berenfeld, R. (1990). Reinforcing properties of ejaculation in the male rat: Role of opiates and dopamine. *Behavioral Neuroscience, 107,* 812–818.

Amano, K., Tanikawa,T., Kawamura, H., Iseki, H., Notani, M., Kawabatake, H., Shiwaku, T., Suda, T., Demura, H., & Kitamura, K. (1982). Endorphins and pain relief: Further observations on electrical stimulation of the lateral part of the periaqueductal gray matter during rostral mesencephalic reticulotomy for pain relief. *Applied Neurophysiology, 45,* 123–135.

Atkinson, B. (1992a). Aesthetics and pragmatics of family therapy revisited. *Journal of Marital and Family Therapy, 18,* 389–393.

Atkinson, B. (1992b). Evaluating qualitative research. *AFTA Newsletter, 47,* 15–18.

Atkinson, B. (1993). Hierarchy: The imbalance of risk. *Family Process, 32,* 167–170.

Atkinson, B. (1998). Pragmatic/experiential therapy for couples. *Journal of Systemic Therapies, 17,* 18–35.

Atkinson, B. (1999). The emotional imperative: Psychotherapists cannot afford to ignore the primacy of the limbic brain. *Family Therapy Networker, 23*(4), 22–33.

Atkinson, B. (2001). Brain to brain: New ways to help couples avoid relapse. *Psychotherapy Networker, 26*(5), 38–45, 64.

Atkinson, B. (2004). Altered states: Why insight itself isn't enough for lasting change. *Psychotherapy Networker, 28*(5), 43–45, 47.

Atkinson, B. (2005). *Developing habits for relationship success* [CD-ROM]. New York: Norton.

Atkinson, B., & Heath, A. (1987). Beyond objectivism and relativism: Implications for family therapy research. *Journal of Strategic and Systemic Therapies, 6*(1), 8–18.

Atkinson, B., & Heath, A. (1990a). Further thoughts on second-order family therapy (This time it's personal). *Family Process, 29*(2), 145–155.

Atkinson, B., & Heath, A. (1990b). The limits of explanation and evaluation. *Family Process, 29*(2), 164–167.

Atkinson, B., Heath, A., & Chenail, R. (1991). Qualitative research and the legitimization of knowledge. *Journal of Marital and Family Therapy, 17*(2), 161–166.

Bargh, J. A., & Chartrand, T.L. (1999). The unbearable automaticity of being. *American Psychologist, 45*(7), 462–479.

Barinaga, M. (1992). How scary things get that way. *Science, 258*, 887–888.

Bechara, A., Tranel, D., Damasio, H., Adolphs, R., Rockland, C., & Damasio, A. (1995). Double dissociation of conditioning and declarative knowledge relative to the amygdala and hippocampus in humans. *Science, 269*, 1115–1118.

Bejjani, B. P., Damier, P., Arnulf, I., Thivard, L., Bonnet, A. M., Dormont, D., Cornu, P., Pidoux, B. Samson, Y., & Agid, Y. (1999). Transient acute depression induced by high-frequency deep-brain stimulation. *New England Journal of Medicine, 340*, 1476–1480.

Berman, P. W. (1980). Are women more responsive than men to the young? A review of developmental and situational variables. *Psychological Review, 88*, 668–695.

Blanchard, D. C., & Blanchard, R. J. (1972). Innate and conditioned reactions to threat in rats with amygdaloid lesions. *Journal of Comparative and Physiological Psychology, 81*, 281–290.

Bornstein, R. F. (1992). Subliminal mere exposure effects. In R. F. Bornstein & T. S. Pittman (Eds.), *Perception without awareness: Cognitive, clinical and social perspectives* (pp. 191–210). New York: Guilford Press.

Bowen, M. (1978). *Family therapy in clinical practice*. New York: Aronson.

Bower, B. (1994a). The social brain: New clues from an old skull. *Science News, 145*(21), 326.

Bower, B. (1994b). Brain faces up to fear, social signs. *Science News, 146*, 406.

Bremner, J. D., & Narayan, M. (1998). The effects of stress on memory and the hippocampus throught the life cycle: Implications for childhood development and aging. *Development and Psychopathology, 10*, 871–888.

Cahill, L., Babinsky, R., Markowitsch, H. J., McGaugh, J. L. (1995). The amygdala and emotional memory. *Nature, 377*(6547), 295–296.

Cahill, L., Haier, R., Fallon, J., Alkire, M., Tang, C., Keator, D., Wu, J., & McGaugh, J. (1996). Amygdala activity at encoding correlated with long-term, free recall of emotional information. *Neurobiology, 93*, 8016–8021.

Cahill, L., Prins, B., Weber, M., & McGaugh, J. L. (1994). Beta-adrenergic activation and memory for emotional events. *Nature, 371*(6499), 702–704.

Carden, S. W., & Hofer, M. A. (1990). Independence of benzodiazepine and opiate actions in the suppression of isolation distress in rat pups. *Behavioral Neuroscience, 104*, 160–166.

Carrere, S., Buehlman, K. T., Gottman, J. M., Coan, J. A., & Ruckstuhl, L. (2000). Predicting marital stability and divorce in newlywed couples. *Journal of Family Psychology, 14*, 42–58.

Carter, C. S. (1992). Oxytocin and sexual behavior. *Neuroscience and Biobehavioral Reviews, 16*, 131–144.

Clark, G. A. (1995). Emotional learning: Fear and loathing in the amygdala. *Current Biology, 5*(3), 246–248.

Consumer Reports (1995). Study on psychotherapy. *Consumer Reports, November*, 734–739.

Cozolino, L. (2002). *The neuroscience of psychotherapy: Building and rebuilding the human brain*. New York: Norton

Csikszentmihalyi, M. (1990). *Flow: The psychology of optimal experience*. New York: Harper/Perennial.

Damasio, A. R. (1994). *Descartes' error: Emotion, reason and the human brain*. New York: Grosset/Putnam.

Damasio, A. R. (1998). Emotion in the perspective of an integrated nervous system. *Brain Research Reviews, 26,* 83–86.

Damasio, A. R. (1999). *The feeling of what happens: Body and emotion in the making of consciousness.* New York: Harcourt, Brace.

Damasio, A. R. (2001). Emotion and the human brain. *Annals of the New York Academy of Sciences, 935*(1), 101–106.

Damasio, A. R. (2002). *The secret life of the brain. Episode 4.* New York: Public Broadcasting Service. (http://www.pbs.org/wnet/brain/episode4/index.html)

Damasio, H., Grabowski, T., Frank, R., Galaburda, A., & Damasio, A. (1994). The return of Phineas Gage: Clues about the brain from the skull of a famous patient. *Science, 264,* 1102–1105.

Davidson, R. J. (2001a). The neural circuitry of emotion and affective style: Prefrontal cortex and amygdala contributions. *Social Science Information, 40*(1), 11–37.

Davidson, R. J. (2001b). Toward a biology of personality and emotion. *Annals of the New York Academy of Sciences, 935*(1), 191–207.

Davidson, R. J. (2003). Seven sins in the study of emotion: Correctives from affective neuroscience. *Brain and Cognition, 52,* 129–132.

Davidson, R. J., Putnam, K. M., & Larson, C. L. (2000). Dysfunction in the neural circuitry of emotion regulation—A possible prelude to violence. *Science, 289,* 591–594.

Davis, M. (1986). Pharmacological and anatomical analysis of fear conditioning using the fear-potentiated startle paradigm. *Behavioral Neuroscience, 100,* 814–824.

Davis, M. (1992a). The role of the amygdala in fear and anxiety. *Annual Review of Neuroscience, 15,* 353–375.

Davis, M. (1992b). The role of the amygdala in conditioned fear. In J. Aggleton (Ed.), *The amygdala: Neurobiological aspects of emotion, memory, and mental dysfunction* (pp. 255–306). New York: Wiley-Liss.

Decker, M. W., Curzon, P., & Brioni, J. (1995). Influence of separate and combined septal and amygdala lesions on memory, acoustic startle, anxiety and locomotor activity in rats. *Neurobiology of Learning and Memory, 64,* 156–168.

Depue, R. A., & Collins, P. F. (1999). Neurobiology of the structure of personality: Dopamine, facilitation of incentive motivation, and extraversion. *Behavioral and Brain Sciences, 22,* 491–569.

de Shazer, S. (1985). *Keys to solutions in brief therapy.* New York: Norton.

de Shazer, S. (1992). *Putting difference to work.* New York: Norton.

Fendt, M., & Fanselow, M. S. (1999, May 23). The neuroanatomical and neurochemical basis of conditioned fear. *Neuroscience and Biobehvioral Reviews, 23*(5), 743–760.

Fisch, R., Weakland, J., & Segal, L. (1982). *The tactics of change.* San Francisco: Jossey-Bass.

Fonagy, P., & Target, M. (1997). Attachment and reflective function: Their role in self-organization. *Development and Psychopathology, 9,* 679–700.

Fox, N. (1994). Dynamic cerebral processes underlying emotional regulation. *Monographs of the Society for Research in Child Development, 69*(2–3), 152–166.

Gendlin, E. (1981). *Focusing.* New York: Bantam.

Gendlin, E. (1996). *Focusing-oriented psychotherapy.* New York: Guilford Press.

Goldhor Lerner, H. (1985). *The dance of anger.* New York: Harper & Row.

Goldhor Lerner, H. (1989). *The dance of intimacy.* New York: Harper & Row.

Goleman, D. (1995). *Emotional intelligence.* New York: Bantam Books.

Gollwitzer, P. M. (1999). Implementation intentions: Strong effects of simple plans. *American Psychologist, 54*(7), 493–503.

Gottman, J. M. (1994a). *Why marriages succeed or fail.* New York: Simon & Schuster.

Gottman, J. M. (1994b). *What predicts divorce? The relationship between marital processes and marital outcomes.* Hillsdale, NJ: Erlbaum.

Gottman, J. M. (1999). *The marriage clinic: A scientifically based marital therapy*. New York: Norton.

Gottman, J. M. (2002). Building the sound marital house: An empirically derived couple therapy. In A. Gurman & N. Jacobson (Ed.), *Clinical handbook of couple therapy* (3rd ed.) (pp. 373–399). New York: Guilford Press.

Gottman, J. M., Coan, J., Carrere, S., & Swanson, C. (1998). Predicting marital happiness and stability from newlywed interactions. *Journal of Marriage and the Family, 60*, 5–22.

Gottman, J. M., & DeClaire, J. (2001). *The relationship cure*. New York: Crown.

Gottman, J. M., Katz, L., & Hooven, C. (1996). *Meta-emotion*. Hillsdale, NJ: Erlbaum.

Gottman, J. M., & Levenson, R. W. (1988). The social psychophysiology of marriage. In P. Noller & M. A. Fitzpatrick (Eds.), *Perspectives on marital interaction* (pp. 182–200). Clevedon, U.K.: Multilingual Matters.

Gottman, J. M., & Levenson, R. W. (1992). Marital processes predictive of later dissolution: Behavior, physiology and health. *Journal of Personality and Social Psychology, 63*, 221–233.

Gottman, J. M., & Levenson, R. W. (1999). Rebound from marital conflict and divorce prediction. *Family Process, 38*, 237–292.

Gottman, J. M., & Levenson, R. W. (2000). The timing of divorce: Predicting when a couple will divorce over a 14-year period. *Journal of Marriage and the Family, 62*, 737–745.

Gottman, J. M. , & Silver, N. (1999). *The seven principles for making marriage work*. New York: Crown.

Guterl, F. (2002, November 11). What Freud got right. *Newsweek*, p. 50

Halgren, E., Walter, R. D., Chrelow, D. G., & Crandall, P. H. (1978). Mental phenomena evoked by electrical stimulation of the human hippocampal formation and amygdala. *Brain, 101*, 83–117.

Hare, R. D. (1965). Temporal gradient of fear arousal in psychopaths. *Journal of Abnormal Psychology, 70*, 442–445.

Hare, R. D. (1978). Electrodermal and cardiovascular correlates of psychopathy. In R. D. Hare & D. Schalling (Eds.), *Psychopathic behavior: Approaches to research* (pp. 107–143). New York: Wiley.

Hare, R. D. (1982). Psychopathy and physiological activity during anticipation of an aversive stimulus in a distraction paradigm. *Psychophysiology, 19*, 266–271.

Hare, R. D., & Craigen, D. (1974). Psychopathy and physiological activity in a mixed-motive game situation. *Psychophysiology, 11*, 197–206.

Hare, R. D., Frazelle, J., & Cox, D. N. (1978). Psychopathy and physiological responses to threat of an aversive stimulus. *Psychophysiology, 15*, 165–172.

Hariri A. R., Bookheimer, S. Y., & Mazziotta, J. C. (2000). Modulating emotional responses: effects of a neocortical network on the limbic system. *Neuroreport, 11*(1), 43–48.

Hausfater, G., & Hrdy, S. B. (Eds.) (1984).*Infanticide: Comparative and evolutionary perspectives*. New York: Aldine.

Heath, R. G. (1963). Electrical self-stimulation of the brain in man. *American Journal of Psychiatry, 120*, 571–577

Heath, R. G. (1972). Pleasure and brain activity in man. *Journal of Nervous and Mental Disease, 154*, 3–18.

Heath, R. G. (1986). The neural substrate for emotion. In R. Plutchik & H. Kellerman (Eds.), *Emotion: Theory, research and experience*: Vol. 3. *Biological foundations of emotion* (pp. 3–35). New York: Academic Press.

Heath, R. G. (1992). Correlation of brain activity with emotion: A basis for developing treatment of violent-aggressive behavior. *Journal of the American Academy of Psychoanalysis, 20*, 335–346.

Heath, R. G., & Mickle, W. (1960). Evaluation of seven years experience with depth electrode studies in human patients. In E. R. Ramey, & D. S. O'Doherty (Eds.), *Electrical studies on the unanesthetized brain* (pp. 214–247). New York: Hoeber.

Hebb, D. (1949). *The organization of behavior.* New York: Wiley.

Higgins, J. W., Mahl, G. F., Delgado, J. M. R., & Hamlin, H. (1956). Behavioral changes during intracerebral electrical stimulation. *Archives of neurology and psychiatry,* 76, 399–419.

Hitchcock, E., & Cairns, V. (1973). Amygdalotomy. *Postgraduate Medical Journal,* 49, 894–904.

Holtzworth-Munroe, H., & Jacobson, N. S. (1985). Causal attributions of married couples: When do they search for causes? What do they conclude when they do? *Journal of Personality and Social Psychology, 48,* 1398–1412.

Hornak, J., Bramham, J., Rolls, E. T., Morris, R. G., O'Doherty, J., Bullock, P. R., & Polkey, C. E. (2003). Changes in the emotion after circumscribed surgical lesions of the orbitofrontal and cingulated cortices. *Brain, 126,* 1691–1712.

Iidaka, T., Terashima, S., Yamashita, K., Okada, T., Sadato, N., & Yonekura, Y. (2003). Dissociable neural responses in the hippocampus to the retrieval of facial identity and emotion: An event related fMRI study. *Hippocampus, 13,* 429–436.

Jacob, F. (1977). Evolution and tinkering. *Science, 196,* 1161–1166.

Jacobs, W. J., & Nadel, L. (1985). Stress-induced recovery of fears and phobias. *Psychological Review, 92,* 512–531.

Jacobson, N. S., & Gottman, J. M. (1998). *When men batter women.* New York: Simon & Schuster.

Johnson, S. (1996). *The practice of emotionally focused marital therapy: Creating connection.* New York: Brunner/Mazel.

Johnson, J. (2004). *Mind wide open: Your brain and the neuroscience of everyday life.* New York: Scribner.

Kagan, J. (1994). *Galen's prophecy.* New York: Basic Books.

Kaihla, P. (1996). No conscience, no remorse. *Maclean's, 109*(4), 50.

Kalin, N. H., Shelton, S. W., & Barksdale, C. M. (1988). Opiate modulation of separation-induced distress in non-human primates. *Brain Research, 440,* 285–292.

Kapp, B., Whalen, P., Supple, W., & Pascoe, J. (1992). Amygdaloid contributions to conditioned arousal and sensory information processing. In J. Aggleton (Ed.), *The amygdala: Neurobiological aspects of emotion, memory and mental dysfunction* (pp. 229–254). New York: Wiley-Liss.

Keverne, E. B., & Kendrick, K. M. (1992). Oxytocin facilitation of maternal behavior in sheep. *Annals of the New York Academy of Sciences, 652,* 83–101.

Keverne, E. B., Martensz, N., & Tuite, B. (1989). B-Endorphin concentrations in CSF of monkeys are influenced by grooming relationships. *Psychoneuroendocrinology, 14,* 155–161.

Kihlstrom, J. F. (1987). The cognitive unconscious, *Science 237,* 1445–1452.

Kirsch, I., & Lynn, S. J. (1999). Automaticity in clinical psychology. *American Psychologist, 54* (7), 504–515.

Kunst-Wilson, W. R., & Zajonc, R. B. (1980). Affective discrimination of stimuli that cannot be recognized. *Science, 207,* 557–558.

LaBar, J.S., LeDoux, J. E., Spencer, D. D., & Phelps, E. A. (1995). Impaired fear conditioning following unilateral temporal lobectomy in humans. *Journal of Neuroscience, 15,* 6846–6855.

LeDoux, J. (1986). Sensory systems and emotion. *Integrative Psychiatry, 4,* 237–248.

LeDoux, J. (1992a). Brain mechanisms of emotion and emotional learning. *Current Opinion in Neurobiology, 2*(2), 191–197.

LeDoux, J. (1992b). Emotion and the limbic system concept. *Concepts in Neuroscience* (Vol. 2, pp. 169–199). New York: World Scientific.

LeDoux, J. (1992c). Emotion and the amygdala. In J. Aggleton (Ed.), *The amygdala: Neurobiological aspects of emotion, memory, and mental dysfunction* (pp. 339–351). New York: Wiley-Liss.

LeDoux, J. (1993a). Emotional networks in the brain. In M. Lewis & J. Haviland (Eds.), *Handbook of emotions* (pp. 109–118). New York: Guilford Press.

LeDoux, J. (1993b). Emotional memory systems in the brain. *Behavioral and Brain Research, 58,* 69–79.

LeDoux, J. (1994). Emotion, memory and the brain. *Scientific American 270(6),* 50–57.

LeDoux, J. (1995). Emotion: Clues from the brain. *Annual Review of Psychology, 46,* 209–235.

LeDoux, J. (1996). *The emotional brain.* New York: Simon & Schuster.

LeDoux, J. (2000). Emotion circuits in the brain. *Annual Review of Neuroscience, 23,* 155–184.

LeDoux, J. (2002). *The synaptic self: How our brains become who we are.* New York: Penguin.

Levenson, R. W., Carstensen, L. L., & Gottman, J. M. (1994). The influence of age and gender on affect, physiology, and their interrelations: A study of long-term marriages. *Journal of Personality and Social Psychology, 67,* 56–68.

Levenson, R. W., & Gottman, J. M. (1983). Marital interaction: Physiological linkage and affective exchange. *Journal of Personality and Social Psychology, 67,* 56–68.

Levenson, R. W., & Gottman, J. M. (1985). Physiological and affective predictors of change in relationship satisfaction. *Journal of Personality and Social Psychology, 49,* 85–94.

MacLean, P. (1990). *The triune brain in evolution.* New York: Plenum

Magarinos, A., McEwen, B., Fluegge, G., & Fuchs, E. (1996). Chronic psychosocial stress causes apical dendritic atrophy of hippocampal CA3 pyramidal neurons in subordinate tree shrews. *Journal of Neuroscience, 16,* 3534–3540.

Mark, V. H., Ervin, F. R., & Sweet, W. H. (1972). Deep temporal lobe stimulation in man. In B. E. Eleftheriou (Ed.), *The neurobiology of the amygdala* (pp. 485–507). New York: Plenum Press.

Mathews, A., & MacLeod, C. (1986). Discrimination of threat cues without awareness in anxiety states. *Journal of Abnormal Psychology, 95,* 131–138.

Mayer, E. A., Naliboff, B., & Munakata, J. (2000). The evolving neurobiology of gut feelings. *Progress in Brain Research, 122,* 195–206.

McEwen, B. S. (1992). Paradoxical effects of adrenal steroids on the brain: Protection versus degeneration. *Biological Psychiatry, 31,* 177–199.

McEwen, B., & Sapolsky, R. (1995). Stress and cognitive functioning. *Current Opinion in Neurobiology, 5,* 205–216.

Menella, J. A., & Moltz, H. (1988). Infanticide in rats: Male strategy and female counter-strategy. *Physiolology & Behavior, 42,* 19–28.

Meyer, B., McElhaney, M., Martin, W., & McGraw, C. (1973). Stereotactic cingulotomy with results of acute stimulation and serial psychological testing. In L. Laitinen & K. Livingston (Eds.), *Surgical approaches in psychiatry* (pp. 245–252). Baltimore, MD: University Park Press.

Monroe, R. R., & Heath, R. C. (1954). Psychiatric observation on the patient group. In R. C. Heath (Eds.), *Studies in schizophrenia: A multicisciplinary approach to mind–brain relationships* (pp. 345–383). Cambridge, MA: Harvard University Press.

Montagu, A. (1978). *Touching: The human significance of the skin.* New York: Harper & Row.

Morgan, M. A., Romanski, L. M., & LeDoux, J. E. (1993). Extinction of emotional learning: Contribution of medial prefrontal cortex. *Neuroscience Letters, 163,* 109–113.

Morris, J. S. (1999). A subcortical pathway to the right amygdala mediating "unseen" fear. *Proceedings of the National Academy of Sciences of the United States of America, 96(4),* 1680–1685.

Nashold, B. S., Wilson, W. P., & Slaughter, D. E. (1969). Sensations evoked by stimulation in the midbrain of man. *Journal of Neurosurgery, 30,* 14–24.

Nelson, E. E., & Panksepp, J. (1998). Brain substrates of infant-mother attachment: Contributions of opioids, oxytocin, norepinephrine. *Neuroscience and Biobehavioral Reviews, 22*(3), 437–452.

Notarius, C. I., Benson, P. R., Sloane, D., Vanzetti, N. A., & Hornyak, L. M. (1989). Exploring the interface between perception and behavior: An analysis of marital interaction in distressed and non-distressed couples. *Behavioral Assessment, 11*, 39–64.

Obrador, S., & Martin-Rodriguez, J. (1979). Analysis of certain responses to therapeutical electrical stimulation of the brain. In W. R. Hitchcock, H. T. Ballantine, Jr., & B. A. Meyerson (Eds.), *Modern concepts in psychiatric surgery* (pp. 95–102). Amsterdam: Elsevier.

Ogloff, J. R., & Wong, S. (1990). Electrodermal and cardiovascular evidence of a coping response in psychopaths. *Criminal Justice and Behavior, 17*, 231–245.

Ohman, A. (1999). Distinguishing unconscious from conscious emotional processes: Methodological considerations and theoretical implications. In T. Dalgleish & M. Power (Eds.), *Handbook of cognition and emotion* (pp. 321–352). New York: Wiley.

Ohman, A., & Soares, J. J. F. (1993). On the automaticity of phobic fear: Conditioned skin conductance responses to masked phobic stimuli. *Journal of Abnormal Psychology, 102*.

Ornstein, R. (1991). *The evolution of consciousness.* New York: Prentice-Hall.

Panksepp, J. (1982). Toward a general psychobiological theory of emotions. *The Behavioral and Brain Sciences, 5*, 407–468.

Panksepp, J. (1985). Mood changes. In P. J. Vinken, G. W. Bruyn, & H. L. Klawans (Eds.), *Handbook of clinical neurology* (Vol. 1, pp. 271–285). Amsterdam: Elsevier.

Panksepp, J. (1986). The anatomy of emotions. In R. Plutchik & H. Kellerman (Eds.), *Emotion: Theory, research and experience: Vol. 3. Biological foundations of emotion* (pp. 91–124). New York: Academic Press.

Panksepp., J. (1989). The neurobiology of emotions: Of animal brains and human feelings. In T. Manstead & H. Wagner (Eds.), *Handbook of anxiety: Vol. 3. The neurobiology of anxiety* (pp. 3–58). Amsterdam: Elsevier.

Panksepp, J. (1991). Affective neuroscience: A conceptual framework for the neurobiological study of emotions. In K. T. Strongman (Ed.), *International Review of Studies on Emotion* (Vol. 1, pp. 59–99). New York: J Wiley.

Panksepp, J. (1992a). A critical role for affective neuroscience in resolving what is basic about basic emotions. *Psychological Review, 99*, 554–560.

Panksepp, J. (1992b). Neurochemical control of moods and emotions. In M. Lewis & J. Haviland (Eds.), *Handbook of emotions* (pp. 87–108). New York: Guilford Press.

Panksepp, J. (1998). *Affective Neuroscience.* New York: Oxford University Press.

Panksepp, J. (1999). Emotions as viewed by psychoanalysis and neuroscience: An exercise in consilience. *Neuro-Psychoanalysis, 1*, 15–38.

Panksepp, J. (2001). The long-term psychobiological consequences of infant emotions: Prescriptions for the twenty-first century. *Infant Mental Health Journal, 22*(1–2), 132–173.

Panksepp, J. (2003). At the interface of the affective, behavioral, and cognitive neurosciences: Decoding the emotional feelings of the brain. *Brain & Cognition 52*(1), 4–14.

Panksepp, J. (2003). Feeling the pain of social loss. *Science 302*(5643), 237–239.

Panksepp, J. Bean, N. J., Bishop, P., Vilberg, T., & Sahley, T. L. (1980). Opioid blockade and social comfort in chicks. *Pharmacology, Biochemistry & Behavior, 13*, 673–683.

Panksepp, J., & Bishop, P. (1981). An autoradiographic map of the (^{3}H) diprenorphine binding in rat brain: Effects of social interaction. *Brain Research Bulletin, 7*, 405–410.

Panksepp, J., Herman, B., Conner, R., Bishop, P., & Scott, J. P. (1978). The biology of social attachments: Opiates alleviate separation distress. *Biological Psychiatry, 13*(5), 607–617.

Panksepp, J., Neson, E., & Bekkedal, M. (1997). Brain systems for the mediation of social separation-distress and social-reward: Evolutionary antecedents and neuropeptide intermediaries. *Annals of the New York Academy Science, 807*, 78–100.

Park, D. (1999). Acts of will? *American Psychologist, 54,* 461.

Patrick, C., Cuthbert, B., & Lang, P. (1994). Emotion in the criminal psychopath: Fear image processing. *Journal of Abnormal Psychology, 103,* 523–534.

Pedersen, C. A., Ascher, J. A., Monroe, Y. L., & Prange, A. J. (1982). Oxytocin induces maternal behavior in virgin female rats. *Science, 216,* 648–649.

Prescott, J. W. (1971). Early somatosensory deprivation as an ontogentic process in the abnormal development of brain and behavior. In E. I. Goldsmith & J. Mody-Jankowski (Eds.). *Proceedings of the Second Conference on Experimental Medicine and Surgery in Primates* (pp. 356–375). Basel: Karger.

Raine, A., Meloy, J. R., Bihrle, S., Stoddard, J., LaCasse, L., & Buchsbaum, M. S. (1998). Reduced prefrontal and increased subcortical brain functioning assessed using positron emission tomography in predatory and affective murderers. *Behavioral Sciences and the Law, 16,* 319–332.

Rasia-Filho, A.A., Londero, R.G., & Achaval, M. (2000). Functional activities of the amygdala: An overview. *Journal of Psychiatry and Neuroscience, 8*(2), 14–23.

Robbins, J. (2000). Wired for sadness. *Discover, 21*(4), 76–81.

Robinson, E. A., & Price, M. G. (1980). Pleasurable behavior in marital interactions: An observational study. *Journal of Consulting and Clinical Psychology, 48,* 117–118.

Rolls, E. T. (1990). A theory of emotion, and its application to understanding the neural basis of emotion. *Cognition and Emotion, 4,* 161–190.

Rosenblatt, J. (1992). Hormone-behavioral relations in the regulation of parental behavior. In J. B. Becker, S. M. Breedlove & D. Crews (Eds.), *Behavioral endocrinology* (pp. 219–259). Cambridge, MA: MIT Press.

Rosenthal, N. (2002). *The emotional revolution.* New York: Kensington.

Rudy, J. W. (1993). Contextual conditioning and auditory cue conditioning dissociate during development. *Behavioral Neuroscience, 107,* 887–901.

Rudy, J. W., & Morledge, P. (1994). Ontogeny of contextual fear conditioning in rats: Implications for consolidation, infantile anmesia, and hippocampal system function. *Behavioral Neuroscience, 108,* 227–234.

Sachser, N., Lick, C., & Stanzel, K. (1994). The environment, hormones, and aggressive behaviour: A 5-year-study in guinea pigs. *Psychoneuroendocrinology, 19,* 697–707.

Salovey, P., & Mayer, J. D. (1990). Emotional intelligence. *Imagination, Cognition, and Personality, 9,* 185–211.

Schore, A. N. (1994). *Affect regulation and the origin of self.* Hillsdale, NJ: Erlbaum.

Schore, A. N. (1996). The experience-dependent maturation of a regulatory system in the orbital prefrontal cortex and the origin of developmental psychopathology. *Development and Psychopathology, 8,* 59–87.

Schore, A. N. (2001a). Effects of a secure attachment relationship on right brain development, affect regulation, and infant mental health. *Infant Mental Health Journal, 22*(1–2), 7–66.

Schore, A. N. (2001b). The effects of early relational trauma on right brain development, affect regulation, and infant mental health. *Infant Mental Health Journal, 22*(1–2), 201–269.

Schore, A. N. (2001c). Contributions from the decade of the brain to infant mental health: An overview. *Infant Mental Health Journal, 22*(1–2), 1–6.

Schurrman, T. (1980). Hormonal correlates of agonistic behavior in adult male rats. In P. S. McConnell, G. J. Boer, H. J. Romijin, N. E. van de Poll, & M. A. Corner (Eds.), *Adaptive capabilities of the nervous system* (pp. 415–420). Amsterdam: Elsevier/North Holland.

Schwartz, R. (1995). *Internal family systems therapy.* New York: Guilford Press.

Seligman, M. E. P. (1995). The effectiveness of psychotherapy: The Consumer Reports study. *American Psychologist, 50,* 965–974.

Shreeve, J. (1995). What happened to Phineas? *Discover, 16*(1), 78.

Siegel, D. (1999). *The developing mind: Toward a neurobiology of interpersonal experience*. New York: Guilford Press.

Siegel, D. J. (2001). Toward an interpersonal neurobiology of the developing mind: Attachment relationship, "Mindsight," and neural integration. *Infant Mental Health Journal, 22*(1–2), 67–94.

Siegel, D., & Hartzell, M. (2003). *Parenting from the inside out*. New York: Jeremy P. Tarcher/Putnam.

Sem-Jacobsen, C. W. (1968). *Depth-electroencephalographic stimulation of the human brain and behavior*. Springfield, IL: Charles C. Thomas.

Sheer, D. E. (Ed.) (1961). *Electrical stimulation of the brain*. Austin: University of Texas Press.

Sprenkle, D., & Blow, A. (2004). Common factors and our sacred models. *Journal of Marital and Family Therapy, 30*(2), 113–130.

Tallis, F. (1999). Unintended thoughts and images. In T. Dalgleish & M. Power (Eds.), *Handbook of Cognition and Emotion* (pp. 281–300). New York: Wiley.

Tranel, D., Bechara, A., & Damasio, A. (2000). Decision making and the somatic marker hypothesis. In M. Gazzaniga (Ed.), *The new cognitive neurosciences* (pp. 1047–1061). Cambridge, MA: MIT Press.

Tranel, D., & Hyman, B. T. (1990). Neuropsychological correlates of bilateral amygdala damage. *Archives of Neurology, 47*, 349–355.

Uvnas-Moberg, K. (1998). Oxytocin may mediate the benefits of positive social interaction and emotions. *Psychoneuroendocrinology, 23*(8), 819–835.

Vanderschuren, L. J. M. J., Niesink, R. J. M., & VanRee, J. M. (1997). The neurobiology of social play behavior in rats. *Neuroscience and Biobeahvioral Reviews, 21*(3), 309–326.

Vanderschuren, L. J. M. J., Stein, E. A., Wiegant, V. M., & Van Ree, J. M. (1995). Social play alters regional brain opioid receptor binding in juvenile rats. *Brain Research, 680*, 148–156.

Van Leengoed, E., Kerker, E., & Swanson, H. H. (1987). Inhibition of post-partum maternal behavior in the rat by infusion of an oxytocin antagonist into the cerebral ventricles. *Journal of Endocrinology, 112*, 275–282.

Watzlawick, P. Weakland, J., & Fisch, R. (1974). *Change: Principles of problem formulation and problem resolution*. New York: Norton.

Wegner, D. M., & Wheatley, T. (1999). Apparent mental causation: Sources of the experience of will. *American Psychologist, 54*(7), 480–492.

Weinberger, D. (1990). The construct validity of the repressive coping style. In J. L. Singer (Ed.), *Repression and dissociation* (pp. 337–386). Chicago: University of Chicago Press.

White, M., & Epston, D. (1990). *Narrative means to therapeutic ends*. New York: Norton.

Weiss, R. L. (1980). Strategic behavioral marital therapy: Toward a model for assessment and intervention. In J. P. Vincent (Ed.), *Advances in family intervention, assessment and theory* (Vol. 1, pp. 229–271). Greenwich, CT: JAI.

White, M., & Epston, D. (1990). *Narrative means to therapeutic ends*. New York: W.W. Norton.

Wile, D. (2002). Collaborative couple therapy. In. A. Gurman & N. Jacobson (Eds.), *Clinical handbook of couple therapy* (3rd ed.). New York: Guilford Press.

Zajonc, R. (1980). Feeling and thinking: Preferences need no inferences. *American Psychologist, 35*, 151–175.

Zajonc, R. (1984). On the primacy of affect. *American Psychologist, 39*, 117–123.

Index

33% Discount with Coupon!

Price of $50 for Purchasers of *Emotional Intelligence in Couples Therapy*

Developing Habits for Relationship Success

*A Workbook for Effective,
Neurobiologically-Based Couples Therapy*

CD-ROM

Brent J. Atkinson

Over the past thirty years, groundbreaking studies on the relationships of coules have identified specific interpersonal habits necessary for relationship success. A structured approach to putting Atkinson's Pragmatic/Experiential Therapy for couples (PET-C), this workbook details each of these crucial interpersonal habits and offers dozens of guidelines and exercises for helping relationship partners implement them.

A Digital Workbook Ready to be Personalized and Published for Your Clients

From the digital files you can generate personalized workbooks that specify the gender of your client's partner and as well as your client's partner's name. Publish as many workbooks as you need. Publish workbook as many times as you need them. *Developing Habits for Relationship Success* is an essential resource for therapists looking to put Pragmatic/ Experiential Therapy into action with their clients.

For Windows and MacIntosh Systems

~~$75.00 USA $105.00 CAN~~ $50.00 USA $70.00 CAN
33% discount for purchasers of *Emotional Intelligence in Couples Therapy*

Mention code OEI 1059 in order to receive the 33% discount

To order
Call **1-800-233-4830** (in the United States) and
      717-346-1442 (outside the United States), or
Email: mcerminaro@wwnorton.com, or
Mail orders to **W. W. Norton and Company, 800 Keystone Industrial Park, Dunmore PA 18512.**

W. W. Norton & Company
New York • London
www.wwnorton.com
1-800-233-4830